A VILLAGE IN SUSSEX

To Anne, Lilian and Brigid
and all the inhabitants of Kingston-near-Lewes
over the centuries

A VILLAGE IN SUSSEX

The History of Kingston-near-Lewes

Charles Cooper

I.B. TAURIS
LONDON · NEW YORK

Published in 2006 by I.B.Tauris
6 Salem Road, London W2 4BU

In the United States of America and Canada
distributed by Palgrave Macmillan
a division of St Martin's Press
175 Fifth Avenue, New York NY 10010

ISBN 1–84511–190–8
EAN 978–1–84511–190–7

A full CIP record for this book is available from the British Library
A full CIP record for this book is available from the Library of Congress

Library of Congress Catalog card: available

Copy-edited and typeset in Berkeley Oldstyle by Oxford Publishing Services, Oxford
Printed and bound in Great Britain by TJ International Ltd, Padstow, Cornwall

Contents

Illustrations

Photographs by Penry Williams

List of Tables

List of Figures/Maps

The maps in Figures 6.1 and 11.1 are reproduced by kind permission of Mrs Margaret Thorburn. Those in Figures 1.1 and 6.1 are reproduced by kind permission of the Ordnance Survey. Figure 11.1 was traced by Mrs Thorburn from ESRO Figg 728, with the kind permission of East Sussex Record Office.

Abbreviations

ACL	Archdeaconry Court of Lewes
Book of John Rowe	*The Book of John Rowe*, ed. W. H. Godfrey, Sussex Record Society, xxxiv (1928)
DNB	Dictionary of National Biography
ESRO	East Sussex Record Office
ESRO LTA	East Sussex Record Office, Land Tax Assessments
Harl. MSS.	British Library, Harleian MSS
Inq. p.m	Inquisitiones post mortem
LP Henry VIII	*Letters and Papers, Foreign and Domestic, of the Reign of Henry VIII*, ed. J. S. Brewer et al. (21 vols, 1862–1932)
PCC	Prerogative Court of Canterbury
PRO	Public Record Office
SAC	*Sussex Archaeological Society Collections*
SNQ	*Sussex Notes and Queries*
SRS	*Sussex Record Society*
Sw. Ct. Bk	Swanborough Court Book
VCH Sussex	*Victoria County History, County of Sussex*
WSRO	West Sussex Record Office
Wiston Arch.	The Wiston Archive in WSRO

Glossary

assart	extension of arable by taking in land from common pasture
close	a small piece of enclosed land, usually around a building
croft	a piece of enclosed land, usually adjacent to a building
copyhold	a form of land tenure: land held as part of a manor by copy of court roll; land held at the will of the lord
demesne	land owned and occupied by the manorial lord; the 'home farm'
engrossing/engrossment	buying up land; economic accumulation, especially of land
furlong	a block of strips in the open fields or laines; also a linear measurement of an eighth of a mile
hide	a measure of land, consisting of four virgates or yardlands, 40–50 acres; also a unit of taxation (see p. 15)
laine/leyne	in Sussex one of the open fields cultivated as arable in the three-field rotational system
leys	land laid down for pasture
messuage	a dwelling-house with outbuildings and land adjacent
rood	a measure of land: in Kingston about a quarter of an acre
severalty	land held separately, not in common
stint	allocation of pasture according to the number of sheep or cattle allowed
terrier	a register of property, including lists of tenants
villein	an occupier or cultivator subject to a lord or attached to a manor; a copyholder
virgate	see yardland
yardland	the holding of a 'full' villein: 10–12 acres in Kingston (see p. 15)
yeoman	originally a freeholder owning land worth 40 shillings a year; later and more loosely a landholder below the rank of gentleman

Acknowledgements

I started writing *Kingston* in the 1970s and completed it in the 1980s. During this period I researched extensively in archives in the East Sussex Record Office, Lewes, and the West Sussex Record Office, Chichester. I wish to express my appreciation for the support and assistance given to me by the archivists and staff in these institutions. My thanks go also to the University of Sussex library and staff.

Because of a number of serious health problems in the 1990s I was not able to prepare the manuscript for publication. However, I have finally managed to achieve this in 2004. Regrettably, poor health and residence abroad have prevented me from consulting new publications of the last twenty years or so. But the book is almost entirely based on original sources (some in print, some in manuscript) and these have not changed. I am delighted that the book will be published and available to people who love Kingston and want to find out more about its past.

The publication of this book would not have been possible without the encouragement and efforts of my sister, Dr Lorraine Lawrence, University of Fort Hare, South Africa, who helped me with editing and some of the proof reading. I owe special gratitude to my cousin, Dr Penry Williams, New College, Oxford, who helped me tirelessly with the selection and review of maps and tables, as well as proof reading the earlier chapters. I would also like to thank John Williams for the original cover design on which the I.B.Tauris one is based and for some maps, and Phillip and Sarah Bentley for redrawing other maps.

I also acknowledge with deep appreciation the efforts of Selina Cohen of Oxford Publishing Services, who prepared what I think is an elegant text.

My thanks also go to Ms Laura Godden in South Africa who undertook the arduous task of word processing the draft for submission to the publisher.

Finally, I acknowledge the love and support of my wife, Anne de Premorel Cooper, without whom none of this would have been possible.

Charles Cooper
Beaumes de Venise
Provence
August 2004

Foreword by Penry Williams

Charles Cooper was trained as an economist and had a distinguished career teaching and researching in Britain, France and the Netherlands. He was born in South Africa in 1936, but having won a Rhodes scholarship to Magdalen College, Oxford in 1957, he made a firm decision not to return to live in South Africa as long as apartheid ruled. On leaving Oxford he worked in Britain, France and, latterly, the Netherlands. From 1969 to 1981 he was a member of the Institute of Development Studies (IDS) at the University of Sussex, becoming its deputy director in 1977. During the 1970s he lived in Kingston-near-Lewes, the inspiration for this book, which he wrote while he was there.

In 1981 he moved to the Netherlands, first as professor of development economics at the Institute for Social Studies at The Hague, and later as director of the United Nations University Institute (UNU/INTECH), in Maastricht. His career covered 40 years of research, teaching and consulting in technology, economics and development in many countries. Cooper always intended to return to this book in his retirement; but tragically he suffered a series of strokes, which made it impossible for him to travel or to work on the sources. As a result, the secondary sources used are limited to books published 20 or more years ago. But the great strength of this book is in its solid base of primary materials, some in print, many in manuscript. It seemed important, particularly for that reason, to make it available to readers interested in the history of the region and to those concerned with the study of manorial history more generally. However, that is not the book's only strength. Cooper writes from the point of view of a professional economist, in particular one concerned with developing communities. His approach does much to illuminate the workings of an agrarian system that has now disappeared and to explain its gradual disintegration. This book is unusual among academic village histories in its great chronological span, from before the Norman Conquest to the enclosures of the nineteenth century. *A Village in Sussex* treats not only of manorial lords, but also of lesser men: tenant farmers, husbandmen, craftsmen and wage labourers. In some instances their flint-built cottages have been located and described. It is written with humour and an agreeable robustness, especially when the author is commenting upon some recent developments in the village.

I should like to thank Mrs Margaret Thorburn whose knowledge of Kingston and its topography was of great help to me in preparing the text; John Farrant, who enabled me to trace several of the footnote references; and Lester Crook, who was of great assistance with the publication. Very sadly, Charles Cooper died on 16 January 2005 at Beaumes de Venise.

Chapter 1

Introduction

This book is about a village in the Sussex downlands. It is called Kingston, or rather Kingston-near-Lewes to distinguish it from the many other Kingstons in England, not a few of which are also in Sussex. It is a history of the village from the time of the Norman Conquest until the end of the nineteenth century.

Lewes, the county town of East Sussex, lies on the River Ouse, about six miles north of the river mouth at Newhaven.[1] It is a market town, with the remnants of a Norman castle on a steep hill in its centre. It has houses, inns and churches of various ages and considerable distinction, set amongst an overgrowth of modern buildings of hardly any distinction at all. The Ouse runs through the lower part of the town. On its way to the sea, it runs between old dykes and across low-lying meadowlands, which were once salt marshes. These were tidal flats in earlier times. They were dyked at various stages, mainly after the fifteenth century. Before that, at high tide, the sea came right up to the southern edge of the town near to the by-pass, built in the 1980s. On either side, to east and to west, the ground rises sharply above the old salt marshes into the chalk downlands, which run along the Sussex coast. These are several hundred feet high. Lewes lies at the northern end of a break in the downs caused by the Ouse.

On the southern edge of the town, there is a second important Norman remnant, a ruined priory church (with some adjoining buildings). Though it was destroyed by orders of Thomas Cromwell during the dissolution of the monasteries, Lewes Priory is still a distinguishing feature of the town.

There are two roads connecting Lewes to the coast, one on either side of the river. The one that runs down the western bank of the Ouse starts in the suburb of Southover (where the priory church and monastery were originally located) and then, running in a winding southward direction, skirts the edges of what used to be the salt marshes. After about one mile, there is a side road running westwards at right angles to the course of the river. This goes into the village of Kingston-near-Lewes.[2] The old part of Kingston village lies in a shallow chalk valley beneath a high point in the downlands.

After the Kingston turning, the main road continues past Swanborough Manor, and to the south into the villages of Iford, Rodmell and Southease, all of which play a part in the Kingston story – especially Swanborough. Today it ends in the modern port of Newhaven.

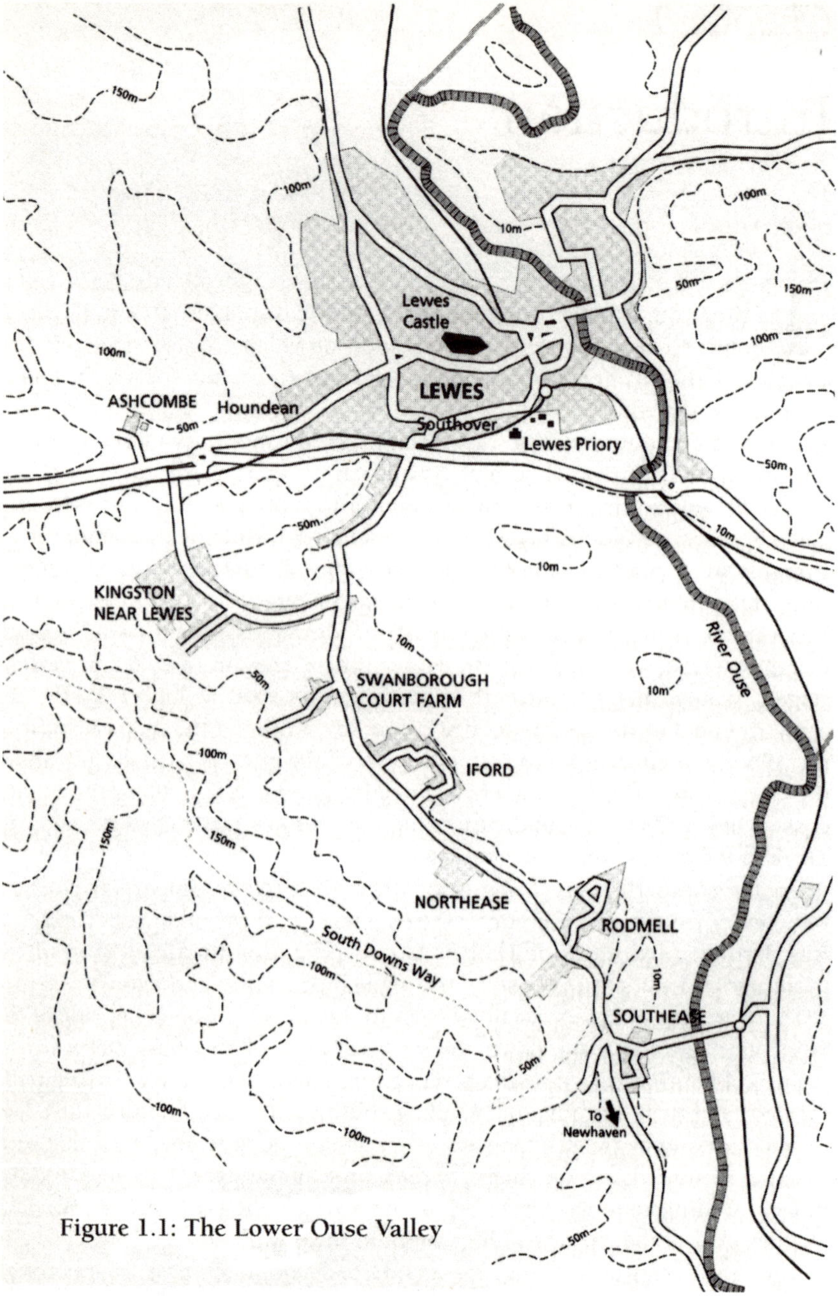

Figure 1.1: The Lower Ouse Valley

This countryside is exceptionally beautiful. The Ouse valley below Lewes is a dramatic break in the long line of coastal downs. Its dykes are stark lines containing the river and there are hillocks standing above the flat meadows. These were once islands above the high tide mark in the salt marshes. The downs are a majestic line of hills, mainly grass covered, but with some sweeps of arable land, sown with various crops and changing in colour and texture with the seasons. The downlands dominate Kingston village, and their lower slopes surround the village with vast sweeping fields, which dwarf it charmingly. Lewes itself dominates the river and the gap in the downlands, and is crowned by the castle keep. Looking southward, across the flat remnants of the old estuary, one sees far off, on the right, the first houses of Kingston in the cleft in the downs. It is indeed 'near Lewes', and that is, as one might expect, an important matter in its history.

But why write the history of a small downland village, which for all its beauty and the splendour of its surroundings is, after all, not unlike many other villages whose stories have already been told? In part the reasons are fortuitous: simply that I lived in Kingston for many years and was intrigued by its age and charm. It happened also that I found in the East and West Sussex Record Offices, pre-enclosure maps that showed the open fields of an earlier and different Kingston, and documents that showed the complicated structure of the manorial system in the village. The medieval past seemed strange and remote, and I wanted to know how it had shaped the village, how it related to less distant history and how things connected up.

This was the start – an interest, which was more antiquarian than historical. If matters had stopped at that point there would have been no need to write the book. The motive to write it grew as it became clear that the documentary records of Kingston are quite detailed, and unusually long – enough to sustain something more than a disjointed record of antiquities. The records start in the early Norman period, at the time of the foundation of Lewes Priory as a Cluniac religious house. The chartulary of the priory has survived. It tells the story of the priory itself, but also incidentally opens up the early medieval manorial history of Kingston village. This is a history of the transformation from earlier Saxon organization to the more formalized logical, and probably more oppressive, Norman form.

The Norman records are the start. In addition, apart from the usual sources for rural histories, there is an unusually comprehensive set of documents showing title to lands in the village over a long period. They were brought together in 1830, from manorial and other records, when the estate of Charles Goring of Wiston purchased virtually all the lands and houses of Kingston. This large purchase happened just at the point when Kingston was transformed from a 'champion' open field village to a system of enclosed fields. The Wiston Archive makes it possible to trace patterns of ownership over long periods – especially important because the manorial records for Kingston are rather poor. Finally, there are some unusually fine maps of the pre-enclosure village, to be found with the Wiston papers, but also in other bundles. In other respects, Kingston is well provided with the more usual documentary sources of English local history.

The existence of these sources opened up the possibility of producing an unusually complete analysis of the village. The main purpose was to describe the processes of socio-economic change, which happened in Kingston, over the long period from early medieval, post-Conquest times, to the last years of the nineteenth century. This long process of change was mediated by changes in institutions, organization, technology and economic accumulation, and I tried to show how these changes combined to make the village what it had become by the end of the nineteenth century. The sources available for Kingston made this a worthwhile and possible undertaking.

The results do not throw up much that is new about the broad sweep of English rural history, but probably the histories of individual villages cannot be expected to do that. The advantage of this kind of history 'in the small' is that it is good at describing causalities and links at a level of detail, which, for example, general rural histories cannot easily reach. This adds a certain amount of richness and immediacy to one's understanding of bigger events.

The changes in the society and economy of the village become clear as one proceeds, and they conform to the changes elsewhere in the rural south of England. After the Conquest, Kingston was a village of villeins. By the Tudor period, it had been transformed in the main into a village of small individual landholders, working their own copyhold and freehold lands. By the nineteenth century, the markets for land and the labour market had brought into being a village of landless wage labourers and of large tenant farmers and landowners. The transformations are not exceptional in English terms; but the precise forms they took were often, if not exceptional, at least particular to the circumstances of the village itself.

These social transformations were related to deeper changes in village life. First, to changes in *institutions*; institutions here refer to 'the rules of the game', the codes by which the village society operated. In the medieval village, the rules of behaviour were given by the manor courts, which essentially determined access to land and labour dues associated with rights in land (for villeins at least), and by village by-laws, which controlled individual uses of the open field system, and which provided the framework for the crucial collective decisions of when to plough, sow and reap and when to leave fallow.[3] In the next chapter, there is an account of the complicated manorial system in Kingston and of the profound changes that took place in how the system actually worked over the long term.

Social change was also related to *organization*. In Kingston, as elsewhere in the countryside, the open-field system, with its probable origins in medieval three-course rotation, was a basic aspect of organization. In this village the open fields, with their multiplicity of acre strips, remained until late; enclosure only came in the early nineteenth century. As a result, changes in the techniques of agricultural production that required larger areas and new, more complex and more frequent crop rotations depended on the extent to which individual landholders had been able to pull together parcels of land containing contiguous strips, or were able to exchange strips with others. As the engrossment of arable land advanced in the late eighteenth and nineteenth centuries, and as the number of owners and occupiers became smaller, this type of adaptation to new technologies became more easily possible.

Engrossment was a fundamental part of *economic accumulation* and growth in the village, part, that is, of the sometimes gradual pulling together of smaller owner occupied landholdings into larger and larger units. This was the crucial economic counterpart of the social transformation of the village from a society of small landholders, often owner-occupiers, to a society of landless labourers and very few large tenant farmers or bigger owner-occupiers, in short, from a village in which economic welfare, however limited, was more evenly distributed to one where it was less so. The main engine of economic change in the village was the concentration of landholdings and changes in the techniques of agricultural production.

The process, which forms an important part of the story in this book, is most clearly evident in the intergenerational histories of the families in the village. These are histories of small husbandman families, which mainly disappeared from the village community, and of the successful yeomen families, especially in the Tudor years, which also eventually gave place to the economically more powerful families, yeomen in their early descriptions but who came to border on the gentry. Once or twice the lines were crossed, but this was an expensive process, ending in a degree of family economic breakdown and often in heavy mortgages on the land. But, even when individual families came to grief economically, the process of concentration of village lands went on. Over the whole period from the start of a market in land, in the fourteenth and fifteenth centuries, there are virtually no instances where landholdings once concentrated in a single ownership were subsequently dispersed. At the end, when the village was finally enclosed in 1830, the Goring family of Wiston came to own everything, and the whole village was worked by a tenant farmer who descended from the most remarkable of the yeoman engrossers of the seventeenth century. In the meanwhile, the village population had been transformed into a small agricultural proletariat of wage labourers and a few cottagers, and the less fortunate who landed from time to time in the poorhouse in Newhaven. The book ends with an account of these last years of the nineteenth century with a few references to the early twentieth.

Chapter 2

Open Fields and Manors

The rural past was not as simple as we like to think and not simple at all in the nature of agricultural decisions. We often mistakenly think of men and women whose lives were ordered by the annual agricultural cycle, who were close to the land because they tilled it directly with simple ploughs, harrows, rakes and spades, and who lived mostly off what they produced for themselves. We tend to build a picture of a topic or elemental way of life. In Kingston Street these perceptions are reinforced by the essential modesty of the place – the withdrawn, self-sufficient quietness it shares with other downland villages.

It is probably wrong to think of past rural life in this way. Life was not necessarily simple because it followed the rhythms of the agricultural year. Even modern farmers could put us right on that. No two years are quite the same, especially not in England. Living under the variant sway of the annual cycle needed constant adaptation because the terms of the game were different every year, and more sharply different before the advent of synthetic fertilizers, hybrid seeds and pesticides. Decisions on when to plough, to plant and reap, how many sheep to pasture, what to do about pests, diseases, blights and new kinds of weeds could not be reduced to rules. They needed then, perhaps even more than now, careful judgement. They were different decisions in each succeeding year.

Nor was it all that simple to live in close proximity to the land. Medieval agricultural implements, for example, may seem extraordinarily basic to us. But perhaps for just that reason they demanded an especially intimate knowledge of the soils of their villages, as well as subtlety and judgement in use. Ploughing, for example, constrained as it was by the power of the ox-team and the limitations of a crude share, demanded complex knowledge as well as strength. Read from Walter of Henley's *Husbandry*, written in the early thirteenth century:

> April is a good time for fallowing, if the earth breaks up after the plough; and for second fallowing after St John's Day, when the dust rises behind the plough; and for ploughing for seed when the earth is firm and not too cracked. But he who has much to do cannot wait for all the good seasons. … At the second fallowing do not go too deep, but so that you can just destroy the thistles, for if you go too deep at

> second fallowing … then when one must plough for sowing the plough shall reach no sure ground. … And if the plough can go two fingers deeper than at second fallowing then the plough will find sure ground … and make fine and good ploughing.[1]

This implies many judgements. Notice, for example, that the depth of ploughing appropriate at 'second fallowing' must be judged so that the plough will be able to find sure ground some *months* later when the time comes to plough again for sowing. The right depth would depend on the structure of soils, which might vary widely in different fields around a single village, as well as on the unpredictable effects of a season yet to come. And, all the time there are compromises to be made with one's best judgement of these matters because 'he who has much to do cannot wait for all the good seasons.' The annual cycle can impose great pressures of time, pressures to get on with the job even in suitable conditions. Tricky and sometimes crucial decisions have to be made.

Nor was it particularly simple to live off the products of one's lands. The choice of consumables was, of course, much narrower, and this might mean that life was simpler in some ways. But production for subsistence has its own complexities. For a poor family – and most Kingston families over the long years from the Conquest to 1900 were poor – there is a complex business of reducing the risks of failure, which even in one year might be a real threat to physical survival.

Even that modesty of Kingston Street is deceptive. Behind the modesty of outward appearance, there was a range of craftsmanship and cunning design. It is no simple matter to build in flint or to design, produce and fit the great timbers, which soar above your head when you stand in one of the big barns at the western end of the street. To conceive and execute the farmyards required intimate knowledge and foresight about how they were to be used. The outward modesty is often a signal that an empirical rural designer had reduced a structure, a barn, cottage or a wall to the basic essentials. He had no way of calculating stresses and strains to achieve this, but it is not certain that a modern designer with all those means available to him would do better. Indeed, he would probably lack the taste and architectural discrimination of his forebears.

To a large extent these realities, which somewhat belie the image of simple rural life in earlier times, are about technical matters – the skills and judgement needed to till, to build and to survive. There were, however, other sorts of complexity, which are less obvious to us now. These complexities arose from the organization of villages, indeed from two particular aspects of village organization: the organization of the land on which villages depended, and the social ordering of life. Let us be more specific and deal with these as they appear in the history of Kingston.

First, the organization of village lands: for by far the greater part of the period from the Conquest onwards Kingston lands were organized on the open-field system, a complicated form of organization that put a set of demands on the community and greatly influenced how people related to each other. Kingston open fields survived with little change until enclosure in 1832.

Second, the social ordering of life: this, of course, was influenced in its own way by the open field organization of the village lands but, more profoundly, it was determined by the incidence of the manorial system on the village.

These aspects of social organization complicated life in the village. They influenced relationships, obligations and rights. They resulted, at various times, in far more complex patterns of existence than our images of the past may suggest. But more important than the contrast between image and reality, the open field organization and the manorial system provided the framework for village life throughout its history. Their effects change drastically from time to time. Open fields had one set of implications for the ordering of life, when land was held by early medieval villeins, and quite another set later on as landlords and tenant farmers dominated. The manorial system of the village was largely inherited from the Norman conquerors who used it to impose rigid feudal obligations on the villagers. Much later it became a mere shell – a residual, failing framework of largely irrelevant formal obligations within which people bought and sold land, rented and leased it, and hired and fired labourers. But for all the fundamental changes in the way the open fields and the manors affected people's lives in the village, they provide the continuing structure within which the changes happened – sometimes slowly, sometimes dramatically. This village – like others – cannot be understood without knowing about them.

The Kingston open fields

The open field system is extremely ancient. Its origins 'lie far back in a past so remote that no direct evidence about it can be produced'.[2] Indeed, Max Weber discusses the use that early German writers made of the open field system to develop their theory of a primitive agrarian communism, which lay, in their view, at the start of agricultural life.[3] The open field system, they argued, was a token of an egalitarian, collective system of organization. It might have been, but there is no need to speculate about the matter. What is significant here is that the system came to England with the Saxons, and although our first clear glimpse of it in Kingston village is from a much later time, there is not much doubt that it was an inheritance from the days before the Conquest.

Kingston lands, as in other parts of rural England, were of three types: pasture, meadowland and arable. The pasturelands lay on the steep downland slopes above the village and on the long level stretches and hidden valleys to the west. From early times it is clear that these grasslands were kept aside for sheep. It is also clear that the number of sheep allowed to pasture on the downland was strictly controlled, and was in proportion to claims on arable land. In medieval transactions involving Kingston lands, the rights to pasturage attendant upon land-holdings in the arable fields are specified. For example, when William Drosey let land to his daughter Lucy in 1339, the property was described as '10 acres in the common fields, 2 acres of meadow and pasture or 2 oxen and 25 sheep in Kingston'.[4] The practice continued through the ages. A grander property, which later became Kingston Manor farm, passed from the Crown to Sir Richard Lee in 1546 – after the dissolution of the monasteries, and had 'common of pasture for 400 sheep on the Downs' attached to it.[5] And the pattern is repeated, with only the smallest holdings in the village (consisting of a cottage and a small amount of arable, often in a strip around the cottage itself) being without an ascription of pastureland. This pattern is quite important. It makes clear that though Kingston flocks were herded in common, the pasture itself was not common land in the sense that anyone in the village could use it freely. In Kingston, 'common of pasture' meant that a person could let his or her flocks graze together with others from the village, but the rights to it were strictly rationed out.

Kingston meadowlands lay to the east of the main highway from modern Newhaven to Lewes. They were on the lowland around the River Ouse. Two things follow from this. First, the meadows were peculiarly subject to flood, and indeed to tidal floods that might cover them with salt water. In consequence, they were built up over the years behind a succession of low dykes, still to be seen. And second, the meadows must have expanded over the years. In the early medieval period, at about the time the Normans appeared on the scene, a great part of the Ouse valley was a wide tidal estuary. Quite large vessels made their way to Lewes. Kingston meadowland must then have been confined to a quite narrow fringe near the Newhaven road. But land was successively reclaimed from the estuary and the meadows expanded. As Farrant has shown, reclamation was not a smooth, even process. There were times when land was lost to the marshes of the estuary. But as far as Kingston is concerned we may suppose that the meadows were defined in a more or less stable way by the early Elizabethan period.[6]

Kingston meadows were given various names over the years. Most title deeds refer to them simply as meadowlands. But there were local names too. On his map of 1773, Marchant the surveyor calls them Kingstone brooks or marshlands,[7] which evokes their origins and perhaps some of the problems of farming them. Individual bits of the meadows have their own names: the Cannels lay below the road to Lewes at the northeastern edge of the village system, the 'Nitch of the Wish' was a seven-acre meadow lying west of the Cannels along the road to the point where it turns and goes southward towards the sea. Between the Cannels and the 'Nitch' was an acre called the 'Drinkers Acre' – for good reasons, as we shall see. Then, further out, to the east of the open fields called the 'Hams' (see Figure 2.1), there were other meadows: the Wish or Wick, divided into strips, part of which was called the

Penny Diddles. South of the Wish lay the Commons – which were held in 1773 in proportion to individual claims to the downland pasture; and south of that again the Slonks, held in strips of individual ownership. To the east of this whole system of meadows lay two further areas – the enclosed brooks of 1773 and the 'Severralls'. These were well out in the Ouse valley, behind low dykes, and were probably later additions that became a stable part of the meadowlands as reclamation proceeded.

Aside from the Commons, most of the meadows were held in individual ownership as part and parcel of holdings in the open fields. Once again there is no sign of common rights. There was, however, a degree of commonalty in the way the part of meadows was exploited. The story centres on the Drinkers Acre and the strips of meadowland called the Wish. It is told in an Elizabethan document,[8] which claims to be 'a true and certeine note how the Drinker doth fall to everymans land … in the parishe of Kingston nigh Lewes at the time of treading of the wish. At which time, whosoever receiveth the same to his part doth pay eight pence to the residue that tread out the wish to make them a drinking.' True and 'certeine' the note may be, but it is also somewhat opaque. The custom seems to have been as follows: on a certain day, the unmown meadows of the Wish were apportioned out to those who held title to them, and they were mown (called 'treading out'). Each year, one of the persons holding title in the Wish also held the Drinkers Acre as an extra bit. The rights to the Drinker therefore rotated year by year among those who had rights in the Wish itself. But rights to the Drinker carried an obligation, albeit an amiable one. Whoever held them must in that particular year pay out eight pence to the others to 'make them a drinking'. The 'true and certeine note' gives a list of some of the more substantial freeholders and copyholders of Kingston who held the Drinkers Acre between 1574 and 1583, and paid their dues to the others. If Elizabethan Kingston needed an excuse for a good party, this surely was it, though it is a fair guess that the custom itself dated from some much earlier time, and reflects the collective behaviour of an earlier community, possibly Saxon?

Pasture and meadow were of course most important to the agriculture of the village: the first because it provided a great reserve of food for sheep, whose dung was crucial for the arable land and who were folded on stubble and fallow whenever possible; the second because of winter feed, and the summer sustenance it supplied for oxen and cattle after mowing. Still, the arable was the heart of the system and it was the arable in Kingston that was set out in the great open fields.

There are two eighteenth-century maps that show the Kingston open fields: Marchant's map of 1773 and a map prepared for the Duke of Dorset in 1799.[9] They both give an exceptionally clear view of the open field village. Figure 2.1 is taken from them.

In the eighteenth century three great fields centred on the village street; they were called laines – tenantry laines to give them full title. West Laine

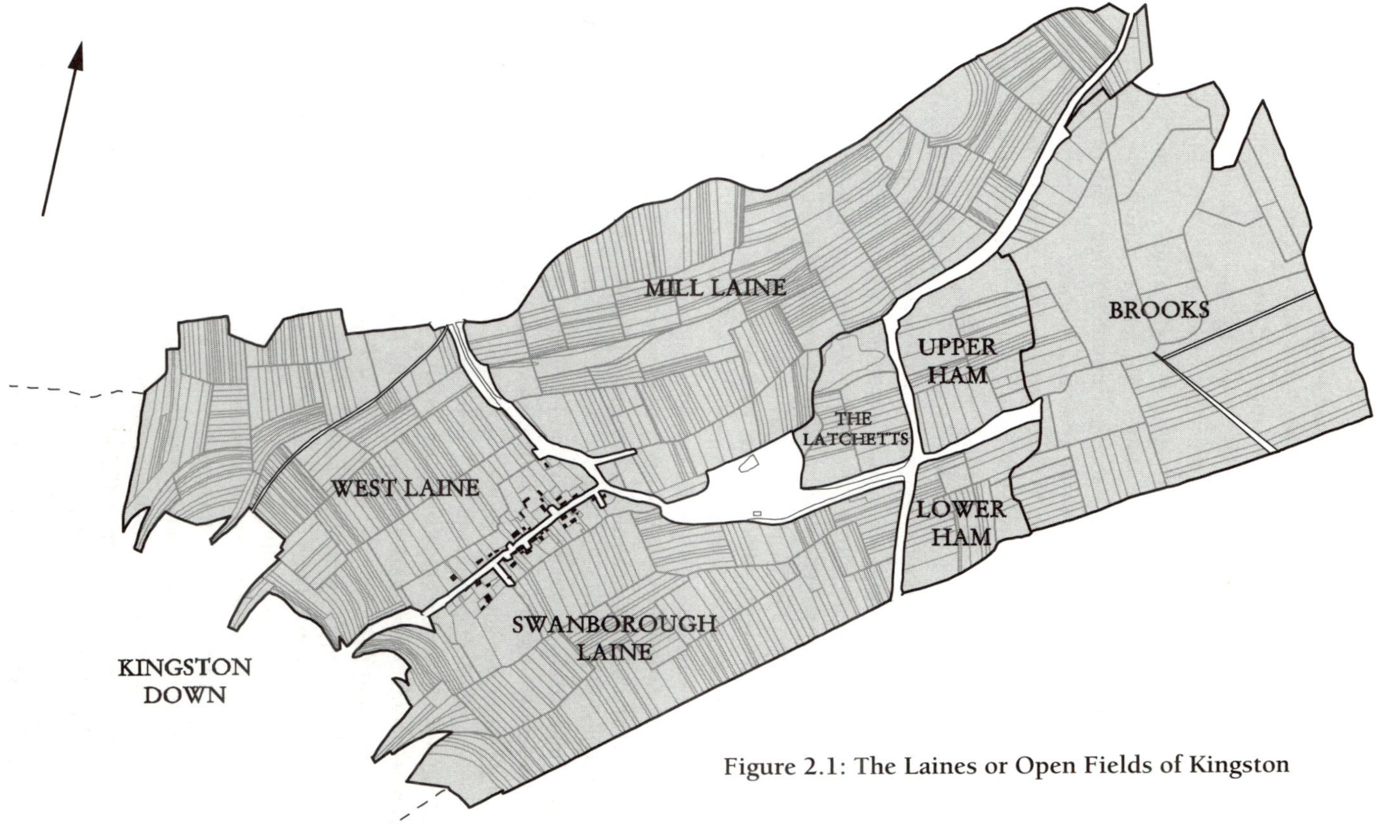

Figure 2.1: The Laines or Open Fields of Kingston

lay on the northwest side of the street in a wide bowl of land that rose steeply up to the ridge in the north, which was crossed by an ancient track called Jugg's Way. To the west it rose steeply too up to the main downlands. Swanborough Laine lay to the south and east of the street. It rises along its whole length to a gentle ridge and its southward boundary lies along the crest of the ridge. To the south lie the lands of Swanborough, which play an important part in the story of Kingston. The third laine, Mill Laine, lay across the road that runs at right angles to the street, and stretched out in part along the slopes that lead to Southover, and in part down the splendid valley that opens out onto the flood plain of the Ouse on the east. In addition to these three great fields, there were two smaller areas of arable. To the east of the Well Green lay the Latchetts, bordering the road to Lewes. And on the other side of the road, lying north and south of the droveway, were Lower Ham and Upper Ham.

There are some other noticeable features of the eighteenth-century village on the maps. One is Well Green itself, a large open area of more than ten acres, which at that time was almost certainly common ground. Marchant's map shows it closed off with a gate on the east and cut off from the village on the west by an unspecified but quite distinct barrier of some kind. Well Green sloped away to the north, particularly steeply in the area of the pond. The other features are both ancient rights of way. One of these is a path, which runs out southeastwards from midway down the village street. It left the street by what was later called Holland's Lane,[10] and crossed the open fields in a direct line to Swanborough. The other right of way (which is still open today) was a cart track, which cut across the south of Mill Laine and ran directly to join the road to Lewes on the east.[11]

The field details in the Marchant and Dorset maps are identical. In Figure 2.2 the details of Mill Laine are shown as an example. West Laine and Swanborough Laine are similarly divided. As Figure 2.2 shows, there are two sorts of division. Each field was divided first into subunits called furlongs. Each furlong was further divided into many parallel strips.

These parallel strips were the characteristic feature of the open field system in England and elsewhere. They were called by different names in different parts of the country – sometimes *selions*, and sometimes just *lands* and other names too. But the unifying feature is that the strips were designed to be that area of land an ox-team could plough in a day – an area that came to be called an acre. Obviously, the area an ox-team could cover depended very much on the heaviness of the soil, so these customary acres differed from the modern statutory acre, sometimes widely. The customary acre in Kingston was about two-thirds of a statutory acre and small, even in terms of the customary acre. Many of them were between half and three-quarters of the local acre.[12] The small acre and the even smaller strips may both result from the general heaviness of Kingston soils and the difficulty of a good deal of the terrain where it borders on steep downland slopes. The point to bear in mind

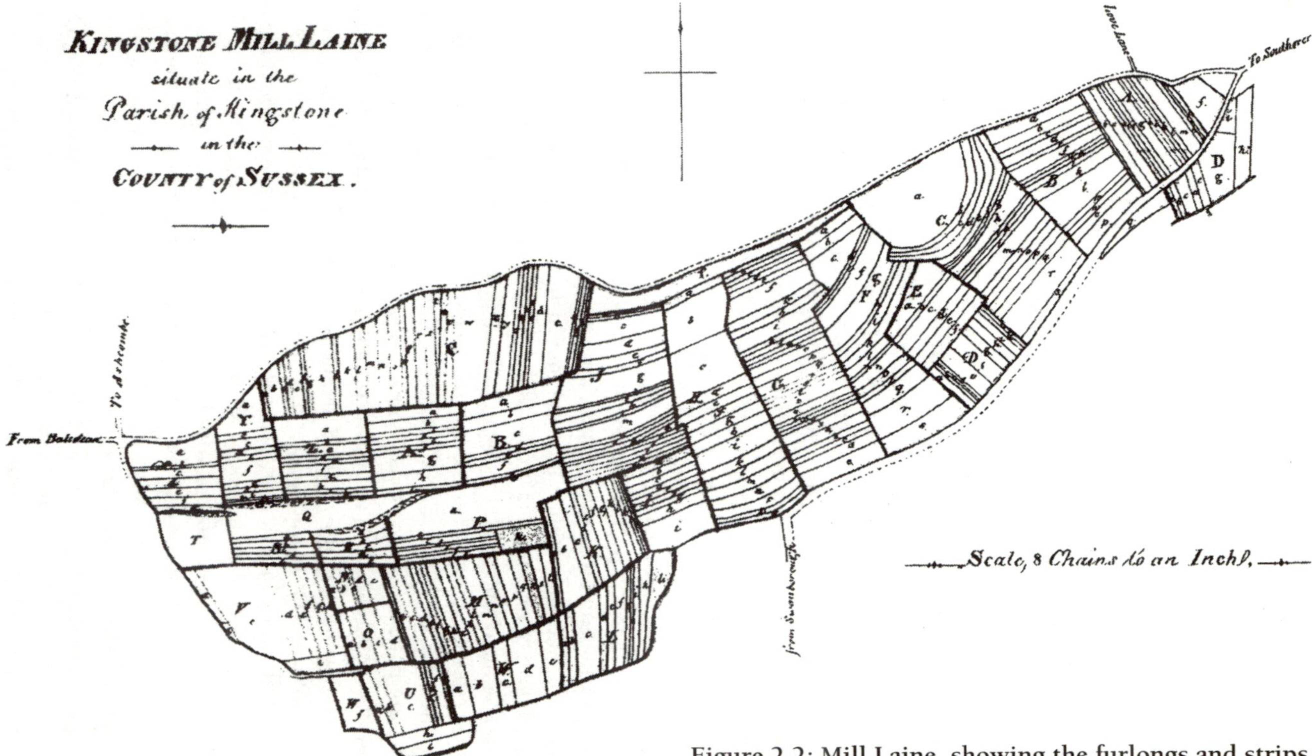

Figure 2.2: Mill Laine, showing the furlongs and strips

is that the customary acre was only partly a measure of area: it was primarily a measure of a day's work for a ploughman's team. This explains varying measurements from one part of the country to another.

What is more interesting, perhaps, is that the customary acre varied within the fields of a village for the same reason. This variation is clear in Kingston from Marchant's terrier, which is simply a detailed listing of all the strips in the laines ascribed to their owners. It is possible to use the information Marchant gives to show how differences in terrain affected the size of the customary acre. For instance, an ox team would accomplish less in a day of ploughing on steep ground than on gentle slopes and, consequently, the customary acre as a measure of work would be *smaller*.[13]

In both Mill Laine and West Laine the customary acre increases in size steadily as the slope of the ground falls off. Swanborough Laine is nearly all gently sloped and there the customary acre has an area not very different from its area on the medium and gentle slopes of Mill Laine and West Laine. The Upper and Lower Hams are very gentle slopes and the customary acre there is large (though larger than one might have expected). The Latchetts are something of an anomaly – they are gently or at most medium sloped and yet their customary acres are quite small. Overall, however, a quite consistent pattern appears that corresponds well with the idea of the customary acre as a measure of labour time. In Mill Laine and West Laine the customary acre was about 20 per cent larger on gentle slopes than on steep ones.

But this leads naturally to a further speculation. If the above argument holds, one might expect that the size of the strips would vary too, for although Kingston strips are mainly a bit smaller than a customary acre in designation, and vary quite a lot even in a furlong, they must in the end bear some relation to the area a team could cover in a day.

Like the customary acre, the area of the strips was greater on gentler slopes than on steeper ones. The correspondence is quite close, except that the medium slopes of West Laine are a bit smaller than one might expect and do not fit the pattern. There is also something of an anomaly in the Hams: the strips in Lower Ham tend to be exceptionally large for Kingston. There is no ready explanation for this, except possibly that by 1773 some strip holders had managed to consolidate adjacent strips into larger areas. The larger strips occur mainly in two particular furlongs where very few owners predominated in 1773. Nor is there an obvious explanation for the generally smaller size of strips in West Laine compared with Mill Laine and Swanborough Laine. Aside from these puzzles, however, the strip story is similar to the customary acre story. Although Kingston strips varied quite a bit in size, they did tend to be about a customary acre in size.

The strips were ploughed from the centre outward, the teams being turned at the end of the furlong furrow on the headlands at the end of the strip. As ploughing proceeded, they had to make a longer and longer traverse across the headland to the other side of the strip in order to take up the next furrow.

As a result of this pattern, the long ridges all faced inwards to the centre of the strip and, as the years passed, strips tended to become considerably higher in the centre than around their perimeters. The strip system is sometimes described as 'ridge and furrow' ploughing because of the raised central ridge it tended to produce. Walter of Henley describes how ploughing was done in the thirteenth century: 'in ploughing go thirty-six times round (the acre) to make the ridge narrower, and when the acre is ploughed then you have made seventy-two furlongs which are six leagues.'[14]

The strip of a customary acre was more or less the unit in which lands were distributed geographically about the village laines, but the basic unit of individual landholding was generally the *yardland* or *virgate*. Both terms are found in Kingston, but not the 'wist', which was used on some manors east of the Ouse,[15] or the term 'ferling', found in the west.[16] The yardland in early medieval times was the typical holding of a 'full villein' from which apparently, he was expected to find subsistence for himself and his family. In Kingston the yardland was small by the standards of the English Midlands, about ten to twelve customary acres, whereas yardlands in the Midlands seem to have been about thirty acres. This small yardland was common in Sussex, particularly in downland manors to the east.[17] As a consequence, that other important conventional medieval measure, the *hide*, which consisted elsewhere of four virgates, was also smaller in Sussex. The Kingston hide was about 40 to 50 customary acres.

Yardlands were, of course, made up of strips, but strips scattered about the village fields in many furlongs. In 1773 there was one farm left in Kingston that in its size and distribution approximated the medieval yardland. Stephen Towner held at that time one and a half yardlands 'of Swanborough Manor'. This holding can be traced back to Elizabethan days in the Swanborough Manor court books in 1578, and it had probably come down in line of inheritance more or less intact from a much earlier time. From Marchant's terrier of Kingston it is possible to work out just how Stephen's holding was spread about the village.[18]

The holding consisted of 23 strips distributed across 20 different furlongs. They were, to say the least, scattered. There was more than a mile between his strips in the furlongs nearest to the street and his furthest strips in the furlongs of Mill Laine, which bordered on Lewes.

The terrier record is of course from 1773 and Stephen Towner, consequently, was no villein. He belonged to that large class of rural people who had come to call themselves 'yeomen', a respectable middle-class farmer, albeit not a very large one. He probably came from an old local family. But times change and so do the relationships of people to the land. The fact is that in an earlier age, such as the twelfth or thirteenth centuries, this yard and a half would have been a common sort of holding for a moderately fortunate villein. And so its distribution in the open field gives a glimpse of some of the problems such a person might have faced in dealing with his land.

Simply remembering where one's land lay was surely one of the main difficulties. It would have been trickier altogether for the villein than for Towner. He at least was literate – villeins were not. So Towner, presumably, kept a list of his strips, with the names of the furlongs in which they lay, and for each furlong, the names of the people who held abutting strips. That is how, for many centuries, strips were customarily specified in titles to land: 23 strips might have 46 abutments. How did Towner's villein forerunners deal with that problem? Whatever the answer, they must have needed very good memories and an extraordinary intimacy with the village fields. It was not, on the face of it, a simple system.

Even Towner must have had his problems in keeping track of his strips and managing their use. And by the eighteenth century there were many larger farmers than Towner for whom these difficulties were magnified. There was John Paine, shown in the terrier as holding 51 strips in 35 furlongs. Richard Relf at this time was a tenant farmer to Mrs Norton and worked some 90 strips or more. Thomas Rogers, who plays a major part in the later history of Kingston, was in possession of 220 strips by the 1780s and in due course added Norton's strips[19] and Paine's also to his ownership.[20] By the end of the 1780s he held more than 360 strips and farmed many others as a tenant; no doubt some of the problems of location and management diminished when holdings grew this big.

But, for villeins, as for the farmers who followed them, many of the bigger agricultural decisions were handled communally by the village landholders and this is a central feature of open field farming and village life.

The three-field system, in Kingston, had its origins in the medieval three-course rotation. Each of the great laines in the open fields would in those early times have been planted in succeeding years to a spring crop and an autumn crop and then left fallow. In any year one out of the three laines would have lain fallow, with the other two under tillage. The three-field system dealt logically enough with this simple rotation, though there is evidence in many places that it grew out of a two-field system,[21] in which land was left fallow every second year. If there was an earlier two-field system in Kingston, it seems plausible from the map that it was based on the West Laine and Swanborough Laine, but we have no evidence of it. At all events, it is clear that the three-field system meant that the individual had little power of decision over what to plant in succeeding years. That was determined by the tradition of the rotation and, given the requirement that the whole of a laine must be in the same rotation, no individual could break with it. The ascription of a whole laine to a given rotation was, it seems, a technical necessity, at least in early times. For one thing, a crucial aspect of the rotation was the grazing of animals, sheep in particular, on the fallow to restore the soil. Since the laines were largely unfenced, even in the eighteenth century, it was simply impracticable that an individual should till strips in an area that others had decided to leave fallow.[22]

But, though the three-field system released the individual from making decisions about what to plant, it also enforced the practice of making other decisions, which might be more open to debate, in a communal way. Everyone must plant at the same time and reaping was also done collectively, at an agreed time. But the most important need for commonalty centred on ploughing. Particularly in earlier times, in the medieval period for example, few individuals in the village owned a complete ox-team. Individual landholders might contribute a beast or two to the plough, but in general not more. Indeed, for an individual virgater there was surely an economic rationality in *not* having a full team to support throughout the year. Ploughing therefore demanded commonalty for economic reasons – and important decisions on when to plough were taken in common. The open field system, in short, led inevitably to a complex set of social obligations. It also required a web of village by-laws, which grew out of precedent, to make it work.[23]

So, the open field system led to complexities of village organization. Many of them were swept away with the open fields themselves at the time of the enclosures, and we who live in a post-enclosure world have no way of recalling them – and perhaps, as a result, we simplify.

The way in which the open-field system works also helps to explain the peculiarities of the strip system. Obviously, if the laines were used in strict rotation, it would be necessary for each landholder to have strips in each laine – indeed desirable that his or her strips should be fairly evenly distributed between laines. The rotation explains one aspect of the geographic distribution of strips, just as the technical and economic facts of ploughing explain their size and shape. What is less obvious is the reason for the distribution of strips between furlongs in each laine. This remains largely a matter of debate, and we shall simply note two possible lines of explanation.

One is that the distribution of strips between furlongs may have facilitated a more flexible use of land. In fact, it opens the way to basing the rotation on the furlong instead of the whole field. Indeed, if furlong rotation were a practice (and it might have been provided sheep could be effectively folded on fallow furlongs), it would require that each landholder should have his strips in as many furlongs as possible, so that if the basic unit of landholding were the yardland, one would expect to find each yardland strip in a different furlong. It is interesting that Stephen Towner's strips were distributed in approximately this way: the fact that there were three Kingston furlongs in which he held *two* strips may be accounted for by his holding a yard and a half rather than a simple yardland alone. There is some evidence of furlong rotation in the medieval period.[24]

The other line of explanation rests on the principle of equity, which was important in village systems dependent on communal decisions. The most obvious way in which it could be assured was by giving everyone access to land of different quality, more or less in proportion to his or her landholding. This would be best achieved by as wide as possible a distribution of a person's strips between furlongs in each laine. And there are other ways in which considerations of equity may have weighed – for instance, in distributing the risks of failure, or in evening out the burden of having to travel a long distance to one's fields, or perhaps most of all in relation to the critical tasks of ploughing and reaping. Both of these were communal – ploughing in particular. *Timing* is apt to be crucial in both activities and it was plainly impossible to plough or reap all the village fields at the same time. Consequently, the more evenly a person's strips were distributed in a field, the more likely they would be to get a fair share, proportionally, of a harvest susceptible to destruction by a sudden deluge, or of ploughing liable to interruption by the weather. But whatever the reason, the facts of the distribution of strips between fields and furlongs are clear enough and their early origin is borne out by the evidence that it was the yardland – the primal medieval unit – that was most widely distributed. That, at least, is a lesson we can learn from Stephen Towner's farm.

The last and obvious questions about the open fields are: How stable were they? How far does Marchant's map of 1773 reflect Kingston, say at the time of the Conquest? What changed and what remained unchanged?

There were certainly some things that changed, for instance the names of the furlongs. The terrier reveals the eighteenth-century names. Some seem to derive from landmarks and places in the fields: the Mill furlong, the Meadow Spotts, Well Croft furlong in Mill Laine; Footway, Highway and Brooks furlongs in Swanborough; the Home Furlongs next to the village; the lovely Greystones and Combe furlongs in West Laine. Others took their names from their shapes or particular relationships to other spaces – 'Between the Links' in Mill Laine, Winding furlong and the Shelf in the West Laine. Still others had names whose meanings are unclear today: the Lagg furlong, for example, or Sneadnore (commemorated still as the name of an undistinguished piece of tarred road). And there were some with names that suggest events or village 'mores' like the Beggars Bush or Sleepers Links.

An Elizabethan survey of Hyde Manor (or at least an eighteenth-century copy of it) survives[25] and shows that many of these names of 1773 were different in 1567. Greystones in West Laine was there in Elizabethan times and so were many others, but the Elizabethans called Winding furlong the 'Long Goore', and Sleepers Links was called, oddly, Hoggland furlong – the sleeping had evidently been done after Elizabeth's reign. Then, also in the West Laine, the Upper and Lower Dene furlongs of 1773 were combined in 1567 and called Denes. There had been a more dramatic change in Swanborough Laine, for if the Hyde survey is to be trusted, it was called South Laine in 1567. And furlong names had altered there too: the Footway furlong of 1773 was Stoneland at the earlier time; the great big Swanborough furlong of the eighteenth century was divided into two, one part called Herd furlong and the other the Headlands. Mill Laine retained its name over these two centuries, but hardly a single furlong name in 1773 is present in the 1567 survey. Clearly field names could be rather transient in the long perspective of Kingston's history.

There are other features of the Kingston fields, which change over the centuries but at the same time show continuities, which point to the antiquity of the system revealed by the eighteenth-century maps. One of these is the disposition of the yardlands in the fields. It was the habit over the ages to give names to individual yardlands or groups of yardlands in the village. There was a duality about the naming of land, which was a natural outcome of the field system. The names of fields and furlongs, obviously, were a way of indicating their location. But they were not very helpful when it came to describing a person's landholding, which consisted of strips in various locations. Consequently, these individual landholdings or parcels of strips were also given names – yardland names.

Many of the yardland names used in the eighteenth century were old. A whole group of them took the names of their Elizabethan or pre-Elizabethan Tudor owners. Howell's lands for example, consisted of a virgate, and are mentioned several times in eighteenth-century documents – in Thomas Rogers's will,[26] for instance. They can be traced back to Robert Howell in 1567, and it is most probable that a Howell held them earlier too in 1524–25. Moreover, at the time that the Howell family held these lands they were called 'Adam's lands', which traces them back to an earlier unspecified time.[27] Then there were three yards of copyhold land called Barnden's, which also took its name from a Tudor family,[28] and Peake is a pre-Elizabethan name that was still used in the nineteenth century for a parcel of six yardlands.[29] Taberer was also a pre-Elizabethan name used up until 1831 for two yardlands and the magnificent barn and close half way down the south side of the street, which became Kingston farmyard in the nineteenth and early twentieth centuries.[30] And there are more besides that bear witness to Tudor owners.

In addition to these, there were three eighteenth-century yardland names that had even greater antiquity: Alfreye's, Diggon's and the lands of Hyde Manor. Alfreye's was the name of six yardlands – which played an important part in the fortunes of the village – and which were almost certainly owned by John Alfrey in the fourteenth century and sold by him to Richard Weyville in 1399.[31] Diggon's was the name given to a group of yardlands owned by the Duke of Dorset in the later eighteenth century. The name came from a very early resident: the de Dyghon family lived in Kingston around 1230 and disappeared from view only after the Great Plague.[32] Finally, the Hyde Manor 'demesne' lands, which played a big part in the eighteenth-century history of the village, originated in a knight's fee of the thirteenth century held by the de la Hydes or atte Hydes.[33]

It is clear that yardlands were designated parcels of strips in the open fields. And, from the fact that the names of groups of yardlands can be traced back for such long periods of time, sometimes up to 600 years, it is a reasonable guess that the patterns of strips belonging to the yardlands remained constant over very long periods too. One needs to be a little careful about this because there are some signs that yardland names could 'shift' from time to time. Diggon's land consisted of one virgate in Kingston Manor in 1619. It apparently passed into the Duke of Dorset's ownership subsequently (Dorset came to own a substantial part of Kingston land as we shall see later), and the duke – or more likely his steward – then attached the ancient name to a whole group of 13 yardlands that he owned in the village.[34] The same type of pulling together of yardlands may have produced the eighteenth-century Alfreye's, though here the evidence is less clear. Title deeds of 1617 describe 'Tenement and two yardlands with one mesneland once Budds; two tenements with four yardlands once Richard Aboore, called Alfreys'.[35]

It is not clear whether the whole group of lands were called Alfreys at the time or whether the name applied only to the four-yardland group. Alfreys probably referred to the whole group and these were certainly the six yardlands of 1700.[36]

Although names could slip from a small group of yardlands to a larger one encompassing the original group, most of the evidence about the yardlands supports the idea that they were parcelled together in rather stable groups over the centuries – and consequently that the strips that made them up also remained the same for very long periods of time. If we consider that a large part of the Kingston yardlands can be traced back to the Tudor period and that some groups of land can be traced back even further to the Norman period, then it is not hard to believe that the maps of 1773 are a rough guide to the field system of the medieval village.

But they are only a rough guide: there is some more detailed information about the village lands that reveals, in the first place, just how stable the disposition of strips belonging to a particular parcel of land actually was – but also indicates the changes that could take place in the open field system. This information is in the survey of the lands of Hyde Manor done in 1567.[37] The survey is a remarkably useful document, even though all that is available now is what appears to be an eighteenth-century copy of the original (which shows evidence of errors). It gives a full list of all the strips of land, which belonged to the manor demesnes, indicating their location in the furlongs as well as the names of the owners of the abutting lands. It can therefore be compared directly with the terrier of 1773 and, together with rich information about the changes in the ownership of land over these 206 years, it is possible to test the idea that the strips that made up any particular holding tended to remain the same over a long period of time.

The results are quite impressive. The 1567 survey lists 86 strips in all. Of these 81 (about 95 per cent) can be located in exactly the same places in the fields from Marchant's terrier of 1773. (They are listed as Norton's lands in 1773, when the manor was held by Mrs Elizabeth Norton). In addition to this, the survey gives the names of the 1567 owners of around 160 abutting strips. Nearly 90 per cent of the owners of abutting lands in 1773 are exactly the people one would expect to hold these lands from the information we have about changes in the ownership of land between the two dates. In total, the survey provides information about the location of around 250 strips in 1567, or roughly a third of the Kingston lands. The comparison with the terrier shows that 92 per cent of the strips of 1567 could be located in the same positions two centuries later through the ownership one would predict from the title deeds, which showed how yardlands changed hands over the ages. In other words, the conclusions that are suggested by the yardland names are clearly confirmed by the survey: the configuration of the open field strips was remarkably stable, and the pattern that Marchant's map reveals is a fair approximation to what the fields were like in a more distant past.

But, as well as this constancy in the configuration of the strips, the survey also shows signs of some interesting changes in the village fields. A close look at Norton's lands of 1773 shows that they included ten strips of land *not* listed in 1567. In other words, although nearly all the 1567 strips can be located on the 1773 map, there are some extra 1773 strips not mentioned in the Elizabethan survey. While this may not seem very interesting it becomes more so when these 'extra' strips of 1773 are located on the map. It turns out that they are all in Mill Laine. It also turns out that they are all to be found in a particular group of furlongs, which are adjacent to one another, lying together in the northwest corner of Mill Laine as Marchant surveyed it. They are labelled X, Y, Z and A, B, C in the map (Figure 2.2.).

Why is this interesting? Simply because it suggests rather convincingly that this group of furlongs was not opened up in 1567 but was added to Mill Laine at some point in the following two centuries. It is the fact that the errant strips of 1773 are situated in contiguous furlongs that leads to this conclusion. If they had been scattered at random about the laine it would have been a different story. There is clear evidence of *assarting* – opening up of wastes or pastures to tillage – probably in the late Elizabethan period, when a good deal of assarting took place all over England, under the pressure of a growth in population.

There are other circumstances that support the idea that there was assarting in this particular corner of the Kingston fields. The first is the geography of this part of Kingston. Immediately to the south of the furlongs in which we suspect there was assarting, there is a very steep slope. The northern parts of the furlongs marked P, Q, R, S, T in Figure 2.2 rise sharply. These are older furlongs, and it would not have been possible to take an ox-team from them to the newer lands above them to the north – although once the slope is surmounted, the slope of the land becomes much more gentle, especially in the big furlong marked C on the map. It is reasonable to suppose from the geography of the lands that the steep slope might originally have formed the northward boundary of this part of Mill Laine and that the ploughmen of

Kingston had been reluctant to use the area to the north until there was strong commercial or other pressure for them to do so. The new lands had to be approached from the track that formed the northern boundary of the laine in 1773 – and this meant that the ox-teams had to be taken up the steep lane that leads from the village to Ashcombe to get there.

The lie of the land then, is consistent with the idea of asserting the Mill Laine – it gives a certain plausibility to the idea; but there is more convincing evidence in the terrier. The fact is that Mill Laine as Marchant surveyed it in 1773 was much bigger than West Laine or Swanborough Laine. Table 2.1 shows this.

The first three lines of the table show the 1773 acreages. Mill Laine at that time was about 50 per cent bigger than either of the others, whether measured in customary or in statutory acres.

From the point of view of a three-course rotation based on whole fields, this difference in size is strange. Unless the fertility of soil in Mill Laine was very much lower than elsewhere in the village, it would have resulted in a strange imbalance in production – with comparatively little corn in the village in those years when Mill Laine lay fallow. It is the case that the yields of corn per acre in Mill Laine were in all likelihood lower than in the other two large laines – but improbable that they were so much lower on the average as to account for the large difference in size. In the days before synthetic fertilizers even modern Kingston farmers reckoned on about a third less corn per acre on the steeply sloping parts of the Mill Laine area than on flatter lands in the Kingston hollow, and had all the lands in Mill Laine been that much less fertile it would account for the difference in size between the laines. But Mill Laine is not by any means entirely made up of steep lands: it includes the lush valley that opens out towards the Kingston brooks, which was high yielding. So it is unlikely that the difference in size could be explained simply by differences in yields.

It is however, easily explained by the assarting that seems to be indicated when the Hyde survey is compared with the Marchant terrier. In line 4 of Table 2.1 there is an estimate of the acreage lying in the assarted furlongs (X, Y, Z and A, B, C in Figure 2.2 worked out from the terrier). When the enlarged Mill Laine of 1773 is reduced by the amounts of these assarts, the estimated area of the laine before the assarts (shown in the last line of Table 2.1) is quite closely in line with the areas of the other laines. Indeed, the remaining differences could quite easily be explained by differences in the productivity of the soil in different parts of the village lands. The assarting that we can infer from the Hyde survey is partly confirmed by the information about the areas of the laines. It may be also that this sheds a light on the way the fields came to be used in later years. If it made sense for extra furlongs to be added to Mill Laine, throwing it 'out of balance' with its two large partners, it suggests that the reasons then may have been that preserving a balance had ceased to be important to the village. Those reasons lay in the use of whole laines at a time in the three-course rotation. Could it be that by the Elizabethan period the villagers were no longer using the laines in quite this

Table 2.1: Acreages of Kingston tenantry laines, 1773

Laine	*Customary acres*	*Statutory acres*
Mill Laine	332.00	203.25
West Laine	201.25	127.50
Swanborough Laine	212.00	137.00
Acreage of assart in Mill Laine	71.50	44.50
Mill Laine before assart	260.50	159.25

way? Had they developed three-course rotation by *furlongs* rather than by whole laines? This is what the assart, if that is what it was, seems to suggest.

At all events it is clear that alongside the signs of continuity – especially the stable configuration of the strips – there are signs of change too, and these need to be in mind as we speculate about the Kingston fields in the more distant medieval past. If lands were recovered from the 'wastes' after 1567, is it possible that there had been recoveries before – in the years between the Conquest and the advent of the Tudors?

Unfortunately one can only guess. There is no evidence. If indeed there were earlier assarts in Kingston, it is very likely that they took place in response to two main forces.

First, as in so many parts of England, there may have been extensions of the arable lands to cope with growing population in the late twelfth and thirteenth centuries.[38] It is a reasonable guess that the Latchetts might have been brought into cultivation at this time, at the expense of an earlier larger patch of waste extending from the Well Green of 1773 right through the highway from Swanborough to Lewes (see Figure 2.1). It is also possible that lands lying north of Well Green, between it and the old right of way (shown as a cart track in Marchant and in the Yeakell and Gardiner map) in the valley below the Mill Laine, were added at this time. The cart track indeed has its own interest. For much of its length it lies accurately along the straight line that is formed if the line of the village street is projected eastwards to join up with the Swanborough–Lewes highway at the point where it turns eastward through a right angle. It is tempting to speculate that this ancient track may have been the earliest access to the village from Lewes. It has the merit of being the shortest route towards Lewes – even if, because it runs down the valley, it is also the muddiest. If indeed the medieval access to the village was by this route, it might well have formed the southern boundary of Mill Laine, and the lands to the south of it, abutting Well Green, could have been added later.

A second force at work in Kingston could have led to assarting – somewhat particular to the village, but not entirely so.[39] This was the effect of the progressive reclamation of marshland in the Kingston brooks, which as we have seen grew considerably from the medieval period. As marshes were turned into village brooklands, it is likely that they created incentives to extend the arable fields. For one thing, the extension of the meadows meant that older lands that might have been suitable for arable farming but had perforce to be given over to meadow to support draught animals and small milk herds might now be put to the plough. For another, the larger meadows would permit the village to hold more draught animals – as well as probably increasing its dairy outputs – and so facilitate the process. At a guess, the Lower and Upper Hams may be the product of such an assarting movement in the wake of reclamation of the marshes. They are certainly located appropriately to give some plausibility to the argument, since they border on the brooks.

All in all then, the Kingston fields at the time of the Conquest were probably slightly smaller and less developed than in 1773. The Mill Laine was certainly smaller (if one accepts the evidence of a post-1567 assart) – and the village open fields were probably confined to the three main laines. This, incidentally, would make it look much more like the open field village of history textbooks. But the Latchetts and the Hams are comparatively small areas. They amount to no more than 10 per cent of the total arable in 1773. If they and the post-1567 assarts are left out, it would mean that the Conquest open fields were about 80 per cent of the area of the 1773 fields, not a great deal of change in 700, or nearly 800 years, for the lands Marchant drew in 1773 were substantially unchanged in 1831 when the village was at last enclosed.

So far we have explored the lands of Kingston in isolation from the lands that lay around. To round out the story, let us take a broader look – a bird's eye view of the village and its neighbours.

The Dorset maps of 1799[40] are not just confined to Kingston. They show how the village lay in relation to other land. The Kingston system lies in a band running from Lewes on its northeast frontier to Woodingdean and Balsdean at the southwestern end. Its points of contact with Lewes are in the area of Southover, which lies at the south of the town, and Houndean in the western part of it. Both were the sites of medieval properties of great importance to events in the village – especially Southover, the location of the priory of Lewes from the eleventh century. The northern edge of Kingston lands bordered on Ashcombe and then Falmer; both were village systems – the former a very small hamlet, the latter a more substantial village with its own developed open field system.

It is, however, the lands to the south that are of greater interest to the history of the village. The Dorset maps show that in 1799, the southern boundary of Kingston lay along a band of land centred on Swanborough Grange. These lands look different from the Kingston lands because, in 1799, they were enclosed in large fields with no strips. The core of the Swanborough lands is the central portion of arable made up of two consolidated blocks: one called Swanborough Court Farm and the other called Stuckles.[41] Stuckles was the smaller part and it appears to have been brought together by exchanges of earlier strip lands – in other words by a very early enclosure. Swanborough Court Farm, which covered nearly 200 acres of arable, had been church lands before the dissolution of the monasteries and belonged then to the priory of Lewes.

The interesting and important aspect of the Swanborough Court Farm lands is that they seem to have been consolidated into a single block for as long as they had existed. Colin Platt explored the lands of Swanborough in the course of his study of monastic granges.[42] In order to locate monastic lands Platt used evidence obtainable from the tithe maps. The point is that the land of some of the great religious houses of the Norman period was exempted from payments of tithe. Although this might apply mainly to the Cistercian houses of England, it was also extended to other orders – and it is clear that the privilege of tithe exemption had been granted to the Cluniac order at the priory of Lewes, at least as far as their lands at Swanborough were concerned. These tithe exemptions (which were of considerable commercial value) were jealously guarded by the orders while they held sway. Afterwards, at the dissolution of monastic lands, their new lay owners inherited them and, no doubt, they were a particularly desirable aspect of the erstwhile church lands. Consequently, Platt argues, it is possible to use the evidence of tithe exemption to locate monastic lands.[43]

The evidence for Swanborough is unambiguous. The tithe map of 1842,[44] drawn up to facilitate the great commutation of tithes in the nineteenth century, shows the great block of Swanborough Court Farm as exempt, 'the said farm and lands having formerly been parcel of the possessions of the abbot and monks of Lewes and having been held by them free of tithes at the time of the dissolution of the monasteries'.[45] The monks, then, had held the land as a great unit, flanked to the east by meadows stretching out into the Ouse valley and to the west by the steep downlands on which they pastured their sheep. So, in the medieval centuries, and right up to the time of the enclosures, the southern boundary of Swanborough Laine, or South Laine, lay next to a consolidated area of enclosures in the court farm. These enclosures must have stood in the sharpest contrast to the patchwork of minute strips that patterned the laines of Kingston itself. And, to the south of Swanborough there lay another area of open fields[46] – the laines of Iford village. Swanborough was a unique area lying between the ancient fields of its northern and southern neighbours. It was an area full of portent for Kingston.

The parliamentary enclosure of 1831 swept away the whole complex of Kingston open fields and, with it, the fields' old names and the yardlands' ancient ascriptions. The 'old' names for locations that still remain are mostly part of the nineteenth-century naming system. Hardly any of Kingston's earlier place names remain. Hyde is commemorated, somewhat misleadingly as it will turn out, by a beautiful house in Kingston Street, and so is Kingston Manor. Perhaps the titles of manors were too grand and impressive for nineteenth-century owners to relinquish them, however irrelevant they may by then have become. Beyond this there is little. Only 'Snednore', once the mysterious name of a furlong remains, attached now with equal mystery to a sad bit of tarred road near to the remnants of Well Green.

The post-enclosure fields that surround the village today have their own grandeur. They sweep across the sites of Mill Laine and Swanborough Laine, broken only by the occasional hedge – crisp stretches of Sussex agriculture. (The old West Laine has disappeared almost entirely under the unhappy postwar housing estate.)

But, for all their splendour, the post-enclosure fields brought large changes to the look of things. The open fields of old Kingston must have looked much busier than today's land. The ploughed and sown strips were discernible, patterning the laines and only melding into one great sweep as the crops matured and ripened and got high enough to hide the patchwork of separate ownerships on which they grew. No doubt too, there were many more people on the land, especially at busy times of the year. And when the land was being ploughed for sowing or for fallow, we might expect that the dust rose from many strips as the Kingston ox-teams heaved through the heavy earth of the valleys and up the steep slopes where the arable encroached the Downs.

The Enclosure Act swept away more than the fields and the names. It also put paid finally to a system of communal cultivation, which had in all likelihood been waning in the century before 1831. The open fields were worked in earlier times to a complex set of rules: rules about the rotation, about the uses of the fallow, about the agricultural activities of the individual cultivators in relation to the community as a whole; and these rules were needed. In such a system there were many small but important matters in which an individual might feel it in his interest to go his own way – but if allowed, the results would be worse for all. Others have studied village rules.[47] The Kingston by-laws have not come down to us intact, but we know they were there, partly because they *must* have been for the system to work at all; and partly because we get a glimpse of them in the manorial records. The 'Book of John Rowe' gives one such tiny glimpse.[48] John Rowe mentions: 'Orders for the ringing of hogges in Kingston (Oct. 36 Eliz.) and against puttings of horses into the comons laynes there before all the corn be carried away in haruest time. (Mar. 39 Eliz. and April 36 Eliz.), the penalty is vs. for every offense'.

There would be no need for such rules if the farmer's unringed hogs put his own arable at risk. But with the strip system, the main risk was to his neighbours and the chances that one of his own strips would be damaged were very small. So a lazy man (or one who felt especially kind to hogs perhaps) might not see much point in ringing, unless the rules obliged him to. And the same owner of enclosed lands would not dream of putting horses out to graze 'before all the corn be carried away'. But, if the danger to one's own corn was minimal and the main danger was to one's neighbours, a careless farmer might not feel much incentive to watch his horses with the necessary degree of care. The open fields needed rules – communal rules to enforce commonalty on those whose social consciousness might not be sharp enough. It is tempting to idealize and see the system as a purely voluntary collective. It could not be so. Whereas the rules might be communally agreeable, obedience to them required some degree of enforcement.

How far enforcement came from the village community itself and how far from manorial lords is a nice question, still debated. There is not much evidence about the matter in Kingston, but there are reasons to believe that the village community might have had a special force in such matters. This is because of the rather curious style of manorial control in the village, which we turn to next.

We may leave the Kingston open fields, temporarily at least, with a final remark: this system of farming was founded in the end on a sophisticated social code evolved by precedent over many centuries. It was not as naive and simple as we may think. Perhaps our visions of the past are too influenced by the simplifications that came with enclosure, for after enclosure the self-interest of individual farmers or their consolidated lands led naturally to the observance of practices that had needed the support of a web of social sanctions in the open field village.

A multiplicity of manors

Manors are rather grand institutions. To our modern minds they give a chivalric patina to rural affairs that tends to obscure the humility of ordinary lives. They evoke images of country gentry and coats of arms, of earls, barons and knights – in short, all the paraphernalia of earlier ruling classes who in their various ways stood for the 'landed interest', which dominated England until the Parliamentary Reform and the repeal of the Corn Laws in the nineteenth century. Perhaps that is why our county histories read as if rural history were largely reflected in the succession of titles to manorial rights: lords are all that matter.

That is not the way to look at Kingston, or at least it is not the way we shall look at it. To understand a village in its times, one must dig beneath the grand events, like changes in lordship, to find the ordinary content of the village today. It is not easy to do this, nor can it be done without guesswork, deduction and large gaps – but it is the purpose of this story.

Even so, manors are important to it. The less grand work-a-day side of the manorial system is that it organized the lives of ordinary people – particularly their working lives. The manor, as much as the open field system, was an essential part of the framework within which ordinary day-to-day matters were sorted out. Ignore the manors from this point of view and the life of the village will seem less grand perhaps, more focused on the ordinary – but it will also be less comprehensible.

The nature of the manorial system changed drastically over the centuries. Its origins are found in England in Saxon times,[49] but it only appeared in its strict and logical medieval form when Normans tidied up the straggling (and possibly more humane) organizations the Saxons had evolved. It was under the Normans that the manorial hierarchies emerged in a comparatively simple and familiar form. Manors were held by lords 'of the King' or of' some superior baron who in turn held lands, which might be scattered all over England, granted by the king. In return, manorial lords and barons had military obligations and, often, civil ones too.[50] The lords controlled the system beneath them. They held part of their lands directly as their own: their 'demesnes', whose product was at the lord's command. A second part was held by unfree people in return for rents in money and, more importantly in the feudal period, for direct labour services. These were villeins, like the villeins who held Kingston yardlands. The lords controlled their comings and goings, their marriages and their careers, and exacted payments when they died before passing rights to their land to their successors.

A third part of the manorial lands was held 'freely' – that is in return for rents or military obligations perhaps, but without obligations on the holder to provide work for the lord's demesnes. They were held by 'freemen', whose lives were not controlled, as were the villeins. Beneath the freemen and the villeins in the manorial social order were cottagers (sometimes called 'bordars') living in tenements with small bits of land attached. These people had comparatively light labour services, more or less in proportion to the smallness of their land-holdings, but in general too little land to provide for themselves and their families. They made up their subsistence by some form of wage labour (perhaps for wages paid in kind in the early medieval days) on the lordly demesnes – and possibly on other lands too. And then, at the bottom of the social pile, were the serfs – unfree, landless and explicitly owned by the lords.

Whether English manors ever had quite the degree of order that all this implies is doubtful. It may be that the refinements of order were as much or more a reflection of a passion for having things in their place on the part of Norman lawyers and bureaucrats as of social realities. The Saxon social distinctions on which the Normans built the system were by all accounts less clearly structured. It is true that the Domesday Book classifies people in the simple feudal hierarchy, but then Domesday is in a sense the first (of many) documents we have from the civil service (some would say still the most useful), and civil servants prefer things to be tidy.

Whether or not Norman manors conformed to this pattern, it is plain that they changed radically with the times. The changes are part of Kingston's story, but their broad outlines are easy to sketch. Villein service was slowly 'commuted' into the payment of money rents as the markets for lordly surpluses grew. The process was slow and uneven. There were times of actual or attempted regression to customary labour service, but by the end of the medieval period – say in the fifteenth century – a labour market had come into being and was to remain. Alongside it, a market in land developed. Land became designated 'copyhold' (from the old 'customary lands' of the villeins, which had been held by 'copy of the Manor Court Roll') or freehold (the lands of earlier freemen), and both kinds were bought and sold. Manorial rights on other matters remained for many centuries – for example, rights to heriot (payment at the death of a copyholder), but many such feudal incidents became redundant or largely symbolic as the centuries passed.

However, in spite of these changes, which amounted to a massive transformation of the feudal system from within, the manorial system remained a part of the rural social framework in other ways. The wide civil powers of manorial lords and their status remained intact long after the feudal order itself had been transcended. And the manors themselves remained important too. Village by-law – so essential to the operation of open-field villages like Kingston – was made largely in the manorial courts, as lords and their 'homage' resolved conflicts or constrained the behaviour of the antisocial, or simply found ways of exploiting the weak and powerless. Above all, perhaps, the manorial court determined title to land. After a transaction, the seller of lands would surrender them 'into the lord's hands', and the buyer would then be 'admitted' with the assent of the lord and the homage – in the case of copyholds after payment of a 'fine'. Even after this procedure had become largely symbolic and the 'fines' themselves merely relics of the ancient feudal incidents on the lands, the civil courts of England continued to use the manorial records as evidence of title to land. So the procedure and the manor courts remained crucial in law.

There are two prevalent generalizations about the medieval manors historians nowadays regard with scepticism; the manorial system in Kingston confirms their doubts in its own small way.

The first generalization is that manors conformed more or less to a type – consisting of demesne lands, copyhold and freehold and embracing the standard social structure of lord, freemen, villeins and cottagers in its entirety. In fact, this 'ideal type' of manor turns out to be rather rare. Professor Postan gives an apt summary of research: 'What emerges from the latter-day view is a pattern of villages and estates in which manors conforming to the classical type were few and far between, but in which manors of a kind were invariably to be found.'[51]

The other generalization – which is to some extent tied up with the 'ideal type' – is summarized in the phrase: 'one manor, one vill'. The idea is simple – indeed probably too simple. It envisages that each village with its system of lands fell under the sway of a single manor – and perhaps also that each manor was made up of a single village, usually of the open field type. For academics, this scheme has the merit of tidiness. If each village fell under a single manor, village law and custom and the 'custom of the manor' would coincide. All tenants of a particular class would be treated alike. All major decisions, agricultural, pastoral or otherwise, would be referred to a single ultimate lordly authority so that conflict could not arise. The attractions of the idea are obvious. Its only flaw is that it does not reflect reality. There were many 'vills of divided lordship',[52] where lands of more than one manor were to be found. Kingston was one example. Indeed, on the western side of the Ouse valley below Lewes the village of divided lordship was the rule – to which there were no exceptions.[53]

The quickest look at seventeenth- and eighteenth-century titles to land in Kingston is enough to reveal an initially confusing multiplicity of manors in the village.[54] A closer look at the holdings of these different manors shows that there was more than one type of 'manor': in fact, there were just as many types as there were actual manors.

The clearest picture of the manors in Kingston comes from the ascriptions of the village lands in the early years of the seventeenth century – at the very end of Elizabeth's reign or in the first years of James I's. This gives a 'photograph' of the manors – a description at a particular point in time, which, however, is good enough to permit inferences about earlier times. The way land was divided between manors was a constant in village life, certainly after Elizabeth's reign and in all likelihood for many centuries before. Table 2.2 shows the way Kingston yardlands in the open fields were divided between manors. It is based on a good deal of detective work, the sources for which are given in the notes.[55]

There were lands of no fewer than five manors in the village. They were: Swanborough, Iford, Houndean, Kingston and Hyde manors. To appreciate the full complexity of the village land system, one needs to bear in mind a point that, once made, is easily overlooked. The lands of these various manors were of course interspersed with one another in the furlongs of the open fields, so that each furlong was a patchwork of strips from different manors.

This interlocking of the lands belonging to different manors can be shown graphically with the assistance of the ascription of strips in the Hyde survey of 1567 and the Marchant terrier of 1773. Figure 2.3 shows the complicated pattern that resulted.[56] It indicates the manorial holdings of parts of two Kingston furlongs and some immediately adjacent ones. Mill furlong lay in Mill Laine between the ancient Jugg's way on the north, and the Swanborough–Lewes highway in the valley to the south. The main windmill for grinding Kingston corn was set at the top of the furlong where it would catch the wind sweeping over the ridge. Horselong Furlong lay in West Laine at its western frontier with the downland. It is just north of the village street. In both furlongs the lands of different manors abut one another in a more or less random manner. A word of warning though: the lands of Hyde Manor are considerably over-represented in these furlongs, since the data on which the maps are based were drawn mainly from the survey of Hyde Manor. This complicated interlocking of strip lands lies behind the more orderly looking distribution of Kingston yardlands between the manors in Table 2.2. Let us return to it.

Table 2.2: Distribution of arable lands in Kingston tenantry laines by manors, *c*.1600

Manor		*Yardland or Farm Name*		*No. Yardlands*
Swanborough:	(1)	Alfreye's		6 (F)
	(2)	Alfreye's		½
	(3)	Addams		1½
	(4)	Boniface		3
		Howells		1
	(5)	Barndens		3
	(6)	Priory Lands		2 (F)
	(7)	Taylors		4
	(8)	Dorsets (ex Skinner, Culpeper, Coppard, Hardman, Bowrer)		15
			Total	36
Iford:	(9)	Taberers		2
	(10)	Hudd's		4
	(11)	Towners		2
	(12)	Bishops		2
			Total	10
Kingston:	(13)	Demesnes		12 (D)
	(14)	Demesnes		1
	(15)	part of Peakes		1
	(16)	Howells (later Bayley's)		1
			Total	15
Hyde:	(17)	Demesnes		9 (D)
Houndean:	(18)	Peakes		5 (F)
			Grand Total	75

Notes: (a) Sources used to compile this table are given in detail in note 55 for Chapter 2; (b) Freehold lands are marked (F), demesne lands (D). All other lands are copyhold, although there is some vestigial uncertainty about (4) and (11).

It shows first of all, a modest village in one particular sense: outside the demesne lands, village yardlands were predominantly copyholds. This can be taken as a rough guide to the proportion of villein landholders in earlier times. If the demesne lands are left out of account 54 yardlands remain. Just 41 of these, over three-quarters of the village lands, were copyholds. And this is likely to be an underestimate of the villein proportion in the early medieval population of the village. In the first place, it is quite likely that some villein customary lands of earlier ages had been enfranchized as freeholds in the centuries intervening up till the Elizabethan time: and second, in earlier times

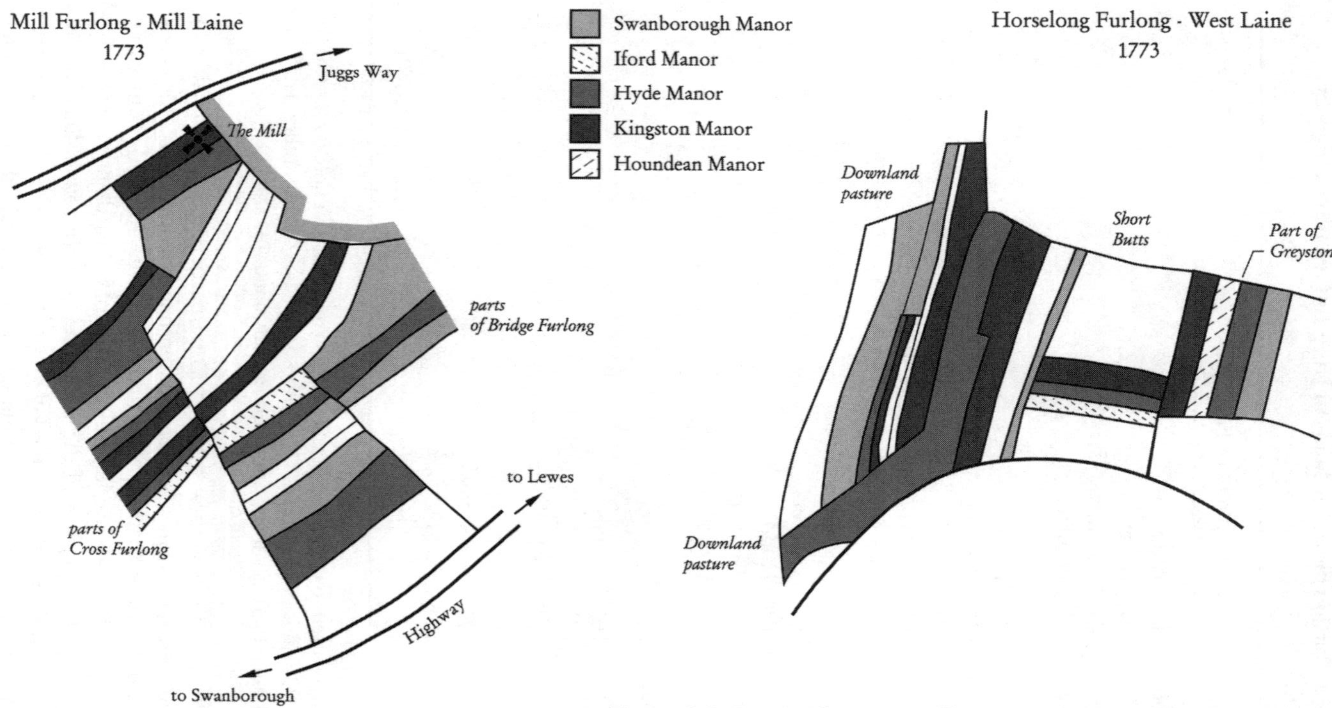

Figure 2.3: Two Furlongs in Mill Laine and West Laine

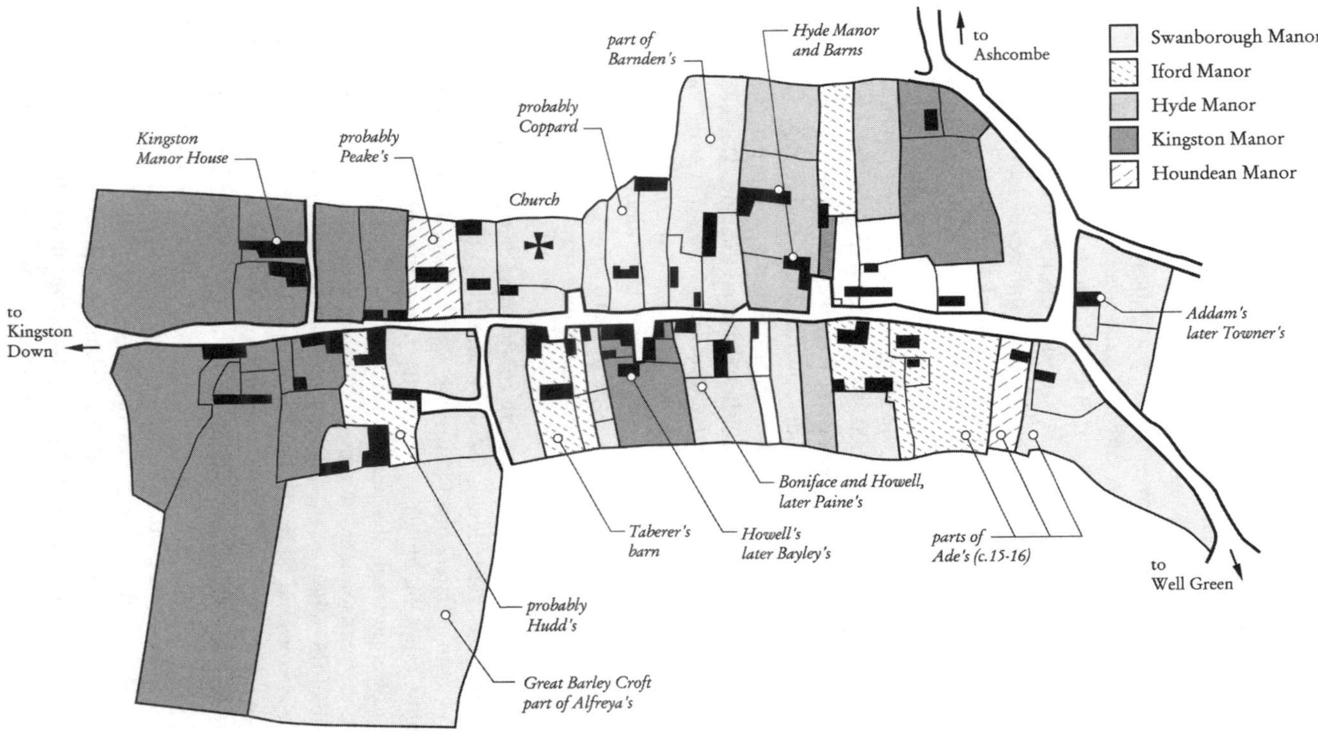

Figure 2.4: Manorial holdings in Kingston Village Street, 1773

it is likely that freeholdings in the village consisted generally of larger blocks of yardlands than individual villein holdings. There is little doubt that Kingston had been preponderantly a village of servile people – as much so or more perhaps than the majority of English villages of feudal days.

Swanborough Manor dominated the village. It had been an ecclesiastical manor, held by the Prior of Lewes until it was wrested from him at the dissolution of the monasteries. In the early 1600s it was in lay hands, of course – but aristocratic ones for all that: the earl of Dorset was lord,[57] and therefore lord over the 36 Swanborough yardlands in Kingston open fields. These yardlands accounted for nearly half the arable lands of the village. If demesne lands are excluded, the manor held more than two-thirds of the village arable and, in particular, just short of 70 per cent of the copyhold, erstwhile villein lands. A large proportion of the Swanborough manorial holdings were copyholds – slightly larger in proportion than for the village as a whole, for even though 15 of the Swanborough yardlands of 1600 were held directly by the lord of the manor, these were not originally demesnes. They were old copyhold lands that Dorset had 'brought back into demesnes' by this time. Before that, however, there had been customary tenants on them: Skinner, Culpeper, Coppard, Hardman and Bowrer. The Hyde survey shows that all the lands Dorset came to hold directly at some point towards the end of the sixteenth century had been held by individual copyholders as late as 1567.[58] In short, in earlier times Swanborough Manor had claimed lordship over a large amount of customary land (28 yardlands to be exact), and a large proportion of the customary lands in the village fields – so also the manor held sway over the majority by far of the Kingston villeins in an earlier age.

It is notable that there were no Swanborough demesne lands in the Kingston open fields. The demesnes – we already know – were in a great enclosed and consolidated block of some 240 customary acres about the Swanborough Grange buildings to the south. In a sense this configuration of lands makes Swanborough the nearest thing to the 'ideal type' of manor in Kingston. A vast consolidated demesne – whose arable lands were nearly a third the size of the whole of the village arable – abutted the Kingston laines, in which the manor held all its freehold and copyhold. There were hardly any Swanborough lands in Iford.[59] The manor embraced all the elements that made up the feudal social order: villeins in some abundance, freeholders and some cottagers too. There was only one respect in which it failed to conform to the type: in spite of its predominance in the Kingston fields, it was not the only manor; it did not fit the pattern of 'one manor, one vill'.

Two of these other manors were like Swanborough in a single respect. Neither Iford Manor nor Houndean had any demesnes in Kingston.

Iford Manor was small. All its lands in Kingston were copyhold but they amounted to less than a third of the amount of arable held by Swanborough. Nevertheless, these ten customary yards appear to have been the sum total of Iford Manor lands outside the demesnes – so it was on an altogether less impressive scale than its large neighbour. In addition, the Iford demesnes, unlike Swanborough's, were at a considerable distance from Kingston, being spread about in the open fields of Iford village, beyond the court farm.

Houndean Manor had hardly any weight in Kingston. Its lands in the village consisted of five freehold yards, though in total Houndean (which had the full title of Houndean Smithwycke) was a substantial manorial property held by Bergavenny in 1600. Its demesnes were in lands along the northeast boundary of the Kingston fields in Mill Laine. In addition to these five yards, there was a freehold tenement in Kingston held by Houndean.[60]

Iford and Houndean differ from the classical type of manor in that their Kingston lands were essentially 'outliers' – they lay apart from the main manorial holdings, in particular the demesnes. Kingston Manor and the 'Manor or reputed manor of Hyde' differed too – but in other ways. They were the only manors that had demesne lands in the village fields. In both cases the demesnes were scattered about among all the other strips of the laines. However, both were small – Kingston held yardlands, substantially less than half the Swanborough holding, and Hyde held only nine yards. And both are remarkable in another aspect: they are comparatively very short of customary lands. Hyde Manor, in fact, consisted simply of demesnes (at least in Kingston – it may be that there were some very few Hyde customary lands in the area between Barcombe and Chailey to the north). Kingston had 12 yardlands in demesnes and only three copyhold yards in addition to them.

As far as the village was concerned, these various manorial holdings centred on the Kingston Street itself. All the main groups of yardlands (listed by their late Elizabethan names in Table 2.2) had associated holdings in the street: houses or cottages or sometimes just barns and enclosed crofts. The strips that made up the ancient yardlands were scattered broadcast about the fields – but each system of yardlands had a natural focus in the heart of the village. It was there that the farmyards lay: storage for grain in the great flint-walled barns, winter protection for draught and dairy stock in cattle yards and sheds (called 'hovels' in this part of Sussex), pigsties, courtyards where poultry scrounged for fallen grain or less delectable bits and pieces, and well kept closes. And among the farmyards there were the 'messuages' of the better off and the cottages and intensively cultivated gardens of the poor, not that anyone can have been particularly rich. Figure 2.4 taken from Marchant's map of 1773 (and therefore no doubt somewhat different in details of layout from the Elizabethan village), shows the main identifiable manorial holdings in the street. This was a busy place – or at least as busy a place as the village could boast. In Elizabethan times – as before – there was no central farmyard such as appeared in the nineteenth century. Each landholding family had its own farmyard. Animals were kept at various places up and down the street and moved about it as the need arose to move them – horses, red Sussex oxen, the occasional milk cow, and smaller animals too.

Even in 1773 the holdings in the street showed signs of the original strips. Particularly in the middle reaches on both sides – north and south – the vestiges of the strips are clear. Elsewhere though there had been a good deal of enclosure and consolidation of land into walled crofts in individual ownership.

The enclosures are clearest at the western end, particularly in the Great and little Barley Crofts (marked 'd' and 'c' by Marchant). These crofts project into the open fields that flanked the village and suggest strongly that there had been exchanges of strip lands between earlier holders and considerable reorganization of lands at some past time. When? It is not possible to say. It may have happened in the earlier Tudor years – but that can only be a guess. There are other places too where enclosure and consolidation of strips appear to have happened: around Kingston Manor house for example, or at the other end of the street on the corners where it joins the way that leads in one direction to Ashcombe and in the other to Well Green.

The holdings of the various manors in the street have their own interest.[61] Swanborough Manor as might be expected, dominated here too. Swanborough held virtually all the lands in the middle section on either side of the street. On the northern side there was a substantial cottage, which has since disappeared, where the copyholder Coppard probably lived in Elizabeth's reign. On Coppard's eastern side there were the copyhold barns and crofts of the Barnden family – a group of lands that acquired the name of Lattendens in later years (though there is no way of saying why). On the south side of Kingston Street still in this middle section, there were various bits of Swanborough land, including particularly the group of houses and barns held by the Bonifaces and Thomas Howell. These became 'Paine's Farm' in the eighteenth century. The barn still stands from Elizabethan days – one of the more precious relics in the street, magnificently timbered.

There were also Swanborough lands at the east and west ends of the street. The Great Barley Croft was part of the freehold group of yardlands called Alfreye's. It is likely that other Swanborough lands between the barley croft and the street were also. Certainly, the great barn and close adjoining the croft belonged to Alfreye's. These too are still standing and in use. At the eastern end of the street there were Swanborough lands in enclosures that came to be held by the Ade family. At the head of the street across the Ashcombe–Well Green way, there was Addam's house and barn, which later belonged to Stephen Towner whose eighteenth-century lands were discussed earlier on, and whose house still stands there.

Iford and Houndean lands in the street were small in proportion to their holdings in the Kingston arable. Iford Manor held a group of cottages, barns and closes at the southeastern end. These were part of Ade's farmyard too – which was made up in Elizabethan days of lands from more than one manor. Iford also held the distinguished barn and cow yard called Taberer's in the middle part of the street (owned by one Wolridge in the Elizabethan period) and, further to the west, a barn and close called Hudd's. Houndean Manor held two 'messuages' at either end of the street, both freehold and with Alfreye's the only freeholds out of demesnes in the street.

Hyde Manor also might be said to have held lands in the street in rough proportion to its smallholdings of arable. The main Hyde holding was the manor house, barn and close on the northern side; the remnant of the Elizabethan manor stands today as a group of cottages.

Kingston Manor to all appearances held much more property in Kingston Street than its proportion of arable. Indeed, since most of the cottages at the eastern end whose manorial ascription cannot be traced for certain were probably part of the manor, it was clearly exceptionally well supplied with holdings at the centre of the village system. Kingston Manor held a mere 20 per cent of the Kingston arable: it probably had about a third or more of the lands in the street itself. These included the big closes at the western end and the manor house, which is still the largest if not the most beautiful of the older buildings left. In fact, the modern Kingston Manor is, said Joseph Cooper, a shadow of its former self,[62] being largely composed as it is of a pair of medium-sized Elizabethan houses. The strength of Kingston Manor, if it had one, seems to have been in the command it had over the cottages of the village. This, we may suppose, is what lies behind the disproportion of its large holdings in the village street.

In short, there were five rather different sorts of manor in the village. Swanborough, with its dominant sway over the villein lands, was the nearest to a 'typical' manor. Thinking back to its medieval past we may deduce that it included a more or less complete feudal 'pyramid' from lord to villein and cottager. And its consolidated demesnes were adjacent to the village that served it. Iford and Houndean, on the other hand, were more tenuously related to the village – though the former included substantial holdings of villein lands. Oddly, the two manors that held demesnes and 'capital messuages' (namely large houses) in the village were just those that had the least claim on villein lands. Hyde had no Kingston villein tenants at all; Kingston had but three customary yardlands. This was not at all the classical form of manor to which Swanborough approximated.

This uneven distribution of copyhold (or villein) yardlands between the manors can be illustrated in another way. By measuring the number of copyhold yardlands per yardland in demesnes for each manor, one gets a reasonable guide to the relative access each had to villein labour. The ratios are illuminating. Swanborough had 28 copyhold yards in Kingston and 24 yards in demesnes in the Court Farm and Stuckles: it therefore had 1.2 copyhold yardlands per demesne yard. Iford, with eight yards in demesnes in Iford village, had ten copyhold yards in Kingston and so 0.8 copyhold yardlands per demesne yard. Kingston had only 0.25 per demesne yard and Hyde none. In spite of the size of its demesnes (which were 60 per cent greater in area than the Kingston Manor open field demesnes), Swanborough

Manor had proportionally much greater access to villein labour than the others: in proportion, it had 50 per cent more villein yardlands per demesne yard than Iford and very nearly *five times* more than Kingston Manor. Kingston Manor, apparently, had some compensating advantages in access to cottager labour in early times, but hardly enough to offset the large assured labour supply that Swanborough must have enjoyed. Kingston villeins belonged in the main to Swanborough.

This curious pattern of differences between the manors of Kingston is of course a puzzle, but for once a puzzle that has a tentative answer. To resolve it we shall need to search through the early Norman history of the village – to ask, in effect, what impact the Normans had on life in Kingston. That is the purpose of the next chapter.

Whatever its origins we may be certain that this complicated manorial pattern – together with the system of social ordering that sprung from the open field system – structured, indeed dominated, village life for long centuries. It added a further complexity to social life, linked to the complications of commonalty we have already noted. Kingston villeins, in early times, cooperated with one another in cultivating the common fields, but at the same time owed allegiance to different lords and up to a point had to follow the customs of different manors. Later, when land came to be bought and sold, an individual might find himself obliged to pay homage in two or even three manorial courts – as did Gregory Ade in the sixteenth century. Each court had its own claims in fines and other manorial incidents. Life was more complicated than it might appear at first glance.

It would be intriguing to know whether the multiplicity of manors meant that communal, village organization was comparatively dominant as opposed to manorial organization. Did the village, as a community, have a bigger say in agricultural decisions than it might have done had there been but one manor court? Unfortunately, there is no evidence for this. One can only speculate, remembering, however, that the multiplicity of manors in Kingston – given the particular form the manorial holdings took – need not have led to conflicts of interest between lords about basic agricultural decisions. Certainly not all the manors had direct interests in the ordering of the agricultural year in the village. As far as the lords of Swanborough, Iford and Houndean were concerned, the village lands were a source of labour and rents at levels that were largely determined by custom. Village decisions would have no effect at all on the way they used their own demesnes, unless villagers made such disastrous decisions about their own cultivation that they turned up for work malnourished or actually died of starvation. In general they did not commit such blunders. If people died of malnourishment, it was due most often to land shortage, bad harvests and ill-starred weather – not incompetence. Why then, if villagers were competent to run their land should lords on more distant demesnes bother too much? The villeins who did homage at Swanborough or Iford Manor courts may have seen them as important places for ordering village affairs, but the lords of those manors probably cared more for rents and labour supply than about the mundane affairs of the village.

For the lords of Hyde Manor and Kingston (who probably was the dominant partner), the story was different. It was only these two manors that had demesnes within the common field system alongside the villein lands. Their lords, or later on the lord's tenants, had a direct interest in the village lands, in their proper and timely organization year by year and in all the crucial seasonal decisions. And this, we may guess, posed some problems, for in their vast majority the villeins who cultivated alongside the lordly demesnes in the open fields belonged to other manors. These villeins owed no homage to lords in Kingston Manor or in Hyde. There is little doubt, of course, that in feudal times they would by and large have known their place. Nor need we doubt that the lords of Kingston could count on Swanborough and Iford for cooperation in the control or coercion of recalcitrant villeins. But even so it is likely that the lords of the demesnes in Kingston or their stewards must have found village communal organization mostly in their interest, at least through the long centuries when there were many individual landholders. The communal system was their most direct means of access to the villeins (and later copyholders) around them – a system they could use to obtain cooperation, if necessary by threat or coercion. So, although there is no direct evidence, it is a plausible guess that the multiplicity of manors in the village indirectly strengthened the communal system of village organization – not because multiplicity weakened manorial power in any fundamental way but because it meant that a well-ordered village system was in the interests of certain lords who, paradoxically enough, had no direct manorial means of wielding power over the servile cultivators around them.

Chapter 3

The Norman Transformation

There is little to be said of Saxon Kingston before the Conquest. The village did not get a separate mention in the Domesday Book: it was included in the entry of 'niworde' – the Domesday name for Iford;[1] but the record of events after the Conquest show that it was there. Beyond that fact, the Niworde record of Domesday and a few reasonable inferences, there is nothing much. Archaeologists have not bothered with Kingston and on the face of it there is no reason for them to do so.

The Domesday Niworde was a countryside area of villeins – 93 in all – whose lands were probably divided between the vills of Iford and Kingston. The villein village of 1086, though it was in all probability as large as or larger than Iford, was not distinguished by any particular features. The chances are that it did not even have a church at the time: there was one church in Niworde, probably in Iford. Before the Conquest, Queen Eddid, wife of Edward the Confessor, had held the lands of Niworde. These are the slender facts we can glean from the written record, but a few guesses are in order too.

One feature of Saxon society, which Kingston probably shared, was the growth of a large servile population: people who held land in return for labour service to an overlord. However, this servile class of Saxon times was never as crisply differentiated as it came to be under the Normans. Where Norman lords could talk in terms of villeins as a more or less homogeneous class of people, the Saxon thegns who had preceded them had had to deal with a more complex social order. The Saxon servile class had more 'degrees' in it than the Normans recognized in their legal documents. There were 'geburs', whose status approximated to the classic villein status of Norman times – but there were others too: 'churls' who had been free and had sunk somewhat into servility but whose degree of servility was less than that of 'geburs'; and others who were less free, who might have risen from earlier slave families. No doubt these degrees counted, both in terms of the amount of servile labour that families were required to provide and also in terms of status – the authority that they might claim in village society. But, even so, the differences were not defined with the precision the Normans later imposed. The Norman concept of the villein class, which is so evident in the Domesday Book, was both more precise than any Saxon classification – particularly with regard to the large distinction between those who were servile and those who were not, and at the same time much less sensitive to differences. Indeed its precision was in all probability something of a legal fiction.[2]

No doubt the little society that lived along the street at Kingston reflected these distinctions. The people who owed labour service on Queen Eddid's demesnes were of different classes; for all that, the Normans blurred their differences in later years.

There was one difference the Normans did not blur. Some people were distinctly free in that they did not owe customary labour services and held land directly of their lords. There are signs that there were such people in Kingston. Two men who held land in Kingston before the Domesday Book was drawn up – but not in 1086 – were Bristelm and Ormar.[3] Both were probably free and in all likelihood Anglo-Saxon. The Domesday record itself mentions a person called Tosard who held land free – almost certainly in Kingston (rather than Iford). Hugh, son of Golde was another who held demesnes, which subsequently became the heart of the dispersed manor of Iford. Tosard and Hugh may have been Normans not Anglo-Saxons. It is likely indeed that they were. But it is also likely that the lands they held had belonged before to independent Saxon thegns, who would have constituted the upper class of Kingston village.

All things considered, the image we can form of Saxon Kingston is at best faint – distantly perceived through the structures the Normans subsequently imposed on it. But whatever doubts we may have about the precise look of Anglo-Saxon life in Kingston, there is one matter on which we can be fairly confident. The year of the Conquest was a stirring, disturbed time in the village.

The year started with the accession of Harold to the English throne and the appearance of Halley's comet. Across the Channel, not far away in Normandy, people connected the two events. The comet was a sign of the justice of William's claim to the English throne and foretold his victory. This particular interpretation reflected the effectiveness of William's propaganda – also perhaps the confidence of Normandy. We do not know if men and women in Kingston had similarly confident interpretations of the strange thing in the winter sky. Were they simply frightened of it? Did they see it as a sign from heaven to justify Harold's distinctly dubious claim? Did they know at all, in those early cold months of 1066, that Harold's succession was a matter of dispute in which the Pope quite soon was to take William's side?

If Kingston villagers were unaware there was a dispute, they became conscious of it soon enough. Before the harvest was in – indeed before the crop was properly ripe – the Saxon militia were called out all along the south coast as Harold prepared himself for the inevitable. This must have struck home in Kingston as elsewhere. The militia, called the fyrd, was supplied by the villages in the proportion of one man to every five hides of arable land. It may be that six or seven men from Kingston and Iford had to join it. They were called out for the customary two months in July – just as everyone was thinking of the harvest to come. If there had been no anxiety in the village before, it must have swelled up then – the more particularly perhaps because if war were afoot, it might come before the crops could be brought home. Armies and crops went ill together even if the army in question were a friendly one. And a ruined crop meant more certain death to many than a war itself.

Moreover, there must in all reason have been a concentration of watching fyrdmen around Lewes. The Ouse estuary then, was excessively vulnerable to attack from the Channel. The tidal waters came up to Lewes itself, and behind and to the east there were natural breaks in the line of downland – opening out to the Weald and the heartlands of the south of England. Vikings had sailed up this estuary in earlier centuries. Once they had killed a group of Anglo-Saxon defenders at 'Saxonbury' on the Southover border of Marchant's Mill Laine. More than a millennium later their bones were uncovered, buried in shallow graves with their armaments by their sides.[4] While people may have forgotten the Viking threat in later years, it must have been clear to them that this great estuary had to be defended against a threat from the sea. Accordingly, the threat must have borne in upon Kingston villagers. The fyrd were on their doorsteps, moving about the Ouse valley lands. Kingston might well be in the line of march of an invading army. It might be at the centre of the line of defence. Neither prospect could have been encouraging.

In the event the summer passed, the crop was brought in and people held their breath as it was stored. But nothing happened. Indeed, in early September the village may well have relaxed as the men came back from their duties in the fyrd – perhaps because their two months were over, perhaps because the Saxon nobles had misjudged the military situation.[5] Whatever the reason, they came back and their return must have led villagers to feel that the threat was over – if only temporarily.

It was not of course. In mid-September Harold's army streamed north to meet a Norwegian invasion under Harald Hardrada. The fyrd was called out again in the south. And then at about 8.30 a.m. on 27 September a great Norman army disembarked at Pevensey along the banks of a marshy tidal estuary very like the Ouse estuary itself.

For two weeks William waited for Harold, prepared his army and pillaged the countryside of Hastings. On 14 October the English crisis reached its culmination. By evening Harold's body lay among the corpses of his house-carls at Senlac on Battle Hill and William, not yet believing his fortune, could look forward to England.

There is no reason to believe that Normans came to Kingston in those two weeks of dreadful waiting – but even so the village had news of what was afoot. News could travel fast. Harold, in York, knew that William had landed a bare three days after the event. Of course, as far as Kingston was concerned, there were no riders to bring the news. Nevertheless, the village was full of expectations. The men had left for the fyrd, again at short notice. And those two weeks certainly gave time enough for news to filter through to people who were desperate to know what was happening. Hastings is only 20 miles away and Pevensey, where looted villages lay in ruin, a mere ten miles. News came through the countryside as men came back from the fyrd.

In the end, particular news of the almighty bloodbath at Senlac reached the village. It can only have brought fear and anticipations of evil. Normans – even more than the English themselves – were close to the Vikings in their ways. Indeed, not forty years before, William's grandfather had played host to a Viking horde that had just completed a most successful ravage of the west of France.[6] Kingston villagers might not have known that, but they certainly knew enough and heard enough about what was happening at Pevensey and beyond to have few illusions about the future. Would the Normans punish the rest of England by pillage? If tense men and women in the village had midnight images of fire in Kingston Street – images that seemed to come from a more distant past before Alfred had settled with the Danes, but were real and present again – if they feared all this, who could blame them? These were the terrible natural expectations of peasants in a losing war. In part, they were amply borne out by what happened in other areas of England after the Conquest – but not, as far as we know, in this village.

In part though, these village fears for the immediate consequences of Senlac obscured any contemplation of the longer term. It would have been natural for Kingston people to concern themselves with the hazards they must face just to survive the coming twelve months and surely that is what quite rightly preoccupied their worried minds. What they could not foresee – indeed would not have foreseen even if universal calmness had prevailed – was the change the Normans were to make to the rest of their lives. The Normans transformed Kingston as they transformed the rest of England, but with some special twists. Looking back from a vantage point of, say ten or fifteen years after the Conquest, a Kingston villein might have been excused if he concluded that Halley's comet had heralded the end of one world and the start of another. In this new world Norman barons displaced Saxon thegns all over England. It was the particular ambitions and obsessions of one of them, which gave a special sting to the experience of the village. He was the Earl de Warenne.

William the Conqueror came over, as we know, at the head of an alliance of Norman aristocrats.[7] He had had problems convincing them to join the invasion but in the end the compelling attraction of wealth greater than any they could hope for in Normandy – and perhaps also the honour to be gained from what had become a holy war – worked its way. Uneasily at first but then with gathering commitment, they worked for the invasion, raised their feudal armies and sailed the Channel.

They were, for the most part, a new aristocracy born out of the vast internal struggles in Normandy and its strife with France, which had ended a mere ten years before the Conquest. This 'most remarkable secular aristocracy produced in Europe during the earlier Middle Ages'[8] was made up of families whose grand territorial names dated back only to the first quarter of the eleventh century, and whose prominence in the decade before the conquest sprung from their successful survival and accretion of wealth and power during troubled earlier years. William's barons were for the most part new men.

Perhaps it was this and their comparatively recent attachments to their Norman lands that made them willing, after some persuasion, to take part in the gamble of the Conquest. A more settled aristocracy, accustomed to long generations of lordship over the same lands, might have felt differently about the affair. Two centuries later in England an unknown writer put down his advice to the settled manorial lords who were for the most part scions of the conquest families: 'The lord ought not to take counsel with young men full of young blood and ready courage, who know little or nothing of business … but he ought to take counsel with worthy and faithful men, ripe in years, who have seen much and know much, and who are known to be of good fame.'[9]

But two centuries of domination of manorial lands had worked their changes. The new men of 1066, forefathers of the Anglo-Norman lords to whom the advice was given, were in a different mood set against a different, shorter and altogether less secure background of events. They were themselves 'young men full of young blood and ready courage'. And so, nothing venture nothing gain, they took the most enormous gamble, setting all their acquisitions in Normandy against the spin of the wheel at Senlac. If they had lost … but of course, they didn't.

William divided out the winnings; the Saxon nobility was comprehensively displaced and their lands shared out, in the first instance to the inner circle of mostly young aristocrats who became the Norman barons of England. This virtually total imposition of lordships from the top down gave English feudalism its special character.

William de Warenne was a member of the inner circle. He had first fought with the conqueror at Domfront in 1051. His relations with his lord were close. He was married to Gundrada, said to be the king's daughter, though there are doubts about the matter. It is possible that she was an illegitimate child of the royal family.

At all events, de Warenne did exceptionally well out of the Conquest. His feudal honour included most of Yorkshire, Norfolk, Surrey and a substantial part of Sussex. Such geographically divided honours were the rule in the conqueror's policy and more generally common in feudal organizations in Europe. They constrained the military power of the great barons: a hundred knights in one area were a much greater threat to central power than if they were geographically dispersed.

In Sussex, de Warenne's lands included the Rape of Lewes and all within it. So the Swanborough hundred was his and also the little vills of Kingston and Iford. The vills themselves were mere specks in the totality of his honour. We must doubt if he even noticed them in the early years or cared much about them later. The immediate preoccupations of exploiting the new lands were left to lesser lords who held lands of de Warenne, or knights he set up with lands held in fee, or stewards and bailiffs on lands he held directly. The particular impacts, which were rather special ones, that de Warenne's lordship came to have in Kingston did not spring from any inherent importance of the village. They were the entirely incidental result of more strategic considerations in de Warenne's mind, and especially the particular interest he so evidently came to have in Lewes and its immediate surroundings. The new, comparatively young lord of Sussex lands (he was very likely younger than the conqueror, who was about 40 at the time of the invasion) brewed schemes for Lewes whose effects were to be felt in a hundred English villages. If they took a special form in Kingston – which they did – it was because of the trick of geography that placed it so close to the focus of de Warenne's attention.

We do not know exactly when de Warenne's reconnoitring men rode into Kingston village but it cannot have been long after the Conquest. They certainly came armed; the fyrd had fought like fury at Senlac. Norman soldiery had reason to play it safe.

Even so, they cannot have been much impressed by the Saxon huddle along the line of the street, nor by what one imagines was a sullen but mostly fearful handful of families waiting for the worst. Probably there was no particular trouble. For the soldiers it was just another village; and for the villagers the devastation round Pevensey was an object lesson in the Norman style.

If they rode over the downland ridge to Lewes, along Jugg's Way, the Normans may have been more impressed by the lands below them. The open fields spread across the Swanborough slope to the south, clustered in the hollow round the street and stretched into the valley, which ran out towards the Ouse. Soldiers they may have been, but they knew how to judge land, and a good deal of Kingston was rich.

But surely, the immediate preoccupation of those first Normans must have been with the Ouse estuary itself. If the tide were in they would have seen a wide inlet of water dotted with a few small islets and marshland here and there. Lewes lay at the head of this and the Weald opened up behind it through the gap. Their recent experiences were fresh in their minds. The similarity to the tidal marshes of Pevensey cannot have escaped them and just as they knew that Pevensey was a vulnerable point – because they had proved it themselves – so they perceived this estuary.

It did not take de Warenne long to act. Very soon after the Conquest work started on the great Norman castle at Lewes and, though the new king was to show some reluctance at the castle-building activities of his magnates,[10] he must surely have seen the point of this one. The first and perhaps always the dominating reason for de Warenne's special interest in Lewes was that he concentrated a good part of his military power there, around the castle. Perhaps the servile men and women of Kingston were mobilized to build it.

But other reasons followed growing out of de Warenne's career after the Conquest, particularly out of his religiosity.

Once the de Warennes, William and Gundrada, had assured their material place in the English world their concerns turned, increasingly it would seem, to their place in heaven. The future life worried them. They had discussed the matter with the new Archbishop of Canterbury – Sir Lanfranc. And Sir Lanfranc with sound Catholic common sense suggested they might found a religious house, 'for (their) sins and the welfare of (their) souls'. The spiritual interests of the hugely wealthy de Warennes and the more immediate needs of the Holy Mother Church could be brought into happy coincidence.[11] Thenceforth, William and Gundrada kept the objective 'in mind and intention'; they were in the market for a monastery. Did William have special reason to fear death? Was the papal blessing of the conquest insufficient? Did it fail to offset the hard realities of Senlac and the devastation of his own lands in Yorkshire that followed? It is more probable that William and Gundrada saw their new wealth as a means to assure a place in heaven commensurate with their place on earth – and followed the fashion of their times.

What followed was a mixture of chance and hard bargaining.[12] William and Gundrada's piety was real enough for them to go on pilgrimage to Rome. They were stopped in Burgundy because of the war 'that then was between the pope and the emperor', and they paused at the monastery of Cluny. Cluny impressed them deeply. They believed in the holiness of its monks. The prior and his brethren paid them honour and the whole experience overwhelmed them. In William's words, 'we began to have … devotion towards that order and that house above all the other houses that we had seen.' The die was cast. As far as William and Gundrada were concerned, *their* decision was made, but not the abbot's. Sir Hugh, the 'holy abbot', had not been at the house at the time of the de Warenne visit and when he heard of their plan he was not overly impressed. The de Warennes wanted three or four Clunial monks from the mother house to come to England. They had rebuilt the old wooden church of St Pancras that stood at the edges of the tidal estuary to the south of Lewes. It was now in stone and de Warenne wished to give it to the immigrant monks he had asked for. Along with the church they would have land, cattle and property sufficient to support 12 monks – and that merely for a start. But Sir Hugh, to their evident disappointment, was unmoved. William wrote years later in his charter: 'the holy Abbot at first was very hard to us about listening to our petition on account of the distance of this foreign land and especially because of the sea.'[13]

This 'Sir Hugh', as it happens, was the great and devout abbot who ruled the mother house of Cluny from 1049 to 1109 and was made a saint by the Church many centuries later. In his time Cluny was in full expansion:[14] by the time de Warenne made his proposal in the 1070s, the abbot had already seen a vast extension of Cluniac houses throughout Europe. Since the beginning of his abbacy a dozen or more new priories had been established or annexed to

Cluny in France alone. And there had been foreign expansion too – perhaps fifteen new Italian houses between 1049 and 1075 and seven or eight in Switzerland, as well as some in Spain. As far as the 'holy Abbot' was concerned then, the de Warenne proposal could not have looked particularly attractive. How could a small church in the back of beyond, and certainly far away from Mâçon (which probably amounted to much the same thing as far as it was concerned), have measured up against the great houses he had seen annexed to Cluny?

In all likelihood the abbot's position on the matter was affected by two things: first, the experience of the previous three decades made it quite clear that Cluny could afford to be choosy; second, the demands this massive expansion put on the mother house probably *obliged* the abbot to be cautious. Although there was a huge and random growth of applicants for the monastic life throughout Europe at the time, Cluny was a centre of experienced and devout, reforming administrators – and they were comparatively much harder to find than aspirant monks.[15] Although Sir Hugh travelled the length and breadth of Europe, there was no question in anyone's mind that his loyalty lay at the mother house. He would not deprive it of the precious resource of its most competent monks without good reason. By the 1070s, Sir Hugh had already turned down other more prestigious offers than de Warenne's; he was before long to turn down William the Conqueror himself when the king asked for monks whom he might turn into English bishops.[16] In context, it is hardly surprising perhaps that the de Warennes ran into difficulty.

It is not at all clear whether they expected it – in fact the tone of the foundation charter suggests not. Perhaps the welcoming priors at Cluny and the brethren who paid de Warenne honour there had a more liberal view about new foundations than the abbot, and gave the Norman too much hope in the absence of the abbot. But, whether William and Gundrada feared such a rejection or not, it must have been a blow when it came. They were asking a prestigious house for monks it is true, but at heart they saw themselves as giving. That, after all, was the point of the undertaking: to make such a gift to the Church as would speed their souls to heaven. Sir Hugh's refusal put the legitimacy of the endeavour in question. It reversed the roles of giver and receiver and, besides, it must have been a wounding experience for a parvenu Norman proud of his new power and lands, however far they might be from Burgundy. In the circumstances, it is a measure of the de Warenne's intentions – and perhaps of William's doggedness – that they pressed on with their plans. King William was brought into the picture and gave his assent to the plan. With this support, de Warenne returned to the abbot and asked anew. Sir Hugh relented at least to the point where it seemed that he accepted in principle that the new foundation might be set up.[17]

Nevertheless, the abbot remained cautious about the plan as well as solicitous of the needs of Cluny itself. Two events followed that nearly led to the breakdown of the whole scheme.

In the first place, while the abbot agreed to send a monk called Sir Lanzo to be prior with three of his brother monks, he would not let them leave Cluny until he had in his hands the deed from de Warenne confirming the grant of the church and lands. Normally, it would seem, it would have been sufficient to leave a document of this kind among the charters of the subsidiary house – in this case in Lewes. But whatever the normal practice, the abbot had his way. He got the deed and kept it. In fact de Warenne was induced to draw up his first charter to the priory of Lewes largely because of this. He says, in the charter 'Sir Lanzo the Prior and my monks pointed out to me that my confirmation that I had made of the things which I had given to them for a start was at Cluny and that they had no evidence thereof.' And, with an explicitness that suggests the recollection of resentment, he remembers the deed 'that we sent to the Abbot and Convent of Cluny because they would not send the monks to us until they had our confirmation and that of the King which we obtained for them of all the things which we had given them.'

The priory was barely established before a second problem arose between abbot and earl. This one threatened to provoke a final crisis, at least as far as de Warenne was concerned. The abbot called Sir Lanzo back to Cluny and kept him there for more than a year. De Warenne fumed in England; his patience was nearly at an end: 'we were so upset that we nearly proposed to give up our intention or to take away our church from them and give it to a greater monastery.' So wrote de Warenne nearly ten years later. The trouble was, of course, that at that time de Warenne would have been hard put to find a greater monastery. The abbot's motives in all this were obscure. Had something happened to confirm his earlier reluctance that led him to undermine the new house? It seems improbable. Sir Lanzo, as his subsequent career in England was to show, was an able cleric.[18] It is most likely that Sir Hugh wanted him for business in Cluny, and simply put the needs of Cluny first.

The dénouement came in Normandy where, says de Warenne, Sir Hugh the abbot 'came to speak with my lord the King'. The purpose of his visit was not such as to give the de Warennes much confidence of their bargaining position with the abbot. It appears to have been at the king's invitation and to have been part of the king's campaign to induce Sir Hugh to give Cluniac monks to be made into English bishops. That at least seems a fair inference from de Warenne's recollections in the charter: 'in our hearing he (the King) asked the Abbot to send him twelve of his holy monks and he would make them bishops and abbots in the land which God had given him for an heritage.' Then, as on other occasions, the abbot turned the conqueror down. Hardly a propitious moment for angry de Warennes waiting in the wings for a chance to talk the abbot into returning one of his more able monks to Lewes.

In the circumstances, William and Gundrada seem to have been well treated by the abbot – though only, as they noted, 'after much urging'. Though there was plainly a seller's market in able Cluniacs, they came away with a written agreement, which, even if a little open-ended, gave them much of what they wanted. The abbot agreed to return Sir Lanzo to Lewes and that plainly was a great step forward from the de Warenne point of view. He agreed also that the priors of Lewes should be permanent and not removed – or at least not unless 'the cause were so just and manifest that no-one could reasonably object'. It would seem that this was the first time the abbot had made such an agreement with a subsidiary house[19] – so, notwithstanding the escape clause, it was a considerable achievement for de Warenne. Another achievement was the abbot's concession that he would not interfere with the affairs of the priory nor with its 'cells' or subsidiary houses, except 'touching the observance or amendment of the order when the Prior cannot amend it himself'. Sir Hugh, it would appear, had not been in the habit of interfering in the domestic affairs of subsidiary houses (except when their priors were away from time to time), so he may have found it easy to grant this.

Finally, the abbot gave his assent to a rather open clause about the longer future: 'if God increased the house and made it into one of the great houses, after the death of Sir Lanzo or his promotion to any greater dignity ... (Cluny) would send as Prior one of their best monks out of the whole body ... the chief Prior of Cluny and the Prior of La Charité excepted.' A cynical view of this is that since it neither made clear who was to judge whether the priory had become 'a great house' nor how to make the judgement, it committed the abbot to very little. That would, in all likelihood, be a wrong view of his intent. In fact, it is more likely that he sought to encourage de Warenne to a deeper commitment of resources so that, having agreed to leave Sir Lanzo permanently in Lewes, he might see an appropriate reward for the Cluniac order. Implicitly, the agreement admitted the possibility that Lewes might be counted among the great houses of Cluny, as indeed it came to be. For William de Warenne, this principle was no doubt important in itself. After all the irritations and blows to his pride he could look forward to treatment that was no doubt more in accord with what he would consider appropriate to this status. However, he had a shorter-term worry on his mind. He feared that the king, having failed to induce Sir Hugh to supply him with monks, would steal Sir Lanzo away to fill a gap in the new ecclesiastical order. He was right to worry. In later years the king did just that.

The whole of this agreement was rounded off with the undertaking that St Pancras would henceforth pay Cluny 50 English shillings per year – and would be freed of all other dues. Whether the 50 shillings helped or not is unclear. At all events, this long discussion and the written agreement that came from it seems to have resolved the problems between the abbot and the de Warennes. Henceforth, de Warenne could look upon his priory as a more or less independent house and a centre of ecclesiastical power in its own right, while enjoying the prestigious link to Cluny.

The development of the priory proceeded with dispatch. A new and ambitious building programme was started to create the monastery and a much larger new church. At its completion it was virtually the size of a cathedral.[20] By then, however, the first William de Warenne had gone to test the notion that founding priories facilitated access to heaven. His son arranged its dedication. In his confirmatory charter to the priory in about 1095, he notes: 'some years having passed in the building of a church at length the work was finished and I was asked by the Prior and brethren to cause it to be dedicated'. The dedication was a grand occasion: the new William de Warenne arranged for three bishops to be present – Chichester, Winchester and Rochester. It had probably taken ten years to build the new church.[21]

Most of all, though, the priory was endowed with lands. The early parts of the chartulary are long accounts of de Warenne's grants of titles to the new house. They make impressive reading. The lands came from all parts of de Warenne's honour. There were Yorkshire manors, lands in Surrey and all over Sussex. There were minor properties like mills for grinding corn, and vast gifts like the grant of tithes on all de Warenne's family income. There were churches in large numbers and the rights to their tithes. And there was a particularly prized piece – a richly endowed subsidiary monastery at Castle Acre (Acra), near to de Warenne's castle in Norfolk. The first William de Warenne had the plans for this monastery in mind when he induced Sir Hugh of Cluny to relinquish control over 'cells' of the priory of Lewes. He was quite explicit about the manoeuvre in his charter: 'this we willed and did because we have always desired to make a house and establish monks at our castle of Acra, which would not be subject to any but St Pancras'. It took a long time to achieve. The monastery at Acra became fully established after the death of the first William, in the lifetime of his son.[22]

The early charters are full of the names of churches, villages and towns all over England. By any measure the priory had become 'one of the great houses' by the time the first William de Warenne died. The second William and the earls who followed increased its wealth. There had been no real need for Sir Hugh the abbot to dangle carrots before de Warenne at their critical discussions in Rouen. De Warenne built the huge ecclesiastical complex of the priory for his own reasons, helped no doubt by the urgings and suggestions of the increasingly powerful prior of Lewes. The view from Cluny changed – partly perhaps because of the understanding between Sir Hugh and de Warenne after Rouen, but partly also as the wealth and power of Lewes grew. In effect the implicit agreement that Lewes *might* become one of the more powerful of the dependent priories became increasingly real as de Warenne multiplied his donations to its support. There were abbeys attached to Cluny that had precedence, but among the Cluniac priories, Lewes came to hold a special place after La Charité. Later in the twelfth century Lewes was one of those five priories that came to be called the 'primary daughters' of Cluny.[23] The growing wealth of the priory opened up splendid careers for worthy (and ambitious) Cluniacs and that helped no doubt to make England seem less remote – in spite of the abbot's aversion to the sea that cut it off from France.

That de Warenne should have sited the priory at the small church of St Pancras was natural enough – for that church was, to use his words, 'below my castle at Lewes'. The gaunt grandeur of the castle on the hill stood in contrast to the gleaming new monastery below. Together they were symbols of the man himself – of his violence in war and his self-absorbed religiosity. The priory was built for the souls of William and Gundrada and their inheritance; there is no hint of any broader concern. And both buildings also stood for his new English wealth: the returns for the measured opportunism that had brought him across the Channel with the conqueror. It was natural in the circumstances that Lewes became a focus of the de Warenne honour. The decision to put the priory there ensured that. It was also full of implications for Kingston.

It is very likely that when the military Normans first surveyed the area called Niworde in the Domesday Book they found a large stretch of land between the vills of Kingston and Iford, which was open and untilled. These were the lands of Swanborough (which means peasants' hill). Later on various speculative legends became attached to these lands – for example that King Alfred's moot of Swinbeorgum was held there. But there is no evidence of any of them, nor is there a sign in Domesday or elsewhere of any Saxon manorial establishments. The legends most probably are no more than that inspired by the subsequent manorial splendours of Swanborough, but without a basis in reality. Is there a village in the south of England where King Alfred did not spend a night, at least? The later evidence all points the same way: these lands were to all intents and purposes empty and unploughed when the Normans came. If they were used for anything it was as pasture for the animals of Iford and Kingston.

In any case, the potential of these lands was clear to the Normans. A look at the good arables of Iford to the south of the Swanborough Laine and Kingston to the north must have suggested that the open area was a fine resource.[24] Like the lands of the two villages abutting it, it encompassed meadows on the east (near the Ouse), a long middle section of ploughable land and a spacious stretch of pasture up the side of the downs on the west. The untilled countryside of Swanborough was a mere fraction of de Warenne's honour – an unexploited speck in relation to his total wealth. Yet he came to know these lands and, if subsequent events are anything to go by, he placed considerable value on them. The fact is that these Swanborough lands were an important part of his first foundation gift to the priory. That circumstance must tell us something of the way he regarded them.

Everything we have recounted about de Warenne's behaviour in those early years points to his commitment to the priory: his extraordinary generosity in giving land and wealth; his concern that as he grew richer, the monastery should grow richer too and the monks more numerous; above all, perhaps, his preoccupation with the permanence of the foundation, reflected again and again in the pre-emptive commitment of his heirs and their heirs to its continued support. It is only to be expected that the man who laid curses in advance on anyone who might contest the entitlements he had bestowed on the priory would select his founding grant with care.[25] He had all the more reason to do so on account of Sir Hugh being so inconveniently awkward about the whole arrangement. De Warenne's choice of Swanborough lands suggests that he valued them in proportion to the importance of the priory in his mind's eye – and that was considerable.

The Swanborough lands were not the only ones, nor at first glance the most important, to be included in the foundation grant. The first deed to the priory granted the church of St Pancras and its appurtenances two ploughlands in Swanborough and one in an unnamed place,[26] and the whole village of Falmer, where Gundrada held three hides. It is dated 1077, nine years before the Domesday record was drawn up.

This deed records possibly the most important title to ownership in the long subsequent history of the Kingston village. Because of the abbot's suspicions or exigencies, or wish to put the Norman earl in his place, the deed was sent to Cluny and remained there. Today it is in the Bibliothèque Nationale in Paris. In view of its place in the story, it had appropriately impressive signatures appended to it, for it was signed not only by de Warenne and Gundrada, but also by the conqueror and Queen Mathilda. On top of that, in order to meet the abbot's demands, there is a confirmation from King William attached to it. This was weighty stuff indeed – and a far cry from the grubby copies from manorial rolls that were the majority of the titles to land in Kingston in following years. Its weight was to be felt. By the time the 'foundation charter' was drawn up many years had passed. The conqueror was dead and his son on the throne; de Warenne was old. The grant was by this time the first among many. But of course the lands are listed in the charter: the manor of Falmer, a hide of land in Burgemera (Balmer), 'and in Swamberga 54½ hides'.[27]

The gift of Falmer manor was, in itself, considerable. Falmer lay over the downs about three miles from the village street of Kingston. It is just outside the northwest boundary of Kingston parish. Even then it was a village of considerable antiquity, which appears to have been 'manorialized' in Saxon times. Some nine years after de Warenne gave it to the priory, it was recorded in the Domesday Book:

> St Pancras holds Falemere of William. The Abbey of Wilton held it in the time of King Edward. ... In the time of King Edward it vouched for 21 hides and now for 18 hides. ... There is land for 15 ploughs. In demesne there are 2 ploughs and 35 villeins and 7 bordars with 13 ploughs. There is a church and 1 serf.[28]

Falmer, then, was an entire manor ('mansionem' in the first charter), fully supplied with villeins. Indeed, since the 'vill' and the manor were coincident, it corresponded more closely to the conventional view of the manorial system than any of the medieval institutions encountered in Kingston itself. It was also a substantial gift – larger on the face of it than Swanborough.

To some extent though, these appearances may be deceiving. Look more closely at Falmer in the Domesday entry. In spite of all the villeins and the large Domesday 'hidage' of the village as a whole, the demesnes in Falmer – that is the lands from which the monks could draw income and produce directly – were limited. They had two ploughlands in demesnes.[29] The Swanborough grant consisted of two ploughlands and villeins. In other words, the demesnes area of Swanborough was commensurate with that of Falmer. And, in addition, the open land of Swanborough was from certain points of view a special advantage to the monks, as we shall see. In their different ways the Falmer and Swanborough lands were of roughly similar importance in the original grant.

A hide of land in medieval days amounted to four yardlands. The foundation charter describes the priory as receiving 5½ hides in Swanborough in the initial grant – an area corresponding to 22 yardlands.

A part of this large arable area was made up of the consolidated demesnes that eventually formed the heart of Swanborough Manor. Carved out of the untilled area between Kingston and Iford, these demesnes had a somewhat special aspect. They were special not so much because the arable was held together in a single unit but because arable, meadows and pastures were all combined geographically. The lands the monks received in Swanborough resembled a self-contained modern farm; they were in that respect unusual at the time. They differed from the lands in Falmer, which were, as far as we can tell, spread about the open fields in the usual way.

This grant gave the priory an opportunity that did not exist in a manor like that at Falmer. Here in Swanborough a monastic community could farm the land directly in its own interests without having to become involved in the temporal affairs and communal decisions of a village. They could control production from their own demesnes without the intervention of a steward or any other manorial official and yet maintain a distance from worldly conflicts that would have been impossible in the communal hurly-burly of the open fields. Swanborough was ripe for direct agricultural colonization by the priory monks. As in other places where such conditions existed,[30] the monastery took its opportunity and set up just such a colony in the form of a grange. There can be little doubt that de Warenne had seen the possibilities of a grange farm at Swanborough from the start and had included the lands in his discussions with Cluny with just this purpose in mind, to make his proposals more attractive.

What might the motives of the priory have been in exploiting Swanborough in this particular way? It is not entirely clear. In part they may have been economic. Certainly, direct control of production from the demesnes avoided the need to support the variety of manorial officials that the priory had to rely upon elsewhere. It is also likely that the monks could be more efficient in the use they made of the land than a steward might be. Their interests and the interests of the house in Lewes were directly engaged. Aside from economic motives there might have been spiritual ones too in the opportunities for 'virtuous labour' that a grange offered. There is not much evidence, though, that the monks took advantage of this, if indeed it was ever perceived as part of the objective. But, whatever their precise motives, it is clear that the priory monks moved onto their Swanborough lands as soon as possible. The Kingston villeins barely had time to catch up with the news that St Pancras church by the side of the estuary below Southover was to be a priory, but now there was building work at Swanborough – just over the brow of the hill from their village.

The monks built a small workmanlike hall out of stone and flint, with a tiny chapel and living quarters attached to it.[31] In part it still stands. It is embedded in the larger structure of a much grander manor house that grew out of it in later years. But its outlines can be clearly seen. Set in the context of the bigger house it seems to speak of virtuous poverty – appropriate to an age of religious survival in which the piety of Cluniac monks played a major part. It was by any measure a colder, harder place to live in than the comfortable and distinguished manor house of today.

But these great demesnes and the little colony of monks that was set up at Swanborough Grange were not the whole of the original Swanborough grant. Two separate pieces of evidence make it clear that the grant included lands outside the demesnes that the villeins occupied.

In the first place, the foundation deed from Cluny says explicitly that the grant at Swanborough consisted of two ploughlands *with villeins*. If there were villeins there must have been lands for them to be villeins on! And second, there is independent evidence from the areas of land involved in the gift. The foundation charter and its later confirmations put the area at 5½ hides of 22 yardlands. Now, by custom, the demesnes area of the Swanborough Court Farm of about 1600 was taken to be 16 yardlands – considerably less than the total amount of the original gift. And these 16 yardlands of arable were all within the boundaries of the tithe-free lands of the original grant. This suggests that the grant contained lands outside demesnes of at least six yardlands of 1½ hides ('at least' because, if anything, one would have expected the amount of arable within the tithe-free demesnes to have increased over the intervening centuries, in which case the original hidage outside the demesnes would of course have been more than 1½ hides). This hide and a half outside the demesnes – if such it was – must have been villein land – and to judge by the later disposition of the Swanborough copyhold yardlands, the chances are very high that it was situated in the open fields of Kingston village.[32]

Other gifts of land in Swanborough hundred followed the original grant. William, 'the second founder', the son of the first Earl de Warenne, confirmed his father's gift of 5½ hides and added: 'I have also granted and confirmed all the other things that my father had granted of the gifts of his barons and other freemen.' Among these 'other things' were 'two hides which Tusard gave them ... and one hide which Bristelm gave and one hide which Ormar gave when they became monks'. There were also some smaller gifts from the barons and other freemen of de Warenne. For example, Warin the sheriff gave two fields beside St Pancras and 'a garden in the vineyard there'. The ways of Burgundy died hard. There is no record of the quality of wine that came from the priory vineyard, but today a respectable wine is grown on the downs not far to the south. Warin also gave 'all his tithe of Kingestona'. Hugh, the son of Golde who will appear again, gave tithes as well: 'the tithe of Hugh son of Golde in Yford. And in Kyngeston the tithe of two hides and the tithe of land he (i.e. Hugh) had in Rottingdean'. For good measure, Hugh had also given the monks the church of Yforde.[33] All these gifts had been given to the priory before 1091.[34] The Swanborough lands among them were attached to the grange.

The Domesday record for Niworde throws a little more light on the various gifts. It reads:

> In Soaneberge hundred ... William de Warenne holds Niworde in demesne, Queen Eddid held it. In the time of King Edward it vouched for 77 hides and a half. When William received it there were only 58. ... These 58 hides now vouch for 36 hides. There is land for 52 ploughs. In demesne are 5 ploughs and one hundred villeins less three and 32 bordars have 34 ploughs. There is a church and six serfs and 2 mills of 23 shillings and 208 acres of meadows. Wood for 30 hogs. ...
>
> Of this land the Monks of St Pancras hold 6½ hides and they have in demesne 2 ploughs and 10 villeins and 3 ploughs. ... Of the same land Hugh has 2 hides and Tosard one hide and a half. In demesne they have two ploughs with 4 bordars. Villeins held these lands.
>
> The whole manor in the time of King Edward was worth 50 pounds and afterwards twenty pounds. Now William's demesne 35 pounds, the monks 3 pounds and the men's 75 shillings.[35]

This is a description of Niworde in 1086. Leave aside for the moment the larger proportion of Niworde lands, which belonged directly to de Warenne at the time, and look at the lands the priory held. In the first place it seems that the area of Swanborough demesnes – two ploughlands – is exactly the same as it was at the time of the original 1077 deed. There had been no extension of this main part of the grange farm. But, second, there are distinct signs that the villein lands attached to Swanborough had increased. There were ten villeins with three ploughs as opposed to the two ploughs in demesne. There is a good deal of doubt about the area of land covered by a plough in Domesday terminology (as for that matter about the Domesday 'hide', which is evidently *not* the conventional field hide of the Lewes chartulary or medieval manorial documents). However, it is probably fair to use it as a rough guide to the relative sizes of different areas; if so, the Swanborough villein lands of 1086 were if anything larger in area than – or at least commensurate with – the demesne.

Comparing the chartulary with the Domesday entry, it seems that this quite large proportion of villein lands was partly accounted for by the bit of village land in Kingston included in the original grant, and partly by the two hides of Bristelm and Ormar that had come to the monastery when they became monks. As the chartulary tells us, Bristelm and Ormar had been freemen (of de Warenne, who of course had confirmed their gift to the priory just as King William had confirmed de Warenne's own gift to Cluny). If they had still held de Warenne land in Niworde in 1086, the meticulous men who drew up the Domesday Book would have noted it as they noted the presence of freemen elsewhere. That they are not mentioned suggests that they had already joined the Cluniac order by 1086; the expansion of the villein lands of the grange at Swanborough suggests in turn that their lands were by this time in villein hands. If this guess is correct, then in 1086 the priory held four hides (or 16 yardlands) of demesnes at Swanborough and some three and a half hides (14 yardlands) of villein lands – the latter being most probably in Kingston.

At the time of Domesday, Tosard (spelt Tusard in the charter of the second William de Warenne) had not yet given his lands to the monks. They followed soon, however, before the death of the first Earl de Warenne in 1091, and like other gifts in the Swanborough hundred they too were attached to the grange. There must be some doubt about the size of Tosard's gift. In the charter of the second earl dated shortly after 1091 it is described as two hides of land – in other words eight yardlands. However, there is another record of these lands in the chartulary that is probably of an earlier date in which a William de Warenne 'gives land which Bristelm held in Swamberga and confirms 12 acres given by Tosard'.[36] Tosard may, of course, have made his gift in two parts. The 12 acres may have been a first instalment. Alternatively, the later entries in the chartulary may have been mistaken. It is not really possible to decide. Other gifts to Swanborough followed. The second earl gave the monks 'a hide and a half of land which Ailwin de Wincestria (Winchester) held in Kingston'.[37] At about the same time he also gave two hides in Iford – one of which a villein (William son of Godwin of whom more later) held and the other of which the monks were entitled to 'have in demesne as their own'. Later, probably in the 1130s, the third Earl de Warenne (yet another William), gave a further three hides in Kingston.[38] In the meantime, the priory had been given the church of Kingston.

Plainly, a substantial amount of land in Niworde had passed from de Warenne to the prior, to be attached to Swanborough Grange farm. In effect, besides enriching the priory, these gifts from de Warenne and his underlings reflect the creation of a new manorial unit, carved out mainly from the villein lands of Kingston. The chartulary sets out this unusual event before our eyes, as it were. And the results tally with what we know of the later manor of Swanborough. In about 1600, Swanborough Manor consisted of 36 yardlands in Kingston village; 24 yardlands in demesne, of which 16 were in the tithe free lands of the court farm and eight in the fields of Iford; and about a yardland elsewhere in Iford. This makes a total of 61 yardlands, which amounts to 15 hides and one virgate. Compare this total area of 1600 with the gifts made to the priory before 1130 or so. The founding gift amounted to 5½ hides; Bristelm, Ormar and Tosard taken together with Ailwin of Winchester gave a further 5½ hides; the de Warennes gave another three plus the two hides that were held by William son of Godwin. Altogether this gives 16 hides – not a bad correspondence with the 15 hides and one virgate of Swanborough some 400 years later, particularly when the possibility that Tosard's gifts were overstated is taken into account.

These early gifts were brought together in a description used in successive confirmatory charters as each earl took over from the last. It reads: 'the church of Kyngestona with its appurtenances and in the same vill 8 hides of land. Swamberga with its appurtenances. The church of Iford and in the same vill 2 hides and one virgate.'[39] At first glance, this confirmation poses a problem. It looks as if the total area attached to Swanborough was only ten hides – the eight hides in Kingston and the two hides and a virgate in Iford. But this is misleading. In fact, we must suppose that the reference to 'Swamberga with its appurtenances' is intended to include the *demesne lands* the monks held around their little hall and chapel. These demesnes, we may assume, included the four hides that came in the foundation grant in 1077 and that lay in the tithe-free central area of the manor, as well as the further two hides or eight yardlands the Swanborough Manor of 1600 held as demesnes in the fields of Iford. If this is the correct way of interpreting the reference to the 'appurtenances' of Swanborough, all is well as far as the total of lands is concerned: the description then implies a total of 16 hides, exactly the amount of all the earlier gifts added together. It leaves a slight unsolved problem, however, since it implies there were 32 Swanborough yardlands in Kingston as against the 36 of 1600, and eight yardlands in Iford as against the single yardland of 1600. There is, as it were, too little land in Kingston and too much in Iford. The shortfall in Kingston is not too bothersome, for there could quite easily have been a subsequent increase in Swanborough yardlands due to assarting in the village fields – for example during the formation of the Hams or the Latchetts or even in the post-Elizabethan assarting in Mill Laine. In fact, the numbers of Swanborough yardlands in Kingston in 1130 are sufficiently close to the numbers in 1600 to make one confident about the idea (expressed in Chapter 2) that the Kingston open fields did not change very much over the centuries between the Norman Conquest and 1600.

The large numbers of yardlands in Iford in 1130 are more of a problem. In 1600 there was only one Swanborough yardland in Iford – the chartulary suggests that there were eight in 1130. What had happened to these lands?

Unfortunately, there is no clear answer. One possibility is simply that the chartulary overestimated the area that had been given to the priory. Recall the contradictory evidence about Tosard's gift to the priory, which although mostly described as two hides of land, is at one point measured as 12 acres – about one yardland. It may be that some mismeasurement of this kind accounts for the large number of medieval yardlands in Iford. Beyond that one cannot go. This, however, is the only inconsistency worthy of mention in the comparison between the Swanborough lands of 1130 and 1600.

Here then is the origin of all those Swanborough yardlands in the Kingston open fields. It is clear that they came from the gifts that the de Warennes made or confirmed from the Kingston lands, and that the process resulted in a considerable reorganization of village lands. It is clear also that it was an unusual kind of reorganization, which intruded a new lordship into the older pattern of village organization. But, to illuminate more clearly the nature of this process and its implications for the village, we need to look a little further – beyond the apparently straightforward business of reallocation of lands between lordships and into the purposes that it was intended to serve.

A main concern of the 'farmer' monks in Swanborough was surely the supply of labour. Compare for a moment the Falmer and Swanborough parts of the first grant to the priory. In Falmer, the monks were given an entire manor in which they held '2 ploughs' in demesne and had the labour services of 35 villeins. In Swanborough the monks also held '2 ploughs' in demesnes, but they had far fewer villeins. Even after Kingston villeins, who owed service to the grange, had occupied Bristelm and Ormar's lands there were only ten working for the monks. This was in 1086, some nine years after the start of the grange. In short, despite the advantages of Swanborough lands for monks because they were a self-contained farming unit, they were disadvantaged compared with Falmer by a shortage of villein labour. This presented problems from the priory's point of view because it limited the possibilities of exploiting their splendid new demesnes to the full.

It is true of course that the monks had other sources of labour to call upon than the villeins. There were a considerable number of cottagers about the Niworde – 32 'bordars' according to the Domesday Book. Though none of these were attached to the grange at the time, it is likely that they formed a supply of labour that any manor in Niworde might call upon in return for a wage. From the bordars' point of view, it is most probable that they required such wage labour to keep their families at an acceptable subsistence level – for what they could produce on their own plots was too little to do so.

Nevertheless, the monks at Swanborough most certainly followed the early medieval pattern in preferring villein labour to other sorts. It was a pattern that was still present some two centuries later when it was clearly reflected in the anonymous *Seneschaucie* – a book that specified the duties of various manorial officials for the guidance of lords. Notice the following instruction about the job of the bailiff:

> And he ought to see and know how many acres of meadow the customary tenants ought to sow and make and how many acres of corn the boon tenants ought to reap and carry, and thereby he can see how many acres of meadow remain to be mowed and how many acres of corn *remain to be reaped for money*, so that nothing shall be wrongfully paid for.[40]

The point is pretty obvious. Villeins – the customary tenants of the *Seneschaucie* – were not paid. The return for their labour was in the form of the customary yardlands they held of the manor, which they cultivated for their own subsistence needs (and usually to meet a rent as well). In other words, the lord's return from a day of villein labour was the sum total of all that the villein produced in that day. In contrast, the lord's return from a day of cottager labour was liable to be less. The cottager had very small labour services and the lord had to pay for any work the cottager did beyond them. This wage, of course, was a cost to the lord, which had to be set against the day's production by the cottager, so reducing the amount of production from the demesne the lord could claim for himself. Unless cottagers were markedly more productive than villeins, it would always be in the lord's interest to use villein labour to cultivate any fixed demesne lands. For the same reason, manorial lords would also have preferred the labour of villeins to that of serfs or slaves – for though serfs had no claim to wages, being owned by the lord, they nevertheless had to be fed – and this subsistence would have to be taken from the lord's demesnes since serfs had no lands of their own. So, given the choice between running the demesnes with serf labour or villein labour, manorial lords must have preferred villeins. The villeins provided their own subsistence from the customary yardlands.

As one might expect, manorial lords – or at least those who wrote treatises for them on the best use of labour on their manors – were sensitive to the advantages of villein labour. Here is some fairly sophisticated economic advice from a thirteenth-century writer: 'And if there is a servant who knows how to do work in the court for which it would be necessary to pay another highly, let him do the work and pay another in his place.'[41] In other words, the (unpaid) villein – called a 'servant' here – should be used as far as possible to perform those jobs that command the higher wages on the labour market, and hired labour correspondingly confined as far as possible to the lower paid – and presumably less skilled – functions. This is no more than good-sense allocation of labour, but of course it is founded on the fact that villeins received no wage and were in a sense paid for anyway by the grant of customary land. Use them to your best advantage, says the writer.

In the early days of the grange, with fairly few villeins, the monks at Swanborough must have relied on such wage labour as they could muster from the cottagers of Kingston and Iford. Obviously these workers had to be paid out of what they produced from the demesnes. And, equally obviously, the monks would have welcomed any opportunity to replace them with villein labourers who would not require such payments – provided the customary lands off which the villeins lived were not taken out of the precious demesne lands in Swanborough. For any fixed amount of demesne lands it was preferable to use villein labour if it could be obtained. It was obtained.

The de Warenne gifts and confirmations to Swanborough Grange were really of two types. Some of the lands they gave – especially the first grant at Swanborough – were demesnes, whose products were intended for the direct benefit of the priory. Others were intended for a different purpose: to support villeins who would provide labour service to the monks on the Swanborough demesnes. The great majority of the gifts of land that followed the first grant were in fact of this type – together with some of the land included in the original grant. The grange farm did not benefit directly from this land; it benefited through the labour services of the people who supported themselves from it. And this means that a good many of the gifts of land to the grange were not in essence gifts of land at all but gifts of labour. Much of the time this fact is left implicit, but for all that it is an obvious inference.

Nor is it always implicit. During the twelfth century the gifts made to the priory by lesser mortals than the de Warennes were smaller than the first series of grants. They are described in greater detail from time to time. It is clear that transactions in people were perfectly acceptable to the spirit of the times. Thus, in the 1170s we find this gift: 'I Henry Count of Eu grant to God and St Pancras ... a bondsman ... whom my brother gave in his lifetime and three whom he likewise gave when he was dying whose names are Lard, Stanard, Teile and Edmund Stumba.'[42] About 1190 there is another gift of a similar type: 'I Aymo son of Robert de Corsle have given ... to God and the Church of St Pancras ... John Blund with all his progeny and 3s of yearly rent ... in pure and perpetual alms.'[43] And in the thirteenth century: 'I Godfrey de Glinda have given and quitclaimed to God ... Ewar de Hamgate my man and neif with all his chattels and all his progeny.'[44] Somehow the sense of perpetuity conveyed by that phrase 'and all his progeny' is especially chilling.

These people deemed suitable as gifts to God for the good of the souls of their masters were of course serfs – men and women who were totally unfree and in ownership. Nevertheless, it is clear from some of the gifts the priory received that villeins were also perceived as owned to a considerable degree, and that it was gifts of villeins as people who would provide labour that lay behind many of the bland looking gifts of land. Thus, in 1175, the Earl de Warenne gave '2 virgates of land in the vill of Brighthelmstone (Brighton) which lands Ailwin the tanner and Aluric Asse hold'. Then the earl adds the following: '*These men* I have given to the monks with the said land, with their wives and children ... in exchange for the mill of Mechinge, which my father gave in alms'.[45] When the earl specifies exactly what he was giving in exchange for the mill, it turns out to be the men and their wives and children – an alternative way of describing the gift of land.

There are records of many other gifts of villein families hidden behind the gift of land (not of course that the de Warenne earls felt any need to hide what the gifts actually meant – it is simply the way many gifts are described that hides their real content from modern readers). A large gift of 1185 is recorded as 'the whole vill of Athelingworth, with the men and stores and stock of the same land.'[46] And, closer to home, there was the gift of Iford lands, which we have already mentioned, but which reads in full:

> I Earl William de Warenne give to God and St Pancras and the Monks … two hides of land in Yfordia which William son of Godwin holds and I give them William himself with his children, so that William may hold from them one of these hides … but the other hide they may have in demesne as their own.[47]

This gift is particularly clear about the two meanings that can be attached to gifts of land. A gift of demesne land was indeed a gift of land in the sense that we would understand today; a gift of villein land was in fact a gift of villeins themselves. This sense of ownership over villeins and the consequent feeling that it was perfectly right and proper to make free of them as gifts to the priory is clear in the second earl's general confirmation of all his father's gifts 'in lands and churches and tithes, in waters, in woods, in ways and paths, in meadows and grazing lands, in men and in all places and all things.'[48]

The gifts of land in Kingston were in fact nearly all gifts of villeins. These villeins held their customary yardlands scattered in strips about the open fields. Consequently, when the villeins were transferred from their earlier manorial claimants to Swanborough Grange, the parcels of strips that made up their yardlands were transferred along with them and were thenceforth customary yardlands of Swanborough. They remained in their original dispositions, scattered about the open fields – but now they were interspersed with lands attached to other manors.

So the intermingling of lands from different manors in the furlongs of Kingston village – as in Kingston Street itself – had its origins in gifts that de Warenne and his men made to the monks. The hard feudal reality behind these intermingled strips is that they reflect the giving of people to the priory – people whose primary manorial task came to be the cultivation of the beautiful demesnes at Swanborough. As far as the monks were concerned, the new manorial unit gave them the best of all possible worlds. It was geographically self-contained and separate from the vills that flanked it – so there was no need to become involved in village affairs. Yet, at the same time, it was close enough to Kingston to make direct use of the village villeins it came to own – for a more advantageous exploitation of the demesnes than had been possible with other types of labour.

******

As far as Kingston was concerned, the needs of the new priory at Southover and the happenstance that men from the village – Bristelm and Ormar – were inspired to become monks turned it into a reservoir of labour for Swanborough Grange. The process was fairly rapid. A large proportion of the villein lands that became attached to the grange were given within fifteen years or so of the foundation of the priory in 1077. Indeed, Kingston villeins were at work on the Swanborough demesnes from the very beginning. In so far as the Earl de Warenne ever thought about the village it was as a place that provided a ready supply of villein labour.

There are indeed signs that this view of Kingston village, though it may never have been worked out very clearly, informed some other actions of the early de Warennes. Take the case of the six yardlands of Houndean Manor held in Kingston, for example. Houndean was held directly by them from the time of the Conquest. We must suppose that one of the early de Warennes simply transferred Kingston yardlands to Houndean, perhaps to increase the supply of villeins available for labour service on the Houndean demesnes – for, although these yardlands were freehold in 1600, they may easily have been enfranchized in the long intervening centuries.

A rather similar reallocation of Kingston villein labour may account for the ten Kingston yardlands that came to be attached to Iford Manor. Iford Manor itself was a strange patchwork affair. It was built upon the lands of Hugh, son of Golde (of the Domesday Book), and passed into the possession of the de Plaiz family at an early date. Here is a portion of a 'post-mortem inquisition' to establish the manorial rights of Richard de Plaiz, who died in 1269:

> The same Richard on the day he died held in demesne in Iford 174 acres of arable worth 12d each; total 8li.14s. Also a messuage with ground round it worth 2s a year. Also 33 acres of meadow worth 6d an acre; total 16s.6d. Also 22 acres of poorer meadow worth 4d an acre; total 7s.4d. There is pasture worth 18s.7½d a year. ... There is 7li.5s.4d annual rent of assize and the annual rent of stock let to farm is 16s.1½d. From the works of Blachington and Wittedene there is 6s.5d and from the works of Kyngeston 8s.11d.[49]

The demesnes in Iford were considerable (they appear to have been larger than two hides). The Kingston lands accounted for a small value for 'works', which at this time was probably the commuted money valuation of the labour services owed by Kingston villeins. Other bits of the manorial holding lay far away in what are today suburbs of Brighton.

The manor of 1269 was a far cry from the small entitlement of Hugh son of Golde in Iford in 1086. Then Hugh held two Geldhides and he and Tosard between them had two ploughs in demesne and a mere four bordars. To all appearances, Hugh had no villeins in 1086 – hence, presumably, no villein lands in Kingston.

But it cannot have been very long before he came by Kingston villeins. The first William de Warenne died in 1089 and the second earl confirmed gifts to the priory that had been made in his father's lifetime. These included the tithes of two hides of land Hugh held in Kingston – villein lands. It looks as though de Warenne had made over two hides in Kingston to his subtenant Hugh at some time after Domesday and before 1089. The rest of Iford Manor – the scattered outliers in Blatchington and Withdean – might well have been attached in the same way. Perhaps the first earl had reason to reward Hugh in a small way.

If these inferences about Houndean Manor and Iford Manor are correct, it would seem as though de Warenne simply extended the policy of attaching Kingston villeins to manors outside the borders of the village itself, from Swanborough Grange, where it started, to other nearby manors. In fact, it could be that this extension was a natural result of the gifts of Kingston labour to the grange; by the time the needs of Swanborough had been supplied and the monks had all the labour they needed, the organizational unity of the old demesnes and the villein lands in the village had been quite disrupted. If we use the state of affairs in 1600 as a guide, the intrusion of Swanborough into Kingston lands left over about 21 yardlands of demesnes. It could be that de Warenne and his manorial officers simply considered that these remnant lands were not worth holding together in a unit anyway, so that it was not of great importance to them if the system in the village were further divided by more reallocations of labour. If there were Kingston villeins at hand to reward Hugh for some service, then let him have them by all means – Kingston, from the manorial point of view, was a mess anyway! It had been gutted of most of its villeins for the benefit of God, St Pancras and the monks.

But whether or not Kingston was a manorial mess, de Warenne and his heirs retained interests in the village. The demesnes of Kingston and Hyde manors are not separately mentioned in Domesday, and it is reasonable to assume that they were together part of the total of demesnes of Niworde in 1086. 'William de Warenne holds Niworde in demesne', says Domesday, 'Queen Eddid held it'. So it is a good guess, that the demesne yardlands spread in strips in the open fields of Kingston had been a part of Queen Eddid's Niworde demesnes before the Norman Conquest. It is a good deal more difficult though to work out how these lands came to be divided between the manors of Kingston and Hyde as we find them later. There is a puzzle to solve and we cannot do better than to set out the three main pieces that have to be fitted together:

1. The de Warennes and their successors appear to have held demesne lands in Kingston village from the Norman Conquest onwards. These demesnes formed the manor of Kingston – though they were not called that until the latter part of the fourteenth century. In 1347 the last of the de Warennes

in the male line died. The de Warenne inheritance passed to the earls of Arundel and Surrey and among the lands there was Kingston Manor.[50] Later, in 1397, Richard Earl of Arundel was proclaimed a traitor and beheaded. The honour reverted to the King (Richard II), who bestowed it on Thomas Mowbray, Duke of Norfolk. In the course of this brouhaha the lands of the erstwhile Earl of Arundel were surveyed and there is an inventory of these possessions at Kingston Manor.[51]

From this point on the succession to Kingston Manor is clear. The Lancastrian Henry IV restored the Arundel family to their lands and the manor passed back to them. In 1411–12 they held it.[52] A subsequent Earl of Arundel and Surrey made the manor over in 1423 to the hospital 'or Almshouse' of the Holy Trinity in Arundel, where it remained until the dissolution (after which we shall see that it can be traced quite straightforwardly).

It is clear then that the manor was held directly by the de Warenne family in the late fourteenth century and also clear that the demesne lands in Kingston had been held directly by the first Earl de Warenne. There is not much evidence, however, about intervening centuries except for the occasional indication that de Warenne held land directly in Kingston.

Thus, in 1100, the third Earl de Warenne granted the Kingston church to the priory; the grant itself suggests that the church had only recently been built.[53] Then in about 1180 Seffrid II, Bishop of Chichester, confirmed 'by (his) episcopal authority' the grant of the church to the monks, along with the churches of Iford and Rottingdean. In the confirmation he makes a remark that throws a glimmer of light on the manorial holding in the village. Seffrid, it appears, was concerned to stipulate that although the churches had been made over to the priory, the vicars themselves retained certain direct rights. He specifies these vicarial rights in Kingston: 'And in Kingston, saving the vicar a messuage to the same church belonging, with two acres of land minus one rood which adjoins to the cemetery and the meadow of the same; and all obventions to the altar, *except of the land of de Warenne*.'[54] It is not far fetched to interpret the italicized part of this reference as indicating that the Earl de Warenne held land directly in the village – and that land must have been the demesne Queen Eddid had held, or at least part of it.[55]

2. This straightforward interpretation of the manorial ascription of the ancient demesne lands in Kingston is somewhat confused by the evidence in the chartulary of St Pancras priory that a senior manorial official of the de Warennes held land in the village. At an early stage, sometime before 1089, there was a 'Warin the Sheriff' who held land in Kingston. This is the same Warin who gave 'two fields and a garden in the vineyard' to the monks and whose gifts are listed among those of the 'barons and freemen' of the first earl. The clue to his holding in Kingston lies in another gift he made to the priory – or rather that de Warenne made for him – for we

read in the chartulary of 'Warin the Sheriff … all his tithe in Kyngestona'. Another sheriff, who also held land in the village, followed this one: the grant of the church of Kingston to the priory is accompanied by a reference to 'one acre of land which Peter the Sheriff gave there (i.e. in the village street) for the making of a church'.[56] This was either in or just before 1100.

Exactly what functions these succeeding sheriffs performed for de Warenne in unclear. It may be that they were in some degree responsible for the law and order of the Swanborough hundred while also performing the duties of manorial stewards to the earl. At all events, they seem to have been succeeded in the holding of Kingston lands by people whose functions were more clearly of the latter kind. Somewhat more than a century after Peter the Sheriff's gift of land to make a church, a family that had taken its name from the village itself appears on the scene. From 1215 a certain Warin de Kyngeston was witness to a number of transactions involving the priory.[57] In 1240 he or his son is described in the chartulary as 'Sir Warin de Kyngeston, Steward of the Earl Warenne'. Then, also in the 1240s, there is a record that a Warinus de Kyngestona held half a knight's fee of the sixth earl in the village of Kingston.[58] As later historians have shown, there is indeterminacy about the amounts of land involved in a knight's fee,[59] but by custom it was supposed to be five hides or 20 yardlands.

The de Kyngeston family of the early thirteenth century were, at least in their manorial functions, the successors of the sheriffs of earlier times: Warin and Peter. It is a reasonable guess that they had also succeeded to a knight's fee (or half of one) the sheriffs had originally held and it is plausible too to suppose that the de Kyngeston family were lineal descendants of the earlier Warin and Peter. If so, we must suppose that at some early year after the Conquest – but also after Domesday – de Warenne had created a knight's fee in Kingston in order to enfeoff one of his more important officials. It is tempting to suppose that all the demesne lands that became Kingston Manor were used for this purpose – but this does not fit the facts. Those demesnes were held directly by de Warenne's successors in 1397, and it is improbable that land once enfeoffed would have passed back into the lord's ownership.

3. The third piece of the puzzle concerns the lands that became known as the demesnes of the Manor of Hyde. Their history is hard to trace, but it is certain that they were not known as the Manor of Hyde until Tudor times. Then, when they came to be held by a Thomas Michell, the manorial title was attached to them (in 1567 according to the 'survey of the manor of Hyde'). Even then the manorial title does not seem to have convinced anybody very much: it appears to have lapsed until much later when the Rogers family purchased the lands in 1782. In 1825 they were referred to as part of the manor 'or reputed Manor' of Hyde.[60]

In the survey Thomas Michell made of these lands he allows a suggestion that they were part of *his* inheritance. This seems doubtful. Titles in the Wiston archive suggest that in fact the lands had belonged to John de la Chambre who had leased them to Michell, his son-in-law, with the proviso that they should be sold on the death of Michell and his wife (which, accordingly, they were).[61] This was not the last time that the lands of Hyde were used to establish a dubious claim to manorial inheritance.

The clearest indication of the constitution of these lands is in a description of them given to demonstrate John de la Chambre's claim to be a freeman juror at the court of the Barony of Lewes – the erstwhile baronial court of the de Warennes. De la Chambre was a juror because he held lands called 'le Hide' in Kingston-near-Lewes, which had been Gartons during the reign of Henry VIII, Hilders before that, and had earlier belonged to the de Rosey family.[62] Elsewhere in this period the lands are described as having belonged – in an unspecified past – to the Hydes.[63] They are variously described as a knight's fee, half a knight's fee and a fifth of a knight's fee. There is not much doubt then about their origin in an enfeoffment, but quite a lot about the amount of military service that had been associated with them.

The late Elizabethan description of the lands of Hyde can be linked through the de Rosey ownership to an earlier date. In 1440 there was a knight's fee in Smithwyke and Kingston that pertained 'to the castle of Lewes', which at that time was held by the heirs of Sayer de Rosey.[64] Smithwyke no longer exists[65] but lay north of Kingston fields in the parish of Westoute; it probably consisted mostly of pasture on the downlands. The de Rosey family who held the lands called Hyde had been in the area for a long time. A Saer de Rosey was excused attendance at the court of the barony and honour of Lewes in 1265.[66] In 1276 he was a juror (along with John de Kyngeston and others) at an inquest post-mortem on the lands of William Bardolph in various parts of East Sussex.[67] And then in 1288 a Saer de Rosey – possibly the same one – 'quitclaimed a corrody' to the prior of St Pancras. This was a strange affair to modern minds. Somehow this Saer de Rosey had acquired the right to two loaves of bread and two jugs of ale daily from the priory. The quitclaim involved the prior paying him a considerable sum of 100 shillings to relinquish the right. Such gifts were not unknown in medieval times. About a century later a more illustrious man, none other than Geoffrey Chaucer, was to be given a pitcher of wine daily – among other largesse – by John of Gaunt.[68]

But, back to the lands of Hyde; they cannot be traced back further than the de Rosey knight's fee except by inference from the name itself – there were de la Hydes in Kingston at the time of the great subsidies of 1297, 1327 and 1332 – and, by the statement in one description of the lands, that they had indeed been held by the Hydes.[69]

These then are the three main pieces of the puzzle that have to be fitted together if we are to have a view of what happened to the ancient demesnes in Kingston village: evidence that de Warenne held the manor of Kingston from the Norman Conquest till the end of the family line; evidence of lands held by Warin and Peter who were called sheriff and of a knight's fee held later by the family de Kyngeston, who seemed to be performing similar civil functions for de Warenne; and evidence of part of a knight's fee that came to be the lands called 'Hyde' and later, though with much less conviction and a touch of pretension, the Manor of Hyde.

The simplest 'fit' and the one we shall follow without more speculation is this: after the Conquest de Warenne continued to hold the demesne lands in the open fields, which had been Queen Eddid's. He and his steward looked after them: Warin the sheriff, whom we may suppose was the first of these and had been, perhaps, one of de Warenne's retainers at the castle. The earl's steward who held land in Kingston – and in all probability lived there – had wider duties than to look after the small demesnes, and the diminishing numbers of villeins who were left to work them, as more and more lands and people were passed to Swanborough. He had to keep an eye on other de Warenne manors, no doubt, at Houndean and Northease; he may also have had responsibility to keep watch over the villeins of the prior of Lewes who made up most of the Kingston population between 1090 and 1100. Warin and Peter, who followed him, were people of considerable power in relation to the villagers. They were the most immediate representatives of the new order.

The earl most probably enfeoffed Warin, the sheriff, and it is a fair guess that the knight's fee held by the de Kyngestons in the 1240s had come down from the sheriffs. The lands for this fee were carved out of the ancient demesnes – about two hides or so. As a knight's fee they carried no rights to villein labour. Such villeins as were not attached to Swanborough, Iford or Houndean manors were left to work the small remnant demesnes of Kingston Manor. They are 'represented', as it were, by the small batch of villein yardlands associated with Kingston Manor in 1600 – three in all. The de Kyngestons and their predecessors on the knight's fee – as indeed Kingston Manor itself – had to hire cottager labour to work the demesnes.

Finally, the most plausible hypothesis is that the knight's fee, which the de Kyngestons had held, passed at some point to that other comparatively wealthy Kingston family, the de la Hydes, or atte Hydes, and the name Hyde stuck to it as it passed down through the succession: de Rosey, Hilder, Garton and de la Chambre/Michell. Eventually, it acquired the title Manor of Hyde, which does not seem to have convinced anyone. Unfortunately, there is no direct evidence to connect the de la Hydes to the de Kyngestons knight's fee. That, of course, is a sad lack. On the other hand, there are facts that point strongly in this direction. If Hyde did not originate in the de Kyngeston fee, where did it come from, since there is no sign of any other enfeoffment? Indeed, if Hyde were not founded on the earlier fee, we would need evidence of a second knight's fee in the Kingston fields. There is none – or at least none except the manor of Kingston itself, and the evidence that the manor was held by the de Warennes directly from the Conquest onwards seems very strong. By exclusion, therefore, we are led to see the de Kyngeston fee as the basis for the manor of Hyde. This would be consistent with the fact that Hyde owed feudal dues to the manor of Kingston in the Tudor period.[70] It is also the only explanation that is properly consistent with the disposition of lands between the manors in 1600.

******

What had the Normans done to Kingston? Many of our inferences are fairly correct, more perhaps than in most English villages.

The villagers themselves – the people who waited on the Normans and who were to become 'villeins' – must have been well aware of the Norman presence from the earliest years. The building programme in Lewes was enough to ensure that first there was the stark castle atop the hill of Lewes, then the grandeur of a new priory. A Kingston villein standing in the West Laine or wandering through the strips of Swanborough Laine towards the river would have seen the priory rising at the edge of the estuary. He would have been able to watch vessels bringing the materials to build it, the stone from Caen in France from which it was made. In the early years such a villein might have wondered at the waste these Normans were prepared to commit. Had not the little church of St Pancras 'below the castle' only just been rebuilt? Why was it necessary to build yet another? As time passed and the grandeur of what was intended became more apparent, this view might have changed; Kingston, it seemed, was to have something very like a cathedral on its doorstep. The old church, clearly, was small out of all proportion to the new lord's intention.

But by the time the full splendours of the priory were apparent the villeins had felt the Norman touch in other ways. The village was progressively turned upside down as more and more villagers were shifted into a new allegiance to the grange of Swanborough. It was not long before the majority of the villeins were obliged to trudge off to Swanborough every morning – with rising sun in the summer, but in darkness in the winter, through the thick chalky mud across the fields. They took the long path that angled out from halfway down the south side of Kingston Street in a line towards Swanborough Grange. They returned by the same route no doubt, in the mid-afternoon, and turned to their own lands on which their families were already working. Others who were attached to Iford Manor probably went the same way to report to the steward of 'Hugh son of Golde' who awaited them in the next-door village. And some may have walked as far as Houndean across the downland to the north. Plainly, the old days were gone – when work for the lord had meant labour on neighbouring strips to one's own in the open fields of the village.

The intrusion of the grange had an effect that can be indicated by the evidence of yardlands. Suppose that all the Kingston yardlands out of demesne were villein yardlands (even though we know this probably was untrue, it is not a bad approximation – for it is likely that most of the freeholds of 1600 were later enfranchisements). On this assumption there would have been 54 villein yardlands to 21 demesne yardlands in the village – counting only what we have called the ancient demesnes in the village open fields. The inclusion of Swanborough added a further 24 demesne yardlands on which Kingston villeins must labour. Furthermore, approximately ten Kingston yardlands became attached to Iford Manor and about six became part of Houndean. So, overall, these Norman adjustments left 38 villein yardlands attached to 45 demesne yardlands in Swanborough, Kingston Manor and the knight's fee of Hyde. This is a rough guide to the change the Normans brought about.

It is a change that probably meant two things for the village, both deriving from the very large increase in demand for labour that it implies. First, if there had been any shortage of labour for cottars before the Normans came, there was none after. Cottars were needed to work the ancient demesnes, particularly after Swanborough had been given the lion's share of villein labour. Cottars were no doubt needed at Swanborough too. It is possible that they benefited from some increase in income as a result – though it was probably not much.

Second, and one suspects much more important in the experience of Kingston, the intensity of labour demanded from everyone must have increased sharply. This must have applied particularly to the villeins as a group: before the grange was set up there had been more than two villein yards to each demesne yard – afterwards there was less than one villein yard to each demesne yard. The lords had the strongest incentives to use villein labour first; the Kingston villeins, we may presume, were exploited as far as possible. If life had been easy before the Normans came, it was no longer so once the priory started to exert its manorial powers at Swanborough.

There were other changes too. To hold this hardening system in place, a new man appeared in the village, enfeoffed as a knight as time went by. Warin the sheriff may well have lived at the top of Kingston Street, on the site of what is today the Kingston Manor house. There are, according to Joseph Cooper, sections of twelfth-century stonework. This Warin, it is fair to guess, was *not* a gentle knight. He had most likely come over from Normandy with his lord. He had stewardship over many Warenne manors at a time when the whole English world – as opposed to the French who ruled it – was restless and resentful. Warin was there *inter alia* to keep a watch on the villeins who lived in their simple dwellings down Kingston Street and who were being hard pressed. Warin may well have had armed men to help him.

The church was built too – in those early years after the Conquest. Indeed, Peter the sheriff had given land for it. It may have been a cause for gratitude among the people in Kingston Street. The walk to church across the fields to Iford or to the old church at Southover before the coming of the priory had been a long one. Perhaps they wondered a little at the apparent contradiction of this generosity from a lordship that, in so many other ways, had surely made life much harder.

Chapter 4

Medieval Glimpses

In the aftermath of the conquest the purposes of the great intersected directly with the lives of the humble in Kingston. A chain of events flowed from the concerns of a Norman magnate for the welfare of his soul. One of these, small in relation to others but big in its significance for the village, was the founding of the monks' grange at Swanborough. Black-cowled Cluniacs, though seldom seen in the village street, were a present force in village life for more than 400 years. They were there forever it may have seemed, in their lonely stone built hall over the brow of the hill. On a still evening after the Angelus had rung, their chant might have reached a person walking in the fields; and every morning a black-clad monk awaited the villeins and cottagers who came to work on the prior's lands. They were there because of the 'intention' of a Norman baron and the uneasy assent of a Burgundian abbot. Their presence signified the special sting the Norman Conquest had for Kingston.

The coming of the grange meant more to the village than the reorganization of the working lives of its inhabitants. In addition, it produced a decisive separation between manor and village. The attraction of Swanborough for the monks was precisely that it gave them the privileges of manorial lordship without attendant needs to participate in the worldly affairs of the village. The grange in effect had little interest in the daily life of Kingston. For the monks it was a positive advantage that all those decisions critical to the proper cultivation of the open fields were taken elsewhere – beyond their ken.

Consequently, for the large majority of Kingston villeins who laboured for Swanborough Grange (or for those attached to Iford and Houndean manors), life was organized around two points – the grange (or the manor) where labour service had to be done and the village community, which, quite separately, decided on the uses of the open fields and on rotations. From the founding of the priory onwards, this duality grew in Kingston as more and more people were 'given' to the grange. It was, it seems, a new complication: to all appearances manor and village had been unified before the Normans came.

But, though the demesnes of Swanborough were away from the open fields, the ancient demesnes that became Kingston Manor and the knight's fee called Hyde were, of course, part of the strip system. The village may have been separate from the manorial system, but there were nevertheless lordly interests in the way the village lands were used. There is no record of the communal organization in the village. As elsewhere in England the ordinary people left no traces of their decisions or of the way they arrived at them. But, whatever system they used, Warin the sheriff, Peter the sheriff and the de Kingeston family who succeeded them as stewards to the de Warenne earls, played a dominant role in it. Indeed, from their standpoint the village system must have presented real advantages: it was a ready-made mechanism for asserting the interests of the lord in a world of villeins whose feudal allegiances were to the grange in the first instance. It was in other words a way of keeping the manorial mess in Kingston in some kind of order. And once de Warenne had enfeoffed his steward in lands made up of the ancient demesnes, the steward came to life. Perhaps the de Warennes saw this as a guarantee that production from their own widely spread demesnes would be properly organized. And, perhaps also, the new church of 1100 became an effective centre for communal organization. Much later on, in the nineteenth century, there were signs that the 'parish meeting' played a central part in the way the village ran itself. The priest and the knightly steward from the nearby castle would have been fully adequate as guardians of law and order – and as insurance that the communal system worked to the lord's as also to the monks' advantage.

For the most part the lords and monks were primarily interested in the supply of labour services free of wages, which the villeins were obliged to supply. It is true, of course, that with the passage of time the feudal organization of labour was transformed. Labour service was 'commuted' into an equivalent rent payment, or one that satisfied the lord. Nevertheless, the supply of labour in exchange for land was to remain a central feature of village life for a long time. As we shall see, it would seem that Kingston villeins were still at work in this way, at least on the grange demesnes, as late as 1330 and after.[1] So, for two or three hundred years after the Norman Conquest, labour service on the demesnes was a dominant imposition on the villagers.

What was it like? How demanding were the feudal masters at the grange and in Iford and Kingston? Sadly, there are few medieval manorial documents for the village and none give an account of what sort of work people had to do. The best we can do is to make inferences from the bits of information that are available about the manors nearby – particularly from the manor of Hamsey a mile or so north of Lewes and only about three miles from Kingston.[2]

William le Byke lived in Hamsey in the 1260s and 1270s. He was a villein owing homage and service to Sir William de Say, lord of the manor. We know a little more about William than this because it happens that he was involved in a prolonged case brought before the Earl de Warenne at the court of the barony and honour of the Rape of Lewes in 1265. William, as he appears from the case, was a contentious, possibly devious man who found himself in a good deal of trouble.

His problems started, by his account, when he stood surety for a lady called Matilda de Wogham (modern Offham, about half a mile from Hamsey) in a debt she owed to one John Snelling, who was probably a Kingston man.[3] Matilda failed to pay the debt and so William was held responsible for it. Unfortunately, though, he could not pay it either and he was made to suffer for it. In January 1265 he brought a case against Matilda and Robert Russel her husband. He complained that he *had* given Matilda the money to pay her debt to Snelling but that she had used it for other purposes. In consequence, he had been excommunicated – no less – until the debt should be settled. Furthermore, Matilda had failed to pay him for goods she had purchased from him, and failed also to pay for ploughing that he had done for her. To crown it all, Matilda and Robert her husband had beaten him up, insulted him publicly in Lewes and damaged his property in Hamsey. William seems to have made his case initially, but not for long. In May 1266, Matilda and Robert brought a case of false witness against him and, to add to the presumably unresolved debt to Snelling, he was fined 12d.

William was still at Hamsey in 1271 when he, together with some members of Matilda's family, the de Woghams, was a witness at the Inquisition postmortem on his lord's manor at Hamsey. It is the Inquisition that gives a picture of what a villein had to supply by way of labour at the time.

William's labour service was based on his 'week works', which he performed in exchange for a virgate of land. First, from 29 September until 1 August the following year he was obliged to work five days a week. These were usually called the 'summer and winter week works'. In William's case they were valued at 2½d a day – which, in view of later evidence, suggests that he worked for half a day for his lord. Then, second, he had 'to find a man', who might presumably be himself, for each day of the eight weeks of autumn – from 1 August until 29 September. These were the autumn week works, especially important because of the harvest. They were valued at 1d a day, implying a full day's work for the lord.

Over and above these regular daily commitments, William had other duties. All the villeins of the manor had to plough one acre for wheat and two for oats – a service valued at 15d. Perhaps it was demesne ploughing done for the de Woghams, who were also villeins, that was in contention between William and Matilda in the manor court.

In addition to ploughing, William had to mow for eight days before autumn (valued at 8d.), and to collect and cart the lord's hay (two cartloads a day for four days valued at 20d.). Over and above this he had to 'find men' to perform other services for the lord: the boon-works (valued 4d.) and a day of work a week over and above his own obligation in the autumn (value 8d). And William paid 14s.6d in rent to the lord at Michaelmas. Since the total value of the works he performed for his lord amounted to about 18s a year, this additional rent of assize was a considerable extra burden. If William had tried to meet it by working elsewhere for wages he would have had to do as much work again as he was already committed to. In fact, the rent of assize was mostly paid out of sales of produce – hence it being timed for the end of the harvest.

William's virgater colleagues on the manor carried similar obligations. Half-virgaters had just half the obligations. Cottagers carried quite heavy week work obligations (about the same as William even though they had much less land), but they paid smaller rents and had no ploughing, mowing or carrying to do.[4]

These labour services were typical for the period. A. E. Wilson notes that 'Sussex custumals point fairly clearly to a burden of five days a week for every half-hide.'[5] The Wiston Manor custumals of about 1300 indicate approximately this level of labour services,[6] though they also contain instances of much heavier dues. Villeins in 'Iryngham', a part of the manor of Wiston, were obliged to do fully twice as much work on the demesnes as William le Byke. But William's load seems fairly typical. Kingston villeins of the time probably did the same amount.

The total of these labour services amounts to a considerable burden. At a rough estimate, William was responsible to his lord for about 180 man-days of labour – not counting the rent of assize or other smaller rents he owed (including a spring-time payment of '25 eggs and two hens' to the lord at Easter). Supposing that the total of working days in the year was somewhat under 300 days – after allowing for Sabbaths and other religious days – this means that le Byke worked for the lord for about two-thirds of a working year, or alternatively had to find other labourers to make up his total. This plainly was a heavy proportionate load, but even so it is liable to underestimate the effect of labour service on the villein. The problem for an unfree labourer like William le Byke was not just that the lord demanded a substantial overall proportion of his working life, but more important that the lord's demands were naturally concentrated at those times of year that were the most critical – during the autumn harvest months. If the autumn weather was at all variable the immediate availability of labour was, of course, critical to the business of getting the crop in. The lord effectively pre-empted this labour supply from his villeins – reducing the risks of harvest failure for his own crops and passing it on to theirs. From this point of view, the viability of the villein family depended on whether they could muster labour at the crucial times of the year – either from their own ranks or alternatively by buying in wage labour from cottagers to replace the villein on the demesnes or to work on the family land.

But other costs weighed heavily on villeins like William le Byke. The rent of assize of 14s.6d, which he had to pay each Michaelmas, is easy to overlook, but for him it was a heavy fixed cost. And there were other payments to be made too, some regularly, like tithes, others less so, like heriots on the death of the villein holder, entry fines, fines on marriage of children and 'amercements' or fines paid to the manor court for infringements of various kinds.[7]

It is possible by virtue of a number of rather heroic assumptions to illustrate the tenuous grip that villein families like the le Bykes had on subsistence.

Table 4.1: Estimates of William le Byke's net annual income from cultivation and how it depended on yields

Yield per acre (bushels)	*(shillings)*	*Rent of assize (shillings)*	*Gross income (shillings)*	*Net income wheat equivalent (shillings)*
5	28.5	14.5	14.0	19.0
6	34.2	14.5	19.7	27.0
7	39.9	14.5	25.4	33.0
8	46.6	14.5	32.1	43.0

Table 4.1 gives some very rough estimates of the welfare of the family. It needs some explanation. First, a number of important assumptions are made. Le Byke is assumed to have held about 12 acres of land – a typical size for the local virgate. Second, the yields of grain he could obtain are assumed to vary between five and eight bushels per acre. It is fairly well agreed that demesne yields in the latter thirteenth century were about six to eight bushels per acre and it has been argued that villein yields were lower.[8] Third, it is assumed that wheat prices were about six shillings a quarter (eight bushels) in the 1270s and barley prices some two-thirds of this.[9] And finally, we assume that William le Byke only planted two-thirds of his 12 acres every year – the other third being left fallow – and that, like his lord, he grew twice as much oats as wheat, presumably because of soil conditions.[10]

However, it is not quite fair to measure le Byke's income in monetary units. Like most villeins, he did not sell all his produce but consumed at least a proportion of it directly. The measures of le Byke's income therefore are merely approximate indicators of his welfare. The main reason for using them at all is to get a measure of the incidence of the fixed rent at assize that he had to pay on his family's welfare. Let us note also that the table only gives an estimate of le Byke's income from the product of the arable land. He had other sources of income too, notably poultry, which may have been a crucial source of protein to him and his family, sheep, which were mainly important for their dung and only secondarily for meat and wool, and perhaps some larger animals as well. Nevertheless, this income from arable must have been by far the largest part of the total and there is some overestimation because the charge for tithes and no doubt some other fixed rents are not included.

The main point that shows up in Table 4.1 is the importance of the fixed rent of assize to the family's welfare. The clearest way of indicating how the fixed rent weighed on the le Bykes is to examine the effect of a fall in arable yields from seven bushels per acre (which was probably very high for a villein yardland) in one year to five bushels per acre in the next. This is a fall of 28.5

per cent in land yield. It would result in a proportionately much greater fall in arable income because of the fixed rent: net income would fall from 25.4 shillings to 14 shillings – in other words by 45 per cent. The main effect of the fixed rent was therefore to make the family's well being critically dependent on the land yields it could obtain.

The last column of Table 4.1 converts the net income of the le Byke family into 'wheat equivalents': it is in other words simply a measure of the amount of wheat their net income would buy at the price of six shillings a quarter. The purpose of this is to give an indication of the family's welfare in more absolute terms. It is unavoidably misleading because the le Bykes neither sold all the produce of their land nor spent all the money income they got from the part they did actually sell on the purchase of wheat on the market. Even so, the wheat equivalent measure of income is a plausible guide to the 'real' value of the arable income. Its applications are worked out in Table 4.2, which shows the amount of wheat equivalent available per family member each day, depending on yields of land and size of family.

This table shows up some of the basic problems of subsistence that a villein family faced. First, it shows the same quantitative sensitivity of family well being to land yields that is evident in Table 4.1. Second, it indicates just how important the sensitivity to land yields could be for the family. The availability of food from tillage is very close to the subsistence minimum at all levels. If 1 lb. of wheat yields about 1200 calories, then about 1½ lbs per day represents a minimum requirement for survival and barely leaves any energy over for work. However, since the le Bykes had some other sources of income and since their family, however big it may have been, would probably have included young children with lower calorie requirements, it is probably fair to take 1½ lbs. of wheat equivalent per day per person as a guide to the minimum required. If this is a fair estimate, it is clear that the le Byke family must have been close to the survival line in the best of circumstances.

Third, the table indicates the basic economic problems facing the villein. An increase in the size of the family had contradictory effects. On the one hand, it increased the number of people available to work on the villein virgate – provided of course the larger family was not made up of a disproportionate number of children. Since the villein landholder was expected to provide about two-thirds of a man-year of work to the lord, often at critical times of the year for the yields of his own lands, it was obviously very important to have extra working hands in the family. Land yields, so important to family income, might well depend on the available labour. A family of two adults and a small child, for example, might be unable to cultivate with sufficient intensity to raise their land yields above five bushels per acre. If so, and if they had no recourse to additional hired labour, they would not be 'viable'; *in short, they might all die.*

On the other hand, the larger the family unit, the more people had to be fed off the land. Obviously a great deal depended on the age structure of the family. A large young family was especially vulnerable – since it might well be that its larger size was not offset by a sufficient increase in intensity of cultivation to make it viable in terms of subsistence. Similarly, as grandparents became too old to work and children left the family unit, the burden of work needed for survival might become too much for two adults to bear. There were plainly many ways in which the family could be at risk even under 'normal' conditions. And they were always at risk if the year was a poor one for agriculture or if a large part of their lands was marginal in the sense of barely providing the additional yield needed to support the additional labour. To put the problem somewhat differently, land yields might rise with the availability of more family labour, but at the same time the vulnerability of everyone in the family to a chance fall in land yields because of poor weather conditions was increased. The margin for survival was never large. The fine of 12d that William le Byke had to pay in 1266 for bearing false witness against his neighbours at Offham looks small enough in today's terms, but in those days it was a lot. In terms of 'wheat equivalent' it might have bought food for a family of four for two weeks or more. In a bad year that might have been enough to make the difference between reasonably healthy survival and malnutrition, disease or possibly death.

Table 4.2: Pounds of 'wheat equivalent' available per day per family member, depending on yields and size of the family

Yields per acre (bushels)	*Number of family members on the virgate* 5	4	3
5	0.63	0.78	1.04
6	0.90	1.13	1.50
7	1.10	1.38	1.83
8	1.43	1.79	2.38

In these later years of the thirteenth century, there is reason to suppose that the Kingston villein families faced much the same delicate calculus of survival as their near neighbour in Hamsey – or at least those among them who held a single Sussex virgate. There are debates among historians about earlier times. Some believe they had been easier and that the feudal pressure on the villein increased in the twelfth and thirteenth centuries; others are less certain. The evidence is mixed. What we seem to see in the case of the le Byke family is a fine adjustment to the business of survival; although there is room for debate, it seems likely that for the most part villeins had lived in this precarious balance since the Conquest.

Nevertheless, there might well have been differences between manors that were of some importance to individual families. Even where the formal obligations of villeins appeared to be identical between two manors, it might be advantageous to be attached to one rather than the other. The villein's obligations, as described in the manor 'extents' or in the Inquisitions postmortem like the one at Hamsey, are in the most general terms:[11] for example, the description of the summer and winter works normally consist of a simple statement of the days owed to the lord. A great deal might depend on how the lord or his officers interpreted the obligations. In short, the intensity of work demanded from villeins could vary from manor to manor.

Broadly speaking, one might expect manorial lords to exert greater pressure on villeins, and others, where they were comparatively few people working in relation to the amount of land to be cultivated. The fewer the villeins, the greater the claims the wage bill would make on the product of the demesnes, and the less the lord's share. So while it was probably always in the interests of the lords to get more labour from the villeins than they might wish to give, it was all the more so where villeins were in short supply.

On this score, the villeins of Hamsey probably had a hard time. There were only eight villein yardlands for about 18 demesne yards: 0.44 villein yardlands per demesne yardland. At Swanborough, by the early years of the twelfth century, the supply was much larger: 1.2 villein yardlands per demesne yardland. It is likely then that Swanborough villeins were less pushed than their counterparts in Hamsey – though they in turn were less well off than the villeins of Falmer, who were very numerous in relation to the size of the demesne they had to cultivate.

It is likely also that the first generation of villeins at Swanborough, the ones who worked the lands in the founding years, were much harder pressed than their successors. They were few in number at first, and the work to be done was considerable. Whatever the trends in the feudal treatment of unfree labourers – whether the general move was towards toughening the demands on them in the later part of the twelfth century or not – the chances are that at Swanborough the Kingston villeins had a harder time in the earlier part of the century than later on.

By any measure then, the community that clustered under the watching eye of the steward-knight at Kingston had a hard time of it in the medieval years, although perhaps not quite as tough a time as the villeins and cottagers at Hamsey endured. It needed little to bring them to the edge of survival. As the centuries passed, the population grew and the pressure on the land increased. Existence became more precarious not less.

By the turn of the thirteenth century and in the early years of the fourteenth, Kingston villagers, as elsewhere in England, must have been at the limits of survival in most years and beyond the limit in any unfavourable season. Perhaps those narrow strips that climb up the steeper westward slopes of the open fields – at the head of Kingston Street – date from this time. Perhaps they commemorate the more desperate years when villagers were driven to cultivate wherever the restrictive technology of the time would let them, at the very margins of possibility. They are long these strips – but so narrow that it can hardly have been possible to pass the teams more than four times to and fro!

The black-cowled Cluniacs at Southover increased in number – there were 100 of them in 1200, somewhat fewer later; though they drew subsistence and wealth from all over England, from dozens of villagers, the needs of the priory were great in proportion and the people in the village had to sweat along with others to keep the monks supplied. The material implications of religiosity then were greater than a man in black telling his beads in the cathedral cloisters at Southover might have realized. His vows of poverty were real enough, but they brought as much poverty to others who never had a choice in the matter.

The hard tidiness of the feudal order – lords and freemen, villeins and cottars and their varying degrees of title to land – was never quite as constant a feature of English rural life as may appear from manorial documents. In fact many of the puzzles about medieval history are precisely about how this 'ideal order', if that is truly how it was perceived, was transformed by evolutionary change.

The formalized feudal organization imposed by the Normans was, from their point of view, an excellent device for controlling the conquered population and, besides, was well suited to the immediate material interest of the conquering classes. The Norman passion for the logical ordering of society, which appears so clearly in Domesday and in twelfth-century records like the Lewes chartulary was not simply a cultural trait distinguishing them from more pragmatic Anglo-Saxons; nor was it only a whim. The conquest itself provided an opportunity for a rigorous reorganization of the existing social hierarchy in favour of the new lords. Any conquering class would have taken the opportunity, no matter how pragmatic their instinctive responses to social matters. And, quite probably, the opportunity had to be taken as a matter of military necessity in the heady but uncertain years after the Norman Conquest.

But from the beginning there were economic and social forces at work, transforming this tidy structure from within and producing a much less orderly society than the Norman lawyers cared to recognize in the documents they drew up. The processes of change were slow and uneven, sometimes wavering, sometimes forceful and directed, but their outcome was clear enough: by the end of the fifteenth century the formal manorial system, though it still had its uses, was more a simulacrum of feudality than a true reflection of social organization. By that time the economic, social and political changes of preceding centuries had produced, not a market economy in the full sense of the term but a world in which markets for labour, land and goods were an increasingly important characteristic of rural economic life.

This long transformation of the feudal system cannot be traced in detail in Kingston. As elsewhere, the record is partial – merely a succession of glimpses that suggest rather than demonstrate what was happening in the village.

Indeed, even great events that certainly touched the community – the Black Death for example, or the Peasants' Revolt in 1381, which involved much of Sussex – are unrecorded. The best we can do is draw some inferences about the changes in Kingston from the more general patterns that prevailed from time to time in England bearing in mind the particular circumstances of the village. The most important of these particularities are the proximity of Kingston to Lewes – it is after all 'Kingston juxta Lewes', less than two miles away – and the predominance of the priory as the source of manorial lordship at Swanborough.

Perhaps the most important economic force at work in general throughout the medieval period was the growth of markets where agricultural production in excess of the immediate needs of the manor could be exchanged for other goods or for any available local manufactures or imported goods. The urban market for agricultural produce had been in existence on quite an extensive scale well before the Norman Conquest, but it grew throughout the medieval centuries.[12] Despite a widely held presumption in favour of manorial self-sufficiency – which was stressed in the thirteenth-century 'husbandry', for example[13] – and despite the instabilities due to prolonged struggles between the barons and the king, the power and attractions of the market place grew steadily. And markets became as important, though in different ways perhaps, for villeins as for lords and freemen. William le Byke at Hamsey must have paid his rent of assize – that substantial 14s.6d per year each Michaelmas – out of the sale of his produce at the market in Lewes. Men and women who worked for wages no doubt bought some of their food there too. The shift towards the marketing of produce was in many respects a necessary condition for the other economic changes of the medieval period.

Lewes was an old market town by the time of the conquest and this is reflected in early Norman records – in Domesday for example, or in a more particular way in the following grant from the first William de Warenne to the priory:

> And of fish and flesh and all other things they wish and require to buy for their own needs and those of their guests, not only in Lewes but also … throughout my lands in all places where a market is held, I grant to the monks forever that every day they may have without hindrance or impediment the pre-emption after sufficient purchases have been made for my own needs and for those of my heirs.[14]

A Norman lord with de Warenne's power was not disposed to let markets work freely until he was sure that they would not work against him. By virtue of his position he could 'pre-empt' – in other words get access to the sellers ahead of other buyers – and so no doubt ensure a ready supply of the things he and his manorial officers needed at a favourable price. William took first crack of the whip and gave the second crack to the priory. Neither pre-emption worked to the advantage of lesser mortals who had come to sell, whether they were villeins from Kingston or manorial servants of other lords. The market place may eventually have undermined the feudal order, but for a while at least a great magnate could find ingenious ways of exploiting it.

The effect of markets on the economy of a village at that time, as for many centuries afterwards, depended considerably on geographic proximity. The transport system was uniformly poor – and particularly so in Sussex. Even in the eighteenth century winter travel across the Weald was regarded as at best vile and at worst impossible. Though the downland tracks may have been a little less villainous than Wealden lanes, they were not all that much better. The proximity of Kingston to Lewes, therefore, and the relatively easy access to whatever markets were held, winter or summer, put the village in a rather special position. Other things being equal one might have expected Kingston to be especially affected by market forces, and by the changes they brought along with them.

But it is hard to escape the suspicion that other things were far from equal in Kingston – and in particular that the predominant role of the priory influenced the extent to which production in the village became immediately directed to urban needs. Being close to Lewes meant being even closer to the priory – indeed within an easy strolling distance. This ready proximity might well have influenced the objectives the prior set for his Cluniacs at Swanborough. As far as more distant or accessible manors were concerned – even perhaps at Falmer – we may suspect that the priors behaved very much as any other manorial lord might have done. If there were reasonable opportunities of increasing income by selling manorial produce for money, they surely took advantage of them. Indeed, since a large part of the priory's manorial holdings were at some distance, some as far away as Yorkshire, it must have been a general rule for the priory to encourage its stewards to sell the products of the demesne for money. But Swanborough surely was an exception to this. It had a fertile demesne right at the doorstep of the monastery; and since the monks themselves controlled it directly it could be used to provide a virtually guaranteed supply of produce to sustain the monastery free of the vagaries of the market. Of course, in a bad year production at Swanborough might suffer as much as anywhere else, but even so it was peculiarly well disposed to provide the priory with a way of hedging against the uncertainties that must have attached to many of its other sources of income. Barons may disrupt the economy by warring against the king or with each other, and income from faroff estates may fail, but the Swanborough demesnes were there to fall back upon in an age when certainties were hard to come by. Surely the appeal to the old instinct of manorial self-sufficiency was too much to resist – all the more so because it made sound sense.

If these guesses are right, the monks at the grange saw themselves producing directly for the subsistence of the mother house in Lewes. They may not have been much concerned about the prices on the Lewes markets. The grange must have appeared as a desirably self-contained undertaking with a narrow but crucial purpose, served all the more certainly because of the assured supply of unfree labour from the village. This view of the grange as largely insulated from concerns about the market ties in, as we shall see, with some of the other aspects of the medieval economy in Kingston. It does not mean, of course, that the village itself was totally unaffected by the market place near by. There were other demesnes and, in time, they must have become more and more oriented towards production for sale. And villeins themselves sold goods on the markets: some in a desperate struggle to find the money for rent of assize, some luckier ones in order to acquire a few more worldly goods. So the market must have influenced life even though the introverted economic purpose of the Swanborough monks might have attenuated its full effects.

A second general factor in the transformation of the medieval economy was the growth of 'demesne farming': this was the practice of leasing out demesne lands to 'farmers' who might be lords, freemen or even villeins but whose main obligation to the lordly owner of the demesnes took the form of a fixed annual rent for the life of the lease. Indeed, the word 'farmer' comes from the Latin root meaning firm or fixed, and it was first used not specifically to refer to agriculture but to any activity in which a person obtained rights to a flow of income in return for the periodic payment of a predetermined and fixed rent.

Two main forces, it appears, led manorial lords to farm out their demesne lands.[15] On the one hand, demesne farming was stimulated by anticipations that the rent it would yield might be greater than the income the lord would get by exploiting the demesne himself, taking due account of the costs of supporting stewards, bailiffs and other manorial officials. In other words, it was encouraged at times when prices were falling compared with wages. On the other hand, demesne farming may also have been a way of reducing the commercial risks incurred by the lord in disturbed times. The most likely explanation for the burst of 'farming' in the middle decades of the twelfth century is that it was a response to the unpredictability of markets at a time when the struggles between barons and the Anglo-Norman monarchy were creating a state approaching anarchy. In more settled times towards the end of the century, prices – and possibly wages also – rose, and the old fixed rents were no longer a satisfactory return to the manorial lords. They returned to the direct exploitation of their demesnes without tenant farmers as intermediaries.[16]

Demesne farming then was very much a response to risk and to the working out of market forces. In Kingston, the risks associated with civil breakdown – whether due to baronial conflicts or to the depredations of lesser lawbreakers – were probably not a major factor. Lewes after all was the military centre of a great magnate and, though in 1265 this very fact made it the focus of one of the greatest baronial armed struggles of the medieval period, for the most part de Warenne's castle stood for law and order. And even if that law and order operated in the lordly interest and was a burden on the villeins, it nevertheless ensured a certain stability in economic life. So we may guess that the use of demesne farming as a way of averting risks was probably not a very important economic motive in Kingston, though the various men who lorded it over the village may indeed have leased their demesnes from time to time, when good commercial opportunities to do so presented themselves.

The great subsidy rolls for 1296, 1327 and 1332 show some signs of demesne leasing in Kingston at that time. The subsidies were taxes on 'moveable property' – an ill-defined category that included farm and household equipment and animals but excluded houses and land. The first three Edwards levied them largely to support heavy military expenditures. Since large numbers of people are thought to have successfully evaded the taxes, the returns give an unreliable measure of the population of individual villages. They are also difficult to interpret because the definition of moveable property seems to have depended on the meaning given to it by local officers – or at least been subject to their judgement. Nevertheless, the subsidy rolls give an invaluable if partial list of villagers and owners of moveable property in villages, as well as some pointers to their relative wealth.[17]

It appears from the rolls that the demesnes of Iford Manor were exploited directly by the lords of the manor in 1296 and 1327 but were quite probably leased out in 1332. In 1296 John de Marmyon was heavily taxed (to the extent of 48s.5½d) in Iford and is known to have been lord of the manor at the time; similarly, in 1327 Richard de Plaiz was among the larger taxpayers in Iford and had inherited the manor from Marmyon. In 1332, on the other hand, the de Plaiz family was *not* taxed in the village: it is reasonable to infer that they no longer held moveable property there and that the manorial demesnes had been leased out in the intervening years.

The same was probably true of the demesnes of Kingston Manor in all three of the subsidy years. At no time was the Earl de Warenne taxed for moveable property in Kingston, though he was consistently taxed elsewhere. In fact his name appears in the lists of village taxpayers in 11 places in the subsidy of 1296 and in 13 in 1332; among other properties, he was taxed for Northease and Rodmell manors in Iford and Rodmell respectively, to the south of Kingston. The absence of an entry for de Warenne in Kingston suggests that he clearly held no 'moveables' in the village, which he would have done had he been exploiting the Kingston Manor demesnes through the agency of his steward. We may suppose that the lands were leased out.

As we shall see, there were substantial taxpayers in Kingston at this time – the de Kyngestons, the de la Hydes. It is quite likely that the de Kyngeston family was installed on the knight's fee, which subsequently became Hyde Manor. The demesnes of Kingston Manor were probably leased out to the de la Hydes.

There are signs of demesne 'farming' then on Kingston and Iford manors.

What about the demesnes of Swanborough Grange? Did the prior of Lewes lease them? Unfortunately, there is no direct evidence on the matter – even at the time of the subsidies. Ecclesiastical manorial lords do not appear to have been taxed[18] and, consequently, there is no entry for the grange farm. All that can be said is that if the Swanborough demesnes had been leased to a lay person there is no indication in the subsidy of any taxpayer large enough to be considered a likely candidate. The evidence suggests that the prior had not leased Swanborough.

That the Swanborough demesnes should not have been leased out is consistent, of course, with the idea that the priory looked upon Swanborough essentially as a source of agricultural produce for its own consumption rather than as a source of money income – a precious and unusually beautiful kitchen garden. If this is how matters were viewed from the cloisters the monks would have had little incentive to lease their demesnes – direct commercial considerations may have weighed quite lightly in the way they looked upon the grange.

The non-leasing of the Swanborough demesnes is also consistent with the architectural evidence at Swanborough Grange, which shows that although the original stern hall was enlarged it appears to have kept its function as an ecclesiastical building with a chapel attached to it throughout the centuries before the dissolution of the monasteries.

In the fourteenth century the hall was transformed by building its walls higher and introducing a second storey. A small gatehouse with pigeon lofts was built to the west. It was not sumptuous, but it was a good deal more comfortable than it had been before. It reflected the expanding tastes of fourteenth-century monks – that decay of monastic austerity that laymen slowly came to deplore, Chaucer not least among them. Even so, there is no sign in this early expansion of the hall at Swanborough of a change of purpose: the chapel remained and presumably the monks remained with it. Kingston villagers probably still trudged over the muddy path to Swanborough to produce food for the feast days, the guest nights and the increasing scale of ordinary living in the priory – a pattern of consumption de Warenne had allowed for long before: 'I grant forever to the said monks the rights of fishing in all my waters of the district of Lewes for the great anniversaries, namely those of the Earls and Countesses of Warenne and for the anniversaries of their Priors and for great feasts and great guests.'[19]

At the dissolution in 1537 the priory was still cultivating the demesnes at Swanborough directly as manorial lord, and showed then the greatest reluctance to accede to the pressure Thomas Cromwell put on the prior to lease the lands.[20] The evidence is flimsy, but still it is hard to resist the conclusion that Swanborough Grange had never or hardly ever been leased out during its long monastic history.

Demesne leasing showed the early sensitivity of the medieval economy to market pressures: the first great wave of leasing in the general record took place within a century of the Norman Conquest. The first swing back to direct cultivation of the demesnes followed as prices rose in the inflationary years of the late twelfth century. But leasing had an importance beyond being a marker of responsiveness to the market, for it opened up new economic opportunities for some. These were people who had some capital and were willing to put it at risk in the form of wages paid out for the support of labourers in advance of the harvest, or as investments in livestock and equipment. They came from various levels of the feudal hierarchy: freemen and the lords of smaller manors may have predominated at first, but later, especially in the later fourteenth century, villein families too had access to land on lease. The de la Hydes in Kingston were freemen; the de Rademelds were freemen in Rodmell. Leasing sometimes allowed men to accumulate wealth in a way that would not have been possible in the stricter confines of the simple feudal order. Perhaps the de la Hydes built theirs on profit from leasing the demesnes of Kingston Manor, so were finally able to buy their way into the knight's fee that came to bear their name. If so, they were not the last in Kingston to found their fortunes on tenancy. Leasing produced a new tenant farmer class, weak at first, limited in number for many centuries, but nevertheless blurring the sharp edges of feudal distinction and pointing the way to the future. But leasing was important also because it was one of the forces behind the most significant of all the changes in the feudal order: the commutation of villein labour service.

Commutation was the procedure by which the lord of the manor released his villeins from their obligations to provide labour service on the demesnes in exchange for payment of a fixed rent in money. The lord could then use the money rent he received to hire labour in place of the villeins. Commutation may have had different causes from time to time, but leasing demesnes was almost certainly one of them.[21] A lord who had let out demesne lands obviously had less interest in villein labour than when he was cultivating the demesne directly, and it is no accident that the first period of commutation coincided with the first wave of demesne farming in the early twelfth century. Nor is it by chance that manorial lords attempted to reassert the obligation to labour service in the late twelfth century when demesne farming was on the wane and the lords returned to the direct exploitation of their lands. They were by and large successful; by the early twelfth century direct labour service was the norm again over much of the south and midland of England.

But demesne leasing was only one factor among many. The late twelfth-century inflation increased money wages as well as prices, and the fixed rents in lieu of labour service that the lords had been willing to accept in earlier decades were a good deal less attractive to them than before. Inflation discouraged commutation – at the least – and it has been suggested that the twelfth-century inflation was responsible for centuries of delay in the liberation of English villeins from their customary labour.[22] It is clear also that commutation could take place on a substantial scale even though demesne farming was declining. Throughout the thirteenth century the lords tended to hold onto their demesnes, but even so this was also the century during which manorial lords, apparently voluntarily, untied the bonds that held the feudal order together and commutation was widespread. Perhaps the reason was that the rapid increase in rural population greatly increased the supply of free labour so that money wages fell: if so, there might have been strong commercial attractions in commuting villein service at a fixed money rent, which would in effect purchase an increasing amount of wage labour as time went by.[23] Perhaps also, the lords realized the inefficiency of unwilling villein labour and the large overhead costs of monitoring the productivity of workers who increasingly resented the time they had to give to their lords, partly because of the growing profitability of their own lands.

The villeins of Kingston experienced commutation too, of course, though the precise course of events is hard to follow. It is possible that commutation proceeded comparatively easily for those who owed service on the small ancient demesnes of Kingston Manor and for the group who worked on Iford Manor. The Kingston demesnes, as a remnant holding of the de Warennes, were not very important to them. They were most likely leased for a good deal of the time. They claimed service from a very few villein families anyway. If there is anything in the idea that villein labour involved heavy overhead costs because it needed more overseeing than wage labour, one would expect the effects of this inefficiency to be most sharply felt on the smaller manors with very few villeins. So the few villeins attached to Kingston may have had their labour obligations commuted quite early. Similarly, those attached to Iford Manor may have been liberated early: Iford is also a small manor and its demesnes were inconveniently far from Kingston village. The Iford 'Inquisition' of 1269 is enigmatic about its Kingston villeins. It mentions only that 'the works of Kingston' are worth 8s.11d – perhaps they were already a fixed rent payment.

And what of Swanborough? It was, of course, a much larger manor with many more villeins than Kingston and Iford, so the problems of overseeing were probably less demanding. It was also an ecclesiastical demesne – and the religious houses were generally conservative about economic changes, slow to commute labour service and quick to reassert their manorial rights when it suited them. And, if the priors were as reluctant to lease the demesnes as we have supposed, their incentives to commute villein service would have been that much less. In the subsidy for 1332, a number of Kingston residents are separately listed as 'villani Prior de Lewes' (villeins of the Prior of Lewes). Quite probably most were villeins who still laboured directly for their ecclesiastical masters at Swanborough.[24] If so, the majority of Kingston villeins might have had longer to wait than most for the greater freedom commutation implied – and had to struggle harder for their liberty in the decisive period of feudal 'reaction' in the later fourteenth century, when the lords tried to re-establish their privileges. Even if there were no men from Kingston in that mass who marched on London in 1381, news of the huge commotion would have reached them. It is not hard to guess where their sympathies lay.

Alongside these developments – the growth of markets, the sporadic incursion of demesne farming and the commutation of labour service – the market in land also evolved. At first it appears to have been mainly limited to exchanges of land held in fee. From about 1250 the entries in the 'Lewes chartulary' quite abruptly change their form. Up till that date, the chartulary was mainly a record of gifts to the priory. Thereafter, the gifts diminish in frequency and size and instead the chartulary turns into a list of transactions between freemen and lords owing homage to the prior as manor lord.[25]

Some of these transactions involve Kingston people or Kingston land. For example, in 1276 Richard de Foci sold half a hide of Iford land to Thomas de Kyngeston[26] and earlier, in 1263, John de Kyngeston had sold 'one tenement and a virgate' in Rustington to William de la Donne – an indication that a freeman with manorial punch like de Kyngeston was able to build up landholdings over quite wide areas.[27] In 1230 an earlier de Kyngeston – Warin – had been involved in a more complex transaction with Ralph de Portesclade. He and Ralph had evidently assumed ownership of a mill at the 'entrance' of Kingston. This was probably on the ridge above Mill Laine, in all likelihood at the site of the eighteenth-century mill. Warin acknowledged that he and Ralph were to share in the mill and made over to Ralph a half of all the profits it might yield: to be paid to him 'by the hand of the miller of that same mill, whoever may be the miller at that time'. They both undertook to provide 'half of the land to support their mill' – presumably to supply food for the miller and his family – and Warin entered happily into a typically medieval agreement in restraint of trade: he promised not to 'raise another mill in the vill of Kingston to the detriment of the said mill', nor to allow their mill to be diminished in any way. An early joint-venture agreement![28]

As time went by the number of transactions in land increased and new types of transactions appeared. As the direct obligation to labour service was steadily commuted into fixed rent payments, freemen of substance became more willing to lease or purchase villein land, held by copy of the court roll, and the land market widened. In 1350, for example, John Scras of Kingston – member of a considerable 'free' family in the neighbourhood – leased two virgates of land from the prior, 'which William Martyn lately held, to hold for the term of 9 years paying 26s.8d (or two marks) yearly'.[29] The rent on it was accordingly considerably above the rent of assize payable on most freehold land. By the close of the fourteenth century the market in land was firmly established and there are records of vast transactions that must have involved villein land as well as freeholds – or perhaps villein lands only. In 1365, for example, John Foxele sold the Earl of Arundel and Surrey (who had succeeded to the de Warennes), '8 messuages, 180 acres of land, 26 acres of meadow, and 52s of rent in Suthenovere, Lewes, Iforde, Westblachyngton, Balesden and Kyngeston by Lewes';[30] in 1399 John Brook and John Alfrey (whose name remained attached to a group of freehold yardlands in Kingston for the next 400 years), sold three houses, 120 acres, meadow and pasture for 500 sheep in Ovingdean, Barcombe and Kingston to Richard Weyville; and along with this Alfrey, Hamme, Starnyden and William Cheyne sold Weyville another 12 houses, 500 acres, meadow and pasture for 1400 sheep in six parishes including Kingston.[31] The market for land had opened up. New men were appearing who bought and sold land across many manors, and whose holdings overshadowed in scale the demesnes of small manors like Kingston Manor or even larger ones like Swanborough. Sometimes they were manorial lords themselves, but it is clear that the freeing of the land from its feudal burdens had created a new world in which lordship, from an economic standpoint, might be overshadowed by ownership – even if ownership was based on lands held by lowly villeins.

Most great events passed Kingston by without perceptible immediate impact on the current of living. It is not clear, of course, how far people in this or any other village were concerned by the larger stream of events or were even conscious of it.

There was, however, one exception, one moment in the medieval years when quite suddenly and to a large extent by chance, the village was as near as may be to the storm centre of English national politics.

In early 1264 Simon de Montfort raised a number of English barons and their men against King Henry III. There was armed insurrection against Henry's misgovernment and usurping of baronial power – it was a crisis point in the long conflict between the monarch and his great magnates – a style of conflict that was profoundly familiar in the medieval centuries. By the spring of 1264 Henry and his son, Prince Edward, were in the field with their forces along the south coast, well placed as they hoped to receive support from France. De Montfort was marching against them. John de Warenne, the seventh earl was with the king – and so, no doubt, was de Kyngeston perhaps with men of Kingston among his retainers.

On a May morning the village heard that the king had come to Lewes and that his forces were encamped in the castle and the priory; they also heard that de Montfort and the barons were nearby so that there was every reason to expect a battle. The monks – appalled as it happens at the rude excesses of the loyalist barons who had spent a more than merry night at the prior's expense – were about their business, preparing for the role they played at such times, for it was a safe bet that many men would need the last rites before long. The monks were ready – and if they had reason to doubt the spiritual preparedness of the drunken warriors around them, that might have made their own part seem all the more important.

How did the village prepare? As best it could, no doubt. The prospect cannot have had much appeal. The winter crop was barely above the ground and there must have been a fair chance that it would go beneath the hooves of one or other army. It hardly mattered which and there was not much to be done about it anyway. But some insurance could be taken against more instant disaster: no doubt the villagers climbed the downs, ready to run if the battle or its consequences should threaten them directly.

From the downs they had an unimpeded view. De Montfort brought his forces from the north and took position on the slopes above Lewes on the northwest. There was a valley between him and the forces of the King and Prince Edward in the priory and castle. A large portion of chivalric England was on the field: flags, pennants and shields bore coats of arms that were then new symbols of birth and status. It was all meant to impress and who can doubt that it did. To villeins on a hillside, still wondering at this disruption of a Kingston May morning, it must have seemed the apotheosis of feudal power. Were it not that men like themselves scurried among the mounted knights they might have believed themselves onlookers at a battle of the gods – a spectacle from another world.

But heraldry on shields and the splendour of warhorses were not safeguards against ordinary human stupidity. The villagers witnessed the foolishness of Prince Edward as he led his knights out of John de Warenne's virtually impregnable castle. Did they wonder a little as they saw the stream of armour and infantry pour out of the gates towards de Montfort's ranks on the hill top? And what did they make of it when King Henry himself led his force out of the priory fastness to charge *uphill* against a more or less prepared enemy?

Prince Edward's charge had the merit that, at least, it caught de Montfort's right flank in some surprise – a surprise that may have been the greater for their disbelief that a commander could waste the trump card of a massive defensive advantage and attack at such risk. Prince Edward accordingly ran through de Montfort's flank – but then overshot and brought his cavalry back down into the valley somewhere behind Hamsey. The King meanwhile, met the weight of de Montfort's centre – well prepared even if astonished as they watched the massive warhorses struggle up the steep slopes beneath them. It was not long before the loyalist knights were on their way back again, turning to fight when they could against the baronial forces coming down the hill behind them. But there was not much they could do: the downward momentum of armoured men on huge horses, the scrambling rush of unenthusiastic infantry trying to get clear of de Montfort's cavalry charge made ordered retreat impossible. The King had been defeated from the moment he launched his men up the hill in support of Prince Edward's hare-brained dash. The rest was rout: knights and men-at-arms scrambled back towards the castle or the priory. Some like de Warenne could not make it and took flight in the direction of Pevensey. Some floundered in the salt marshes on the seaward side of the priory and drowned there within sight of Kingston village. A small number it seems streamed over the ridge above Mill Laine escaping past Kingston towards the downland.

The Cluniacs in their black habits soon beetled over the battleground administering the last rites, seeking out the wounded to bring back to the priory and arranging for bodies to be moved away for burial. They were busy. The Kingston villagers were not. There was nothing they could do but wait and hope that the victorious army would not break out in a massive looting spree. By all accounts it did not. A truce was soon signed and, apart from a little preliminary incendiarism in Lewes, they seem to have behaved well. The battle resulted in Henry signing the mise of Lewes, and opened the way to a brief ascendancy for de Montfort. A year later a wiser king and prince defeated him at Evesham, where de Warenne too regained some of the honour he had lost by his precipitate rush to Pevensey. In the meantime, de Montfort had laid the foundations of a parliamentary system, the point of which might well have seemed a little obscure to the Kingston villagers who had seen it in the making.

In some ways the battle of Lewes was a fair reflection of the preoccupations of the great in medieval times. They had a day for sporting their new heraldry, a chance for display of chivalry and glory at feats of arms. The fight itself was a part of that most medieval of conflicts: the clash between barons and the monarch.

For their part, the villagers who watched the turmoil were representative of the vast majority of humbler lives lived out beneath the surface of large events. The battle affected them only because of the unlucky chance that it happened to be fought out on their doorsteps. All the rest – de Montfort's parliamentary achievement for example – was a bit beside the point to them. The hard business of subsistence remained their central preoccupation as it had been before. The lords had their field day and went away; the villagers remained behind, nursed the crops, ploughed the fallow and found a little time perhaps to enjoy the occasional splendours of the English spring. It may be that the battle lingered on in children's games. Aside from that, and the memory of an unwelcome fright, it was gone.

Some thirty years after the battle of Lewes, we get a first clear view of the medieval village with the help of the subsidy rolls. These are lists of village taxpayers for 1296, 1327 and 1332. They do not include all the families in the village, for there is some evidence that poorer families were not systematically taxed[32] and there was also evasion. But, unreliable and incomplete though they may be, the subsidy lists are useful. They bring us face to face with the early fourteenth-century inhabitants of the Kingston Street.

In Table 4.3 the Kingston lists are set out alphabetically and in such a way that family names that are repeated in two or more of the tax collections can be followed over the thirty years covered by the rolls. The lists are slightly adapted from the originals. First, the lists for Swanborough hundred in 1296 include a number of 'jurati' under a separate heading. The 'jurati' were apparently a panel of assessors for the district. Two of the 12 'jurati' have been included under Kingston in the table, since from later rolls and other evidence it is fairly certain that they were taxed in the village (Philip de Dyghon and Richard de la Hyde). Other 'jurati' may also have belonged to

Kingston, but there is no clear evidence about them. Second, in the 1332 subsidy there is a separate heading for the 'villeins of the Prior of Lewes' under

Table 4.3: Entries for Kingston village: subsidy rolls, 1296, 1327, 1332

1296		*1327*		*1332*	
–		Regino Benne	1–6	Margaretta Benn	1–8
Nicolas Bouar'	1–0	–		–	
		John Bryning	3–3	–	
Wm Denn	1–1½	–		–	
Wm Denn Jnr	1–8	–		–	
Cristian de Dyghon	2–0	–		–	
Philip de Dyghon	2–5½	Philip de Dyghon	1–0	Philip de Dyghon	?
–		Reginald Dounyng	4–11	Roger Dunnyng	8–0
Deryld Fis	5–0	Martin Fysch	4–0	Martin+	4–8
Wm Fis	4–2½	Alice rel' Martin Fysh	1–0	Will Fysch+	4–8
John le Fys	5–0	Wm le Fysh	4–0	–	
–		John le Fysh	4–0	–	
–		–		Reginald Gibb+	3–0
–		Robert Hildelote	3–0	John Hildelote	3–0
Will Horsman	1–7½	–		–	
–		–		Laurence Hulk+	1–2
Richard de la Hyde	2–10	Simon de la Hyde	5–11½	Simon de la Hyde	6–8
John de Kyngeston	16–1	Isabel rel' de Kyngeston	6–8	Gilbert de Kyngeston	6–8
–		Philip de Kyngeston	6–8	Philip de Kyngeston	9–0
Wm Lenwer	2–4	Wm Lewer	1–0	–	
Wm Martyn	4–4	Julia rel' Wm Martyn	2–0	Robert Martyn+	0–1½
Robert Martyn	1–1	Peter Martyn	2–0	John Martyn+	0–4
Robert Peres	3–1	Wm Peres	1–0	–	
Rel' Prepositi	3–8½	–		–	
–		–		Wm Pope+	1–0
fil' Ralph de Rademeld	6–0	Ralph de Rademeld	3–0	Ralph de Rademeld	4–0
Anwis Ruck	2–4	John Ruck	4–11	John Ruck	5–4
–		–		Wm. Scot+	1–0
Snellyng	1–10	–		–	
–		Ralph Sprot	2–6	Ralph Sprot	9–0
Rel' Stappere	1–4	–		–	
–		Laurence Tor	3–0	Laurence Tor	1–8
		Ralph le Tor	4–0	Ralph Tor	2–10

+ Denotes villeins of Lewes Priory, 1332.

Swanborough hundred. All these names, barring one, have been included under Kingston village. The single exception is John de Swambergh – who is left out because he is shown to have been in the subsidy roll of Iford village in 1327 and, from his name, may well have lived near the Grange itself.

The subsidy rolls show the amounts of tax the various village families paid on their 'moveable property' and, since the tax was 'one-eleventh' in 1296 and 'one-fifteenth' in the other two subsidy years, it is possible to work out directly the value of their moveables. Take the de Kyngeston family as an example – if only because they were the richest in the village. In 1296 John de Kyngeston owned 'moveables' worth £8.11s.6d; in 1327 his widow owned £5 worth and Philip de Kyngeston a further £5; in 1332 Philip de Kyngeston's moveables were assessed at £6.15s. and Gilbert's at £5. There were other families with comparable amounts of moveable goods – like the de la Hydes or the Sprots – but none with more.

Moveable goods included a mixture of things – household equipment, agricultural equipment and livestock – and it is not easy to interpret these amounts. The de Kyngeston family taken together owned moveables worth between eight and fifteen pounds over this 30-year period. What does that mean? They were plainly the richest in the village, but how rich exactly did that make them?

One standard of comparison for measuring the wealth of the de Kyngestons is the wage rate for agricultural labour at the time. There are manorial documents that give valuations of the work obligations of villeins in money terms and, while these may not be a precise measure of the wages paid to 'free' labour (which at the end of the thirteenth century, a time of commutation, may well have been below the manorial valuations) they are a guide.

The Hamsey Inquisition, which reveals the feudal labour burden carried by William le Byke and his villein colleagues in 1271, also mentions the value of their labour services to the lord of the manor.[33] So, in the eight weeks of autumn when the villeins were required to work all days of the week in the interests of the lord's harvest, each 'work' (or day's labour) was valued at 1d. Mowing 'before autumn' was valued at 1d a day also; and so was the extra labour of 'one man for one day of each week', which le Byke was required to find for the lord throughout the harvest months. In fact, the only exceptions to this valuation of 1d for a day's labour are: first, the 'winter and summer works' that le Byke owed his lord between the end of September and the beginning of the next August, which were valued at ½d a day; and, second, a variety of special additional obligations that were valued more highly than the standard 1d a day – ploughing at 5d a day, for example, or carting hay at two cartloads a day for four days valued at 20d. The first exceptions, the low value put on the winter and summer week-works, is probably explained by the fact that le Byke worked half days only during the seasons when general farm work aside from ploughing was slack.[34] The second group of exceptions have in common that the villeins were required to provide equipment as well as labour to the lord; accordingly, the lords valued these 'works' correspondingly higher.

A similar pattern to this occurred elsewhere in the neighbourhood. In 1296, the year of the first subsidy, a villein called Henry Wernefalst at Willingdon was valued at 1d a day for regular duties of the demesne, at 2d a day for harrowing, 3d a day for carting and 6d a day for ploughing.[35] Similarly, wage rates on the estates of the Bishop of Winchester for 1300–19 give an average of 3.85d for threshing a quarter of wheat. By convention, two bushels of wheat could be threshed in a day – for 'one work' – so that the wage rate implied by this valuation is somewhat below the 1d a day in the other manorial documents (and may be a fairer reflection of actual 'market rates' for labour, as opposed to the manorial valuations).[36] All in all, a rather stable pattern appears. John de Kyngeston's wealth in 'moveables' might be compared with a more or less standard wage rate of 1d a day.

It can also be compared with some other contemporary valuations from the Hamsey Inquisition of 1272. For example, it appears that the net income that could be anticipated from one acre of wheat was approximately 6d a year and from an acre of oats 3d a year.[37] Meadowland, which was comparatively scarce in Hamsey, partly because tidal flooding was a perennial problem, was worth 12d a year. Another rough standard is that a *freehold* tenant holding a yardland in East Sussex at this time paid approximately four to five shillings rent a year to the lord of the manor.[38]

How does John de Kyngeston's wealth in moveables in 1296 measure up against these valuations? It was worth the equivalent of about *nine years* of ordinary agricultural labour (assuming a working year of about 240 days). It was also roughly equal in value to the annual net income from 90 yardlands of arable demesne lands put down to wheat – that is approximately 1000 to 1300 acres. Alternatively, it was equal to the freehold rents on 35 to 40 yardlands. Remembering that the tax did not include some major items of 'capital investment' like the value of John's house and lands (though it did of course include his livestock, which in Kingston might have been a rather large part of de Kyngeston's assets), these valuations suggest that the family was comparatively rich. Such an accumulation of property would have been beyond a villein family like the le Bykes, whose annual income – whether in money or in goods for family consumption – left little over for accumulation beyond the bare necessities of a draught animal or two and a few sheep. It would have been quite unthinkable for a cottager who depended on wages, together with the kitchen crops and poultry he might raise though the intensive husbandry of his small patch of ground, for the subsistence of his family. Against such standards, the de Kyngestons were clearly a substantial, well-founded and secure family – fairly typical probably of a senior manorial servant to a great lord.

In relation to others of their class, the de Kyngestons were not especially rich. For example, in 1327 the de Say family were taxed on moveables worth £15 in Hamsey, while in 1296 John de Marmyon had been taxed on £26 worth of moveables in Iford. The de Plaiz family, who resumed the manorial lordship of Iford Manor after de Marmyon, were consistently richer (in terms of moveables) than the de Kyngestons – though not by very much. The de Kyngestons, it would appear, were about as rich as most small manorial lords in the neighbourhood, and a little poorer than some. The wealth of a lord like de Warenne was of course great, out of all proportion to the amounts of property that such smaller families had been able to accumulate.

In their relations with the little village community in the street the de Kyngestons were essentially feudal. Others may have bought land on the newly widening market to enhance their social standing, or used their initially favourable place in the feudal order to build themselves higher still, but there is little sign of such economic preoccupation among the de Kyngestons. The first of the family to appear on record is Warin, who was witness to gifts to the priory in 1215. This Warin, or quite possibly his son of the same name, was a witness again in 1230, in 1235 – when he was present at the time Gilbert de Say of Hamsey gave his serf to the priory – and twice in 1240.[39] In the second of these records of 1240, the reference is to 'Sir Warin de Kyngeston, Steward of the Earl Warenne',[40] and at about the same time there is evidence that a Warin de Kyngeston held a knight's fee in Kingston.[41]

The de Kyngestons continued to figure in the lists of witnesses in transactions involving the priory throughout the thirteenth century and on into the fourteenth. One or two Philip de Kyngestons followed the Warins in 1240 and 1260.[42] Shortly afterwards, at the time of the subsidies, the first John appears on the scene and a succession of at least two Johns is followed by the appearance of a Gilbert – once again standing as a witness to a transaction involving priory lands, in 1352. Thereafter, the family disappears without trace: perhaps there was simply a failure in the male line, such as brought the de Warennes to an end; or perhaps the bubonic plagues that followed the Black Death of 1347 depleted the de Kyngestons.

Whatever the reason for their eventual disappearance, the de Kyngestons had been feudal masters in the village for at least a century and a half – and if our earlier guesses about their relationship to the 'sheriffs' of conquest times are correct, for considerably longer. Their position seemed to depend on the role they played for de Warenne as stewards to his manors and surrounding lands. As far as Kingston was concerned, this made them effective masters of the ancient demesnes in the open fields. They held responsibility to de Warenne for Kingston Manor when it was not farmed out on a lease; they held the knight's fee that became Hyde Manor in their own right. Their interests in communal agricultural decisions were paramount. The Cluniacs at Swanborough claimed the labour services of the majority of the villagers, claimed their tithes also and appointed their vicar, but they deferred to the de Kyngestons over the cultivation of the open fields of their own village.

The family had wider duties too, for though they may not have accumulated lands as others had done their particular responsibility to de Warenne automatically implied a considerable status. They were regularly witnesses to important transactions at the priory and obviously had a close relationship with the Cluniacs, a relationship that must have been important to the prior during those long years in which the demesnes at Swanborough depended on the labour services of Kingston villeins. They were stewards for a lot of the medieval period. They were also coroners. Between 1271 and 1279, John de Kyngeston was a coroner in the rapes of Arundel, Bramber and Lewes – a position of considerable public responsibility. His son succeeded him: the hundred rolls of Edward I record the appointment.[43]

But firmly founded in feudal privilege and responsibility though they were, the powers of the de Kyngestons must have eroded with the passage of time and under the influence of the broader economic changes going on around them. In Kingston they were at their peak just so long as they were stewards and the lands of Kingston Manor were held directly by the de Warenne earls – for then their feudal responsibilities as 'managers' of the manor demesnes were at a zenith. But when those demesnes were leased, the de Kyngestons were turned into rent collectors for the earl and, though they continued to hold the knight's fee and so had their own vital interests in the ordering of communal life, their unique position in that ordering was gone. The lessees of the demesnes were rent payers, so perhaps a cut beneath the de Kyngestons, but still they had the rights to cultivation of the demesne strips in the open fields and so also the rights to a voice in communal decisions commensurate with the scale of the lands they cultivated. And, when commutation of labour services became more general in the village, the status of the de Kyngestons waned further. Obviously they must have remained superior people, but it is reasonable to suppose that their feudal functions simply diminished in importance.

Meanwhile, other families found alternative routes to fortune and position as they took advantage of the economic opportunities of the times; these opportunities were not written into the feudal organization of life but appeared in its interstices as the unsuspected powers of the market were asserted.

The de Rademelds are a good example. The subsidy roll (see Table 4.3) shows that they held a substantial amount of moveable property in the village – £3.6s worth in 1296 – but it understates their economic position and, no doubt, their social position too. They were a family of freemen who originated in Rodmell village lying to the south of Kingston in the Ouse valley, and they had started to acquire land long before, freehold land we must suppose, wherever they could obtain it in the neighbourhood. They appeared on the scene as early as 1199, in the reign of the unfortunate King John, and in a time when the de Warenne earls still felt constrained in the interests of precision and proper order to address their proclamations to 'all their men, French and English'.[44] In that year there is a record that Ralph de Rademeld was admitted to four acres of land he had obtained from John de Benefeld in Northease, just north of Rodmell, where the omnipresent de Warenne family were manorial lords.[45] In 1203, while barons like de Warenne were already rumbling towards the crisis of Magna Carta, this Ralph de Rademeld got his hands on a further two virgates in Rodmell itself.[46] And though the record is doubtless incomplete, the pattern of family progress was set. A later Ralph (possibly a son, but more likely a grandson) was admitted to 'a messuage and a carucate' (probably a hide) in Ovingdean, a small village lying close to the sea and adjoining the far southwestern boundary of Kingston. This was in 1263.[47] In 1270 he made a larger purchase from Matthew de la Cumba, another substantial freeman: 'a messuage and two virgates' in Kingston and 'a messuage, a mill and 100 acres' in Hamsey nearby.[48]

Parcels of land in Northease and Rodmell to the south of Kingston, in Ovingdean to the southwest, in Hamsey to the north and in Kingston itself, made up a rambling but considerable empire. The resources to bring these lands together must have come from successful exploitation of the favourable markets and low wages of the thirteenth century. If they were sufficiently commercially minded, men who held land in fee were well placed to accumulate more. The de Rademelds were not the only ones to take advantage of chances when they appeared. The de la Cumbas, for example, had a similar empire in the Ouse valley earlier in the century; like the de Rademelds they held lands in many manors and villages. By the time of the subsidies the de la Cumbas had shifted the centre of their commercial interest northwards and were large landholders in the hundred of Barcombe.

The de Rademelds exploited most of their empire by leasing their lands and the rest by taking charge of cultivation themselves. Although their scattered lands were as big as the demesnes of most manors, they did not of course add together into a manor in any sense of the term. Indeed, the de Rademelds owed homage in manorial courts in every village where they held lands – though of course as freemen they stood high above the villeins and, as large landowners, they might have been richer than the lords themselves. But since they were not lords, the de Rademelds could not call on a manorial system of stewards and bailiffs to manage their lands for them. The only choices they had were to use the land directly themselves – which was difficult if it were far away – or to lease it out to subtenants and take their income as rents. The de Rademelds apparently chose to live on and work their Kingston lands, to set up younger members of the family on the smaller parcels in Northease and Rodmell, and to lease the lands in Ovingdean and Hamsey.[49] It was rent income from their dispersed estates that accounted for their wealth (as well as their own efforts on their free lands in Kingston), and for their superior status in the community. And rent incomes made it possible to expand the empire further still. In 1355 John de Rademeld, together with a partner, got admittance to another set of properties: 'one-third of two messuages, 200 acres, 40 acres of meadow, 200 acres of pasture and 40s of rent in Hamsey, Barcombe and Rodmell'.[50] By this time, after the ravages of the Black Death and the shortages of labour and labour tenants that it caused, commutation had become more general; John de Rademeld's additions must have included villein lands; that is the implication of the rather large amount of rents included in the purchase.

In building up their wealth on the basis of 'farming out' newly acquired 'free' land, the de Rademelds and families like them were following a route that the manor lords of the twelfth century had charted. If the lords could lease out their demesne lands and live off the money incomes they yielded, it was surely open to an acquisitive freeman to buy his way into lands and to follow the lords' example. But while the de Rademelds may have seen the leasing of demesnes by the lords as an example they could follow, there were others who exploited the availability of demesne lands on lease more directly as tenant farmers.

The de la Hydes were freemen in Kingston who had built their quite considerable wealth on tenancies on the demesnes of Kingston Manor. Over the comparatively short period covered by the subsidies, the taxable value of their moveables grew sharply. They were taxed on 31 shillings in 1296, 75 shillings in 1327 and 100 shillings in 1332. Since prices were fairly constant over this time, these figures leave the strong impression of an economically successful family rising rapidly in the hierarchy of wealth in the village. But though the de la Hydes enjoyed access to more wealth (and presumably were willing to spend time and effort in diligent cultivation to ensure it), their status in the village probably did not depend crucially upon it. They were well established – a substantial free family that had been almsgivers to the priory in the 1240s.[51] Ralph de la Hyde and Ralph Dyiun (Dyghon in the subsidy), both of Kingston, each gave 'all their share of the land of Niwehokland in the Parish of Chaggelegh' to the monks. Chaggelegh is Chailey today, a parish lying 15 miles to the north of Lewes in the Weald. How the de la Hydes had come by these lands so far from home is unclear, but the mere fact that they had lands to give is an indication of considerable economic security and feudal status. That the de la Hydes, like the de Kyngestons, were part of a comparatively small group of local freemen who frequented the priory and were trusted by the monks confirms this impression. They appear as witnesses in a number of land transactions at the priory in the thirteenth century; they were accepted as standing surety for others in debt.[52] They do not, however, appear as major landholders at the time of the subsidies, nor do they figure in any large transactions in land in the style of the de Rademelds. This lack of involvement in land ownership suggests that their comparative wealth was based on successful tenancy – and in Kingston this can only have meant tenancy on the demesne of Kingston Manor.

De Kyngestons, de Rademelds and de la Hydes in their different ways were all quite clearly near the top of the social pyramid in Kingston. It is less obvious that the de Dyghons were too. In the subsidies the de Dyghons appear as a rather poor family. In 1327, Philip de Dyghon's moveable property was valued at 15s – a fifth of the de la Hydes and, as we shall see, less than some villein families. Moreover, there is no sign in the subsidy rolls that the de Dyghons had property elsewhere in Sussex. Yet, there is no doubt about their superior status in the village. They were, along with the de la Hydes, one of a small minority of freemen who had given alms to the priory (the lands in Chailey that in the 1240s they seem to have shared with the de la Hydes); they were frequenters of the priory and appear as witnesses well into the fourteenth century;[53] and, in 1296, Philip de Dyghon had been one of the jurati who made the assessments of taxable value or, perhaps, checked the fairness of social position – signs that the de Dyghons could expect a certain degree of deference from the majority of villagers. Accordingly, there is a touch of mystery about them: how was it that 'free' status had not assured their wealth? Had their wealth dissipated from the heady days when they gave land in alms to the monks – or were they always comparatively poor? And there are other questions too, particularly about their name. It is (like most others) variously spelt: Dyghon, Dyiun, even Digeon. Whereas other names in the French form – de Kyngeston, de Rademeld, even de la Hyde – are easy enough to understand, de Dyghon is less clear. It is possible that it came from Dijon – or is that a preposterous suggestion? If it did, was the status of the de Dyghons preserved intact, in spite of poverty, because of some communal memory that they could claim the closest affinity to the early overlords who crossed the Channel? All surmise, of course, but hard to resist – and all the harder in the light of the fact that in 1832, some 600 years after the first record of the family, there was still a Kingston yardland called Diggon's land. Was it pure chance that their name, among all the dominant medieval names in the village, should have been preserved in the folk memory?

Aside from these pure speculations, the facts about the de Dyghons point to a more certain conclusion: wealth, economic pre-eminence, was not in itself the touchstone of social status. In a world where feudal rankings still counted, differences in wealth between the de Dyghons and other freemen who were on their level do not seem to have disadvantaged them in terms of their social role – their access to the priory, for example, or their position as judges and arbiters in the minor but momentarily important matter of who should pay what taxes in 1296. Nor apparently could men of lower rank but greater wealth – men of whom we know very little like John Bryning, Roger Dunnying, John Ruck and Ralph Sprot (see Table 4.3) – aspire to a comparable position to the de Dyghons' in the ordering of village affairs. Whoever these others may have been (and it is possible that some villeins of Iford and Kingston manors had benefited by commutation), they were definitely not part of that small circle of village notables who were called in from time to time by the priors of Lewes to give opinions, stand surety or lend their names to local transactions in land. That circle in all probability defined the people who 'counted' in medieval Kingston, with the exception of the de Rademelds who stood outside it, perhaps because they were comparatively 'new' people whose allegiances to many lords and villages diminished the degree to which any single lord relied upon them. People like the de Rademelds who built their wealth by accumulating 'free' lands in many manors may have paid a price in terms of local influence.

Wealth was neither a passport to influence nor, if one were born with a name like de Dyghon, was lack of it a disqualification. But in a village where no one was very rich there is no doubt that a bit of it was very welcome. In the thirteenth and early fourteenth centuries access to wealth – the possibility of accumulating a few resources for immediate comfort and as some security against poor seasons – was highly dependent on access to land on the right terms. Freemen had that kind of access and could exploit the rising food prices and falling real wages to the full. What is especially interesting about the subsidy roll for Kingston though is that it shows that some villeins had been able to grab a share of landed prosperity even though they may have held their virgates on disadvantageous, 'le Byke-like' terms.

In general, the subsidy lists are not very informative about the unfree of the village. There is, of course the great advantage that the 'villani' of the prior of Lewes are separately listed in the return for Swanborough hundred in 1332 – but there are still two problems. On the one hand, there is no indication of who were villeins in the other manors that held land in the village; the lists cover Swanborough villeins only. On the other hand, in the returns for Wiston,[54] the subsidy rolls for Swanborough certainly give a fuller list of freemen than of other classes and leave out altogether the poorer inhabitants, whether villeins or cottars. At a guess there may have been as many as 15 to 20 families in addition to those shown in Table 4.3 in 1332,[55] all of them villeins or cottagers and all poorer than the families listed in the return (except perhaps for a few comparatively richer tax evaders). In short, there was a large class of Kingston villagers whose personal wealth was negligible and who in one way or another – as poor villein or wage-earning cottager – were living close to the limits of subsistence.

Yet, as the subsidy shows (Table 4.3), there were some quite rich villeins as well. Martin Fysch was a Swanborough villein taxed on moveables worth 60s in 1327. He was much poorer – or better at evasion perhaps – in 1332, but another Fysch, Will by name, was taxed on 70s in that year. William Martyn was taxed on 47s 8d in 1296, though his family were considerably poorer in 1327 and 1332. These families owned about the same amounts of moveable property as the freemen of the village; they were not as rich as the de Kyngestons or the de la Hydes of course, but certainly richer than the de Dyghons. There are some other indications of their economic status in the chartulary records. For example, in 1350, John Scras, then of Kingston, leased two virgates of land from the prior, which William Martyn, scion of the Martyn family of 1332, had held in villeinage. And the Martyns not only held two virgates; they also had what must have been an excellent house. In 1352 there is a charter 'by which the Prior and Convent of Lewes granted to Alice who was the wife of Simon atte Hyde, a tenement which William Martyn formerly held in Kingston, to hold for the term of her life paying 26s.8d.' In his lifetime William Martyn held the tenement in villeinage. Gilbert de Kyngeston, John atte Hyde and John 'Dyionn', among others witnessed the lease to Alice de la Hyde. Plainly, William Martyn's house was good enough for a comparatively rich freemen family like the de la Hydes to judge it suitable for their widowed mother,[56] and that perhaps is a measure of how far the Martyn family had closed the economic gap between themselves and the upper level of Kingston society.

The Fyschs, Martyns and Gibbs were a tiny proportion of the villein families in the village – somewhat over 10 per cent perhaps. But it is interesting, nevertheless, that they had succeeded in raising themselves economically to a level not far from that of the freemen. How could this have been done under the exacting conditions of servitude that circumscribed their lives? How did they raise themselves so strikingly above the poverty of their fellows?

Villeinage had one potential advantage compared with the conditions under which cottagers lived. Villeins held land and, in the thirteenth century, the profits on commercially exploited land were high and rising. For the most part it was hard for villeins to take advantage of these conditions. Their service obligations to the lords reduced the amount of effort they could put into cultivating their own parcels and though they, like the lords and freemen, could take advantage of the fact that real wages of labour were low and falling, the burden of heavy rents of assize and the weight of other feudal payments greatly reduced their opportunities for saving out of income. Nevertheless, even under these adverse circumstances, the possibility of accumulating at least a little wealth did arise from time to time. It depended partly on the size and structure of the family and partly on market conditions. If, by chance, a sequence of profitable years coincided with a period when the villein family consisted of an unusually high proportion of people of labouring age and was not too large it might well save out of income. Whether such savings could be turned to good account for the future depended no doubt on other strokes of fortune – for example, on whether a virgate fell vacant at the time when family fortunes were running high. Such combinations of good luck were rare, of course, but in a century when landholders had the advantage they must have occurred and, once established on a larger number of strips in the open fields, the villein family would have had better chances of staying comparatively wealthy, indeed of getting richer. William Martyn, whose house and lands had reverted to the prior in 1350, had two virgates. This not only reflects his comparative wealth but it also explains in part why he was richer than the mass of villeins in the village.

Other favourable circumstances could push a villein family upwards. By the fourteenth century, or before, laws of inheritance determined the succession to villein yardlands and they might, in their fickle way, have allowed a small inheriting family to acquire access to additional land. Service to the manor lord might have helped. Villeins served as bailiffs, and in a number of other roles, and it is conceivable that additional service or special skill in dealing with the community in times of strife might have won admission to more land. Commutation, if it came at the right time and in exchange for a reasonable rent, might also have helped. William Martyn had almost certainly had his labour service commuted by 1350 – and perhaps long before. The grant of two virgates on lease to John Scras required that Scras should pay rent of 26s 8d (or two marks) 'at the terms at which the said William used to pay his rent while he was alive'. This, as we have remarked, was considerably more than an ordinary rent of assize and was plainly intended to give the prior a return on the virgates commensurate with the value of labour service that had once been attached to them. So perhaps an early commutation on favourable terms and access to a second virgate by inheritance or favour of the lord accounted for the success of the Martyn family. And commutation may account for the comparative wealth of a number of other taxpayers in Kingston who cannot be identified as freemen but who held property valued not far below that of some of the more influential families who were free.

******

This glimpse of Kingston society in the middle of the medieval centuries shows a structure that is a good deal more complicated than one might have expected, more complicated also than it had been in the early Norman period.

The feudal institutions and their guardians were ever present, of course: Swanborough Manor and the Cluniacs; Iford Manor and the de Plaiz family; Houndean – of which there is little to say because then, as after, its weight in the village was slight; Kingston Manor under lease or under the steward; and Hyde, the knight's fee. It is an impressive catalogue, an ordered array of lordships great and small, all directed to this single rather humble community. Kingston was never short of feudal institutions; the people were laden with them.

It is true too that the central features the Normans imposed were still there. The majority of people were poor and unfree as they had been before – and at a time when population and labour supply were growing some may have been worse off. Cottagers in particular depended on wages to reach the margins of subsistence and, in the thirteenth century, wages tended to fall. Furthermore, in 1300 these villeins and cottagers were still deferential to people whose superior positions in the community were founded on their feudal rank: men like de Kyngeston, very much the lord's man, carrying responsibilities in a wider world, which was extraordinarily remote to the villeins and common people, and holding a knight's fee; and de Dyghon, a freeman of distinction if not wealth.

In the meantime the workings of the medieval economy had brought changes at both the top and the bottom of this social order. At the top the increasing profitability of land produced new patterns of differentiation among those who held it on favourable terms, especially freemen. If, in 1300, the de Dyghons were representative of the older type of freeman, the de la Hydes and the de Rademelds surely stood for the new – men who had grasped the opportunities of the time. To all appearances, the de Dyghons were settled on a virgate or so, paid homage to Swanborough and seemed satisfied enough to stay as they were, enjoying the influence and occasional responsibility that went with their old status. The others had been less settled in their ways. Demesne tenancies brought the de la Hydes growing wealth and influence. The de Rademelds exploited the fact that free lands were increasingly being bought and sold to build an empire that rivalled a manorial demesne in arable area if not in feudal privilege. New ways were opening up by which families with some initial social advantage could raise themselves and, by the time of the subsidies, these four in their different ways shared a certain social eminence in the community.

They all had names written in the French form (though the de la Hydes were sometimes called 'atte Hyde' in the English way), which reflects the continuing, but waning, importance of a distinction that had been accepted for two centuries after the Conquest. French was the language of the socially dominant; even in 1300 men who did business with the priory may have been expected to use it, however roughly. Doing business with the priory was, it seems, often necessary. That magnificent institution with its cathedral church, cloisters, living quarters and prior's lodge enclosed in 33 acres of gardens and vineyards was a natural focus. Whether or not they owed homage to the prior the men who dominated the Kingston community were called there again and again on matters of local importance.

At the bottom of the social order there were changes too. We have seen that, because of commutation, inheritance, lordly favour or good luck, by 1300 a few villein families had reached levels of wealth that were at least commensurate with those of freemen – Martyns, Fyschs, Gibbs and perhaps others too. The majority remained poor and excessively vulnerable to the vagaries of the seasons, but some had climbed out of the poverty trap.

This changing community lived along Kingston Street, but we can only guess at where they had their houses. The de Kyngestons, for example, held the knight's fee that was called Hyde's in later years. Much later, in the Elizabethan period, these lands had a 'manor house' associated with them that lay on the north side of the street about half way along (marked 'Hyde Manor and barns' in Figure 2.5). It is likely that this was the headquarters of the de Kyngeston family in medieval times, so the chief house in the village. Today there is nothing left on the site that can prove the theory, though a row of timber-framed cottages is the distinguished remnant of a new wing built onto the 'manor house' some time before 1567.[57]

The de Rademelds were probably freemen of Houndean Manor.[58] If so they may well have lived in the house that was later linked to 'Peakes' yardlands (see Figure 2.5). The front wing of the existing house has been dated to the fourteenth century: it has heavy, extremely aged timber frames, which, as in so many other downland houses, are hidden by the outer flint facing; the interior walls are wattle and daub and there are vestiges of an old solarium. It is quite probably the house de Rademeld occupied.

The de Dyghons and de la Hydes are even harder to 'place'. De Dyghon was apparently a freeman of Swanborough Manor. In 1600 the Swanborough freeholds consisted of the six yardlands called 'Alfreys'. There were houses associated with these lands just across the road from 'Peakes' and the de Dyghons probably lived in one of them. There are two possibilities for the de la Hydes. They may have lived in an earlier house on the site of the present 'Kingston Manor' as lessees; this house was certainly associated with the Kingston Manor demesnes after the dissolution. It is possible, however, that the site was only developed into a large dwelling in the Tudor period, in which case it is likely that the de la Hydes lived close to the de Dyghons.

Villeins and cottagers lived in smaller homes along the street. They cannot be traced, even by guesswork, but they nevertheless were the continuing majority of the community. Despite the new prominence of a few enterprising freemen, Kingston was a humble village in the early 1300s – a community of villeins and cottars in the main. The importance of the social changes lay not so much in their magnitude at the time as in the future they foretold.

Chapter 5

New Lords for Old

In the early fourteenth century a new kind of economic order had spawned within the feudal organization and was growing with a vigour that may have surprised and dismayed both the lords whose power was founded less on wealth than on homage and the villeins who 'knew their place'.

The change that had most effect on ordinary people, and that produced the most social dissension in the late fourteenth and fifteenth centuries, was the change in the status of villeins through commutation. The substitution of fixed money rents for labour service made it possible for some villein families to survive poor harvests and bad seasons. The 'success' of people like the Martyns, the Fyschs and other families of middling wealth in Kingston pointed the way that poorer villeins, who still owed service to their lords, wished to follow. The many lords who conceded commutation to their villeins in the thirteenth and early fourteenth centuries were no doubt motivated by self-interest, but they started an irreversible social process when economic circumstances and lordly interests changed. It was a painful process because it involved a conflict of interests – and it took a long time to complete. Though we cannot follow its progress in Kingston, we can trace it in the broader stream of English rural history and see its results in the village.

The feudal system was especially well adapted to a world in which there was plenty of land and a scarcity of labour to cultivate it. In these circumstances, it assured manorial lords a ready supply of low cost labour where a market system would have burdened the lords and benefited the workers with a high wage rate. But these were not the circumstances of the second half of the thirteenth century. By that time there had been a substantial growth of population and in most parts of England there was an abundance of labour in relation to the amount of land – precisely the contrary situation to that for which the feudal system was 'intended'.

The large numbers of people without land who required work in order to subsist brought the wage rate down. In a sense, the lords no longer needed the panoply of feudal restrictions to assure a supply of cheap labour. The market was doing that job for them and, although this by itself cannot 'explain' commutation, it does at least indicate why manorial lords were not necessarily ill disposed towards it.

But the population expansion came to an end. By the early years of the fourteenth century the population was pressing hard on the available food supply, and it may be that excessive exploitation of the land was forcing yields down.[1] Together these changes meant that the agricultural population was increasingly vulnerable to adverse harvests and, from the second decade of the fourteenth century until its middle years, the frequency of bad harvests was high. Population growth slowed down and probably declined. We get a hint of the penury that came with a really bad year in the Kingston district from a report on a tax levy in 1340. The tax collectors had to account for 'losses of value' in the taxes they collected, over the amounts they had been able to extract in previous years. In the villages immediately adjacent to Kingston, the reason for tax losses was that land had simply not been cultivated: the explanations make grim reading:[2]

Rottingdean:	240 acres uncultivated because of 'the debility of the land and the inability of those who used to cultivate it';
Falmer:	120 acres not sown, 'from the poverty and inability of the parishioners';
Rodmill:	80 acres unsown, 'because they have not the means of sowing them';
Iford:	110 acres unsown, 'from the poverty of the land and the poverty and inability of the cultivators'.

The unsown areas were large in proportion: 110 acres amounted to about 15 per cent of the arable area of Iford including the demesne lands of Swanborough; if the demesnes are left out (probably the failure to sow was confined to villein yardlands in the open fields of the village),[3] the unsown area amounted to about a quarter of the arable. Falmer was afflicted to a similar degree. That such a proportion of land should have been left uncultivated in villages where the majority of people were generally not far above the subsistence line was a signal of disaster.

The tax collectors' reports hint at what had happened. There had been two very bad years in a row. The first (1339) is known to have been an exceptionally wet year in which flooding ruined the crop: it is likely that the 'debility' and 'poverty' of the land mentioned in the report was in part due to the dereliction the flooding left behind. But this was the least of the problems it caused. The ruin of the 1339 crop had two other consequences that were severe enough to affect the 1340 cycle. First, people had obviously been driven so far as to eat their precious stock of seed corn. Lack of seed was noted as a reason for idle land in other parts of Sussex and the report for Rodmell – 'they have not the means of sowing them' – may be interpreted in this way. It was comparatively easy for this kind of crisis to arise in medieval times. Yields were generally so low that corn output was only three to four times the amount of seed sown.[4] Consequently, in an average year people had to store about a quarter to a third of corn output to ensure a normal crop the next season. In a poor year, like 1339, it was necessary to store an even larger proportion of the smaller crop as seed to ensure the next year's planting. Obviously, in very poor times the immediate needs of survival would make it impossible to hold back this fixed amount of seed corn needed to ensure the next year's output: people faced the grim choice between starving now or eating into the seed corn and putting next year's crop at risk. In 1339 they were driven to eat a large proportion of the seed so that land was left unplanted in 1340. The second consequence of the dreadful crop of 1339 followed from these circumstances: people were apparently too weak physically to deal properly with the spring planting of 1340. That at least is what the frequent references to the 'poverty and inability of the parishioners' signify – in other references in the report it is made clear that 'inability' implied sheer physical weakness resulting from famine. If they had declined so far at planting time, it is difficult to imagine what state they were in by harvest. And 1340 was not much better, for not only had less land been sown but also the weather was still poor. It would not need many experiences like this to reduce village populations cruelly. Kingston itself is not listed in the report. Possibly the record is lost, but it is hardly likely that Kingston villagers escaped famine while people living within a radius of two miles were suffering extreme duress.

Recurrent agricultural crises like these are thought to have started a decline in population in the first half of the fourteenth century, but their effects were minor compared with the dreadful consequences of the pestilences in its second half. The Black Death, which swept England in 1348–49, was the first and most severe of a series of plagues whose cumulative effect was to reduce the population by nearly a third, leaving lords with empty villein lands and landholders without wage labour and transforming, in the cruellest way, the relationship between the amount of labour and the amount of land that had characterized the thirteenth century.[5] The disappearance of the dominant families of the early medieval period from Kingston – the de Kyngestons and de Dyghons in particular – was possibly one small local result of the disaster.

These great demographic changes resulted in shortages of labour to work the lands – shortages that persisted for at least a century after the Black Death and until the early Tudor period. Their first consequence – in the half-century after the Black Death – was to produce a persistent conflict of interests between those who held land and needed labour to make it profitable and those who had labour to offer. For those who held land the problem was that the wage rate for agricultural labour had a natural tendency to rise, threatening their profits. For labourers it was a struggle to keep hold of the slender advantages of the higher wage rate in the face of a series of attempts by landholders to keep it down.

In a sense, the decline in the labour force recreated just those conditions that feudal organization was peculiarly well adapted to control in the interests of manorial lords: a shortage of labour in relation to the amount of land. And, in the second half of the fourteenth century, the feudal organization was still in place despite economic and social change. It was natural that manorial lords should try to meet the threat of rising wages by reasserting rights to labour service from villeins that their predecessors had been happy enough to commute for fixed rents. Their very limited success was due to resistance from villeins, to the undermining force of the labour market that had come into existence in the preceding 150 years, and to the fact that manorial lords with an interest in the direct cultivation of their demesnes were no longer the only group of landholders. Men like the de Rademelds or the de la Hydes in Kingston were not lords. It was not necessarily in their interests that manor lords should reclaim the labour services of their villeins. De Rademeld and others like him depended on rents and hired labour for their incomes and were threatened by the rising wage rate. A successful bid by manor lords to pre-empt villein labour by a return to labour services would quite likely push up the wage rate even further by decreasing the supply of labour available to work for wages compared with the demand for it. Politically and socially, conflicts of interest between different types of landholder – particularly between the lords of the manors who held land by feudal privilege and the freemen landholders whose status depended on wealth and whose wealth depended on high rents and low wages – diminished the possibility of a systematic return to feudal labour dues.

But whatever the different views about the reassertion of labour service, there was one matter on which landholders of all kinds probably agreed. From all their points of view it was desirable that the increase in wages should be checked. It is not surprising therefore that the main political response to the Black Death was a statute of labourers setting maximum wages that might be paid for various kinds of work: 'against the malice of servants who were idle and not willing to serve after the pestilence, without excessive wages'.[6] This, rather than an attempt to reaffirm manorial rights to villein labour, reflected the collective interest of the widening class of landholders.

Neither the statute of labourers nor the lords of the manors' attempts to claim labour service worked in the long run. The wage rate was driven up through much of the fifteenth century because there *was* a labour market and all types of landholders competed in it; labour service could not be re-established partly because the lords had great difficulty retaining 'customary tenants' in the face of higher wages and partly because the villeins resisted so successfully that commutation became general during the fifteenth century and was virtually complete at the outset of Tudor rule in 1485. And, once again, the widespread leasing of demesne lands, as manorial lords responded to falling prices and profits by leaving cultivation to tenant farmers, furthered commutation. Whether or not the prior of Lewes leased the Swanborough demesnes, the villeins and cottagers of Kingston shared in the advantages of the commutation and higher wages that eventually followed the trauma of the Black Death and succeeding plagues.

Despite the great reversal in the growth of population, other developments of the early medieval period continued through the late fourteenth and fifteenth centuries. Acquisitive freemen like the de Rademelds expanded their untidy empires of lands in many manors and vills. By 1340, while the whole area about Kingston was destitute by famine, a de Rademeld had acquired a 'part' of the manor of Rodmell[7] – a step up the social ladder as well as a new source of rents. Then, in 1355, John de Rademeld, together with an unknown person (whose name is obscured in the 'fine'), was admitted to substantial lands in Hamsey, Barcombe and Rodmell.[8] And others followed the path the de Rademelds had trodden for so many generations: John Alfrey in partnership with others put together a straggling 'estate' of lands in Kingston, Ovingdean, Rottingdean and Rodmell to the south of Lewes, and Hamsey and Barcombe to the north.[9] Alfrey and his colleagues were in search of rents that could be obtained from wool production: although there were 580 acres of arable among these lands, they are chiefly notable for the 1900 sheep leazes attached to them. These lands were sold to Richard Weyville in 1399; he then proceeded to build an estate of almost baronial scale. In 1400 he married the daughter and heiress of the de Rademelds and brought their Hamsey and Rodmell lands together with those he had bought from John Alfrey.[10] Weyville became an important absentee landlord to Kingston tenants, for he did not live in the village.

By 1400 an increasing supply of erstwhile villein lands affected the land market. These 'customary yardlands' had their disadvantages from a commercial point of view. Commutation freed villeins from labour service and, if the lord of the manor agreed, made it possible for their lands to be bought and sold. But many of the disabilities that had attached to the villeins themselves remained attached to their yardlands. Commutation was obtained in exchange for a fixed rent on the land – so the manorial rents on old villein lands were a good deal higher than the virtually nominal rent of assize for free land. In addition, there were special fines on entry and other dues – like heriots – and, for a while at least, manor lords tried to keep up their income from land by increasing feudal incidents on land above their conventional levels. Because of these disabilities and because villein lands were formally held at the will of the lord, the distinction between them and lands held 'in free' was carefully made. The villein lands were called copyholds: title to them consisted of a copy from the manor court roll recording the proceeding of the court at which the person holding the land was admitted to them and 'paid homage to the lord'. Despite their disadvantages, however, copyholds were bought and sold with increasing frequency from the late fourteenth century onwards – as commutation became firmly established in law and people's minds. Commercially acute freemen whose wealth lay in land empires were no longer restricted to transactions in lands 'held in free'; they could buy and sell copyholds as well. Weyville's empire must have included copyholds in Kingston as well as freeholds. Later in the fifteenth century, as prices rose, the old feudal rents on copyhold that were fixed in terms of money became much less of a burden. An active market developed in copyholds. Commutation not only freed people; it freed land as well.

General movements like these, which shaped English rural society, played their part in Kingston – but local changes also affected the form of village society in the fifteenth century. These were mostly associated with the ancient demesnes, which lay in strips about the open fields. In the first half of the fourteenth century these demesnes were divided into a knight's fee held by the de Kyngestons and the demesne lands of Kingston Manor on which the de la Hydes were tenant farmers.

At some point in the late fourteenth century the knight's fee passed from the de Kyngeston family to the de la Hydes – and as time passed these nine yardlands became known to the villagers as Hyde's. There was an obvious convenience attached to the name; it distinguished these lands from the demesnes of Kingston Manor, whereas calling them de Kyngeston's had the obvious disadvantage that it was confusing. Hyde's they became and Hyde's they were to remain for at least five centuries thereafter – in name though not, of course, in ownership.

In fact, ownership seems to have changed fairly quickly for the times and the changes had implications for the social 'shape' of Kingston. By the early fifteenth century, the lands called 'Hyde's' had passed into the hands of Sayer de Rosey,[11] a member of an old freeman family with similar proclivities for assembling lands to those of the de Rademeld family. The de la Hydes were Kingston people; the de Roseys were not, even though they had owned village lands long since.[12] The de la Hydes had occupied the knight's fee themselves and, as members of the small cabal of freemen who frequented the priory, lent a certain feudal distinction to the village. The de Roseys had just as much, perhaps more, social status, but they did not occupy the land; they leased it out. And, as far as can be judged, their fifteenth-century and Tudor successors to Hyde's – first the Hilders and later the Gartons – also leased it.[13] Where there had once been a freeman family with nearly two centuries of Kingston history behind them, in the fifteenth century and indeed in the sixteenth there was a tenant farmer.

There were also changes in the lordship of Kingston Manor – that vestige of de Warenne land left over after the early barons had met the labour requirements of their new priory. The last Earl de Warenne died in 1347. The honour of de Warenne passed by a rather complex succession to Richard, Earl of Arundel, and along with it came the small manor at Kingston.[14] This Richard died in 1376 leaving an elder son, also called Richard, who succeeded to the earldom and a younger, Thomas, who became Archbishop of Canterbury. The new earl, however, was a contentious man.

In 1386 this earl, together with other great barons, was party to a successful attempt to curb the power of Richard II and to diminish the king's favourites who were, in their estimation, much too influential. What Arundel, Gloucester and Warwick had started by threat of arms, the so-called

'Merciless Parliament' completed with some show of legality. A pack of royal advisors were declared guilty of treason and dispatched. The king accepted these decisions at the time, but only for want of any alternative and he never forgot. The quarrel between the king and Arundel continued. It reached a peak in 1394 when, in the midst of a dispute about military policy, the king's mother died and Arundel, in what was probably a studied insult, failed to attend the funeral. He was put in the tower and only released on a huge bond of £40,000 against good behaviour. But neither he nor the king behaved well. In 1397 the king correctly perceived that Arundel, old, warlike, unrepentant, was again about to move against him together with his old companions in king baiting, Gloucester and Warwick. By a variety of trickeries – at which Richard II was considerably gifted – the barons were brought to book. The parliament, which they had used against the king's favourites in 1388, was now used against them. They were charged with high treason and Arundel would have been hanged, drawn and quartered had the king not ordered the axe instead. He died on Tower Hill in September. The king passed his lands, including the poorly regarded and unimpressive little manor in Kingston, to Thomas Mowbray, Duke of Norfolk.

Kingston villagers were aware of what had happened to the Earl of Arundel. There may even have been some regrets for, although a bloodthirsty 'hawk' of a man, he had been their distant lord for a long time. But, beyond a few regrets, the change in lordship is unlikely to have made much difference in the village, which is a measure of the distance that lay between baronial conflicts that affected the government and the ordinary life of its villagers. Possibly the most noteworthy consequence of Arundel's execution was the appearance in the village of lawyers whose task it was to survey the lord's possessions[15] before they passed to Norfolk.

The surveyor's lists of the earl's possessions in the village suggest rather strongly that he had been cultivating the Kingston demesnes directly rather than leasing them out before his death. They also give a picture of the yields and the equipment of the manor.

In the first place there were stocks of products. The earl had been put to death in September; the survey therefore probably records the crop that had been harvested just before his demise. The main stocks were 27 quarters of wheat (at 5s a quarter) and 80 quarters of barley (at 4s). This amounts to a total of 856 bushels of grain from the demesnes. A century and a half later the demesne area for Kingston Manor was given as 150 acres – customary acres of course.[16] Since only two-thirds of this acreage was sown (on the three-field system of Kingston), this suggests that the yields on the demesnes had been about eight and a half bushels per acre – assuming that all the grain in stock belonged to the harvest that had just been completed. This is a quite high yield for the time but possible in a good season. In addition, there were stocks of pease (five quarters) and three cartloads of hay. In total, the stocks were worth a little short of £24, which, remembering that it represents gross revenue, relates sensibly to the annual valuations of other manors of similar size in the vicinity.

Next, the survey gives a list of the livestock held at Kingston. These were less numerous than one might have expected. There was one mare and 11 oxen – enough to provide a plough of eight with three over to put together with village teams; and there were 200 wethers. The shortage of sheep is particularly noticeable. In the sixteenth century Kingston Manor had pasture for 400 sheep and there is no reason to believe that there was any less at the end of the fourteenth; evidently, the lord's flock had been allowed to decline, or perhaps had not yet been built up after the last lease of the demesnes. Aside from pasture animals, there were 11 pigs and 17 piglets.

Finally, there is a list of implements. It shows the comparatively sparse capital equipment used for cultivation at the time. The main items were 'a plough with three iron chains, a wagon with wheels, and two harrows'. These were valued at 5s. Then there was a 'courtpot' (probably a kind of barrow), a 'retrop' (not identifiable), a winnowing-van, and an iron spade and shovel, which together were worth 2s. Finally, the lord had 26 hurdles for folding sheep, a polysyn, which Salzman identifies as a pitchfork, and a sack – worth all together 3s. There is no record of any harvest implements, which suggested to Salzman that the lord was still dependent on the communal labour of the village at that most important time of the year.

In 1397 then, this small but apparently fertile estate, along with a vast collection of other lands spread all over England, passed to the Duke of Norfolk. But only a few years later they were back in the possession of the Arundels. In 1411 a new king made his peace with Thomas, son of the fierce earl who had been butchered by Richard II, and the land, including Kingston Manor, came back into the family.[17]

But the manor did not remain in it for long. Years before, the first earl Richard, who had inherited from the de Warennes, had wished to set up an almshouse in Arundel attached to the college of the Holy Trinity, which earlier Arundels had endowed. He died before he could carry out the plan, but his son pushed it forward. The almshouse for 20 poor or infirm people who were to live to a strict, almost monastic, rule was set up in 1395, two years before the earl was beheaded. When Thomas Arundel had his family lands returned to him, he considerably enriched this 'hospital' by a succession of gifts, especially after 1415.[18] In 1423 he gave the lands of Kingston Manor to the college. Kingston, which had borne an ecclesiastical lordship for nearly four centuries, now had another. From this time on until the dissolution of the monasteries monkish lords held virtually all Kingston lands.

At the time of the gift to Holy Trinity the Kingston demesnes were leased out. There were two tenants for life – John Hanslap and John Kelsale – who were to be left undisturbed by the change in lordship. The Kingston demesnes remained on lease for all the time the hospital held them.

With commutation, the slow growth of a new and broader class of landholders, demesne leasing, tenant farming and new manorial lords, how did the changes that followed the decline in population in the late fourteenth century affect Kingston? What can we infer from them about the village society in the fifteenth century? How, at the outset of the Tudor period, did Kingston differ from what it had been in 1332 when the subsidy roll gives a privileged glimpse of its medieval form?

There were certainly changes in the look of the village. The open fields of course remained much as they had ever been: Kingston was cradled in the chequered pattern of the great 'laynes' the Normans had founded and the ways of cultivating this majestic sweep of arable had not changed much either. A fourteenth-century visitor to fifteenth-century Kingston may have wondered a little that the villagers could afford to leave some of the older marginal furlongs out of cultivation, but otherwise he would have felt at home as he looked down on the busy strips.

He may have felt less so in the village street. Here, in the sheltered fold running from the downs into the valley he would have found the 'messuages' and 'tenements' of his successors grander and more substantial than in his day. For the most part the fifteenth century was a better time for the comparatively poor than the fourteenth had been. The real value of wages had risen, so wage labourers benefited; and commutations at fixed money rents had set free the smaller villeins to enjoy more of the product of their own labour on their own lands. The lord's dues had fallen in value and consequently so had the burden on the ordinary people. Some of this increase was taken up in higher levels of consumption – higher that is than the penurious levels before the Black Death – but some had been used to improve the houses people lived in. There was more timber framing, more flint-work, more mortar, less wattle and daub, and less turf. By the fifteenth century the village houses were more permanent and, though there were no chimneys and smoke still curled from roof-holes, they may already have had something of the form that was to shape the village in Elizabethan days – a form that is still discernible in the modest but confident beauty of the remnant cottages of today.

The village was also more ordered in the fifteenth century than it had been in the fourteenth. The great barns had appeared and the cattle yards around them were walled. Flint walls brought greater order, both in *fact* – since smaller animals were easier to control – and in *appearance*. They defined the street; they traced the outlines of property; quietly, unobtrusively, they kept things in place.

Yet, though the physical appearance of the village suggested greater wealth, security and well being than in earlier medieval times, it had become more humble in other ways. In the early fourteenth century there had been quite important 'feudal' people at the top of the social hierarchy. By the second half of the thirteenth century they were no longer there. Where de Kyngestons, de la Hydes and others had once ruled the roost, in 1450 there were tenant farmers. And though they were 'tenants for life', as were John Hanslap and

John Kelsale in 1423, they were nevertheless more 'ordinary' than their predecessors – closer to the ordinary people who were in the majority. Depending a little on his outlook on the world, our fourteenth-century visitor may well have thought the new Kingston a better founded, less vulnerable and happier place than in his day, but he would also have remarked that it was less distinguished by men and women of 'rank'.

In part, this change in Kingston society was a reflection of the times. By the end of the fourteenth century a wider cross-section of people were on the look-out for 'farms' – simply because the more even distribution of wealth in rural areas meant that people who in earlier times would not have had the capital resources needed to take on tenancies had now acquired them. So, an economic activity that had been restricted to richer, established freemen like the de la Hydes was accessible – in the fifteenth century – to 'smaller' families like the Hanslaps and Kelsales. It is unclear who they were, but they may have sprung from among the poorer free families of medieval times or from the richer class of villeins whose beginnings were evident in the village in 1330. They were early representatives in Kingston of the new 'yeoman' class. There were increasing numbers of them as the fifteenth century went by and it was only to be expected that tenancies in Kingston – on the demesnes of Kingston Manor and also on the 'lands called Hyde's' – would pass to them in the fullness of time.

But is this all that can be said about the change? Was it merely the chance outcome of a new statistical fact, just a reflection of the greater numbers of people of the middle rank looking for tenancies?

In earlier medieval times the small, tight-knit circle of dominant families depended for their influence and position on the priory at Southover and the castle in Lewes. As far as the priory was concerned it was most convenient to have a senior feudal person like de Kyngeston in the village as well as a network of freemen. These people could be relied on to ensure that village affairs followed an orderly course because it was in their own interests to do so. And, while the demesnes at Swanborough depended upon Kingston villeins for labour, order was needed. The monks held a manor court at Swanborough, but it was reassuring to know that communal affairs were watched over by people whose purposes the prior could trust.

The castle was an important focus in another way. Until well into the fourteenth century it was the main residence of the de Warenne family and this made Lewes a natural centre for men and women whose place in the world depended on access to the magnate. The de Kyngestons were such people. As far as the de Warennes were concerned, there was an obvious convenience in having Kingston, barely two miles from the castle, as the base for a senior feudal office-holder with important local functions – hence the knight's fee. As far as the incumbents of this knight's fee were concerned, what reason in the world could there be to move from this place with its splendid geographic access to the fountainhead of local privilege, the more especially as favoured access brought more 'honour' and power to the family as time went by? Medieval Kingston was as close as may be to a great centre of local power; Kingston's elite drew on that power and was held in place by it.

From the middle of the fourteenth century onwards the basis of these relationships between the village elite, the priory and the castle was progressively transformed by the passage of events. The changed social structure of the fifteenth century village was as much a consequence of these transformations as of the simple fact that there was a ready supply of farmers ready to take up tenancies. What precisely happened?

First, commutation weakened the link with the priory. The monks at Swanborough were as conservative in their social views as other ecclesiastical lords. They held onto the demesnes as a home farm and were reluctant to lease. But even the most conservative of lords gave way in the end before the demands for commutation and the priory was no exception. As time passed the monks relied less and less on villein labour from Kingston and more and more on people who came to the grange to work for wages. Their preoccupation with the orderly conduct of their reluctant unpaid workforce in the village diminished as the unpaid workforce itself got smaller. The monks no longer had the same need for the eyes and ears of their trusted freemen to watch and listen for discontent and rebellion; they, like many other lords, may have found that the disciplines of the labour market were quite as effective in getting work out of people as direct feudal control had ever been. As the years passed new men were admitted to the freeholds of Swanborough Manor in Kingston. They did not take on the roles their predecessors had played because those roles were no longer necessary. By the fifteenth century the priory's main interest in Kingston was in the feudal rent it yielded to Swanborough Manor – rent that consisted in large part of conventional fixed payments given originally in return for release from labour service. The manor court was quite adequate to the task of collecting them.

Second, in the middle of the fourteenth century there was a quite abrupt change in the importance of Lewes Castle to the village. The last in the long line of de Warenne earls only used the castle occasionally as a residence. Its importance as a centre of local power probably declined accordingly. Then, in 1347, there was a more decisive change. On the death of the last de Warenne the earldom passed to the earls of Arundel and Arundel effectively displaced Lewes as the geographic centre of what had been the honour of de Warenne. The old link between the knight's fee in Kingston and the nearby castle lost a good deal of its meaning: the village lost such advantages its location may have given it in the eyes of men who built their fortunes on access to great lords. For the people who held the knight's fee in the fifteenth century it was just land, advantaged only by the comparatively light payments due on it and by a touch of ancient feudal distinction. Whoever held it was eligible to be a juror at the court of the barony in Lewes,[19] but its main advantage was the rent it yielded.

So a number of changes – some particular to Kingston, some more general –

accounted for the changing order of the village and its less grand outlook in the fifteenth century. The villagers probably had little reason to regret the passing of the influential families of the past. To the fifteenth-century 'folk memory' the fourteenth must have been seen as a time of hunger, destitution and, above all, pestilence followed by long struggles for commutation and to maintain the advantages of the higher wage. The rural elite had not played a particularly lenient or constructive role in the story; the old Kingston elite had as much interest as any in keeping the wage rate down and in implementing the statute of labourers, if at all possible. Why should the ordinary villager of the fifteenth century have looked back with regret at their departure?

The image of the fifteenth century shifts and changes according to different perspectives: for poor rural people it was in general a better time than had gone before; it was more peaceful, less painful and penurious and, above all, perhaps freer. For emerging landlords, as also for the growing class of tenant farmers, it was a time of opportunity, constrained only by the dismaying tendency for wages to rise, reducing the yield on land. That declining yield on land meant less prosperity for the older feudal classes and for them it was a less rewarding time. For the monarch and his great magnates it was a time of political instability and military frustration. After the brilliant victories of Henry V, his successor became involved in a wasting series of losing wars, which a kingdom that was less wealthy than it had been in the early fourteenth century and less disposed to taxation had to finance. In the eyes of many of his subjects Henry VI dissipated his inheritance of French possessions and sucked his people dry with taxes in doing so. Then, in the second half of the century up to 1485, the old baronial class ripped itself apart and ultimately despoiled its wealth and political power in the wasting conflicts for the throne we call the Wars of the Roses.

By and large, the effects of this armed chaos that passed for government left ordinary rural people undisturbed. Kingston was not much affected by the Wars of the Roses. It was made up, in the main, by the kind of people who did quite well out of the economic changes of the fifteenth century – villeins who gained commutation, smaller freemen and tenant farmers. Overall, it was probably a peaceful time, with new opportunities for the more enterprising and reasonable security for all.

But it was not entirely so. In the years before 1450 Kingston people shared in the growing disenchantment with the king and his government, in the disaffection his taxes produced and in the disillusion at his inability to hold the great English possessions in France. On top of this they had special local reasons for concern at the course of his policy. Throughout the French wars and especially after 1435 the king's forces were largely unable to defend the south coast. The French raided English ports with impunity; they were able to plunder the coastal settlements virtually at will. Kingston, though six or seven miles from the sea, was vulnerable. It was within range of a determined strike.

This was not an entirely new experience for the village. There had been similar trouble with French raiders in the past and if, in the 1440s, there was no one in the village who participated in the defensive actions of 1377 it is certain that tales of them were still current. In that year, in the course of an earlier war, the prior of Lewes himself had led a force against French invaders and fought a skirmish with them on the downs near Rottingdean. The prior was captured and later ransomed. His men fought with great courage, especially one of his French servants 'who fought so stoutly, fiercely and persistently against his fellow Frenchmen that his stomach was pierced by their swords and his bowels dropped to his feet. Disregarding this injury, he pursued the enemy, trailing his intestines far behind him.'[20] There must have been Kingston men who saw this extraordinary exploit and if it is true that Londoners of Chaucer's circle discussed it with admiration at the time,[21] it is even more likely that it passed into the oral tradition of village history. It did not necessarily inspire villagers to deeds of valour against the French; it may have focused their minds on their vulnerability and the nasty consequences that could follow from French seaborne guerrilla warfare. When the French nuisance recurred in the 1440s, people along the Sussex and Kent coastlines found in it yet another reason for discontent. Far from winning the war in France, the government seemed to have brought it home to England.

By the middle of the century discontent with government reached a flash point. In late 1450, a year after the French had broken the ineffective and disadvantageous truce Henry had made with them in 1444, Jack Cade – usually described as an 'Irish adventurer' – raised a revolt in Kent. Cade's rebellion was a strange affair. It brought together the gentry, yeomen, local officialdom and the mass of rural labourers, and it appealed to a heterogeneous set of discontents. These cohered around a characteristically medieval objective. The king was not at fault: his advisors were. The king must be rescued from his evil counsellors. The purpose was sufficiently open to interpretation for the rebellion to bring together men who in many other ways had conflicting interests. It started in Kent, but soon Sussex was raised too and men marched from all quarters to join Cade in the Kentish countryside south of London.

For a short while Cade's rebellion was a real danger to the established order. It brought together some 25,000 people. It had sufficient leadership to defeat an admittedly incompetent royal force at Sevenoaks. Within a little short of a week from 1 July, Cade made his base at Southwark and his men entered the City. They executed Lord Say and Sele, a man of profound unpopularity. If they had not made the stupid, undisciplined mistake of looting London homes and turning Londoners against them, they might have built themselves a powerful base for negotiation with the king. As it turned out, London defeated Cade. On 6 July a force of Londoners prevented his men from entering the City. A vicious battle ensued on London Bridge and Cade was forced back to his Southwark base at the White Hart Hotel. From there he was able to use the threat of his presence to negotiate pardons for his followers – though not apparently for himself – and in the end these proved sufficient to disrupt the movement. Men went home to Kent and Sussex. They came home to Kingston too. Cade was at large for a short while but was discovered hiding in a garden in Heathfield in East Sussex. He was killed while escaping and, in the unattractive fashion of the times, he was cut into pieces and parts of his body sent for public exhibition about the towns of Kent and Sussex.[22]

The promises of pardon were kept and the lists of people on them from all over Kent and Sussex reveal how widespread support for the movement had been. There were many from the vicinity of Kingston. Members of the Culpeper family, certainly gentry, had taken part. The constables of Lewes were pardoned as a group, as were the constables of Swanborough hundred; they had presumably called out the local militia in support. Most surprisingly, perhaps, the prior of Lewes had sanctioned the revolt. Among the pardons we find 'John (Danyell), Prior of the priory of St Pancras and the convent of the same place, and all the men and servants of the same priory or convent'. Were there copyholders of Swanborough Manor among 'men' of the prior? We must assume so.

Next to these the lists contain names of ordinary people who made up the main body of the rebellion. Many came from parishes south of Lewes. In Piddinghoe and Meeching (modern Newhaven), at the mouth of the Ouse, a carpenter and several labourers were involved; so was a husbandman called John Allecock of Southease. Further north, at Iford, a yeoman called John Machyn had taken part, together with a whole family of Holybons, some of them yeomen, some labourers. In Smythwick, that small attachment of Kingston, there was a husbandman called Richard Elyot. And, in Kingston itself, John Hylder, yeoman, had joined the march.[23] Hylder was a village notable: he held the knight's fee called Hyde.

These people had followed in the great armed throng that marched behind Cade. Some of them may have been in action against the king at Sevenoaks. They had massed in Southwark, south of the great city that many of them had probably never seen before. They crossed the wonder of London Bridge, which with its superstructure of houses and stalls was more like a medieval street across the water than a simple river crossing. They had gawped at the crowded buildings of the city; some of them perhaps had joined the looting. They had seen the quasi-judicial beheading of a great lord and the furious struggle in which whatever hopes they had of their rebellion began to fade. With some relief, perhaps, they straggled home to Sussex when they were sure of pardon.

From Culpepers, the prior and the constables to the minor gentry, yeomen, husbandmen, craftsmen and labourers, the rebellion had been astonishingly comprehensive in the classes of people it drew on – and this was the case, of course, throughout Kent and Sussex. Its ultimate causes remain something of a mystery. It differed from that general run of medieval revolt in which a great and rebellious baron called on his men to serve his cause. There were no barons here; they are noticeable by their absence. In the Lewes vicinity, the prior was the only person who seems to have mobilized men by the exercise of lordship – and this, in the general pattern of the uprising, would appear to have been exceptional. Yet, the rebellion differs also from that other type of revolt in which a distinctive class interest was involved – the sort that was identified by the Peasants' Revolt of 1381. This was no simple struggle of a single class. It drew its inspiration from a wide coincidence of discontents, a disaffection so general and accepted that it was sufficient to validate the use by constables of their powers to raise militia – an action that suggests something more than an instantly spontaneous uprising in which men reached for their swords, axes and pitchforks in a frenzy of thoughtless assent. The considered, if hasty, decisions of 'respectable' men with much to lose were involved, and this has the feel of forethought and planning about it. Who did the planning? Cade alone? Yorkist plotters? Men who truly believed they must rescue the king from his advisors and his scheming French wife; men who believed the king had been suborned? Cade's rebellion remains unexplained in many of its dimensions. We can only take it as a signal of a very general anger and disillusion.

How sustained that anger was remains uncertain. The men who came back to Kingston – and there were certainly more than just those whose names are on the record[24] – brought stories to amaze their neighbours. When they straggled back, the street was alive with groups of people hurried in from summer fields to elbow for a listening place. The tales of violence and of London that they heard while standing in Kingston's chalky dust must have lived on in their memories. But there were few subsequent signs of anger and no further trouble. The village that watched the dawn of the Tudor monarchy in 1485 was a peaceful enough place, though different of course in important ways from the medieval village of 1332.

******

It would be false to suggest that the early years of Tudor rule produced any discontinuity in the pattern of life. They did not. The early Tudor village was a creation of fifteenth-century changes, which continued. Those changes resulted in a more fluid and in some ways more complicated society, and this is reflected most of all in the systems of land tenure – the outcome of interactions between the older feudal economic order and the new and less discriminating market forces that had unfolded.

First, though men and women of senior feudal rank no longer lived in Kingston in the fifteenth century, the old manorial system was still in place. Everyone who held land in the village, from commuted villeins to freemen 'empire-builders' (some of whom might have been lords of other manors), owed homage to the court of one of the Kingston manors and if they held copyhold land it was 'at the will of the lord', irrespective of whether the holder were free or villein. The manors continued to draw rents of assize, rent on copyhold in exchange for old labour services and other feudal dues from all village land, even though as time passed these fixed money payments became largely symbolic. The tangled manors of Kingston were still the intact framework of life.

Second, though not present or represented in village society, lordly people still held the ancient demesnes in the open fields. Arundel and the monks of Holy Trinity succeeded to Kingston Manor and a succession of the grander freemen to the knight's fee of Hyde. Generally speaking, these demesnes were leased out, mostly as undivided units. They were comparatively big 'parcels' – fifteen yardlands in one case and nine in the other. They made space for two tenant families who were 'big' in Kingston, more powerful economically than the general run of people and, after the monks at Swanborough, the largest employers of wage labour.

Third, increasing amounts of village land had come into the hands of men intent on building land empires. The de Rademelds, who had originally lived in the village, were the first representatives of this new class; Alfrey, seemingly based at East Grinstead,[25] and Weyville at Hamsey or perhaps Rodmell came later; and others we cannot trace followed them. These men were purely landlords, as distinct from manorial lords with lands to lease – even though some of them came to hold manors as well. They were, to all appearances, acquisitive and opportunistic – more capitalist than feudal. Because their lands spread over many manors they did not usually have large amounts of land in any single village. There may have been several such landlords in possession of Kingston lands. They had an interest in bringing yardlands together into larger farms – a process called 'engrossing', for which the simplest explanation is that fewer tenants meant less bother for the landlord. However, their holdings were a good deal smaller than the demesnes. These parcels therefore provided an opportunity for smaller tenant farmers who had more limited capital resources than the larger farmers on the demesnes.

These empire builders took over many copyhold yardlands. A fourth aspect of the village tenure system was the continuing presence of people who held their old villein lands directly 'at the will of the lord' by copy of the court roll. They were not necessarily a homogeneous group. Some were smallholders with a virgate or less. Others were more like the successful villeins of earlier times, with two or three virgates. As copyholders, such people belonged more to the feudal order than to the new system of tenant farming, but there was no clear distinction: richer copyholders could take small tenancies and progress to larger ones too when they had the resources to do so and wished to expand the arable at their command.

Finally, there were similar new complexities in the world of the cottagers and the landless, though there were few truly landless in the fifteenth century. Some cottages were still held on traditional terms, namely directly from the manor lords in return for rents. These had land attached to them in walled enclosures around the 'tenement' itself. Others had passed to new landlords and were included in the leases of tenant farmers who often sublet them to wage labourers. There are signs – particularly in the smaller cottages associated with Kingston Manor house at the end of the street – that some were virtually without land.

The fact that the old elite was no longer represented in Kingston did not mean that there were no social 'degrees'. There was a social structure, which corresponded to a considerable extent to the pattern of tenure. Large tenant farmers were plainly above the people to whom they paid wages, or the smaller copyholders. Larger copyholders had higher status than small and so on. But this hierarchy differed from the older feudal one in at least two ways. For one thing, it was based more on wealth and income than on feudal status. For another, it was much more fluid: a copyholder on old villein lands could rise through smaller tenancies to large; freemen might hold copyhold lands if the terms were right; small copyholders or the sons and daughters of larger ones might work for wages on a tenant farmer's land. There were, in short, new opportunities, chances of advance that had not been there to the same degree in feudal times. They existed because the old order had been subverted in various ways that allowed other forces to operate: by commutation of labour service and leasing out of demesne in the first instance; later on it was by the appearance of the new landlords who comprehensively exploited the possibility of subtenancy that always existed in the manorial system and, in so doing, opened up smaller tenancies than the manorial lords had on offer. In Kingston, as elsewhere, the start of the Tudor monarchy coincided with a time when social mobility among rural people was greater than it had ever been. This, together with the absence of villeinage, made rural England something of a wonder to the rest of Europe. It was part of what Tudor people had in mind when they boasted with characteristic exaggeration of English 'freedom'. The basis for this new society had been laid long before: its beginnings can be discerned in the glimpse of Kingston we get from the subsidies in 1296 and 1332; its growth was assured by the successful social struggle against villeinage that followed in the wake of the demographic disasters of the fourteenth century. By the second half of the fifteenth century it was there to stay.

There are no records of the names of Kingston villagers in the first Tudor monarchy but in 1524, the sixteenth year of Henry VIII's reign, royal enquirements for revenue (largely for war against the French and the Scots) once again provide us with a list of village taxpayers. This list, from the so-called lay subsidy roll of Sussex, is in Table 5.1.[26]

As with the earlier subsidy rolls, there are reasons for being careful about the conclusions one draws from the list. The tax itself was complicated because it was payable on annual income from land, on the value of goods, or on wages,[27] though people did not pay tax under all three headings but only where their liabilities were greatest. This makes it impossible to draw any simple conclusions from the amount of tax actually paid, for it is merely a rough guide to comparative wealth. Aside from this difficulty, it is unclear

Table 5.1: Taxpayers in Kingston village in 1524 (amounts in shillings)

Richard Adam	2	Robert Segrave	2
John Lybben	2	John Dewe	3
Robert Howell	10	John a More	1
Richard Howell	1	Thomas Thetcher	1
Richard Alcoke	3	Will Austin	2
Thomas Picombe	5	Will Ellis	1
Richard Picombe	1	Richard a More	1
John Piccom	5	Will Wodschore	1
John a Wod	10	Richard Marwycke	1
Robert Pet	1	John Ashurst	1
Richard Harris	1		

whether the list includes all villagers; there are reasons to suspect that the poor are left out. The tax on wage earners appears to have been levied at a flat rate of 4d, yet there are no four-penny taxpayers in the list. It seems that Kingston wage earners were left out of the subsidy – though it is unclear why this should be so.

Some patterns show up clearly nonetheless. In the first place, two families stand out above the others in terms of wealth: Robert Howell's and John a Wod's. These were the two large tenant farmers on the old open-field demesnes of Kingston. From later evidence, the Howells, who were to play a considerable role in the Elizabethan history of the village, were farmers on the lands called Hyde's;[28] the a Wods therefore were presumably tenants to the hospital of the Holy Trinity, which at this time still held Kingston Manor. If each of these families was taxed on its 'goods' rather than its annual income (which is plausible since large tenant farmers could be expected to hold numbers of livestock and hence be liable for more tax on goods than on other counts), their liabilities for 10s tax payments each suggests that they were 'worth' about £20. This was somewhat greater in monetary terms than the valuation of John de Kyngeston's 'moveables' in the early fourteenth century, but since there was substantial inflation at the time it amounts to a good deal less in real terms. Insofar as any comparison of wealth over such a long period has a meaning, it looks as if the Howells and a Wods were not as well off as their grander feudal predecessors.

Beneath these two larger tenant families there was a group of middling wealth: we might list Richard Alcoke, Thomas Picombe, John Piccom and John Dewe (Delve) at the top of this group and Richard Adam, John Lybben and Robert Segrave beneath them. It is likely that Piccoms and Picombes were branches of the same family; Picombes stayed on in Kingston for a long time, as we shall see, and were remarkable, even for Elizabethan times, for their inventiveness in varying the spelling of their name.

This middling group was made up of smaller tenants and more successful copyholders who had branched out and added to their arable by taking tenancies. Their natural predecessors in 1332 had been the more successful villeins, like the Martyns and Fyschs – people who had acquired a second or third virgate and who might from time to time have taken on tenancy. But, in 1524, the difference was that the landlord class increased in size and acquired more land. There was, accordingly, less room in the village for the independent copyholder, but more opportunity for a small number of successful families like these.

The independent copyholders were nevertheless still there. The majority of those taxed at one shilling were probably essentially virgaters, holding land 'at the will of the lord' in the old way, though of course with commuted labour services. They extended their livings from time to time by working for wages – or at least setting their sons and daughters to do so as the family grew and the pressure on their 12 acres became too great. As smallholders with land held directly from the manor lords they were the nearest group to a peasantry to be found in the English rural world. Most of them were regarded as 'husbandmen', a class of person who at this time stood distinctly below the 'yeomanry'. Most probably only the a Wods and the Howells would have had a claim to be yeomen at this time – though it is possible that some of the middle group, perhaps the larger ones like Thomas Picombe and John Piccom, were so regarded.

The most powerful people in the village world are not included in the list. They lay in the background, as it were, because they did not live in the village. They were the manor lords and the landlords pure and simple.

The manorial lordships are fairly easy to trace. The priory, as ever of course, held Swanborough: and Kingston Manor, also in church hands, was still in the lordship of the hospital of the Holy Trinity. Houndean had been divided, by virtue of a complex succession that is of little immediate interest, and was held in 'moieties' by the Earl of Dorset and Lord Bergavenny (the Nevill family). The Kingston lands attached to Houndean were in Lord Bergavenny's half. Iford Manor had passed down through the de Plaiz family for centuries, but by 1524, because of a failure in the male line, it had progressed from Lady Bergavenny (a de Plaiz), to the Lewknor family, gentry who provided a long line of members of parliament for Lewes. The knight's fee of Hyde is more of a puzzle. At this time it was either held by the Gartons or, perhaps, was still in the Hylder family. A John Hylder, possibly descended from the 'yeoman' who set forth from Kingston in the Cade adventure in 1450, lived in comparative wealth at Iford in 1524.[29] About a century later a Hylder lived in Kingston and when Robert Croham (alias Peterson), the last prior of Lewes, died in 1554 the descendants of Richard Hylder were left a small sum of money.[30] But whether Hylders or Garstons held the knight's fee at the time, it is plain from the subsidy roll of 1524 that neither family lived in the village and that the demesnes were leased out.

The manorial lords between them had feudal claims on all the village lands and those who leased the open field demesnes of Kingston Manor and Hyde were landlords as well. But there were other landlords who did not hold manors – the commercially oriented landholders who followed in the tracks of the de Rademelds, the Alfreys, the Weyvilles and their kind. There is no track of them in the records for 1524, so we do not know who they were, but this landlord class of 1524 was clearly beginning to enjoy the increasing returns to land as real wages fell from about the first quarter of the sixteenth century – probably because of population increases.[31]

The Henrician subsidy roll reveals something of the social structure of early Tudor Kingston, but it also shows that there had been a complete change of dramatis personae in the village. The list of 1524 in Table 5.1 does not include a single name from the list of 1332 (Table 4.3). Apparently all the village families had changed. Though this transformation over two centuries is not surprising, it does contrast with a certain view of the constancy of rural life, which is apt to invade modern perceptions of the past. In fact, there was a good deal of mobility in rural society even in the early medieval period and, after the disruption of the Black Death and the subsequent incursion of markets in land and labour, this geographic mobility was enhanced. Kingston had experienced it to a higher degree than most, but it was not exceptional.

Mobility there may have been, but the Kingston families of 1524 for the most part had their origins in other Sussex villages, which were not far away. And since at least some of them can be found in the neighbourhood in the early medieval subsidies, it appears that, though most families moved, they did not move very far or very rapidly. Indeed, some Kingston people were branches of families, which remained established in *other* villages for very long periods.

Of the two main tenant farming families the a Wods are easier to trace than the Howells. There were many atte Wood, a Wood, and a Wod families in Sussex at the time of the earlier subsidies (1296–1332), but one in particular was established at Hamsey.[32] They were still there in 1524 and remained on into Elizabethan times.[33] John a Wood of Hamsey and his wife Elizabeth died in 1541: John a Wod of Kingston was probably their second son.[34] The Howells are harder to track. Their name appears in 1296 and 1332 in West Grinstead, 25 miles west of Lewes. Much later, at the time of the subsidy and towards the end of Henry VIII's reign, the family name was found mainly in Eastbourne, about 15 miles southeast of Lewes and near Eastbourne in Willingdon.[35] The Kingston family was probably a junior branch of these Howells.

Among the 'middle' group of families, the Picombes were present in villages on the outskirts of Lewes in 1296 and 1327 and were named in Barcombe in 1332. Barcombe is about three miles north of Lewes.[36] By 1524 Kingston seems to have become the main base for the family, though there was a Pecham family in Iford in 1542 that may have been related.[37] John Picombe died at Kingston in 1546, Richard, described at the time as 'the elder' died in 1559, but the family remained in the village long after.[38]

The other middling families cannot be traced in the earlier subsidy rolls. In one case (the Adams) this was because the name occurs so frequently that it is impossible to sort out any connection to the Kingston family, and in the others because their names do not occur at all. However, three of the families – Adams, Alcokes and Delves – can be located in later records. Like the a Wods and the Picombes, they came from villages north of Lewes, but whereas the a Wods and Picombes are first encountered in Hamsey and Barcombe within a couple of miles of Lewes, the Adams, Alcokes and Delves were all based near Uckfield about ten miles to the north. Like the a Wods – but not the Picombes – the Kingston parts of these families were all minor, both in numbers and in wealth, compared with the branches that remained in their 'original' villages.

The Adam's family appears to have come from Fletching – a few miles from Uckfield. In 1502 a Thomas Adam died there, leaving his lands to his son Richard. Richard was 21 at the time and died in 1525. By the time of his death he had added to the Fletching lands and also held land in Cliffe in Lewes.[39] These are most probably the forbears of the various Adams families who appear later; at Eastbourne, where William Adam died in 1546, leaving inter alia, money to support the poor of Wilmington; at Battle (John Adam, d.1552); at Tarring Neville, a beautiful village near the mouth of the Ouse (also a John Adam, d.1552); and, of course, at Kingston, where Richard Adam lived in 1524.[40]

The Alcokes seem also to have been based in Fletching. The earliest record shows a Richard Aucocke who died there in 1535.[41] The family was present there in considerable numbers in the last years of Mary's reign and in Elizabeth's.[42] They were mostly 'husbandmen'. John Awlcoke, probably a son of Richard Alcoke of 1524, died in Kingston in 1558. In the manner of his times he left money at the discretion of his executors for masses of remembrance: 'I will to be done and prayed for the welth of my Soule and all cristen sowles of the day of my buryeng in masses and derige to be sayed or song … with bred and drynke to be gewin and distributed to the poor people.' And, similarly in tune with the times, he left 2s 8d for the repair of the village church.[43]

Delves were found near Uckfield too – in Little Horsted and in Buxted. In Little Horsted there are wills for Richard Delve, who died in 1505 and for Thomas (died 1542). In Buxted, Alicia Delve left a will in 1512.[44] At some point a branch or branches of the Delve family moved south. In the subsidy of 1524, Thomas Delve of Iford was taxed at about the same rate as the richer tenant farmers of Kingston, and a good deal more than his poorer kinsman in Kingston. But, poorer though he may have been, John Delve was well connected for a Kingston man of his time. He had married Agnes, the daughter of a rich Ringmer man called John Thatcher.[45] And he plainly had a fairly close relationship with the prior of Lewes, for in 1555, when Robert Peterson the erstwhile prior died, he left money to the descendants of John Delve of Kingston.[46] These were most probably married daughters – in 1524 Agnes and John were described in John Thatcher's will as having female children only. The Delves had a way of being more explicit than most about their precise intentions regarding the foods they wished to have distributed to the poor at their funerals (and anniversaries). Thus, Thomas Delve of Little Horsted insisted on 'brede beff and mony to the valew of 10s'. He had been remarkably generous in distributions to 20 of the poorest households in Framfield, ten in Uckfield and ten in Isfield: 'a cast of brede and a pounde of bef and a peny in monye'. When John Delve of Kingston died in 1544 he left instructions that at his anniversary the poor people should receive '4 bushels of whete, a calf and 2 sheep'. Delve's anniversaries must have provided some relief for the poor of Kingston.[47]

Delves, Alcokes and Adams belonged, like most Picombes, to the fortunate families who benefited from access to rented land – as well as holding copyholds in their own right. But from where had the poorer families come?

The poorer taxpayers of 1524, who were not necessarily the truly poor of the village, seem to fall into three main groups. First, some were offspring or cadet branches of richer families in the village. There were poor, as well as relatively rich, Howells and Picombes. Second, a larger group had connections that are either very difficult to trace or were related to families elsewhere in similar circumstances. John Ashurst, for example, was probably related to a 'husbandman' of Laughton[48] five miles east of Lewes; William Ellis may have descended from a family in Cliffe in Lewes;[49] Richard Harris probably had family connections in the Weald to the east of Laughton;[50] the a Moore family abounded but was particularly well represented in the Westmeston area in the later years of Henry VIII;[51] Robert Pet, William Austin and Will Wodscore cannot be linked to any nearby villages.

The third and in some ways the most interesting group among the poor families consists of the Thatchers and the Marwyckes. They are worth distinguishing because both probably descended through cadet branches from richer yeoman families.

By 1524 members of the Thatcher family were among the larger landlords in the Lewes district. This branch appears at the turn of the fifteenth century. In 1498 John Theccher – a 'gentleman' – died in Ringmer, a few miles east of Lewes; in 1512 Agnes, who had been his second wife, passed away in Southover, that growing suburb around the priory.[52] From their wills it is clear that the family had been based in Willingdon in the fifteenth century – the village just north of Eastbourne where Howells were also to be found. John Thatcher left 13s 4d 'to the church wirkes of Wyllyngdon'. Agnes left 10s for similar purposes and also a substantial 40s for the repair of one of the parish roads. Thatchers were present in Willingdon much later too in Mary's reign.[53]

Though Agnes moved to Southover, Ringmer and its surrounding area became the family base. In the next generation two Thatcher brothers built on the wealth of their fifteenth-century ancestors. Thomas Thatcher, the younger of them, based himself at Westham, a Wealden village near Ringmer. He died a wealthy man in 1536. He left bequests to churches in neighbouring villages, including Ringmer and, of course, Willingdon, where he was buried. John Thatcher, the elder brother, died in 1526 and was even wealthier.[54] He was to be buried 'in an new chapell attached to the chauncell of the Parish Church of Ryngmer which I have there … builded'. Masses and dirges were to be sung in a multiplicity of churches, and most particularly at the priory of St Pancras. Thatcher's claim on the solicitude of the prior was considerable. At his death the monastery had a debt of £300 outstanding to him. He made bequests to virtually all the churches of Lewes – of which there were many – as well as to village churches in the Weald between Ringmer and Eastbourne. His death did not pass unsung. His progeny continued in Ringmer: later, in 1574, another John Thatcher died there leaving lands in many Wealden villages – Ringmer, Mersham, Laughton, Glynde, Hurstmonceux, Westham and Pevensey. He had married 'upwards' to the daughter of a Wealden knight, Sir Edward Gage of Firle.[55] Other Thatchers married into the Culpeper and Lewknor families. They were, in their way, the apotheosis of new Elizabethan gentry, whose wealth was founded on 'land empires' scattered in the interstices of the manorial system, and eventually in manors as well.

These Ringmer Thatchers stand far above their counterparts in the Ouse valley. Thomas Thatcher of Kingston was followed by William Thatcher who died in 1558, and John Thatcher who died in Iford in 1546. Besides his lands, William left 4d for the 'poore mennes box', money for two masses in the village church, and 'to the hyghe Aulter of the church' a careful 2d 'In the Recompense of my tythes forgotten'.[56] By comparison, when John Delve died in Kingston he had five priests say masses for him at burial and thereafter on anniversaries.

The Marwyck story has some similarities, though the Marwycks were never quite as successful as the Thatchers had been. They abounded in Hamsey and Barcombe and later in Lewes as well. Thomas Marwyck died in Barcombe in 1529; Edward, who was probably his brother, was connected to Kingston, since he had married a daughter of John Picombe.[57] He was perhaps progenitor of the Kingston family. Edward, in 1537, left 40s to the priory, being a 'brother of their chapter'. The Barcombe family and their relatives in Lewes were 'yeomen'; their ancestors can be traced to the eighteenth and nineteenth centuries.[58] In contrast, the Kingston family left no wills and disappeared from the village by Elizabethan times.

What images of contemporary Kingston society does all this suggest? Do these family connections have any particular features?

A number of the early Tudor Kingston families appeared as minor branches of larger, richer families based in other nearby villages. This is true of the bigger tenants (a Wod and Howell) as of the majority of middling families (Adams, Alcokes and Delves). It is also true of at least two of the poorer group (Thatchers and Marwycks). It is as if – with the exception of the Picombes and possibly some of the poorer ones – Kingston people tended to be part of wider families whose 'centres of gravity' lay elsewhere, even if never too far away. The village, it seems, was something of a haven for less privileged cadet branches.

Why this should have been so is hard to say. If indeed it is a feature that distinguishes the village from some others it may be explained by the disposition of Kingston lands. Even the largest parcels in the village, Kingston Manor and Hyde, were not very big. The holdings of the individual absentee landlords were smaller than these, and Kingston also had a larger proportion of unattached copyholds than some other villages. This prevalence of small tenancies and the large proportion of virgate copyholds could have been an attraction for the younger sons of yeomen with only small amounts of capital.

There remains, of course, a further question: how is this putative high proportion of small tenancies and copyholds itself accounted for? Why was Kingston distinguished from some other places in this way?

One part of the explanation is clear enough. There simply were no large parcels of demesnes in the open fields. The Normans opened up the large demesnes associated with the village at Swanborough and these remained in the hands of successive priors. Such demesnes as there were in the open fields – the 24 yardlands of Kingston and Hyde together – had been split into two distinct parcels because it suited a Norman baron to divide them in order to create a knight's fee. It made sense for de Warenne to do this in the early twelfth century because the old demesnes of Kingston had probably appeared to him as the remnant of a dismembered manor, bereft of villeins in the interest of a new priory. So the social structure of Tudor Kingston was accounted for in part by decisions taken 450 years before.

But this was only in part. The other feature of Kingston, which made it a natural base for cadet branches, was the frequency of small tenancies and individual copyholds. If indeed there were more of these in proportion in Kingston than in some other villages, why was this so?

It is possible that the answer might be found in the priory's policy towards commutation of villeins. Most Kingston copyholds belonged to Swanborough Grange and it is possible that the priory, like other ecclesiastical lords, had been slow to commute the labour services of their villeins. If so the villein lands of Kingston would have remained inaccessible to outside purchasers for longer than most; inaccessible that is to the new landlords who were putting their intermanorial estates together in the early fifteenth century. Villein lands had very restricted 'marketability' while they had labour services attached. New landlords had limited opportunities for 'engrossing' lands into larger tenancies in Kingston because of ecclesiastical conservatism. And, as more

Kingston copyholds slowly became available, they were likely to be taken by different absentee purchasers from those who had already bought up small parcels in the open fields. Hence, the small tenancies compared with the pattern in other villages where villein lands had become available earlier and in greater amounts. Hence also, quite possibly, the high proportion of independent copyholds – too small and dispersed to be of much interest to larger landlords. Once again, the features of Kingston society in the sixteenth century owed much to its earlier history and, ultimately, to the enthusiasm of William de Warenne in 1077 for his soul and his new priory.

Because of the division of its land, early Tudor Kingston had found no truly dominant families to replace its medieval elite. It had no equivalent of the a Woods and Marwycks of Hamsey, or of the Adams of Fletching – and certainly there were none to match either the opulence of the Thatchers or their longevity as a Willingdon family. Kingston's yeomen were poorer than in many other villages. It follows that the economic distance between them and the richest was less than in many other places. There was a more even distribution of income, for the great of Kingston were not very great. It is difficult to assess whether this made life easier for all or not. The poorer members of rich families are not necessarily better disposed to the truly poor than are the rich themselves. Sometimes they feel the need for social distance more sharply than their richer cousins.

One thing is plain from all these family connections: Kingston was not isolated. The community had blood and marriage ties in many places, albeit mostly within a radius of ten to fifteen miles to the north and east. Though some of the family links were distant and weakened, others were not. The Thatchers of Kingston were further from their Ringmer relatives than the facts of geography suggest, but others had closer family links: the Adams, Alcokes and Marwyckes, for example, and the Delves with relatives in Iford might well have kept their connections with Little Horsted. Nor were direct family links the only ones that mattered: the families intermarried. John Delve brought rich John Thatcher's daughter home to Kingston. How did the Kingston Thatchers deal with that? John Picombe married into the Marwyck family. Richard Adam's mother married a second time to Henry Lawrence, a yeoman of Southover,[59] and Richard had a half-brother there. Kingston, clearly, was part of a wider community.

This, among other things, accounts for another feature of the village: the apparently high mobility of its population. Of the Kingston families of 1524 only two were deeply rooted: the Howells and Picombes. Both were still present two centuries later. The others moved on. By the last quarter of the sixteenth century they had gone and others had taken their places. In 1524 Kingston was at the beginning of a new set of changes.

******

For the most part, the experience of change in the medieval period had been slow and progressive – a protracted transformation of the structure of village society, which, though it ultimately produced the distinctive village of the early Tudor times, had been barely perceptible to the successive generations of people who lived through it. And this style of slow transformation was to be characteristic of Kingston in the centuries ahead.

The Tudor period, however, produced one of those comparatively rare, abrupt changes that from time to time interrupted the even progress of events. Henry VIII, in his profound preoccupation with the succession, broke decisively with the Vatican and laid the first foundations of the reformation Church of England. Then, from 1536, when the rupture was final and the English crown was in dire need of revenues, Henry, tutored by his clever and dislikeable minister Thomas Cromwell, set about the dissolution of the English monasteries and the alienation of their lands to the monarchy. After a first sweep, which took in the smaller monastic establishments, Henry and Cromwell turned their attention to the slightly more prolonged business of dismantling the larger ones. This was mainly accomplished by 1540. In a very few years the crown took over that major share of English lands that men like de Warenne had over centuries given 'in perpetual alms' to monastic houses. And, in an equally brief span, the crown sold the rights to these lands and manors into private hands. The outcome was a sharp acceleration in the economic and social transformations that were already under way – particularly an abrupt increase in economic opportunities for the 'new men' of the Tudor age.

Inevitably, the dissolution of the monasteries had a particularly marked effect in Kingston. In part, this was a natural consequence of the fact that in 1538, when Cromwell turned his attention to the priory of St Pancras, about two-thirds of Kingston lands were in monastic lordships. Swanborough Manor held the major part of these and they had been monastic for more than 450 years; the remainder were the lands of Kingston Manor, which the hospital of the Holy Trinity had held since 1423.

But this was only part of the story. Monastic lords held many other English villages in even greater proportion and, though the dissolution certainly meant a change in lordships on quite a grand scale in the village, this was not in itself a singular experience.

The more particular effects of the dissolution in the village resulted directly or indirectly from the proximity of the priory. A direct result of that proximity was the fact that after more than four centuries the priory was in the simplest physical sense a part of village life. It was after all a vast and beautiful medieval building visible from the open fields. Its great, spired church stood out above the walled gardens, cloisters, prior's lodge and monastic dormer grandly disposed about it. For many in the village it was a sign of the lordly power that tonsured men in black habit exercised from Swanborough – a power that had once been almost absolute and that, though much reduced by 1538, was still to be reckoned with. Moreover, many villagers worked for wages at Swanborough and in the priory garden; in fact the priory was the largest employer of village labour. Its disappearance as an establishment therefore meant something more than a mere change of lordship. In Kingston, the dissolution meant the end of a dominating institution that had directly affected the way ordinary people lived and worked for centuries.

The less direct results of proximity were probably more important in the longer run. Because the priory was close to Swanborough, the priors had come to regard the manor, with its splendid enclosed demesne, as a sort of 'home farm' – a direct source of supply to the mother house in Southover. In consequence, these demesnes were in the service of the priory. They were not part of the increasingly commercial world of tenant farming and landlords, which Kingston had become. They were isolated and, however desirable, inaccessible to acquisitive men on the look out for rewarding tenancies. Above all, the dissolution was to end that isolation, just as it was to bring the less impressive but nonetheless desirable demesnes of Kingston Manor into the market place.

However important the dissolution was to become, the villagers were almost certainly unaware of the protracted series of events that preceded the dismemberment of the priory itself. These involved Robert Peterson, the last prior, who had taken the ecclesiastical name of Robert Croham, and Thomas Cromwell and his emissaries. They were of a kind that the prior might well have wished to keep to himself, for he was consistently in the disadvantageous and somewhat inelegant position of fighting a battle that could not be won. Robert Croham had the privilege of considerable education – he had been at Gonville Hall in Cambridge (now Caius College) – and was a more energetic prior than most who had held office at Southover. Whereas a majority of his predecessors had simply learnt to live with the mounting indebtedness of their house,[60] Croham had at least concerned himself with its improvement. He was involved in efforts to drain the tidal marshes in the Ouse valley where, of course, the priory had direct interests[61] – and he had visited Flanders to inform himself of drainage techniques.[62] But whatever his qualities he was in no position to match the all-powerful Cromwell – or even to stand up to Cromwell's shabbier henchmen when, from time to time, they intervened in events. Croham, like abbots and priors all over England, was in no position to resist a process that the overwhelming majority of English people seem to have accepted and that started from the king himself. There is no reason to suppose that the lord of Swanborough Manor revealed his embarrassment to the 'homage' of his manor court.

The downward progress started in the course of Richard Layton's tour of ecclesiastical houses in 1535. Layton, as he appears from his reports, was unpleasant. He pursued the supposed evil-doings of a succession of unfortunate churchmen with an enthusiasm that would reflect ill on him even if his 'discoveries' were real. 'The flippant tone of this man's reports and the excessive profusion of his foul accusations renders his evidence when unfavourable almost worthless', says the *Victoria County History*.[63] In August 1535, Layton was at Farley, a cell of St Pancras, where he accused the prior of having eight whores and suggested that many of the monks indulged themselves similarly.[64] He mentioned his forthcoming visit to St Pancras with some relish, for a young monk at Farley had told him that 'unnatural crimes are at Lewes'. Unnatural crimes were Layton's stock in trade. It is no surprise that when he arrived in Lewes in October he was able to write to Cromwell that he had found what he called 'corruption of both kinds'. But there are no details of these corruptions because matters altogether more exciting than the supposed sexual proclivities of the Southover monks carried Layton onwards. He had somehow induced the sub-prior to confess to 'treason in preaching'.[65] The sub-prior had presumably preached against the king's marriage to Anne Boleyn – an action that had been made treasonable under the Act of Succession of 1534.[66] Layton, plainly, was in his element and all the more so when, as he reported to Cromwell, he succeeded in dragging a further 'confession' from the monk that the prior had known of his crime. So the prior was implicated and Layton was able to confront him with his complicity. He describes Robert Croham as grovelling before him, begging forgiveness and beseeching him not to tell Cromwell of the goings-on at the priory. Layton gives a lofty description of how he summoned Croham to the court in London.

We shall never know the truth of the interview with Croham, for Layton cannot be trusted and there is no account by the prior. But whether or not he grovelled it is clear that the prior went to London shortly afterwards. In August of the next year he wrote the first of a series of letters to Cromwell in which he referred to a discussion they had recently had in London. There is no mention of the sub-prior's treason. It disappears from the record. Perhaps Cromwell merely used it as a means of pressure against Croham in what followed. The matter was not raised in the prior's letters to the minister.[67]

The letters and the events to which they related concerned Swanborough and they are revealing in two ways. They indicate how the prior looked upon his manor; and they show also how attractive these demesnes were to others.

It appears from the correspondence that the prior had committed himself in 1534 to lease the manor demesnes to a certain Edward Shelley and that Cromwell had, at that time, supported Shelley's request to have them.[68] However, Cromwell had second thoughts on the matter – very probably because, as his mind turned towards the dissolution of the larger monasteries like St Pancras, he perceived that he might make rich pickings of the priory lands and preferred to have them unencumbered by tenants. At all events, on the occasion of Croham's visit to London, Cromwell gave him strict instructions *not* to lease Swanborough demesnes, described as the priory's own 'manurance lands', necessary for its maintenance.[69] Moreover, he gave Croham the strange, characteristically devious command that he must hold onto the Swanborough lands notwithstanding any letter to the contrary that he, Cromwell, might write! Precisely what tortuous purpose this complicated instruction was meant to serve remains a mystery; it reflects perhaps some subplot in a political life founded on manoeuvres large and small. It also suggests that Cromwell found the Swanborough demesnes rich enough to care about.

It was, however, bound to lead to confusion. By August 1536 Cromwell had apparently changed his mind. He came to feel that this advantage lay in obtaining the lease on the Swanborough demesnes for himself. Perhaps he sought in this way to ensure that when the lands were alienated from the priory they would be free of tenants with life-long claims on them. Perhaps he feared that Croham might seize whatever chance there might be to install a relative or well-disposed member of his monastery as tenant, so ensuring for himself by indirect means a continuing interest in the demesnes. Cromwell knew well enough that abbots and priors all over England were attempting to sustain their interests and security in this way.[70] Perhaps the threat of implication in 'treason' was too weak to hold Croham in check, or Layton's evidence was too slim to stand up even in the biased processes of a Tudor treason trial. Cromwell, so it would seem, was disposed to make doubly sure of Swanborough.

Whatever his motives, there is no doubt that his command threw poor Croham into confusion. How was he to respond? A short while before he had been sternly instructed to ignore any attempts to obtain a lease of the Swanborough demesnes – even one that might come in writing from Cromwell himself. But here he was faced with a demand for just a lease from the originator of the instruction. He wrote back reminding Cromwell of the earlier instruction and expressing his unwillingness to lease. Most of all he was concerned to impress on Cromwell the importance of the demesnes for the priory itself. This demesne, says Croham, 'is the only thing I have for the maintenance of the house' – a cry he was to make again in the near future. It indicated the part the Swanborough demesne played in the economy of the priory. Notwithstanding the mass of other leases yielding rents (most of which had to go in meeting the continuing debts of the monastery), Swanborough was perceived as the provider: the source of food for the community at Southover.

The issue between Cromwell and the prior was hardly raised when other eyes turned with interest towards the land. Sir Thomas Audley had succeeded Sir Thomas More as lord chancellor and he, with the king's support, wanted to lease.[71] Swanborough was attracting the attention of rather important people. Cromwell, faced with royal support for his rival, withdrew and became the recipient of desperate letters from Prior Robert who sought at all costs to keep the demesnes under the direct control of the priory. On 31 August 1536 he wrote to Cromwell repeating his assertion: 'I have nothing but the said farm and grange and parsonage to maintain my house.' Consequently, he urged Cromwell to do whatever possible to avoid the lease going to Sir Thomas Audley. Then, a fortnight later after receipt of an unhelpful reply from Cromwell, he wrote a letter that admitted his defeat. Audley could have the lease, though not for two years; Cromwell would recognize that the lease 'will cause the decay of my hospitality and lack of hay and straw for the house'. Then, in a slightly disingenuous way that suggested some royal displeasure may have been expressed about the delays in coming to an agreement, Croham put the blame elsewhere: 'My delay has been caused by the untowardness of my brethren.' Croham made one last attempt to hold the land before greater happenings overtook this whole sequence of events. In October he wrote to Cromwell that Shelley, who had been promised the lease long before, had revived his claim upon hearing that Audley was to have the land. Perhaps Croham hoped that some rivalry between Audley and Shelley might slow the whole process.

But by this time Cromwell and the king had started a greater business. In fact, neither Audley nor Shelley obtained admission to Swanborough before the priory itself was dissolved; less than a year after this correspondence with Cromwell, Prior Robert was undermined: in November 1537 he surrendered the priory together with its main 'cell' at Castle Acre in Norfolk and lands in fourteen English counties into the hands of the king. The priory was no more; it had lasted for 460 years, but notwithstanding the fearsome curses that William de Warenne and his successors had laid on any who might put their great gift to religion in question, King Henry undid it at a stroke of his pen. He dealt generously with the monks and prior. They all became pensioners of the king and the 'servants' of the priory, among them a Richard a Wood, seem to have been given a type of redundancy payment: a Wood received 7s 6d from Cromwell. In all there were 22 monks and 80 servants at the monastery when it was dissolved. In February 1538, some four months later, virtually all the priory's possessions, spread over the length of England, were granted to Thomas Cromwell. They included, of course, the priory itself, its church and messuages, its Swanborough lands and the manor, and the vicarages of Falmer, Kyngeston and Iford, which had once been in the gift of the lords de Warenne and had been granted to the priory. They included also that other part of the original de Warenne gift to the priory: the lands and the 'vill' of Falmer.[72] Cromwell, for the moment at least, was the new lord of Swanborough Manor. The quite humble families of Kingston who owed homage in the manor court might well have wondered at the radical change of fortunes that had brought them under the lordship of such a mighty (and no doubt frightening) personage – even if the only evidence they had of him was a new steward in the courtroom at Swanborough Grange.

The last act of the old Cluniac regime at the priory came in the form of a sad, unavailing letter from Croham – now just Robert Peterson once again – to Cromwell. It is not without significance that the prior's 'last request' was about Swanborough. He wrote: 'I beg your favour that my brother may be your farmer at Swanborough. Because I have been brought up in these parts, I am desirous to spend the living I have … at the late priory of Lewes in such lodging as your farmer may spare'.[73]

The letter was signed at Lewes while the erstwhile prior was still in the lodgings at Southover. Prior Robert could not bring himself to leave his splendid house or face a future in which the ancient monastic lands at Swanborough would be inaccessible to him. It was a mournful plea, the more so because it was refused. Robert Peterson left the priory soon after and took up a rectory at Bury near Chichester. He remained there until he died in 1555. In his will he remembered old servants of the priory and close associates, among them Francis Pouncer, William Goodfellow, Richard Botting and Adam Taylor of Kingston; he also left small sums, as we have seen, to 'the heirs of Richard Hylder and John Delve'. When he left Lewes for Chichester, the last link with Cluny was broken. The monks were gone from Swanborough and tough-minded new men moved in to take their places.

Although Cromwell's ascendancy was to be short, it was also eventful and he wasted no time in taking possession of his new lands near Lewes. He appears to have divided them between those that were leased out 'to farm' and those that were cultivated directly under the supervision of his manorial servants. Swanborough Manor demesnes were in the latter category. Cromwell held onto them for his own use. Other lands and property were leased out. Nicholas Jenney, a yeoman farmer, was granted a lease on the priory itself as well as the 'tithes of Kingston' and neighbouring villages. He was installed as farmer at Falmer village, where in the latter part of 1538 he was granted the whole of the demesne land, which included the sheep leaves on the Downs. Jenney was sufficiently impressed by the wool-producing capacity of his new lands to contemplate the production of cloth. 'The farmer is minded to occupy (himself) with making a cloth,'[74] wrote Polsted, who was managing affairs for Cromwell at the time. Later, in 1540, Jenney was granted a new lease for 21 years; he had pasture and herbage for 1840 sheep in Falmer.[75] Jenney installed himself in the monastic buildings. He died in 1549 in Southover, leaving his wife 'tholle Apparell of the Lodgynge chamber next adionying unto the great dynynge chamber … within the late dissolved Monastery of Lewes'.[76]

This substantial yeoman had hardly been established at the priory before it became clear just how direct an interest Cromwell had in his new possession. In 1538 his son Gregory, together with his wife and a quite large retinue, arrived at the prior's lodging and settled in. 'The house and situation please us much,' he wrote to his father, adding, 'the gentlemen of this country have welcomed me and entertained me with presents.'[77] Gregory Cromwell was set upon a long stay, and it was therefore a sensible precaution for local gentry to ingratiate themselves.

Unfortunately, the rats of Lewes had their own less pleasant presents in store. A few weeks after Gregory's arrival plague broke out and, shortly, the people of the town had a taste of the ways of their new lord. Whatever advantages Southover had as a place to live were vitiated by the fact that it had a large churchyard – indeed, generations of feudal notables had been buried either in the priory or in the churchyard of St John's nearby. Naturally, as people died of the plague in Southover, they were brought to these places for burial. Thomas Cromwell, in London, reacted immediately. He ordered the corpses to be buried in the yard of St Anne's Without, on the west of Lewes and well away from Gregory and his family. St Anne's parishioners not unnaturally objected, 'not having plague in their parish,' but Nicholas Cholmeley was able to write to Thomas Cromwell: 'henceforth none shall be buried in the church or churchyard within the precinct of your house here in Lewes.'[78] Gregory was well looked after, though the unhappy people of St Anne's may have had their own views about the price they had to pay on his behalf. Cholmeley, one of Cromwell's household, contemplated moving Gregory to Swanborough at this time but decided against it since it was 'thought to be too little for Mr Gregory's company'. Though Gregory and his companions stayed on for a while, the plague in the end drove them back to London. They appear to have left by the end of 1538. Cromwell held onto the Swanborough demesnes though and it is likely that he had in mind to set up the grange as a living place. His concern about the fortunes of Swanborough before the dissolution makes a certain kind of sense in the light of these later events.

Kingston villagers were, of course, fully alive to all these events. The monks were gone; there was the steward of a new great lord at the manor court; a large tenant farmer was installed at the priory where he dined every night in the monastic dining room; Falmer demesne was let out to the same man who had vast flocks on the Downs nearby; Master Gregory, the lord's son, appeared in Southover and established himself in the prior's lodging. The world must have seemed upside down. Perhaps some more conventional spirits wondered a little at the sacrilege that all these lay people, intent on their own material well being, might commit in the great religious centre nearby. And perhaps some anti-clerical enjoyed the prospect. They possibly felt that the village owed little to the priory, which had lorded it over them for so long and, even if the new lord's behaviour to their neighbours in St Anne's did not suggest that he was any better, there was some pleasure to be taken at the discomfiture of the easy-living monks who had been thrown out of their vineyards and gardens into the harsher world.

But the excitements of the first months of Cromwell's lordship paled before the events of 1541. In that year Cromwell set about the physical destruction of much of the old monastery. This singularly Philistine undertaking, which had its counterpart in many other parts of England, was an act of policy. If it did not actually guarantee the irreversibility of Henry's dissolution of the religious houses, it did at least reduce the dangers of what he and his ministers might have seen as a recrudescence of the old Catholic monastic life. From the moment of the dissolution at Lewes there had never been any doubt about Cromwell's intentions: the lease to Jenney granted him the use of the site of the monastery except for 'the Frater and other buildings to be destroyed within three years'.[79]

The dismal business started at Southover with the arrival of an Italian 'engineer' called Portinari accompanied by seventeen workmen. They had their orders directly from Cromwell who kept in touch with progress throughout. Portinari had hardly arrived at the priory before he made his first report. 'I found the church much larger than people thought,' he wrote,[80] but estimated that he would have it down in eight to ten days. Cromwell wrote back immediately asking for details of the size of the building; later, in his reply, Portinari gave them. It was indeed a large church. Its overall length was 420 feet, which is commensurate with Notre Dame de Paris; its width varied from about 70 feet to 150 feet at the transept; the nave was 63 feet high and lined with 32 columns of which eight were 'very large', about 14 feet in diameter; the walls were ten feet thick and the steeple 90 feet high.

Portinari gave Cromwell an indication of how this great building was to be destroyed and his methods are of some interest because they are still used at times in major demolition. The technique was simple in principle, though complicated to carry out in practice. He intended to dig deep under the foundations of the great east end of the Church – in fact to mine under it. The underground gallery created under the church would be propped up with balks of timber – then, when the undermining was judged sufficient to the purpose, the supporting timbers would be burned and, if the job had been properly done, the huge walls would break and collapse.

The Italian knew his job. By 24 March he wrote to Cromwell that much of the church was 'thrown down'; he was working with the man he had brought from London to melt down the roofing lead.

This gigantic destruction must have been clearly seen from the Kingston fields, from the furlongs that ran out along the hillside to Southover, and by any villagers who were curious enough to move closer and watch from the meadows near the priory. No doubt the smoke and flames from Portinari's fires filled the Southover air and made a kind of funeral pyre for the church. And the whole enterprise was consummated when the east end, which had stood for 400 years and echoed to at least a hundred thousand masses, broke with a roar and the dust of tons of Caen masonry billowed into the smoke. The process was repeated until the work was completed. As the flames from the last fires died beneath yet another fallen wall, the church was reduced to a pile of debris, the frater was rubble and so too was the old dormer and the cloister where choir monks had said their breviary. If there had been any in Kingston who had doubted the finality of the dissolution, their doubts were now dispelled. The Italian engineer had done the job he had come to do.[81]

Portinari's achievement – or to be fair Cromwell's and the king's – was to destroy one of the finer pieces of Norman church architecture in England. It is hard now to recapture the priory church. All we have are the bald facts about its size and a few hints about its architectural relationship to the abbey church at Cluny itself. But it is clear that St Pancras belonged in its basic concept to the great period of monastic revival, when Cluny spread its religious power over Europe: a period that produced the loveliest Romanesque churches of France. So it is not too fanciful to imagine that it echoed some of the singular beauties of Vezelay or the clarity of religious purpose of St Amant-de-Boixe in the Charente. Whatever later decay may have done to the Cluniac order at Southover, their church itself came from days when belief had been a simple matter, and perhaps its Norman arches had conveyed something of that simplicity of spirit and sureness of mind.

But, whatever nobility of concept was expressed at St Pancras, by the summer of 1541 it was largely reduced to disordered masonry, ruined tombs and the remaining traces of the Italian's mining operation. Only the prior's lodge, now inhabited by Jenney and his family, was left in one piece, standing in what at the time must have looked like a battlefield. The remnants could serve only one purpose: the masonry itself could be sold off for building stone and that, indeed, is what happened. The priory became a kind of man-made quarry. Lewes builders and gradually villagers in Kingston bought its stone. The vestiges of Tudor building in the street contain substantial sections of Caen stone. And here and there is the occasional block in some humble cottage such as the Howells'. Most were bought from the new lords of Southover, but it is likely that people in the village took the odd load for occasional repairs to walls and buildings in a somewhat less formal manner. The end of the priory left its own particular mark in the village; the villagers' shock at what had happened was not enough to stop them putting the remnants of the old to good use.

The mining of the priory was among the last of Thomas Cromwell's undertakings. His career ended suddenly, as political careers often did under Henry VIII. He lost favour with the king, at least partly because he had played an instrumental role in Henry's strikingly unsuccessful marriage to Anne of Cleves. Within a few short months of the destruction at Lewes, his political enemies had arranged his attainder for high treason. Before 1541 was out Cromwell was dead; his astonishingly extensive estates reverted to the king and the king proceeded to grant them to others.

Anne of Cleves was prominent among the beneficiaries. In her case, Henry had resolved his marital dissatisfactions by the comparatively mild procedure of nullification, and Anne's compliance was secured by grants of land, particularly from the ample estates that so conveniently became available at the death of Cromwell. The grants were made on the condition of her renunciation of her marriage to the king as 'never consummated'.[82] They included lands and manors in Essex, Surrey and Suffolk as well as in Sussex; she was especially attracted to her Sussex possessions, for she came to live in the main street of Southover (in a house that has now been turned into a museum). So Anne of Cleves came to hold the manor of Falmer as well as the manor of Southover, which comprised the lands immediately surrounding the ruined priory and the derelict buildings. She also took possession of the farm of Ovingdean, abutting Kingston parish on the west. In Kingston itself, she was granted the rectory and the advowson of the vicarage along with a portion of the tithes on 'Dygon's lands'.

Swanborough Manor was excluded from these grants to Anne. The manor had, of course, reverted to the king at Cromwell's demise and Henry granted it to William Earl of Arundel, apparently as part of an exchange of estates.[83] William was given 'the manor or lordship of Swanborough' and the grant especially mentions 'the windmill … called Cranedowne Myll', which stood atop the hillside of Southover Laine, as well as rights of pasturage of 400 sheep on Swanborough Down, the stretch of downland above the old grange the monks had built. It included manorial rights over 'all lands in Kyngeston near Lewes … belonging' – the yardlands in the open fields held by the freehold and copyhold landlords and owner-occupiers of Kingston village. The Arundels were lineal successors to the de Warenne family, so, after more than four centuries, the lordship of Swanborough had come back into the family that had originally given it to make a priory. But the Arundels did not hold it for long. Within quite a short time they sold their rights in the manor to the Caryll family.

While the destiny of Swanborough Manor had been tied to great people and great events, the story of Kingston Manor, which had also been in monastic ownership, was much simpler and more humble. When the hospital of the Holy Trinity at Arundel was dissolved Kingston Manor reverted to the king. It remained in royal hands until 1546. Then it was granted to one of Henry's courtiers: Sir Richard Lee who had been knighted two years before. Lee was a comparatively minor servant of the crown. He had his rewards for his work as 'Surveyor of Calais and Guisnes' between 1536 and 1543, and as general receiver of the Court of Wards and Liveries.[84] He had no particular interest in Kingston Manor beyond the money it was worth and so he sold it immediately to John Crane of Kingston who, though described as a husbandman in the early deed, was clearly a local yeoman farmer.[85]

The dissolution, then, had some special impacts on Kingston village, mainly because of the immediacy of the monastic hold over it, and Portinari's explosions under the church of St Pancras must have lived on in village memories for many a long year. They were, after all, the clearest symbol of the ending of a very ancient order in village life. These immediate effects, for all their high drama when set in the context of a mainly regular rural life, were less important for the future shape of Kingston society than the changes in lordship – and particularly in the accessibility of land – that resulted from the dissolution.

The varying patterns of land tenure and the organization of land inevitably had implications for the social structure of the village. It had always been so. That Kingston in 1524 was mainly a village of comparatively poor 'cadet' families was in good measure the outcome of a particular history that had by chance resulted in a preponderance of smaller tenancies along with small copyholdings. The pattern of landholding was not the only thing to determine the nature of village society, but it was always important. The dissolution created new opportunities for ambitious people through the changes it brought to Swanborough and Kingston manors; these, quite as much as the disappearance of the Cluniacs and the ruination of their church, were part of its lasting influence.

Their significance at Kingston Manor was clear within a short time. After centuries of distant de Warenne and Arundel lordship, followed by the equally distant lordship of the monks of the Holy Trinity, it came to be held by a local yeoman who moved into the village. For the first time in its history Kingston had a 'lord of the manor' living in the street alongside the tenant farmers and copyholders and, though John Crane could have been much the same kind of person as those who had been tenant farmers on the Kingston demesnes before, the fact of his lordship most certainly meant that he and his family were perceived in a way that his predecessors never had been. Kingston Manor and the manor farm came to have a new kind of dominance in the society of the street.

The changes at Swanborough were doubtless less immediate in their effects on the village. Within a few years of Cromwell's demise, the demesnes that had been a home farm to the priory became available for leasing. Here, indeed, was an excellent opportunity for a rising yeoman in search of a rich tenancy to further his wealth and fortune. In the middle years of the sixteenth century, as the commercial profitability of land increased all over England, rising local capitalist farmers, yeomen or gentry could use a tenancy at Swanborough to build fortunes. It took some time before the effects of this new opportunity became evident in Kingston village; the first tenants at Swanborough were based mainly at Iford. But the time was not far off when men who had enhanced their wealth by judicious and skilful farming at Swanborough turned their eyes to lands in Kingston that might provide a more permanent base for them and their posterity.

Chapter 6

Yeomen and Gentry: New Ascendancies

By the start of the Tudor period the medieval manor had been thoroughly and, in European terms, uniquely transformed. The manor still counted, of course. Lordship carried social distinction, especially in a time when 'new men' with new wealth sought to define their status in relation to older families. Lordship also carried power in local affairs outside the limits of the manor itself. And manorial custom and court records still largely determined the nature and security of claims to land and to title. The common law on such questions was growing up from precedent founded on the experience of the manor and it would be wrong to underestimate the manor and its functions. Nonetheless, while the manorial system provided a framework of regulation for rural societies, actual social and economic developments in rural England were everywhere determined increasingly by the force of the markets that had come into being with the gradual disintegration of feudal relationships.

In the century and a half that followed from 1500, a particular set of circumstances much affected the direction in which these markets operated. After the medieval decline the population started to grow again with a new vigour.[1] The numbers of people in relation to the area of productive land increased and, though there were some advances in the techniques of agricultural production, these were not radical enough to keep up with the increase in the demand for output. The results were predictable and familiar: the profitability of holding land or of farming it as a tenant increased steadily. The prices of agricultural goods increased, albeit with many ups and downs, over the whole period while the increased supply of labour kept wages down.[2]

The beneficiaries of this shift were, of course, the older landed classes and also those acquisitive families that had built up landlord estates in the midst of the old manorial system. They were manor lords with large demesnes to lease or farm in their own right, and people who held blocks of freehold and copyhold lands outside the demesnes, sometimes scattered far and wide in different manors. Beneath them there were smaller landholders who benefited too, freeholders and copyholders who had retained their title and achieved security of customary tenure. It was the accumulation of wealth by the variety of landowning classes that ultimately contributed to what W. G. Hoskins called the 'rebuilding of rural England'. Where monastic splendours and the castles and manors of great magnates had dominated rural architecture before, the houses of the new gentry, of yeomen, even the expanding and improved cottages of the smaller copyholders, then became the characteristic mark of English villages.[3]

Those who suffered were the mass of people who lived off wages: cottagers, landless rural labourers and, increasingly, people who laboured in growing industries. It was inevitable that as the population grew and productivity in food production failed to keep pace, real wages should not only grow less rapidly than the returns to land – than profits and rent – but should actually decline. Between 1500 and 1650 the real wages of agricultural labourers in the south of England were reduced by very nearly a half. There is room for controversy about whether the wealth of the country as a whole was rising or falling over this century and a half, but there can be no serious doubt that the material welfare of its poorest classes (who were quite likely an increasing proportion of the whole population), fell off steadily and, in bad years, disastrously.[4] The Elizabethan poor law, which provided for the support of destitute people out of a rate levied on the parish landowners, was in one sense necessary to public order in a rural society of manifestly growing inequality. The village realities that lay beneath the surface of the splendid achievements of Elizabethan and Stuart England were harsh indeed. But the effects of market forces on English villages were a good deal more complicated than this. Though the prices of grain, which constituted much of the real income of poorer people, rose, often sharply, from the second quarter of the sixteenth century, the prices of some other agricultural products went up even more. Wool prices had increased to high levels by the middle of the sixteenth century and stayed high for the rest of it. Meat prices increased in the second half of the century. The increase in wool prices resulted from the high demand for English fine and worsted cloth at home and abroad, and the consequent growth of a thriving wool industry even before Tudor times. Meat prices mainly rose because of increasing demand from the newly rich landowning classes and those benefiting from industrial profits.

There is little doubt that the rising prices of wool and meat resulted in increases in these pastoral productions in proportion to the output of grain for direct human consumption. There is some disagreement, however, on two other matters related to the shift to a larger proportion of pastoral production.

In the first place, it is unclear whether the increase in pastoral outputs was at the expense of arable farming. Did the increased production of fine cloth and meat mean that less grain was produced for the English poor? If so, the profitability of wool and meat production ultimately reduced the real wages of the poor more than demographic pressure did. But the answer is unclear. Even if all productive land was in use to some degree, which was not the case in sixteenth-century England, an increase in pastoral production need not reduce arable output. Within limits, the more intensive pasturing of animals on land that could not be used for crops might provide more manure for the open fields in their fallow seasons. And the conversion of arable to pasture could even increase crop production, depending on how it was done.

If tired ploughlands were turned over to pasture for three or four years – into what were called temporary leys – their productivity could be greatly increased when they were cultivated again. The practice of temporary leys spread during the sixteenth century; they allowed a greater increase in crop production than would have occurred through a simple extension of arable land using the old three-course rotations. Once again, the effect of the expansion in pastoral production depended on its scale. If it were small enough, the temporary conversion of erstwhile arable need not have disadvantaged the production of grains for consumption by the poor; if it were larger, the temporary leys would become permanent and there would be less of those crops that provided the bulk of the 'real incomes' of the poor.[5] It is unclear whether the overall increase in sheep and later cattle was large enough to undermine a complementary growth in grain production, or actually small enough to facilitate it. The debate is about whether real wages, or more simply the incomes of the poor, would have fallen more or less without the increase in pastoral production. That real wages actually fell, and fell steadily over 150 years, is not a matter of contention.

The second source of disagreement is about the changes in the organization of agricultural production associated with the shift to wool and meat, and the extent to which these worked to the disadvantage of the economically weak in the interest of the strong.

In many parts of the country, especially where population was comparatively dense, an increase in the production of wool and meat necessitated the conversion of arable land into pasture. Even where this was done on terms that did not prejudice the total output of grain in a village, such conversion always involved reorganization. In principle, an open field village in which individual landholdings were spread in strips could be converted by turning over blocks of arable to pasture, and then reapportioning strips elsewhere in the open fields. In practice, this would be a complicated operation; therefore, conversion and intensification of pastoral production were much more frequently the outcomes of actions by individual landlords and lords of the manor, who were able to make decisions over larger areas of open-field land, than small copyholders – and whose incentives to turn to pastoral production were greater. Such conversion at the instigation of landlords and manor lords was a commonplace of rural experience in the Tudor century. The controversies are mostly about its extent, the terms on which it was done and its implications for village people.

Pastoral farming had three features that implied that its extension in an open field village would in nearly all cases produce abrupt change.

First, there are economies of scale in pastoral production, which were not present in arable farming in the sixteenth and seventeenth centuries. Flocks had to be large to take full advantage of the labour of the few skilled shepherds. Not only did flocks (and herds) have to be large, but it also had to be possible to graze them on large and unified areas of land; otherwise the possibilities of reducing costs by the effective use of only a few herders would be much diminished. Consequently, to be economically effective, the extension of pastoral farming into erstwhile arable lands, even if it were done on the basis of temporary leys, required not only the transformation of large areas of arable but also the formation of consolidated blocks of land. Though these consolidations could be accomplished by agreements between smallholders, they were more easily achieved if only a few people were involved. A large landlord who held title to a big proportion of the land in a village could, if he were able to reduce the numbers of his tenants on the arable, push through a consolidation more easily than could smaller landholders. Large landowners, irrespective of whether or not they were manorial lords, did just this. And manor lords had advantages in this respect too, whether or not they were landlords in the new commercial sense. Depending on the customs of the manor and the terms on which copyholders had access to their yardlands, manor lords could use their residual feudal powers to reclaim customary lands in the interests of consolidation for pastoral farming. In a word, conversion and consolidation were often accompanied by what came to be called 'engrossment' – the amalgamation of what had been a number of individual landholdings into a single large one, which could then be leased out to a pastoral farmer.

Second, pastoral production was often accompanied by 'enclosure' – the physical separation of newly consolidated lands by hedging them off. There was more than one motive for enclosure. It might be done simply to separate consolidated lands from the open-field system around them, which was a necessary step because intermingling the old system of production on the open fields with the new pattern of lands turned to pasture, or the alternation of temporary leys, would be quite impractical. It might also be done in the interests of greater efficiency in the control of animals – to lighten the task of the shepherd or cowherd so that he could control larger numbers of animals. And, finally, enclosure was also a way in which a new commercially oriented pastoral farmer could separate his animals from the village flock, perhaps to ensure better care and attention, perhaps also to avoid the periodic epidemics that afflicted the village animals.

All in all though, enclosure was not in itself a source of fundamental change. It was for the most part the outcome of the more basic changes that flowed from consolidation and engrossment. Enclosure only impacted directly on village life where it took place on common land on which cottagers and labouring families had hitherto been able to maintain an animal or two. Even so, for Tudor contemporaries and their Stuart successors, the word itself (enclosure) became a general term to describe the ills that followed from the transformation of village life.

The third important feature of pastoral farming – the one that probably caused most concern to Tudor governments – was that it required much less labour per acre of land than arable production. Where pastoral production was pushed to the point of permanent conversion on a large scale, villages became depopulated for want of employment. The aspect of deserted villages and the distress of populations thrown on the poor law and into destitution moved Tudor pamphleteers to vivid and heartfelt outcries against 'enclosure'. It also moved Tudor governments to a long series of legislation against conversion and engrossment – mostly called anti-enclosure legislation – in the interests of social stability in the countryside.[6] Sir Thomas More, that most eloquent and motivated opponent of enclosure, expressed the matter in words that have not been forgotten: 'Your sheep, that were wont to be so meek and tame, and so small eaters, now, as I hear say, be become so great devourers, and so wild, that they eat up and swallow down the very men themselves.'[7]

There is no question that the increase in pastoral production had a strong impact, yet nobody claims it was the only factor causing rural reorganization. Landlords, for example, undertook engrossment without any intent to convert the engrossed lands from arable or to consolidate them. They simply wanted to take advantage of the greater profitability that could be got by putting farms in the hands of fewer, more capable large tenants rather than spreading them between less well-capitalized small ones. Engrossments that reduced opportunities for small tenancies created as much resentment and concern as those that resulted in conversion.

A history of a single small village in Sussex can show the incidence of the broader changes in a particular case. Kingston does not lie in that area of England where it is now accepted that the impact of conversion to pasture was greatest. The 'crowded' Midlands almost certainly experienced the biggest problems; Sussex, with its large areas of downland pasture, could naturally encompass more animals than lands that were already worked to the limits that the techniques of the time would allow. Still, Kingston and its surroundings show signs of the changes that came between 1500 and 1650, and their incidence there is important to our main purpose: the description of change in the social organization of the village.

The area around Kingston was certainly caught up in the current of change. Downland pastures were prime countryside for sheep rearing and Kingston, like neighbouring villages, had plenty of them. When Marchant drew up his 'terrier' of the parish many years later in 1773, he found that of a total area of 1642 statutory acres, 865 were on the downland and devoted to pasture, and a further 186 acres were brookland, mainly meadow that provided hay for winter feed. This means that very nearly two-thirds of the productive land in the parish was devoted essentially to pastoral production.[8] There is good reason to believe that the apportionment of land between animal and crop production was much the same during the sixteenth century as when Marchant made his survey. And, nearby in Iford, on the demesne lands of Swanborough and in Falmer, the proportions were much the same.[9] All in all, it is no surprise to find that when Nicholas Jenney, the farmer at the priory, obtained the lease of Falmer Manor and village from Cromwell in 1541, his access to the demesnes gave him herbage and pasturage for 1840 sheep. And it is a sign of the times that he declared his intention to Cromwell's agent of setting up a fulling mill because he was 'minded to occupy the making of cloth'.[10] In Kingston itself there was pasturage for about 2000 sheep on the downs in 1546.[11]

The downland clearly was excellent sheep country. But were the sheep 'eating men'? There is indeed some evidence in two villages abutting Kingston parish of that process of depopulation, which Sir Thomas More so vigorously deplored.

Balmer village was just north of Kingston parish. It is listed in the Domesday Book and appears in the first chapter of William de Warenne as part of his grant to the priory.[12] It is likely that Burgamera, as it was then called, was part of the original grant to the priors and that is the village whose name is indecipherable in the deed de Warenne made out to Cluny.[13] It was assessed in the subsidies of 1296, 1327 and 1332,[14] when it was a village of villeins about the same size as Kingston. It was a hamlet within the parish of Falmer, which lies a mile or so away, but was substantial enough to have its own chapel.[15] By the middle of the sixteenth century it had decisively diminished in size, so much so that the chapel was demolished and whoever was left living there must have walked to church along the downland footpath that links the village to Falmer. Today it is a desolate and beautiful place, the site of a few tired cottages and a great farmyard near the crest of the downs, looking out on a sweeping view to its parent village at Falmer across the valley.

Balsdean lay deep in the downs to the southwest of Kingston parish and was part of Rottingdean. It has a similar history to Balmer. It appears in the early de Warenne grants to the priory, was assessed as a quite substantial settlement in the medieval subsidies and experienced a huge crop failure recorded in the official enquiry of 1340.[16] Unlike Balmer, Balsdean was the site of a manor. In 1558, Thomas Gratwyke of Seaford died in possession and it passed to his son;[17] it remained in the family until the seventeenth century. A small part of Balsdean land and pasture was part of the demesnes of Kingston Manor.[18] The parish at Balsdean was still active in 1579, but probably much reduced in size,[19] and it cannot have been long after that that the village ceased to exist. Today there are only traces of the chapel building. Like Balmer it is a place of mysterious desolation, but where Balmer is near the top of the downs, Balsdean lies in one of those remote inland valleys enclosed by the downlands near the coast.

Both these villages were, in their different way, marginal. Balmer was a mere hamlet in Falmer, peopled entirely by the comparatively poorer villeins of the parish at the time of the medieval subsidies, and therefore in all probability made up of comparatively poorer lands in the parish. Balsdean was disadvantaged by remoteness, never very large and apparently severely afflicted by the decline in arable in the appalling agricultural years around 1340. Lands like these probably remained under-utilized after the Black Death, and neither place was as heavily populated in the early sixteenth century as it had been in high medieval times. It is fairly certain that pasture invaded the arable here in the Tudor period, that there was depopulation and that, however precisely it was carried out, it was not very difficult for its instigators to accomplish.

But in Kingston itself the position was different. Here there is little evidence of enclosure or conversion. In Marchant's map of 1773,[20] there are certainly no large enclosures on the pasture. The downlands above the village to the west remained a huge unbroken stretch crossed by lonely rights of way, which followed the contours of the high ground and circled the isolated blind valleys where only shepherds went. The deeds of Kingston lands in the Wiston archive make it clear that these high pastures continued to be in common use by all with claims to arable land: whether by title or tenancy. The individual's right to pasture was, as ever, proportional to the amount of land he or she held in the open fields, and there had been little or no attempt to transform their claims into consolidated areas of pasture under individual control. When Peter Crane came to hold Kingston Manor at the end of Henry's reign, his 15 demesne yardlands of arable gave him rights to 400 sheep leazes on the downs, and so it was for each group of village yardlands.[21] Altogether Kingston people owned many sheep, but they grazed together as a village flock. There are signs of this in the lease Thomas Cromwell made to Nicholas Jenney, the 'farmer at the priory', in 1541. Included in it were rights to farm a small amount of arable in Kingston itself – strips that altogether made up about two or three yardlands in the village fields, which the ancient priory had held directly in the village (and which later came to be called 'priory lands' in Kingston parlance). These gave him the rights to pasture for a few animals and the deed makes it clear that his animals would graze 'amongst the cattle of Kingston-near-Lewes'.[22]

But, of course, the onset of pastoral farming, conversion and enclosure could take other forms than the appearance of large enclosed pastoral farms on hitherto open grazing. A common symptom of conversion was the appearance of enclosed areas within the arable lands of villages where before there had been open fields with strips. These enclosures, sometimes quite small, facilitated the alternation of periods of arable farming with the laying down of the land to temporary leys for grazing, a practice that naturally broke into the three-common communal rotation that was traditional in strip farming.

Iford, which was in so many ways the sister village to Kingston, shows distinct signs of such enclosure in the arable. Part of Iford arable lay strung out along the southern boundary of the ancient enclosed demesnes of Swanborough. In Dorset's map of 1799 [23] these lands are shown divided, not into strips such as pattern the open fields of Kingston, but into discrete and enclosed units generally between five and twelve statutory acres in size. There were 32 of these units, which were called yardlands but of course bore no resemblance to the yardland of dispersed strips found in Kingston open fields. These lands lying in the Iford fields are sharply distinct from the open field systems in Kingston, and must surely be the product of enclosure to facilitate the extension of pasture in the form of temporary leys. They were farmed in severality – that is to say each unit was held by three or four villagers together and these landholders shared out the product from it in proportion to their recognized claims; alternatively, when the land was used as pasture, each would have rights to put on it a number of animals proportionate to his or her claim. So, for example, a quarter of each of these enclosed bits of land in Iford was apportioned to the farm called Stuckles, which had become attached to the Swanborough demesnes by Tudor times. Severalty preserved one advantage of the open field system – the facility with which it ensured equity (not equality) in access to land of differing quality in the village. But it was at the same time a system of landholding that was much more amenable to the introduction of temporary leys than the traditional open fields.[24]

The enclosure of the arable in Iford shows the signs of a reorganization in which a number of landholders exchanged their claims to individual strips for shares in consolidated 'crofts'. In Kingston, though, such incursions into the arable were rare indeed. Marchant's map shows only a few crofts. At the head of Kingston Street to the northwest there were two – the Barley Croft and the Great Barley Croft – which were clearly the result of enclosure of older strip lands. But both were quite small: a mere seven and a half statutory acres. The Slonk Croft and the Clover Croft along the road to Lewes measured eight and eight statutory acres respectively. They were probably enclosed and cultivated in severality. Then, in the brooks where the village meadows lay, there were bits of land that were enclosed and similarly cultivated, but as far as one can judge they had never been part of the arable.[25] And that, as far as enclosures in the arable were concerned, was that. No more than about 20 acres of Kingston lands were enclosed in this way, compared with more than 250 in the northern part of Iford. Conversion to temporary leys was negligible in the village. Such other evidence as there is all points in the same direction – economic incentives to increase pastoral production did not result in incursions into the arable in Kingston. Elsewhere, and quite nearby, it might well have been the case that 'sheep ate men', but in Kingston it seems they did not. The close correspondence of the individual strips described in the Hyde survey of 1567 and those in the Marchant map of 1773 points to a stable disposition of village lands over a long time,[26] and shows no signs at all of conversion of pasture to arable after Elizabeth's accession. Indeed, all the evidence suggests that Kingston arables were *extended* in Elizabeth's reign by asserting from the 'wastes' rather than diminished by invasions of sheep and cattle. And if there were such an invasion in the years before the Elizabethan period it left none of the traces one would expect to find. Kingston arable retained its integrity and the open fields remained, while surrounding villages felt the impact of the shifting market for rural outputs far more directly.

It would surely be wrong to imagine that Kingston was unique. Many other parishes along the downlands and elsewhere were doubtless comparatively undisturbed by the thrust towards animal production. As Brian Murphy points out, permanent conversions of arable, depopulation and the various social ills Tudor people so often and so loosely attributed to 'enclosure' were mostly concentrated in the Midlands. There the incursions of sheep and cattle were much more general and it was probably the disruption and deprivation of ordinary people in that region that caught Thomas More's saintly attention and pity.[27] Sussex was not especially afflicted by 'enclosure'. Even if Kingston village was not unique, it is still interesting to speculate why – when Iford experienced the incursion of temporary leys and Balmer to the north and Balsdean in the west were depopulated by pastoralism – it should have escaped any significant incursion on its ancient open fields.[28]

It is possible that Kingston's special position had something to do with the pattern of landholding. Conversion of arable to pasture almost always involved accommodating a number of landholders. The arrangement could take the form of an agreement on more or less equal terms to exchange strips in the open field to allow land to be consolidated. It could and sometimes did have a more coercive aspect, as when a manorial lord was able to re-establish his residual feudal power of possession over copyhold or customary lands, or when a landlord was able to rid himself of tenants-at-will so as to engross lands into a larger farm prior to consolidation, conversion and enclosure of old arables. In all cases, whether conversion resulted from simple voluntary arrangements or involved the exercise of economic power by dominant people, the fewer the number of people involved the easier it was to accomplish. If Balsdean and Balmer had been depopulated by conversion, the reason could be that neither place had ever been fully *repopulated* to early medieval levels after the great declines in population of the fourteenth century, so that reorganization of the lands was facilitated by the fact that there were comparatively few people with whom to deal.

From this point of view the prospects for conversion of the arable in Kingston were poor. For one thing, the Norman incursion had left a bemusing multiplicity of manors in the village. There was hardly a single furlong in the open fields in which the strips were ascribed to fewer than three or four manors, so that any rearrangement of village lands would inevitably require the assent of several manor courts. Even in an age when the real economic power of the manor was in decline this was a daunting prospect for a would-be 'converting' landlord. And, quite aside from these manorial complexities, the subsequent history of the village, especially the dominant conservatism of the priory before dissolution, had produced a particular pattern of landholding that made reorganization more difficult to accomplish than elsewhere. In 1524 Kingston appeared as a village of small tenancies and small individual landholders – a pattern that had made it a favoured spot for the poorer cadet branches of yeoman families. Though Kingston landlords belonged to powerful families with large estates, their individual holdings within this particular village tended to be small. Proportionately for the size of the village, there were many independent landlords as well as many manors. And, outside these lands farmed by tenants there were independent copyholds held directly of manor lords by the customary tenantry. These too were small, and customary tenants therefore numerous. The multiplicity of manors and the historic process that had produced a multiplicity of landlords and customary tenancies all worked against reorganization of the arable, whether by agreements or by some degree of enforcement. This accounts for the absence of any signs of large-scale conversion, and the very few indications of Tudor or earlier enclosures in the village. In effect, Kingston kept its medieval shape. Marchant's eighteenth-century map shows us a village in which the disposition of lands had been but little disturbed by the transformations that changed the geography of other villages.

That Kingston kept the integrity of its open field system, and especially that it maintained the proportions of arable and pasture in more or less their medieval pattern, had some considerable advantages for its Tudor inhabitants. The poor of the village, who mostly worked for wages, did not find the demand for their labour lacking, as happened in villages where pasture took over. Small copyholders – the elements of an independent peasantry – also probably held out longer here than elsewhere. Village society was perhaps less rapidly transformed than in some other places. In the longer run there were probably costs to pay for this. By Elizabethan and Stuart times people had come to recognize the possibilities of increasing arable yields by the use of temporary leys – an alternation of pasture with arable on a cycle of three or four years, which of course could not easily be encompassed in a three course rotation open-field system. No doubt Kingston farmers found partial solutions to the problem, perhaps by agreement to turn individual furlongs to leys from time to time. But, in the main, Kingston villagers had to forego the advantages that could be gained from the limited but important technical advances of the early seventeenth century. In the same vein, they were poorly placed to exploit the much later and more radical changes in practice of the eighteenth century. However, the villagers of Tudor times were pleased enough to hold their old open fields intact and, from what they could observe about them, they had reason to be.

Nevertheless, it would be misleading to suggest that the Tudor century left Kingston unchanged. Rural change was not confined to the transformation of arable lands into pasture. The growing force of markets, especially the increasing profitability of landholding they brought, had other consequences too. One of these was the engrossment of farms, which, though often a prelude to consolidation and conversion, was not always so. Engrossment took place *within* the arable lands of English villages as well. Even when there was no reorganization of the land from its traditional disposition in strips, furlongs and fields, engrossment obviously meant change. In particular, it reduced the numbers of smaller tenancies and opportunities for smaller less well-capitalized tenants. It could advantage landlords partly because it reduced the irksome managerial problems of rent collection, partly because it reduced the risks of defaults in rent payment (larger tenants were more likely to have the resources to cover their rents even in bad years), and partly because larger tenants were in general more successful farmers and so could sustain the profitability of the land.

Though conversion played hardly any part in sixteenth- and seventeenth-century Kingston, engrossment did. Indeed, it could be argued that the history of the village from Elizabethan times right through until the nineteenth century was predominantly a history of engrossment. Kingston engrossments took their own special forms, often more complex than the common pattern, with landlords seeking their own advantage dominating the process. That happened in Kingston, but so did other things. The open fields retained their old shapes, the strips remained and the land looked much the same as it had always done, but farms were getting bigger and changes flowed from that. To illuminate these we must start with a view of Elizabethan Kingston, a clearer and more informed view of the patterns of landholding than can be got from the evidence of 1524. We move on to 1567, the year in which an invaluable survey was made of the lands of Hyde. Elizabeth I had been on the throne for nine years.

By 1567 Kingston had lived through Mary's attempt at counter-reformation in its own way. What this entailed for the village is unclear, but we may guess that the times were insecure and tense. The area of East Sussex around Lewes was firmly Protestant, indeed, if anything, inclined to be Puritan. Lewes was one of the towns Mary chose for an exemplary burning of 14 people whose obstinate adherence to Henry VIII's church was a threat to her policies. Kingston of course knew of this horror and people from the village probably stood in the old market in Lewes to watch the executions. For the most part rural people held their peace in the face of such events and waited for better times. Elizabeth's accession no doubt was a welcome relief for them. How then did the village appear at the outset of the great Elizabethan age?

First, there were the manors. By this time – indeed well before – the economic importance of the manor had diminished in ways already described. But how did these changes look from the village street? How had the relationship between the manors and the villagers changed from their point of view?

Long before, medieval Kingston villagers who were customary tenants of Swanborough Manor, or any other, had felt the economic weight of that relationship in no uncertain terms. The feudal rents, which originated in the commutation of labour service, were a significant burden on most family incomes. The differences between freehold tenancy, with its formal obligations to a small rent of assize, and customary tenancy, with these larger rents as well as other 'feudal incidents', were marked. By Tudor times this was changing and certainly by Elizabeth's reign the change was radical. There was of course no more servility. For all practical purposes villeinage had gone even if, as Dobb points out, the House of Lords rejected a bill to free villeins as late as 1537.[29] But, more to the point, because the old medieval rents were mostly fixed in money terms, the weight of feudal rents on customary tenants or copyholders diminished as the prices of agricultural goods rose and as the profitability of the land increased. By the middle of the sixteenth century the incidence of these old rents was so low in Kingston that the differences between freeholders paying only rent of assize and copyholders with their extra manorial burdens was small, so small as to be negligible. It is true, as Tawney strongly argued,[30] that copyholders might have had less security of tenure than freeholders, and manor lords with ambitions for larger farms could exploit this; it is true also that lords were able in some instances to increase the fines on entry, and other payments like heriots, in partial compensation for the declining value of their manorial rights, but there are no obvious signs of such feudal reassertions in Kingston.

These changes had a number of effects on village life, but one in particular is significant here. As time passed by, the importance of the manors to village society lay much less in the power of manor lords to control directly the economic destinies of people and much more in the fact that manors had large demesne lands attached to them. These lands formed the basis for big farms, or became the holdings of gentry and yeomen, who came to live among the copyholders and independent husbandmen of the village itself. Seen from the village street in Kingston, the manors were important mostly because they were the centres of the biggest landholdings in the parish and only secondarily as seats of power.

One consequence of this shift in focus was that, as the sixteenth century passed by, the relative importance of Kingston Manor and the demesnes of Hyde grew in terms of their immediate impact on the shape of village society compared with Swanborough. Swanborough's earlier dominance had been feudal – derived from the old system of relationships. Kingston and Hyde on the other hand had demesnes in the village fields. They became the centre of operations for the largest landholders in the village and that, by Elizabeth's reign, was a more important social fact than ancient feudal privilege and a villager's obligations to pay homage at the manor court. The lord of Swanborough Manor became more distant, less relevant to daily life than in the not so remote past, although, as we shall see later, events at Swanborough were to play a central part in Kingston's history from time to time.

Swanborough Manor passed briefly to the Earl of Arundel after the dissolution of the priory. In 1557, Arundel relinquished it and the king and queen – Philip and Mary – admitted John Caryll to the lordship. Caryll was a Catholic, but in all other respects the family was typical of the rapidly rising gentry of the Tudor period. Their wealth may have been partly based on land, but it was also drawn from new opportunities for professional advancement in London. John Caryll's father had been a 'serjant at law' – a barrister of high rank, the kind of person for whom there was much work and wealth to be got from it in litigious times.[31] His son put this wealth into land, as was sensible and proper at the time. John Caryll lived in Warnham in the Sussex Weald where he had a manor house. He held manors and land all over Sussex as well as in Suffolk and Hampshire,[32] and settled down as a country gentleman while his brother Richard pursued a commercial career as a mercer in London. For Caryll, Swanborough was one manor among many. It was left, with his other properties, to his grandson John, who was then nine years old (in 1566). The executor of his will, Edward Caryll, was asked to use part of the income from Swanborough for the 'upkeep of the manor house at Warnham',[33] perhaps indicating Caryll's priorities and attachment to his Sussex home.

In 1567 then, the lord of Swanborough Manor was a ten-year-old boy who played in the gardens at Warnham and did his lessons. He was in the guardianship of his uncle. A tenant farmer cultivated the demesnes of Swanborough, far away from the centre of their lives; we do not know who he was, but most probably he was from one of the larger families at Iford. A steward held the manor courts where customary tenants from Kingston paid homage for their yardlands. The small feudal rents from Kingston lands and the large commercial rents from the privileged demesnes helped to keep the house at Warnham in its accustomed splendour, but Kingston saw little or nothing of its new lord.

The little boy grew up to become John Caryll, Esquire, a gentleman. He was in his time a quite substantial gentleman too. Years later, in 1588 as England and Elizabeth faced the prospect of the Armada, the queen sought loans from Sussex gentry 'for the better withstanding of the intended invasion of this Realm, upon the general preparations made by the King of Spain'. Among the larger loans there was one for £100 from John Caryll.[34] Recusant or not, Caryll naturally did his part to keep an alien monarch out of England. He died at Warnham in 1614.[35] He had, however, relinquished his lordship of Swanborough long before. In 1584, when he had come of age and was managing his own affairs, Swanborough was sold to Thomas Sackville, the first Baron Buckhurst, subsequently the first earl of Dorset.[36]

Though the Carylls only held Swanborough for 27 years, their accession was a sign of the changes that came in Tudor times. Consider the succession to Swanborough in the two busy decades after 1537. In that time the manor had passed from the ancient feudal lordship of the prior of St Pancras, through Cromwell's grasp, then to the Arundels, who were as representative as any family of the old aristocracy, and so to the Carylls, new gentry. The

Carylls brought rich skimmings from London's mercantile wealth back to the profitable countryside. But they were not the only representatives of change: the Sackvilles at a higher social level (they were distantly related to the queen) had also newly risen in power and position. Baron Buckhurst was among the comparatively small group of peers Elizabeth created and also, as it happened, the start of a long family line.[37] Swanborough was to remain in Dorset lordship – always as absentees – for more than two centuries. The demesnes were firmly committed to tenancy.

Changes in the lordship at Swanborough after the dissolution had little immediate effect on life in Kingston. As ever, the manor court claimed homage from its Kingston tenants. And, in the old way of manor courts, it administered the resolution of village disputes, creating or calling on precedent in village by-law. So, for example, in 1585 the court required the lord himself, Thomas Sackville no less, to 'mend his fences with John Howell', a customary tenant whose family name had figured prominently in the village in the time of Henry VIII. And, in 1580, Gregory Ade was licensed to 'pull down posts and rails of a certain customary fence between his property and that of Peter Towner, to remake it'. And the court claimed its rents no matter how small and gave instructions for the upkeep of customary property: in 1580 the bailiff was ordered to distrain John Eversfield, a gentleman, for a rent of 12 hens due on three yards of land four years in arrears; later John Barnden agreed to pay a similar rent for two and a half yards of land, again four years in arrears; and Agnes Howell, a widow, was ordered to repair her customary house in Kingston against a penalty of 10s.[38] The court was no respecter of persons in such matters. Barnden was a substantial local yeoman, Eversfield one of the larger landowners in East Sussex and Agnes Howell a poor lady of the village. But in all these matters the manor court was following its usual ways, undisturbed and in substance unchanged by the new lordship. For the moment Swanborough's impact in the village was limited simply because the manor held little or no land directly in the village fields.

The post-dissolution changes in lordship at Kingston Manor, however, had more immediate implications. When the manor passed briefly to Sir Richard Lee in 1546, it consisted of a substantial amount of Kingston property in demesnes. There were five messuages, of which one was the large house at the head of the street. The arable consisted of 150 customary acres or about 18 per cent of the land in the open fields, and attached to it were 20 acres of meadow, 30 acres of marsh and common of pasture for 400 sheep on the Downs. The land lay mainly in Kingston, but there were some outlying bits, mostly pasture in Balsdean.[39] These were the lands that John Crane bought from Lee for £150 in 1546. He moved into the village with his wife Joan and Richard their son to become the lord of the manor, and surely the most important single person in the village. Kingston Manor had transformed from a distant lordship and a tenant farmer to the new lord who had weight in village decisions about cultivation in the open fields.

In their own way, the Cranes were just as much the product of Tudor times as the Carylls. They were yeoman farmers who had attained a degree of success above the average. In 1524 the family had been centred at Southease, a village to the south of Rodmell: Thomas Crane, probably father to John, was assessed at £3 in the subsidy.[40] A branch of the family clearly remained in these more southern parts, for in 1552 a John Crane – not the one who had settled in Kingston – died in Piddinghoe, a village on the banks of the Ouse a mile or two from the coast.[41] But the Kingston Cranes stayed on at the manor house for the greater part of Elizabeth's reign. John died in 1555.[42] His son Richard inherited the manor but had no chance at all to enjoy his lordship; he died about a year later, leaving the manor to his infant son Peter aged three, and no doubt in the guardianship of his mother.[43] So in the early years of Elizabeth's reign there were two manors in Kingston in the lordship of minors: while rich little John Caryll grew up at Warnham, Peter Crane, not so rich but a little older, was growing up in Kingston. Peter was granted lordship of the manor in 1575 at his majority: there is a warrant from the crown to the Sussex escheater in that year.[44]

Peter Crane married Joan, a daughter of the powerful Newton family, who had moved from Cheshire in the time of Henry VIII and taken up residence at the priory.[45] He stayed on at his manor in Kingston until 1594, when it was sold to the same Thomas Sackville who had taken over Swanborough Manor from the Carylls in 1584.[46]

In these years at Kingston Manor the Cranes made their modest contribution to the 'rebuilding of England'. The Elizabethan house hiding behind its high flint walls at the head of the village street dates from their times. It was built to suit their manorial lordship and, perhaps also, to measure up to the status implicit in a marriage to the Newton family. It made copious use of stone from the ruined priory, which had by that time come into the possession of Joan Crane's parents, and, full of priory stone, it remains the largest Elizabethan building in the village – though not perhaps the most beautiful. It is still called Kingston Manor House.

The dissolution of the monasteries had opened the way to these new Tudor lordships at Swanborough and Kingston manors. As far as Houndean and Iford manors were concerned, this abrupt redistribution of landed property left them largely unaffected. Houndean, which held some freehold yardlands in Kingston, continued in the divided lordship of Bergavenny and Norfolk, and remained so for the whole of Elizabeth's reign.[47] Iford remained in the Lewknor family until the death of Sir Roger Lewknor in 1543. Thereafter, the manor appears to have been divided between his two daughters, Katherine and Constance. These moieties followed complicated successions,[48] which did not have immediate bearing on events in Kingston.

On the other hand, the succession of ownership on the old knight's fee of Hyde did affect Kingston. Hyde, in a different way from Swanborough and Kingston, seems to show up some of the assertiveness of new Elizabethan landholders. Successions on the lands called Hyde's are among the more teasing questions in the history of Kingston village. Hyde originated in the knight's fee, which the Earl de Warenne created in the early years after the conquest. It was the earl's concern to have his own man in the village that led, in the first place, to the division of Queen Eddid's old Saxon demesnes between a part that remained in his own hands – as Kingston Manor – and a part that was divided off and passed to the de Kyngeston family. From them it went to the de la Hydes and then on through medieval years to other families.[49]

At some point in its Tudor history this ancient parcel of Kingston strips came into the possession of John de la Chambre of Rodmell.[50] De la Chambre was in line of succession of an old 'gentle' family in East Sussex, which had held the manor of Eastbourne for a number of generations. He lived at Rodmell and held lands there, and at some point in his later life he appears to have purchased the Rodmell manor, which had passed through the medieval de Rademeld family to Weyville. He also succeeded in his father's lands in Laughton – lying to the east of Lewes. The de la Chambres were linked by marriage in the sixteenth and seventeenth centuries to Sussex gentry like the Scrases, the Newtons and the Culpepers.[51]

It is unclear how John de la Chambre came by the lands of Hyde. They were neither inherited nor in the entail in his father's will, so he must have bought them. He was entered as juror at the court of the barony of Lewes 'for lands in Kingston-near-Lewes called le Hide'.[52] Perhaps he bought them for his daughter Jane on the occasion of her marriage to Thomas Michell. Michell and Jane took occupation of the land in 1567 and John de la Chambre specified that he had leased these lands to his daughter and son-in-law for their lives, to be sold only after their deaths.[53]

Henceforth, this Thomas Michell appeared as a major landowner in Kingston. He was the elder son of the cadet branch of a substantial Sussex yeoman family based mainly at Cuckfield to the north of Lewes. His Cuckfield cousins inherited large manorial properties,[54] which had been in the family for long generations. And, though he himself acquired a considerable amount of land in Cuckfield,[55] it may be that the sense of being a comparatively less advantaged relative stayed with him through his life. At all events, when he and Jane de la Chambre moved into the lands of Hyde in Kingston, he had them surveyed and that survey shows signs of a pretension that spilt over into deceit. The heading reads as follows: 'A Survey of the Manor of Hyde in Kingston by Lewes, now the inheritance of Thomas Michell, gent: son and heir of Mary Michell deceased daughter and heire of … taken the XXVI the day of May in the ninth year of the Reign of our Sovereign Lady Queen Elizabeth by the said Thomas.'[56]

There are oddities about the way this is put: on the one hand Thomas calls himself son and heir of Mary Michell, which he no doubt was, but this is put in juxtaposition to the description of Hyde as 'now the inheritance of Thomas Michell, gent'. The natural interpretation is that he had inherited the lands of

Hyde from his mother and it is fair to conclude that Thomas meant the heading to be seen in that way. It was, of course, misleading. Hyde had come to him through his marriage; it was not by any stretch of the imagination an 'inheritance'; it was a lease for life; it had nothing to do with the fact that Michell was son and heir to Mary. It is as if Thomas had found a form of words that did not quite make the false assertion, that preserved the bare bones of truth but that nevertheless contrived to convey an impression he wanted people to have, but that was false. We may wonder whether the Kingston yeomen who witnessed the survey – 'Thomas Michell, John Barnden, Richard Martyn, John Bowrer and others' were taken in – for it was presumably they among others whom Michell set out to impress.

They might have been more surprised to find Hyde described as a manor. That, as far as one can tell, had never been done before and it may be that solid John Barnden and the others shared a grin or two to discover a new manor in their midst. True, the claim was not entirely outrageous. It did not offend, for example, against the rules of the game as set out by early Jacobean lawyers:

> For should any man at this day alott and appoint out any competent quantity of land, and divide the same into desmeasnes and tenement lands ... and perfecting the rest which ... is said to belong unto a mannor, yet will all this not make a mannor, for it is the office of time by long continuance to make and create the same.[57]

That Rathbone, the Stuart lawyer, should have perceived the need to write this down suggests that other men than Thomas Michell were pretending to manorial lordship by means of real deceits. Hyde at least was a demesne of long antiquity; although it had no customary yardlands, there were other manors that had none and were no less manors for that. So it was not a large deceit to call Hyde a manor. It offended only against the fact that it had never been a manor before – neither in Kingston minds nor in papers and documents that described it. Michell's ascription did not meet the criterion of 'long continuance', for there had not been long continuance in calling the 'lands called Hyde's' a manor. However, the ascription met his need to claim a lordship. Perhaps the heading on his survey was as much intended to impress his Cuckfield relatives as anyone else!

Thomas Michell was neither the first nor the last Englishman to embellish simple economic success with the accoutrements of feudal status. And, because he was at such pains to have his survey, he left behind him an invaluable record of village lands. And not the least of his record was the account it contained of his 'manor house':

> The site of the said Manor:
>
> Inprimis the Mannor Howse by a Hall of the old Buildinge and other

> old Howsinge on the West End of the said Hall: And on the East end of the said Hall a Parlor and a Buttery newly builded ... with Glasse Windowes: There is more a Kytchinge on the Sowthe Syde of the said Hall with Howses of Basement in the same with a lyttele Court betweene the Hall and Kytchin: Also there is a Gate Howse on the East Syde of the said Howse: and on the Sowth and West partes is an Herbery inclosed adjoining to the said Howse: Item, there is also two Barnes of Stawle and a Stable on the North and Est syde of the said Howse: And an Inner Close betweene the said Howse Barnes Stawle and Stable: – And an outter Close lyinge on the North Syde of the said Barnes: The which outter Close lyeth on this wise ... it adjoineth to the Lands of John Barnden on the West and to half an Acre of Land of Newtons of Lewes on the Est which half Acre of Newtons lyeth to the West Layne on the North and to the Highe leading through the Town of Kingston on the Sowth.[58]

For all its charm, this is a complicated and in some ways confusing description. It is confusing chiefly because it describes a house lying on the north side of the street: that much is plain from the description of the abutment to Newton lands. If Newton lands ran down to the street at the south, then obviously, the land on which the 'manor house' itself stood must also have the street on its southward border. The confusion comes in because the house that is called Hyde Manor House today lies on the *other side* of the street – to the south in other words. Figure 6.1 shows how the modern Hyde Manor House is placed on the site of of the house owned by Thomas Rogers.

But, an exploration of this copy from the Marchant map of 1773 also shows where exactly the house described in Thomas Michell's pretentious survey was sited. It must have been on the site marked 'k' lying on the north side of the street. There are three reasons for this. First, this site shows precisely the configuration of three closed areas lying each to the north of the other and abutting the street to the south, as the description of 1567 sets out, and it is the only site on the north side of the street in 1773 that meets this description. Second, and perhaps most telling, this site was owned in 1773 by a Mrs Norton[59] and it is clearly established that Mrs Norton held what had come to be called 'the manor of Hyde' at that time.[60] And third, there is the evidence of the buildings that remain on the site: despite much building in recent years, the remnant buildings fit in with the description of 1567. The large building shown in Marchant's map of 1773 in the first closed area abutting the street still stands today. At first glance, it appears to consist of three pretty cottages – charming in their tile-hung way, but not especially distinguished. But at a closer look, and especially a look inside, it is clear that this is a building of some importance. It is splendidly timbered internally, in heavy and beautifully carpentered oak. At its northern end is a large inglenook leading to an elegant Tudor chimneypiece, all of which is heavy in priory stone,

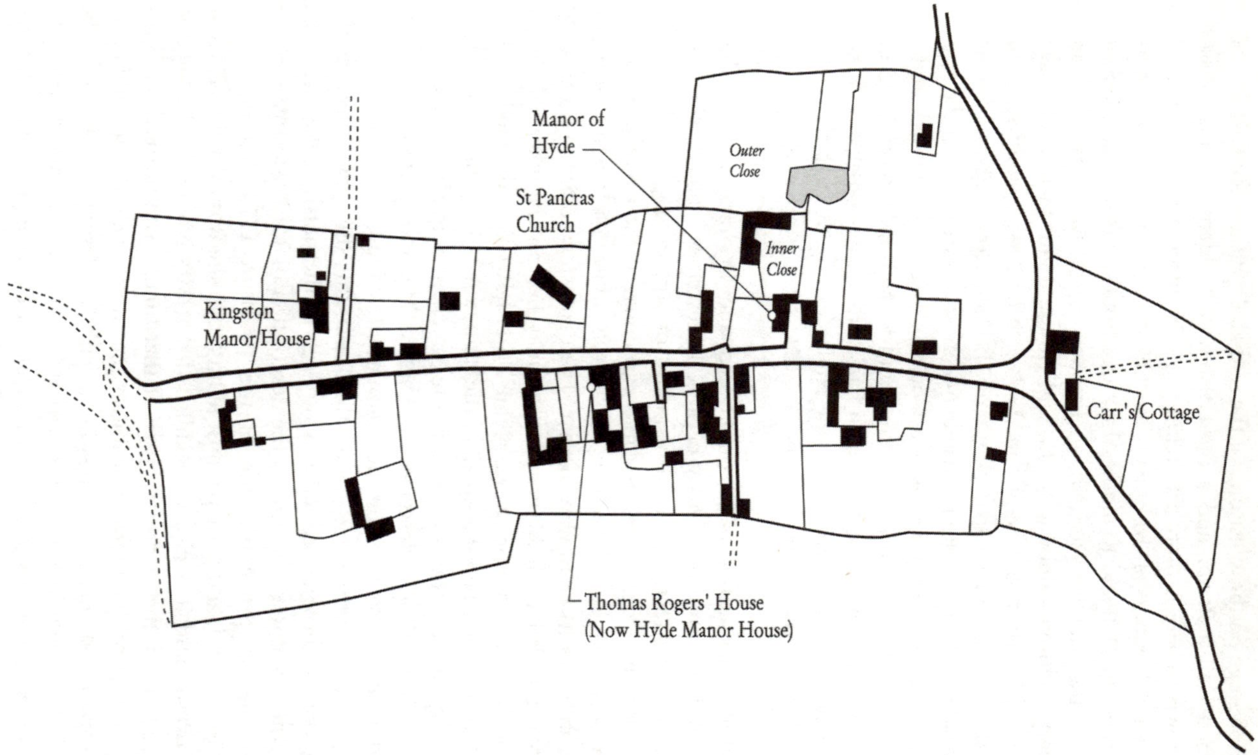

Figure 6.1: Kingston Street, 1879, showing the location of the house of T. Rogers

so heavy that it must have been constructed while such stone was still readily available in the years immediately following Portinari's destruction. It is clear that the cottages are a later addition and that this indeed is Thomas Michell's 'parlor and buttery newly builded' of 1567.

The buildings that stood in the second close (to the north) until quite recently also fitted the Elizabethan description. Within living memory there were stalls and stables all around the close and until some ten years ago there was a splendid barn in exactly the position shown by Marchant and required to fit Thomas Michell's description. It was pulled down, sadly, to make way for an undistinguished modern house.

From the survey description of 1567 and the map of 1773 it is possible to reconstruct the ground plan of Michell's 'manor house'. The 'Old Hall', which was most likely a medieval building and the centre of the house, has since disappeared. So have the old buildings on the west. But these, together with the kitchens and 'Houses of Easement' lying along the street, formed the 'Lyttele Court' of which Michell speaks. The inner close, where a man on horseback might dismount and hand his horse over to the groom, lay behind the house, set off by the great barn and closed in by 'stawles'. Behind that again there was a closed field, large enough to use occasionally as a paddock for riding animals and giving on to the wide sweep of strip lands in the West Laine. John Barnden's land lay down one side and Newtons of Lewes down the other. The complicated description of 1567 unravels rather well when it is set in this little group of closes taken from Marchant's map.

So, here is yet another mystery about Hyde Manor. The evidence from Michell's survey and from deeds and extant building is unambiguous, showing that the 'manor house' further down the street, which is called Hyde today and which had that name in the nineteenth century also, is something of an impostor. It is not the old manor house and there is, as we shall see, independent evidence to confirm this.[61] There is a roving manor house in Kingston. As it turns out, the moving of Hyde manor house, which happened much later on, was itself a revealing event in the later history of the village. It is a climax in the story of Kingston in the eighteenth century.

Michell's 'manor house' of 1567 was, along with the reconstructed Kingston Manor House at the head of the street, a focal point in the village. Although it is not possible to be certain it is likely that this place, particularly the 'old hall', which is mentioned in the survey, had been the main dwelling associated with the knight's fee from the very beginning – therefore probably the de Kyngestons' house and, after them, the Hydes'. In all those medieval centuries when Kingston Manor was run by a steward of de Warenne, or a tenant farmer of the Earl of Arundel or of the hospital of the Holy Trinity, this old Hyde property had been the home of the man who held the knight's fee, the most powerful family in the village. Its present superficially nondescript appearance belies the importance it had in the minds of medieval and Tudor people in the village. Michell's claim to manorial power might be an exaggeration, but there is no doubt about the powerful associations of the place he made his home.

Thomas Michell held the nine yardlands of Hyde – the demesnes of his newfound manor. He also held strips of land, mostly 'gardens', in the street and at least two houses, which he listed as part of his demesnes and which were most probably leased by wage-earning families.

Michell enjoyed his manor, and whatever grandeur it gave him, to a ripe age. He died nearly sixty years after taking possession, in 1624.[62] He and Jane lived both in Kingston and on their Cuckfield lands, for he was always 'Thomas Michell of Kingston and Cuckfield'. Jane outlived him and even married again – to Stephen Ridge of a wealthy yeoman family in Iford. She probably died in 1630 when, in accordance with the will of her father, the property reverted to the de la Chambre family. John, the father, was dead, of course, and Hyde passed to his surviving and ageing daughters or their descendants: Mary, Ann and Elizabeth. It was sold to John Alchorne, Ann's son, for £1000 and remained in the Alchorne family for the next 150 years.[63] Over those long years the property seems to have decayed. When it passed in the latter part of the eighteenth century to Mrs Norton, an Alchorne descendant, the grand house Thomas Michell described had mostly gone. All that remained was the existing wing, the part that had been built in Tudor times with the help and reinforcement of priory stone from Caen. Michell's Kingston glory had decisively departed and, however well it might have served his purposes, his 'manor' was something of a relic. It was to be revived much later by another man of equivalent social ambition, and for rather similar motives. But even then the old house, which had been such a focus of Kingston village life for so many centuries, was never brought back to its former centrality. With the passage of time it became a line of cottages. Where de Kyngestons had ruled the roost and ruled the village too, ordinary working people came to live in the midst of Tudor beams. But in his lifetime – for the whole of Elizabeth's reign and for a whole decade of Stuarts – the old 'Hyde Manor House' served Michell well enough.

So much for the manors, for in Elizabeth's time manor lords were not the only power in the land. The landlord class had grown over many centuries. Its first emanation was the early emergence of men who built up empires of lands in many manors in the early thirteenth century in Kingston. By Elizabethan times, investment in land and landlordism on large and small scales was in many ways a more important aspect of *economic* organization in rural life than manorial lordship. The landlord class had spread out to embrace many different kinds of people. The accumulation of lands was a natural outlet for the economically successful, especially in the sixteenth century when land profitability was increasing fairly consistently. Manorial lords and successful yeomen built up lands or took over the land empires of their medieval forbears; urban merchants and families who accumulated wealth in new industries like textiles or iron-making brought their money back to the land.

In early Tudor times, in 1524 for example when the subsidy was taken, it is difficult to identify the landlords of Kingston. They are as it were behind the scenes. By Elizabethan times they were much more evident.

Among the largest individual landlords in the immediate vicinity of the village were, of course, the manor lords themselves: Caryll, for example, who leased out the Swanborough demesnes and, as it happens, Thomas Michell who never cultivated the demesnes of Hyde himself but 'farmed' them out to a tenant, Thomas Howell.[64] And, though the Cranes always worked the 15 yardlands of demesnes in Kingston on their own account, they had lands elsewhere in East Sussex, which they leased out. There is no line of distinction to be drawn between families who had manorial lordships and were landlords too and those who were simply landlords. Landlordism had spread out to include a whole segment of the economically strong.

Aside from the manor lords then, there were other substantial absentee landlords from Kingston who had bought their way into the freehold and copyhold yardlands in the village open fields.

The Eversfields were the largest Kingston landlords outside the manorial demesnes during the Elizabethan period. They were an economically powerful family with lands in many parts of Sussex.[65] Their centre was at Fletching, where they held the manor of Torrying Peverell. It was the Eversfields' good fortune that their manor lands contained iron ore. Their considerable wealth was derived in good part from the boom in the Wealden iron industry, which lasted through most of the sixteenth century: the Weald had the richest ores then known in England and abundant supplies of wood for ordinance.[66] With these ingredients the Eversfields accumulated capital that went back into the land and a knighthood to embellish their wealth. Kingston was one of many places in which they chose to buy land.

The first record of the family in Kingston comes from 1553. Nicholas Eversfield died in that year and in the 'post-mortem inquisition' he is shown as owning 'lands in Kingston-near-Lewes'.[67] They passed to his son John who was in possession in 1567 when Thomas Michell burst upon the village scene so full of enthusiasm and pretension. John Eversfield died in 1595 after more than fifty years as a Kingston landlord and the lands went, in turn, to his son Thomas.

The Eversfields engrossed lands in the Kingston open fields. They started, in the 1530s perhaps, with six yardlands called Peake's, which were held by Houndean Manor and which had been brought together in the first place by a freeholder of Houndean called Bannester or by one of his predecessors.[68] To these six yardlands, an Eversfield – most likely John who had taken over the estate in 1553 – added another six, taken this time from the lands of Swanborough Manor. By the 1580s, John Eversfield was in possession of that group of yardlands villagers called 'Alfreye's' – after the landlord of the fourteenth century[69] – and there is some evidence that Eversfield had bought these lands from two independent yeomen,[70] so reducing the number of separate landholdings in the open fields. At all events, when Michell took his survey of Hyde in 1567,[71] the Eversfields owned about 12 yardlands – an area of open-field strips nearly equal to that held by the very young lord of Kingston Manor in his demesnes. Forty years later John Rowe recorded that Eversfield was the owner of 12 yards of land in the village.[72]

By Kingston standards 12 yardlands constituted a large landholding and, in so far as the Eversfields leased them out to a single farmer, the basis for a big tenancy. With a fixed area in the open fields, one could only create a big tenancy by reducing the numbers of smaller ones and that, we must presume, is what the Eversfields did. Even though they may from time to time have divided their yardlands into more than one tenancy, they nevertheless contributed to the general transformation of the village from a place of small tenants and yeomen to a place of fewer bigger farmers and more wage workers without much land of their own. The Eversfields were neither the first nor the last agents of this transformation. In later centuries other men would build on the foundations they had laid.

Other Kingston landlords belonged to families just as powerful as, or more so than, the Eversfields, but they held less Kingston land. Culpepper was a weighty name in Sussex. The Culpeppers were a vastly wealthy 'gentle' family based mainly at East Grinstead. Like the Eversfields they held lands in villages all over Sussex. They were manor lords, landlords and held the advowsons of village churches, which might be the envy of men qualifying for the new Elizabethan clergy in their Oxford colleges. In Kingston, the Culpeppers of Wakehurst held 'certain lands called Culpeppers lands'.[73] There were perhaps four yardlands,[74] a mere speck in the Culpepper empire but a fair sized tenancy for Kingston, and a name of enough importance for villagers to attach it to the lands for more than a century. By 1567 though, the Culpeppers had sold out. The Newtons of Lewes, a comparatively new family to Sussex whose daughter married Peter Crane later on, bought their yardlands and attached two more to them that they had acquired from a yeoman family called the Skinners.[75]

The Newtons came from Cheshire and were a younger branch of the family from which the great Sir Isaac later descended.[76] William Newton settled, as we have seen, at the old prior's lodge in Southover in 1544. Some 15 years later he purchased the lands and house called East Mascalls in Lindfield. A little after that the poor Newtons decided they had had enough of the prior's lodge. It was cold, draughty, somewhat derelict and, however well adapted it might have been in earlier times to the life-styles of successive priors, it was unsuitable for the needs of an Elizabethan family. In 1572, therefore, William Newton set about building a new house. He obtained the right to use very large amounts of priory stone, which were still readily available, and he used it to build a splendid house set amid gardens along the little Winterbourne stream in Southover. This was Southover Grange – still one of the beauties of Lewes and in many ways a quite unique structure, for Newton built an

Elizabethan country house in town. The family lived between East Mascalls, which lies quite close to Cuckfield, and the new Southover Grange. East Mascalls was, of course, the centre of their rural life, but it is not at all surprising that they should have come to hear of yardlands for sale in Kingston, just down the road from Southover, or that they should have bought out 'Culpep's Lands'. This they did and, by bringing them together with the two yardlands the Skinners had owned, created a single 'farm' of six yardlands. The Newtons made their modest contribution to the engrossment of the open fields.

Eversfields, Culpeppers and Newtons were among the grander and richer Sussex gentry. Along with the Carylls, these families made contributions to the loan the queen raised among Sussex gentry to finance her defences against the threatened invasion by Philip of Spain.[77] But there were less grand Kingston landlords not numbered in these august ranks. The Skinners, for example, held two Kingston yardlands before 1567. They were a yeoman family based in villages near Eastbourne;[78] one branch of Skinners, the Kingston landlords, had established themselves in Balmer by 1524 and took part in the gradual extension of that village's pasturelands.[79] The Shoesmiths held two yardlands in Kingston in the early 1580s.[80] Shoesmiths had legitimate claims to be regarded as gentry. They had a coat of arms and a pedigree, which could be traced to 1387 on lands near Laughton to the east of Lewes.[81] But, in terms of the fine distinctions of the sixteenth and seventeenth century, the Shoesmiths were yeomen regardless of the appropriateness of the label; they were not a hugely wealthy family in, say, the Culpepper tradition. And, last but not least, the Hardmans held four yardlands in Kingston at the beginning of Elizabeth's reign. The Hardmans were local yeomanry based at Falmer and Balmer where their tax assessments in 1524 and 1525 indicate a considerable degree of economic success, perhaps the outcome of growing flocks on the Downs at Balmer, where the village itself was in decay.

All in all these absentee landlords of Elizabethan Kingston are a fair cross section of the kind of people who did well out of the changes of the time. Kingston had its iron-master landlord (Eversfield) and had grand landlords whose wealth came from urban power and commerce as much as from the land (Culpeppers and Newtons). It also had its powerful yeoman landlord in Robert Hardman of Falmer who, it is fair to guess, had done his bit towards the depopulation of neighbouring villages in the Downs and the replacement of men with sheep. And it is possible to detect the contributions these landlords made to the enlargement of tenancies in the village during the sixteenth century: the Eversfields by bringing together 12 yardlands into a single farm, displacing three or four tenancies with one or two; the Newtons on an altogether smaller scale by combining Culpepper's lands with Skinner's to make a farm of six yardlands where there had been two before. These landlords were not much concerned about whether the land they held was freehold or copyhold. It is true that the greater part of Eversfield's was freehold; in fact the family had taken up virtually all the Kingston freehold lands by 1580 or so. But the Culpeppers, Skinners, Newtons, Shoesmiths and Hardmans were pleased enough to hold copyhold lands, in effect to be 'customary tenants' of the various manors in the village and to pay homage at the manor courts as feudal ritual required. This in its way is a measure of the changes that had come about – a sign that wealth in lands was now far more important than manorial status as such. No stigma attached to a Culpepper who became a tenant on lands that had once been servile; what mattered more was to have possession of land and the commercial rent it would yield. The landlords cared little about how their new farms related to the manors. Eversfield's 12 yardlands were divided equally between Houndean Manor and Swanborough Manor. For Eversfield that mattered not at all; what mattered was to find a good tenant farmer capable of making a profit and paying rent without default.

But for all the importance of the landlords, Kingston was by no means reduced to a village of landlord and tenant. The forces that had helped to preserve the integrity of the open fields against incursion from pastoral production probably also helped to create and maintain a space in village lands for independent landholders – a village yeomanry with their own considerable importance in the way Kingston evolved. These were the large and small peasants of Kingston, mostly customary tenants of the various manors. Table 6.1 shows the place they held in the open fields in the early years of Elizabeth.

It is clear from the table that in 1567 or so about half the lands in the open fields were held by what we might call owner-occupiers – families who held the land they worked as freeholders or copyholders and owed no landlord rent. If the old demesnes are excluded (the lands of Kingston Manor and the Hyde) the proportion of the ordinary freehold and copyhold in owner-occupation is a little lower than half. This pattern of 1567 is probably not greatly different from the pattern of 1524 in its broad outline: the main change is the demesnes of Kingston Manor, which had been tenant farmed in 1524 before the dissolution but were held in 1567 by the Crane family who worked them directly. Otherwise, the overall distribution of yardlands between those worked on tenancies to landlords and those worked by 'owner-occupiers' was much as in Henrician times.

But though the broad distributions of the yardlands between these categories had not changed much, there had been some marked changes in the landholding patterns *within* each category. Some of these, notably the reductions in the number of tenancies available because of the formation of larger farms by the new landlords, have been discussed. It is clear though that, alongside the changes in the organization of the lands held by landlords, there had also been changes in the pattern of landholding among the independent landholders. For one thing only a few of the names from the 1524 subsidy list appear among the 'families on their own lands' in Table 6.1: the

Howells, the Picombes and the a Moores (others of 1524 may of course have been among the tenants to Kingston landlords but they cannot be traced). For

Table 6.1: Landholding in Kingston open-fields, circa 1560–70[82]

Landholders	*No. of yardlands*	*Notes on manorial ascription*
A. Landlords		
1. Eversfield	12	6 yards Swanborough freehold 6 yards Houndean freehold Alfrey's and Peake's
	1–2	Kingston copyhold
2. Michell	9	Demesne of Hyde
3. Newton of Lewes	6	Copyholds of Swanborough, formerly Skinner and Culpepper
4. Robert Hardman	4	Copyholds of Swanborough
5. Elizabeth Shoesmith	2	Probably copyholds of Swanborough
6. Caryll	1–2	Ex-priory lands
B. Families on their own lands		
7. Crane	12	Demesnes of Kingston Manor
8. Gregory Ade	6	4 yards Swanborough – Taylor's 2 yards Iford – Bishop's all copyhold
9. Picombe	4	Iford copyhold called Hudd's
10. Barnden	3	Swanborough copyhold
11. Coppard	3	Swanborough copyhold
12. Bowrer	2	Swanborough copyhold
13. Towner	1–2	Houndean freehold
14. Wolridge	2	Iford copyhold called 'Taberers'
15. Adams	1½	Swanborough copyhold
16. Robert Howell	½–1	Swanborough copyhold
17. Thomas Howell	1	Probably Kingston copyhold
18. A Moore	1	Swanborough copyhold
19. Boniface⁺	2½	Swanborough copyhold

⁺ Antecedents on this land cannot be traced

another, there are new names, new copyholders with quite substantial lands, who, had they been present in 1524, would most certainly have appeared on the list of taxpayers: the Ades, Barndens, Coppards, Bowrers, Towners and Wolridges, of whom the Ades and Barndens were the largest. And it would seem also, that the incursion of some of these newer yeoman families as owner-occupiers had in a comparatively modest way resulted in a certain amount of engrossment quite independently of the engrossments by the landlords of other lands. The Ades in particular had put together a large holding of six yardlands, displacing at least two earlier owner-occupiers and possibly more; the Barndens and Coppards may well have created their three-yardland holdings in the same way.

Of all these independent yeoman families, the Ades were the strongest economically in 1567, and were to remain a dominant Kingston family for the next two centuries. They were of considerable traceable antiquity and, interestingly, had always kept their roots in the Ouse valley. More than two centuries before their appearance as Kingston landholders, the Ade family was well established in Iford. In 1327 Thomas Ade was taxed in the early medieval subsidy; in 1332 he was taxed again (at 3/–) and a Juliana Ade also (at 2/4). The amounts they paid put them among the better off Iford families of the time – almost certainly freemen.[83] By 1524, when the Henrician subsidy was taken, there were no Ades in Iford, but they were among the largest taxpayers in Rodmell a few miles south, and there were four separate Ade families in that village at the time.[84] Rodmell had indeed been described as their village of origin.[85]

However, sometime after 1524, but well before Elizabeth's time, the Ades moved north from Rodmell. The main branch of the family became re-established initially at Iford, where they were to be for centuries: the long line of Ade graves in Iford churchyard attests to their solid economic achievements as well as to the size and robustness of their families. The Kingston Ades, headed by Gregory, were (as ever for Kingston) a cadet branch of the Iford family, but they moved into Kingston at much the same time as the main movement of the family from Rodmell.[86]

Gregory Ade, who bought the Swanborough copyhold yardlands called Taylor's and the Iford yardlands called Bishop's, set up his family home on properties lying at the corner of Kingston Street and Well Green Lane (see Figure 2.4). There, mingled with a house and barn of Peter Towner's and a house that came into Thomas Michell's ownership in 1567, the Ades built up their farmyards and settled down to work their 60 or 70 strips in the open fields. It was appropriate that they should guard the entrance to the street, for they were to be among its more constant inhabitants for the next two centuries.[87] In time they acquired Peter Towner's house and barn as well as Michell's house (which they probably leased in 1567), so they came to hold the whole stretch of property around this southward corner of the street. Today there is still a farmyard on the property, which the Ades bought from Towner (see later, also Figure 2.4), and the remnants of old stalls that were in all likelihood cattle sheds on the old farm. Gregory and his wife, later called 'Old Jane Ade', had come to found something of a yeoman dynasty in the village. They stood for a tradition that was not that old in the village itself, but was known as age-long to the villagers: the tradition of the independent yeoman who grew large; sometimes this happened through tenancy, seldom through landlordism, but nearly always through a tenacious attachment to his own lands, preserved through thick and thin with all the acumen at his command. At another level, and in another language, Ades were, in the peasant world of Elizabethan Kingston, part of a 'kulak' class, but probably never quite as exploitative of the misfortunes of their neighbours as their Russian counterparts.

The Barndens, who were also comparative newcomers to the village in the late 1560s, were very like the Ades. They too were an ancient family in the Ouse valley. Nearly three centuries before their arrival in Kingston there had been 'Berndons' in Rodmell village: Mabel and Reginald Berndon were taxed there in 1296 – and heavily too; Laurence and Reginald Berndon were in Rodmell in 1327 and 1332 and in those years there was a Jourdan Berndon in Rottingdean, along the coast to the west of modern Newhaven.[88] By that time too a William Berndon was to be found in Iford. By 1524 the Barndens were firmly established in Piddinghoe,[89] where they were taxed at rates commensurate with those paid by Ades in Rodmell. There was also a branch of the family in Southease, the little village just south of Rodmell: between 1555 and 1559 Richard, Thomas and Elizabeth Barnden died there leaving wills.[90] Elizabeth left substantial amounts to the 'high altar' and to the poor of Southease, Telescombe and Piddinghoe, as well as a 'barrel of malt' to the high altar at Piddinghoe church. By 1559 a somewhat less wealthy branch of the family had set up in Kingston: Richard Barnden died in the village in that year leaving 8d for the poor box and 20d for repairs to the church.[91] This Richard was probably the father of John Barnden who held land in the village by 1567, and was listed in the Swanborough court rolls in 1583 as agreeing to pay 6s for '12 hens' due on three virgates of lands 'late Picombes'.[92] The Barndens were set to occupy these lands in Kingston for nearly a century. It is clear though that they held the close lying next to the old 'manor house' of Hyde, where Thomas Michell brought his wife Jane de la Chambre – and it could be that they had a home nearby, if not on this site. The Barndens were successful and somewhat acquisitive yeomen: in 1589, there is a record of John Barnden of Kingston acquiring lands in Streat from Thomas a Moore of Telescombe.[93]

The other 'new' small copyholders of 1567 are more difficult to trace in detail. Richard Coppard held three yardlands. He was related to a Rodmell family (so again an immigrant from the southward villages in the Ouse valley).[94] The Coppards – and probably the Bowrers also – lived in a house near the village church, which has since disappeared.[95] The Bowrers, Towners and Wolridges cannot be traced. Wolridge occupied the house at the splendid farmyard called Taberers, halfway down the street on the south side.[96] The fine Sussex barn on the site today dates from his times at least. The Bowrers appear on the Kingston scene but disappear again. The Towners remained in the village; the family reappears as owners of various properties later on but there is no way of telling from where they had come. From the standpoint of influence, permanence and status in the village, the Ades and Barndens were the more important by far of the new owner-occupiers.

But what do we know of the older families? Howells, Picombes, Adams and a Moores, all of whom had been in the village in 1524, were still there in 1567 and later. They were independent copyholders. They were also preponderantly *small* landholders and, in this sense, representative of a somewhat older, late medieval and early Tudor Kingston.

The Adams, for example, held 1½ yardlands. They lived in the cottage at the crossroads of the street with Ashcombe Lane and Well Green Lane (see Figure 2.4),[97] which has a view straight down the street. They lingered on there until late in Elizabeth's reign.

The Howells had a somewhat grander Kingston pedigree. They had been a dominant village family as tenants of Hyde Manor before the dissolution of the monasteries, and in 1567 Thomas Howell remained as 'farmer' at Hyde after Michell took over the knight's fee on lease from John de la Chambre. By 1567 he had also acquired land on his own account and held a small amount of Kingston copyhold.[98] He was not the last Kingston tenant farmer to use the resources he had managed to accumulate through tenancy in order to purchase village land.

At the same time the Howells had proliferated. By 1567 Richard Howell, the son and heir of Thomas,[99] was in possession of an orchard opposite the Ade households on the northern corner of the street. And besides, Robert Howell, a brother of Thomas, had acquired a copyhold yardland of Swanborough Manor and also owned the lovely isolated cottage bordering on West Laine and lying to the north of the main village, which is called 'Shepherd's Rest' today.[100] This little cottage – of all the lands members of the Howell family held from time to time – was to remain the longest in their ownership. Some three centuries later an immediate descendant of the Howells was still in possession as the last small copyholder left in Kingston.

But, for all their longevity as a Kingston family, the Howells never quite achieved that grip on landholding that the Ades managed to acquire. When the Ades settled permanently in their yardlands and held onto them, the Howells, though ever present, came and went as landowners. It is as if the multiple branches of the Howell family were especially subject to fortune: moving from successful tenancy to the ownership of copyhold in the good times, and out of ownership into tenancy again in the bad. The signs of this instability were present even in 1567: by that date the Howells had relinquished the four copyhold yardlands of Iford Manor called Hudd's, which they had owned before.[101]

The Picombe family were similar to the Howells in more than one respect. They too had a substantial ancestry, if not in Kingston then in nearby Barcombe (see Chapter 5). Like the Howells, there were several branches of Picombes in the village even in 1524 (Table 5.1). And, just as Howells came and went from one piece of land to another, so did the Picombes. Prior to

1567, perhaps at the time of Henry VIII's subsidy, the Picombes held the three yardlands Barnden had taken over by the time of the Hyde Manor survey.[102] By 1567, the lands called 'Hudd's' were held by John Picombe and were to remain in the family through the seventeenth century,[103] but other pieces of Kingston land that came into their possession from time to time were apt to slip out of their grasp by sale or by inheritance through female lines of the family.

The a Moores, who held a single yardland in 1567, were perhaps representative of a type of small copyholder who had been more numerous in earlier Tudor times. They were, however, soon to disappear from the village altogether. In 1558 Thomas Howell was admitted to this yardland, which he had evidently bought from John a Moore.[104]

Beneath the independent copyholders, who occupied their own lands in the open fields, were those people who depended mainly on wages for their livelihood and who hardly shared at all in the prosperity that flowed from the generally high profits on land. Indeed, since the level of real wages fell for a century and a half after 1500, we must assume that labourers in Kingston as elsewhere drifted closer to impoverishment and the limits of subsistence as the decades passed by.

Who were the wage workers of Elizabethan times? Unfortunately, they left no direct records through which to trace them. We can only infer a few aspects of their lives from other sources. It seems that there were two distinct classes of people who sought to sell their labour to the tenant farmers and the larger independent copyholders.

In the first place, there were families who held cottages in their own right: people who had a dwelling, a garden and if they were fortunate an orchard or a very small parcel of arable land, and who owed nothing to a landlord but held directly from one or other of the manors. To judge from later deeds, there were five or six copyhold cottages in the village. Some of them stand today. The families who lived in them, though poor, were able to produce a little of their own subsistence. Consequently, even though they had to find wage labour to make ends meet they were at least protected against the harsh effects that flowed from the fact that the price of their labour fell in relation to the price of basic foods. No doubt, their cottages and orchards were cultivated to the limits of intensity. And some were supported against the worst effects of the falling real wage in another way, for it seems that among these independent cottagers were cadet relatives of economically stronger village families. The extended family still operated in rural England of those times; in really bad years, while more vulnerable people were at or below the limits of subsistence, this small minority could rely on uncles, aunts and cousins to ensure their survival. So, for example, Richard Howell held a cottage and orchard in 1567, and was most likely head of just such a family at the time, and it seems that there were also Picombe cottagers in the street.

Then there was a second group. Some Kingston cottages were held by manor lords in demesnes or as part of the property of the landlords. The Cranes at Kingston Manor, for example, held five cottages.[105] These were not independent copyholds at all; they were dwellings for domestic servants and labourers. Some of them still stand at the head of the street on the north side. They had very small gardens and there were, as far as we can tell, no arable lands or rights to pasture attached to them. And, at the head of the street on the south side there was another group of cottages, which are no longer there. These were part of Eversfield's lands. The tenant farmers to the Eversfields, the primary tenants as it were, could use these to house their workers.[106] The families who lived in them were subtenants – either explicitly if they paid a rent for their houses, or implicitly if there was some allowance made against wages. Their tenancies were evidently less secure than those of the 'customary' cottagers who held by copyhold of the manor. They were more dependent on their wages alone for subsistence and hence more vulnerable. They were less likely than the independent cottagers to have relatives among the yeomen in the village, and so more reliant on charity and goodwill rather than the sense of family obligation to see them through when times were bad. They were, in short, the poor of the village, the people for whom Elizabeth's law of 1576 made a compulsory levy on landowners and who were the most likely to land up in the village poorhouse. And, after the draconian legislation of earlier times, they may have seen the new law as a relief, at least a fair guarantee against starving in times of dearth.[107]

In its broad outlines this village society of Elizabeth's reign was not very different from what it had been in her father's reign. The basic structure of manorial lordships, rising landlords, tenant farmers, independent yeomen (some of whom might be tenants at the same time), cottagers and less privileged labourers was still in place. The outlines are clearer in 1567 than in 1524, but the picture itself was not that different.

A closer look, however, suggests changes in the finer structure of village society, which, though in themselves not much, were important for the future because they show the direction in which things were going.

The manor, as in Henry's time, was less important for feudal attributes of lordship than for the access it gave to demesne lands. Yet in Kingston, that most Tudor of all transformations, the dissolution of the monasteries had given a new importance to Kingston Manor. It had, circuitously, given access to the Cranes, a yeoman family suddenly turned into manorial lords who came to live in the village in the place of tenant farmers. The manor house at the head of the street was rebuilt to reflect its new status, or more correctly the new status of the Cranes. And in their wake came Thomas Michell with his de la Chambre bride, claiming manorial status too and filling the old house of Hyde with a new assertive presence, quite in keeping with the times. The Cranes, sequestered behind their high flint walls at the head of the street, and the Michells, coming and going between Kingston and Cuckfield – and filling the courtyards and the 'inner close' with their movements – were more dominant than their tenant predecessors had been. The village was a less humble place for their presence.

The landlords appear more clearly than before. They were natural successors to medieval estate builders: Kingston landlords like Culpepper, Eversfield, Newton and Caryll were among the greatest of the new Sussex gentry. At the same time they reflected the new sources of wealth and accumulation that opened up in Tudor times: the Eversfields made money out of iron, the Culpeppers out of the law as well as lands and merchandise, the Newtons were as much urban as rural, and Robert Hardman, a yeoman grown to landlordism, furthered his way by pastoral farming in Falmer and, most probably, contributed to the depopulation of Balmer in just the way that Thomas More deprecated so profoundly. Above all, though, the Kingston landlords, or two of them at least, engrossed the village lands: the Newtons in a modest way by bringing together the lands that had been owned by Culpepper and Skinner to make a Kingston estate of six yardlands; the Eversfields more drastically by pulling together the freeholds of Alfreye's from Swanborough Manor and Peake's from Houndean to make a potential tenancy of 12 yardlands; 12 yardlands rivalled the demesnes of Kingston Manor and surpassed those of Hyde. Eversfield, though paying homage to two manor lords of Kingston, had in effect created the largest landed estate in the open fields of the village. The landlords had changed things since Henry's day and others were to build on what they had done.

Engrossment by landlords almost certainly meant that there were fewer tenants, for one of the main purposes of engrossment was precisely to reduce their number and to create opportunities for richer farmers who might be more reliable rent payers. Following the pattern of these and later times, it is likely that the tenants of these Kingston landlords were independent yeomen in the village. Ades, Barndens, Howells, Picombes and others, with their knowledge of the fields, furlongs and strips, must surely have been natural tenants to choose. Younger families who stood in line to inherit from landed copyholders and had a bit of family wealth behind them, as well as the experience of local land, were obvious candidates.

There had also been changes in the 'small' lands of the village – the lands held by independent copyholders. The Ades had come into Kingston, and after the manorial families they must surely have stood near the top of its small society. They too had done their bit of engrossing; Gregory Ade and 'Old Joan' held six yardlands, and paid no rent apart from feudal dues to Swanborough and Iford manors. They cultivated lands with hired labour where in earlier times two or three peasant families had worked. Barndens, who were to increase their holdings in the sixteenth century, and Coppards too, invaded the smaller copyholds. Between them the new landlords and acquisitive yeomanry were changing Kingston from a village of small copyholders and tenants, even if the process was slower than in some other places.

Somehow, the older yeomanry, the Howells and Picombes in particular, seem to have been less successful economically. By sheer weight of numbers both families were a prominent part of Elizabethan Kingston. Howells and Picombes were not only yeomen, they were tenants too and also cottagers – families who spread across the social spectrum of the village. Yet, they did not show quite that tenacious grasp on land that was to be so characteristic of the Ades. They increased their lands from time to time, only to lose them again – only to be reduced to smaller holdings. They never quite crossed the border that separated successful Ades and Barndens from families like the a Moores, who later vanished from the village; Howells and Picombes, for one reason or another, were in a kind of no-mans land.

The incursion of larger tenancies and larger yeoman holdings probably did not reduce the demands for labour in the open fields. Since there was virtually no conversion to pasture and since the old three-field system was retained in its integrity, it is likely that just as many people were needed for labour as before. The difference in Elizabeth's time was that more of the labour came from wage workers who, through the agency of the larger individual holdings, replaced family labour. If Kingston was a richer village in 1567 by virtue of landed families like the 'gentle' Cranes, Michells and yeoman Ades, it was by the same mark a poorer one because of the proportionately greater number of landless or cottager families. It was becoming a less equal place; it was, in all these ways, moving towards its future.

Chapter 7

Engrossment: Comings and Goings at Kingston Manor

Among the many changes that complicated rural life in the sixteenth and early seventeenth centuries, two in particular had a certain pride of place. They were closely related to one another – so much so that there is perhaps a degree of artificiality in distinguishing them. The first, and most obvious, was that the pattern of demand for the outputs of English agriculture changed and changed drastically: prices moved in favour of pastoral production – wool in the latter fifteenth and early sixteenth centuries, and meat later on. The new gentry and enrichened yeomanry wanted beef and mutton on their tables, and this demand sustained the pressure for pastoral outputs as the growth of demand for wool slowed down in the second half of the sixteenth century.

The second change, less immediately obvious, was that there were limited but quite important modifications in farming practice. By the sixteenth century it was becoming plain that the relationship between arable and pastoral production might be altered from its medieval balance – and altered to the advantage of both. The old three-course rotation left little opportunity for the land to regain heart. The practice of turning land back to pasture for temporary spells of two or three seasons emerged by chance in medieval times, when manorial lords had problems finding tenants to fill their manor lands. It had, however, taught men that the fertility of the soil could in the long run be better maintained by ploughing it less; and, moreover, the gains in yield were sufficient to allow for arable and pastoral outputs to be expanded simultaneously, even though the amount of land under plough at any time would be less than under the old systems. The practice of the temporary ley was not a dramatic technical breakthrough. Sixteenth- and seventeenth-century yields did not rise in a particularly striking way, but they did at least rise at a time when pressure on arable land was growing and when the old system by itself might well have sickened the land, as it probably had in the early fourteenth century.[1] Possibly there would have been pressure to extend pasture in England, even if the structure of demand itself had changed much less sharply.

In the neutral and clinical language that economists like to use, these changes in demand and in the techniques of production required a shift in the allocation of land. In fact, the 'natural' forces of the market were inducing people who held land to seek just such a shift. The problem, though, was that the shift also required the transformation of an ancient system of rural organization. The old three-field system was more than just a way of organizing cultivation: it was the cornerstone of village community. And, since by and large the reallocation of the land towards pasture could be done more easily if the old system was dismantled, it inevitably involved social disruption with attendant pains and conflict. While market forces might have their value in pointing the way towards a more efficient use of resources, they take no account of the losses and disruption that people experience in making the transition.

The villages around Kingston show the differing degrees to which Tudor reorganization of the land impinged on different communities. Balmer and Balsdean were depopulated in the interests of pasture. Falmer, most probably, was invaded and diminished without being destroyed. In the Norton part of Iford, where there were Swanborough Manor lands called Stuckles, people accomplished a transition, by all appearances through mutual consent among landholders and the practice of severality. If there were 'losers' in Iford, they were most probably among the wage labourers because the extension of pasture – whether temporary or not – probably meant that the amount of labour needed for any area of land was less. In Kingston, on the other hand, the movement towards pasture made no headway at all.

These pressures towards new patterns of land use had another consequence – easy to overlook but in the long run most important for the development of Kingston. They considerably enhanced the commercial attractiveness and profitability of the demesnes of Swanborough Manor compared with neighbouring lands.

The Swanborough demesnes as we have seen had always been unique because of their attachment to the priory at St Pancras. They had become consolidated into a single block of land.

Some 500 years later, however, consolidated and enclosed areas like Swanborough commended themselves for other far more mundane reasons than those that might have sparked the interest of the Cluniac abbot. The demesnes were large. When surveyed in the late eighteenth century, they were 570 statutory acres in extent.[2] This was just a little more than a third of the size of the whole of Kingston parish. At the time of the eighteenth-century survey exactly half this area was sheep down and, with the stocking intensity current in Elizabethan Kingston, this would have provided grazing for 800 sheep or more. About 40 per cent of the area was arable, which meant that the arable acreage was a quarter the size of all the arable in Kingston parish. But, of course, where Kingston arables were divided into open fields, the demesne arables of Swanborough were in separated enclosed fields, varying in size from four to forty acres, but mostly in the region of 15 acres. The remaining 10 per cent of the demesnes lay in the meadows and brooklands of the Ouse valley. The whole area was splendidly drained; the soils, though heavy, were fertile; the downland slopes were steep, but covered in rich turf for sheep.

To a certain extent, this eighteenth-century allocation of the demesnes is misleading. The whole attractiveness of these lands in Tudor times lay in the fact that the pattern of land use could be easily changed from one proportion to another. Where the integrity of the Kingston open fields fixed the ratio of arable to pasture quite rigidly, the use of the Swanborough demesnes could be changed freely without meeting any obstacles such as village organization, the rights of other landholders or the resistances of labourers who did not wish to be eaten by sheep. Swanborough fields could be set to temporary leys, which broke into the three-course rotation but increased yields in the end. They could be turned freely to more permanent pasture for sheep and cattle if prices for pastoral outputs seemed set to rise steadily against those for crops. They could be turned back to arable again if the farmer had guessed wrongly at how the market would behave, or if the demand for corn kept prices relatively high for a few years at a time. Whatever attractions the consolidated demesnes might have had in medieval times, they were sharply enhanced by the shifting demands and new methods of the sixteenth and seventeenth centuries. The large enclosure the priors had valued for their own purposes came to be prized by yeomen and gentry for reasons the Normans and their churchmen could not have dreamt of. Swanborough simply was more profitable per acre when acres were scarce – and since it was large, larger indeed than any holding in nextdoor Kingston parish, it promised large incomes and the possibility of wealth to anyone who had access to it.

It is not surprising in the circumstances that, even before the dissolution of the priory, powerful men at King Henry's court should have sought to persuade the jealous and reluctant prior to give them a lease on the demesnes – men like Sir Thomas Audley or Thomas Cromwell himself. That, perhaps, is a measure of the economic merits of the demesnes. The dissolution opened these lands up, prised them away from monastic grip and handed them to lay lords who sought to exploit them through tenancies. As we have seen, they went first to Arundel and then to the Caryll family, based to the north of Lewes at Warnham.

Just how successful Carylls were at taking advantage of the economic opportunities at Swanborough we do not know. There are no records of their tenant farmers and no signs of their influence in the villages around. It is as if Swanborough's potential was never fully realized in the Caryll period. Perhaps the Carylls had difficulty finding the right men as tenants – finding the correct formula for exploiting the advantages of the demesnes to the full – for though the demesnes represented a splendid chance of advancement for a tenant, the economic and managerial preconditions for working them successfully were demanding. To get the most from these lands a tenant must of course be well capitalized, indeed must be rich. He had to be able to put forward large sums for wages, seed and equipment to make the land yield. He needed large flocks to take full advantage of that great slope of downland above the arable. Above all, perhaps, he needed commercial acumen – an ability to be right more often than not about next year's prices – combined with an ability to manage land and workers. There were or course such men about in Caryll's time. The Ades in Iford and Kingston, for example, if they were rich enough, could have brought a vast fund of knowledge about farming in the Ouse valley to the exploitation of Swanborough. So, probably, could many others. But perhaps the Carylls were poorly served by their stewards and never found them.

In 1584, after about thirty years at Swanborough, the Caryll family sold out to the newly ennobled Sackvilles – created Lord Buckhurst in 1567, and the earl of Dorset in 1604. A new era opened at the manor.[3]

There was a certain symbolism about the departure of the Carylls and the accession of Dorsets that is hard to resist. The Carylls belonged to the old religion. They were recusants and even identified as one of those powerful Catholic families who provided lines of entry for English Jesuits returning from their training at Douai to say illegal masses in secret rooms in English country houses.[4] Had Swanborough, so close to the sea and near the Ouse, been a point of entry for the priests? There is no way of knowing, but it was certainly well placed for the purpose.

At all events, by 1584 Elizabeth was at the outset of a sequence of undertakings, which were to confirm the new religion in people's allegiance and in great measure discredit the old. In the following year the inevitable war with Philip of Spain broke into the open; the Catholic cause became fatally identified with a foreign and enemy power. The queen turned more harshly on Catholic plotting and finally, in 1587, destroyed the temptations of a Catholic succession by executing Mary, Queen of Scots. Then, in the following year after much nervous delay, the Armada came down on England. Beacons flared along the south coast to mark its progress. Kingston people, like others in the vulnerable villages near the sea, prepared to deal with Spaniards and saw from the top of the seaward downs the inventive destructiveness of Drake's ships in harrying the Spanish men-of-war. With the defeat of the Armada, the sea was open to the English in a way it had never been before – and the old order, the order for which Caryll stood, was decisively disestablished. England was to be Protestant henceforth. Men like Dorset, close to the queen, enrichened and made powerful by the changes of the times, stood for the future. The departure of the Carylls was the final breaking of Swanborough's links with its Catholic past, and it came at a time when the country in its vast majority was similarly breaking with the old way of belief.

The Elizabethan Buckhurst contemplating his new manor, which of course was one among a great many he held in Sussex, was most unlikely to have turned his mind to such matters. His purpose at Swanborough was simple enough: he or rather his steward must find a tenant farmer who could handle the place so that it yielded a safe and predictable flow of rents worthy of its merits. He needed a rich, able person to do the job.

Buckhurst found his man and started a business relationship that was to have consequences in villages all around. The man was called John Vinall. He was found, it would seem, at Falmer, where he was probably the tenant farmer on the demesnes. He came to Swanborough in 1589[5] – four years after Buckhurst had taken over the demesnes and just one year after Howard and Drake had defeated the Spaniards and given Elizabeth and most of England a new confidence. Perhaps some of that confidence had rubbed off on Vinall, or perhaps he never felt the lack of it.

Who was he? Many years later in 1639 when, by virtue of sustained economic success, the Kingston Vinalls could claim to be gentry they were granted arms[6] and this question seemed a little hard to answer: 'John Vinall of Kingston, gent., is of good birth and anciently descended, which was the son of John, which was the son of William, which was the son of William of the same place and country, who was anciently descended from Vynehall in the same country.'[7] The pedigree of 1639 is a bit vague, as those of the new gentry were apt to be. This second John Vinall of 1639 was the son of the man who had first come as tenant farmer to the Buckhursts in 1589. He was 55 when he received the grant of a coat of arms. His ancestors – the various Williams – had not been 'of the same place' though they were certainly 'of the same country'.

In fact, the new tenant farmer of 1589 most probably sprung from one of the Vinall families that were by then established in Wivelsfield, Cuckfield and Fletching. They were already numerous in that area of Sussex – which is the area where assertive old Thomas Michell at Hyde Manor had come from – by the middle of Henry's reign.[8] John Vinall of 1589 had moved to Falmer some time before. His son, who later received a 'grant of arms', was born there and was aged five at the time his father took up a tenancy on the Lord Buckhurst's Swanborough estate.[9]

But, beyond these bare facts, there is not a great deal to be said about them. John Vinall who came to Kingston in 1589 was a yeoman – and that is a good enough description of the family's origin. The rest, right down to the nineteenth-century efforts by some local historians to find an ancestry for the family, is mostly a search for a kind of legitimation. By the record of subsequent events, John Vinall was clever and acquisitive and became rich enough to found a family dynasty. In some important ways, he was to change the shape of the village.

However, the initiative that gave impetus to Vinall's Kingston career and eventually brought his family to the Restoration list of 'Sussex Gentry' came from Lord Buckhurst and not from Vinall himself. In 1594, ten years after he had purchased Swanborough Manor and its demesnes from the Carylls, Buckhurst, far away at his country seat in Kent, decided to buy Kingston Manor from Peter Crane.[10]

The circumstances of the sale are unclear, but we can perceive their outlines. When Peter Crane, the yeoman who had inherited Kingston Manor from his yeoman father, sold out to Dorset he was still comparatively young –

about forty.[11] He was married to Joan Newton, daughter of the powerful 'gentle' family in Lewes, and when he left Kingston Manor it was to become overseer to the lands of the Newton family.[12] Perhaps, on balance, there was more to be gained as overseer to the lands of the rising gentry than as a small manor lord in a small village. In 1621, 27 years later, Richard Crane – Peter's son – was a substantial landowner in Lewes borough.[13] The Cranes had made their choice – Kingston was to see no more of them. Buckhurst, on the other hand, had only started to be interested in the village.

Buckhurst's undertaking in Kingston was not confined to the purchase of Kingston Manor. Within a few short years he extended his landholdings in the village in a dramatic way. The 12 yardlands of Kingston Manor – a part of the ancient demesnes of the village – were only a beginning. By 1602 the lord had bought his way into less distinguished bits of the Kingston arable. To quote John Rowe, he held '4 yards sometimes Harmans', '5 yards late Coppards and Joane A. Bowrers' and '6 yards called Skinners and Culpeps late Newtons'.[14] So, over and above the old demesnes he had bought from Peter Crane, Buckhurst had acquired a further 15 Kingston yardlands.

This was engrossment on a scale that the village had not seen before. The Newtons had pulled together six yardlands from two previous owners to create a larger farm; the Eversfields had engrossed 12 yardlands; but Buckhurst had beaten them all. In a short space of time he brought together 27 yardlands, well over a third of the arable of the village. As the sixteenth century turned to the seventeenth he was by far the largest landowner in Kingston.

For Elizabethans – indeed for many historians of their times – engrossment was a heinous agrarian offence. For those who concerned themselves with such matters, it was not perhaps as grievous as consolidation, enclosure and the conversion of arable lands to pasture, but it was an offence nonetheless. And the reason is clear enough. Engrossment was a threat to smaller landholders. It took land from copyholders and small tenants and made it available for large well-capitalized and rich farmers. So historians struggle over the extent to which engrossment 'dispossessed' copyholders (the old customary tenants) and disadvantaged small farmers. How in these terms did the engrossment in Kingston affect matters?

Obviously, Buckhurst's incursion into the open fields displaced copyholders. It is most unlikely though that it involved dispossessing anyone – if 'dispossession' is taken to indicate the use of power in defiance of custom to eject someone who would otherwise have wished to stay on the land. Consider who the duke's displaced copyholders were.

The Newtons of Lewes were too powerful themselves and too well connected to be subjected to any arbitrary reassertions of manorial power from Swanborough. Buckhurst could not have dispossessed them even if he wished to. Robert Hardman was displaced, but he too was a most unlikely candidate for dispossession. What the Hardmans lacked in urbanity they made up for in economic strength. They were well-founded yeomen in Falmer who probably knew a thing or two about dispossession themselves, for their wealth lay in part in flocks that grazed on pastures that had once been the arables of the customary tenantry of Balmer. It is difficult to imagine the Hardmans being pushed unwillingly from their lands. Only the two small 'owner-occupiers' Coppard and 'old Joane Bowrer' show the characteristic vulnerability an unscrupulous manor lord might exploit – but there is no evidence at all that the manor lord did so. We must presume that his engrossment was based on the power of his purse, not on manorial lordship and the re-enactment of ancient feudal privilege. His erstwhile copyholders left their Kingston yardlands because he bought them out and they were, no doubt, happy enough to take their money and go. For Newtons and Hardmans, the sale of lands in Kingston was merely a small rearrangement in their comparatively large estates. For Coppards and Bowrers more may have been involved. There is no evidence of what happened to these two after they left the village. Coppard had relatives in Rodmell and he may have turned in that direction; Joane A. Bowrer was an old lady, a widow and presumably the end of her family line.

Though Buckhurst's engrossment of Kingston was, as it were, fairly done and not susceptible to charges of ruthlessness and inhumanity to copyholders, it raises questions, particularly the question of how the earl was able to buy up yardlands from five separate landholders within so short an interval. The likelihood is that the purchase of Newton's, Hardman's, Coppard's and Joane A. Bowrer's lands took place at more or less the same time as the purchase of Kingston Manor. What induced these landholders to sell, in effect, simultaneously?

In part, circumstance may have helped the new lord. It could be that the whole process started at Kingston Manor. Here in the manor house was Peter Crane – uncertain in his mind about how much longer a minor lordship at the head of a muddy winter street would satisfy the inclinations he felt towards a more sophisticated urban life. Or perhaps Joan Crane, neé Newton, brought up at the centre of such wealth and urbanity as Lewes could muster, was the restless one. At all events, once the Cranes decided to sell out – or accepted a proposal from the duke that they should do so – the Newtons, in turn, may have felt less interest than before in *their* six yardlands in Kingston. While their son-in-law was a manor lord in the village he could be relied on either to farm their lands as a tenant or act as their overseer. Once Crane decided to move, the family interest in what had become an odd outlying bit of their estate probably diminished so that Newtons and Cranes became predisposed to sell at much the same moment.

Still, there is no reason to suppose that the Cranes, Newtons or any of the others were at all inclined to sell their lands below the market rate. The obvious implication of Buckhurst's engrossment was that he was not only *able* to pay and to pay well for lands in Kingston, but also, for one reason or another, was *willing* to do so.

We get an inkling that he was willing to pay a good deal for access to Kingston lands from the circumstances surrounding the purchase of Kingston Manor itself. Buckhurst paid Crane £1500 for it in 1594.[15] Now, 48 years before, Peter Crane's father had bought the manor from Sir Richard Lee for £150. In money terms therefore Buckhurst paid ten times as much. It is true of course that inflationary pressure was considerable throughout the Tudor period and especially in this second half of the sixteenth century, but even so an increase in the money price of land by a factor of ten in about fifty years was considerable. The general price level of agricultural outputs over the same period had gone up but only by a factor of two and a half.[16] Even allowing for the possibility that Sir Richard Lee had sold out too cheaply in 1546 and for the fact that the Cranes had undoubtedly improved the manor, it would seem that Dorset paid Crane a goodly price. And this is considerably confirmed by the fact that when the next earl of Dorset sold the manor in 1623 to John Morley of Glynde,[17] he was only able to raise £1550 for it. This was little more than 3 per cent above the amount paid to Crane 29 years earlier in 1594 and, in the meantime, agricultural prices had increased by at least 25 per cent. Prices are of course volatile things and it is risky to rest too much argument on them, but it seems fair to conclude that in 1594 Dorset was strongly disposed to buy up Kingston yardlands at above their current market value (in the case of Kingston Manor perhaps 20 per cent above) and that this disposition explains the scale and success of his engrossment of the open fields.

Still, even the enormously wealthy Buckhurst was no doubt guided by commercial considerations rather than whim when it came to the purchase of a not very remarkable manor and dispersed parcels of hard-worked arable land in a remote Sussex village. The Buckhursts must have had reason to believe that they were onto a good thing. Why?

We can only guess at their reasons. It is possible, for example, that they anticipated greater increases in agricultural prices than most other people did. Prices were certainly rising steeply in the 1590s. But this sort of general explanation does not really meet the puzzle of why Buckhurst, of all people, should buy his way into unenclosed (and apparently unenclosable) lands in Kingston when he might easily have purchased lands elsewhere that were already consolidated. By engrossing land did he hope to establish a strong enough base to consolidate and enclose in Kingston? Perhaps, though surely after ten years in possession of Swanborough Manor his steward and tenant farmer, Vinall, would have been well aware that Kingston was rather intractable to enclosure. At all events, the engrossment remained just that: an engrossment. He never accomplished consolidation or enclosure in Kingston. The village remained unrepentantly committed to its open fields and strips; it remained what had become known as a 'champion' village.[18]

The most plausible explanation for Buckhurst's policy lay closer at hand, in Swanborough. It was, simply, the presence of John Vinall. Without much doubt Vinall had made the best possible use of his first few years at Swanborough as tenant on the advantageous demesnes. By 1594 he had already demonstrated the brilliance and acumen as a capitalist 'farmer' he sustained throughout his subsequent career. Moreover, as events were soon to show, Vinall was ready to expand his operations by extending his tenancies beyond the Swanborough demesnes and Stuckles. An enterprising, well-capitalized tenant farmer was not only able to take profit on his own account in a time of rising agricultural prices, but he was also a precious asset for any lordship. He could farm larger areas, making the administrative business of rent collection less onerous. His ability and wealth were a guarantee to the landlords that the rents would actually flow as they should. The risks of default were much reduced, being underwritten by the skills and resources of the tenant himself. And, if the tenant were held on a lease of not more than seven years, the landlord could hope to share in tenant success by increases in rent. In this, of course, the landlord had to be judicious because excessively greedy increases would drive the tenant elsewhere. But, given duly modest aspirations on the landlord's part, a modus vivendi could be found between a landlord and a competent tenant at a higher rent than could be got from a financially weak, technically inadequate farmer.

As later developments were to show, up to this period Vinall was the most successful tenant farmer in Kingston's history. If he had more successful predecessors their names and accomplishments are lost to us. He was also one of the more successful tenants on the Buckhurst rent roll and it is quite plausible that the lord, together with his overseers and stewards, might have regarded himself as having a special asset and commercial advantage in the Kingston area. Vinall could have been the reason why Buckhurst was impelled towards the lands of Kingston village. And Vinall's skills, which had been proven on the demesnes at Swanborough, were possibly the reason for paying more for the land than it was worth. Those skills and abilities were some assurance to Buckhurst that Vinall would be able to produce surpluses on Kingston lands large enough to generate rents and profits that would cover the high costs the duke incurred for his engrossment. We discern the outlines of an implicit partnership between the first Baron Buckhurst and the rising capitalist yeoman – a partnership that induced the baron to make himself the largest landowner and biggest engrosser in Kingston village.

But, whatever the precise purposes Buckhurst had in mind, it is certain that his purchase of Kingston Manor and 15 copyhold yardlands in the open fields was the initiative that brought the Vinall family into Kingston where they were to be the dominant village family for much of the next 120 years. The move was timely as far as John Vinall was concerned in 1594. He had farmed Swanborough demesnes and Stuckles for five years and was ready to extend himself to larger undertakings. When Peter Crane moved out of Kingston Manor, John Vinall and his family moved in, not just to 'occupancy' of the manor's demesnes but also into the manor house at the head of the street.

They became Kingston people.[19] In this initial period, the Vinalls were Buckhurst's farmers, not only on Queen Eddid's ancient demesne at Kingston Manor but also on the 15 copyhold yardlands that had been bought from Newtons, Hardmans, Coppards and Bowrers. Since Vinall retained the tenancy of Swanborough and Stuckles, which had given him his start, his accession to these lands turned him into a farmer on a unique scale for the village. All together, he farmed 50 yardlands in Kingston and at Swanborough and Iford: 50 yardlands amounted to perhaps 600 statutory acres, possibly more, of which a substantial proportion were the enclosed and flexible lands of Swanborough. No Kingston family living in the street had ever achieved access to such an area; indeed, none before Vinall had had the wealth in the form of working capital to finance the seeds, labour, equipment, herds and flocks such a large enterprise demanded.[20] Vinall was a new phenomenon for Kingston. To cap it all, in the 1590s his tenancy gave him control over more than a third of the village arables. His weight in all matters requiring communal decisions was commensurate.

The pattern of John Vinall's tenancies changed over the years. However, virtually throughout his life (he died in 1625[21]) he remained tenant to Lord Buckhurst on the farms at Swanborough, Stuckles and Kingston Manor. These lands formed the base from which Vinall occasionally branched out into other tenancies.[22] By 1614 he appears to have relinquished his tenancies on Dorset's copyhold lands in the Kingston open fields. Instead, he was farming the demesnes of Iford Manor. John Rowe mentions 'John Vinall thelder … who albeit he dwelt in Kingston yet he occupied Swanborrowe farme, Stuckles and the Demesnes of the Manor of Iford all lyinge in Iford, and his servants lodged in Swanborrowe house'.[23] In 1618, the accounts of Edward Lyndsey, at that time the steward to the earl of Dorset on many of his Sussex manors, confirms the pattern of Vinall's tenancies. He paid rent to the duke for the 'scite and demesnes' of Swanborough Manor and Kingston Manor and farmed Stuckles.[24] The lands the first lord Buckhurst had bought from Newtons and others were by that time occupied by another tenant, Edmund Bowker.

Though Vinall's tenancies in Kingston open fields were of course reduced in size by his move to the demesnes of Iford Manor, his social position in the village was in no way diminished. He remained 'farmer' on more than 600 acres of arable and he remained at the manor house. From Rowe's remarks we can deduce that he was rich enough to hold the manor house at Swanborough as lodging for his 'servants'. No other Kingston family could compare in terms of personal wealth. He was in demand for public service and, as one might expect of a man whose mind was given to running a substantial capitalist farming enterprise, he acceded reluctantly. John Rowe tells the story:

> The Constable of his hundred [Rowe means Swanborough hundred], was aunciently chosen by tourne out of ech borrowe, but when Westout had none inhabitants of sufficiency to vndergoe that office,

> the elleccon fell by course betwene the other two burrowes. [The other two boroughs in question were Iford and Kingston.] And in successe of time Steuen A. Ridge onely beinge left in Iford able to discharge the constableshipp – all thother inhabitants of any reasonable hability beinge remoued to Kingston where then dwelt at the least a dozen fitt for that seruice ... the steward, not thinkinge it reasonable or fittinge that the said Steuen should execute the saide office eu'y second yeare and yet desirous to obserue ye auncient custome, elected John Vynall thelder to serue the constableshipp for Iford. ... Whereupon John Vynall complayned at the Quarter Sessions as of a wronge and breach of custome; but all the judges – vna voce – answerred that the eleccon should stand, and the custom was not broken.[25]

The steward's problems in finding a person in Iford other than Steven A. Ridge who was fit to be constable of the hundred are interesting. The constable, who was unpaid, was required to apprehend civil and criminal offenders and refer them to the justices of the peace. His job was not particularly demanding in terms of skill, though it is plain from Rowe's remarks that convention required he should be someone of social status – a yeoman of some wealth. For more practical reasons he also had to be a person who was not too advanced in years. Even though the constable was not expected to rely on his own physical strength to carry out arrests, he might very well find himself in situations requiring some degree of athletic prowess. Steven A. Ridge was the only man left in Iford who met the qualifications of this not especially demanding or honorific public post. That, perhaps, was an outcome of enclosure and engrossment in Iford. Norton, the north part of the parish, had been enclosed for some time. Steven A. Ridge himself had engrossed at least 12 yardlands in the southern part of Iford and probably farmed much of the rest as a tenant. In 1614 the Ade family held a good deal of the rest of Iford land and it could be that the family heads (William Ade and John Ade) were advanced in years and had moved in with their Kingston relatives on the corner of the street, while leaving Steven A. Ridge to farm their strips. That Rowe thought there were at least a dozen people in Kingston fit to perform the service is in part a reflection of its comparatively undemanding nature and in part an exaggeration. That Iford had lost many of its yeomen farmers, who had removed themselves to Kingston, reflects the fact that Kingston's resistance to enclosure and consolidation led to better opportunities for smaller and middle yeomen than in a village where the land had been more extensively reorganized.[26] At all events, John Vinall's reluctance to perform what was probably a rather thankless public service seems clear. We may take his objection to the breach of custom with a pinch of salt. Vinall was probably not a great defender of custom unless his interests dictated that they should be defended. More likely, his concern was that, apart from the unrewarding nature of the task, it would distract his attention from those 600-odd acres of arable under his command. Old John Vinall was surely never short of things to do. In the end, the quarter session judges in Lewes dismissed his appeal: the vast amount of land he occupied in Iford was judged a good enough justification for requiring him to take his turn at the job instead of Steven A. Ridge. Unwillingly, he did so.

Apart from such minor disturbances, the pattern of John Vinall's Kingston career was more or less unchanged until the very last years of his life. He remained committed to tenant farming and apparently never moved into land-ownership on any significant scale.[27] Tenancy had served him well. He and his family, including his eldest son John, lived in comfort in the manor house in Kingston and, through the long years of rising prices and profitability, they no doubt became steadily richer.

Then, in 1623, a new earl of Dorset reassessed the family's Kingston investments. While holding onto the 15 copyhold yardlands the first earl had acquired in the 1590s, his successor sold Kingston Manor and the demesne lands attached to it. John Morley,[28] a member of the Morley family of Glynde, which lies behind the downs to the east of Lewes, bought it.

This was a decisive move for the Dorsets. From this point forward they held onto the copyhold yardlands but never extended their Kingston holdings beyond them. To some degree the Dorsets seem to have lost interest in Kingston. Perhaps, as John Vinall grew older, his ability to extract profitable surpluses from the strip lands of Kingston declined and, with it, the commercial attractions of Kingston Manor.

The implications of the sale of Kingston Manor from the Vinall point of view are unclear. It seems that the family continued as tenants to Morley – at least for a part of the next decade; they certainly continued as tenants on the other lands they farmed in Iford and Swanborough. Perhaps the sale was not a major disturbance.

Nevertheless, from about this time, the Vinall family policy changed: they began to move towards the ownership of land. Old John Vinall died in 1625. His son, also John Vinall, took over the old man's tenancies at about the age of forty and kept the family anchored in Kingston. He married Mary Ade in 1628[29] and, by doing so, reinforced the family commitment to Kingston, for the Ades were deeply rooted in the village by this time. And, in the period following his father's death, the younger John Vinall began to think of mobilising the wealth his father had accumulated in order to buy his way into land.

In 1634 he got his first big opportunity. Morley, at Glynde, decided to sell Kingston Manor. John Vinall bought it from him at the considerable price of £2500 – 60 per cent more than Morley had paid for it 11 years before, in a period when the rise in agricultural prices was, if anything, slowing down.[30] But, for Vinall, Kingston Manor and the manor house probably had a value somewhat above the ordinary. He had grown up there and his family had lived there for 40 years. If there were to be a switch from tenancy to ownership, what better way to begin? From 1634 Kingston once again had a resident manorial lord living at the manor house. The Vinalls partially withdrew from tenant farming at about this time – presumably because so much of their capital was tied up in the manor – and settled down to what was a second phase of life in Kingston. It was a phase in which respectability and the social status associated with manorial lordship became proportionately more important to the Vinalls than they had been before. Old John Vinall, the patriarch tenant farmer who had spent 36 years farming the Swanborough demesnes and other lands and so had made the foundations for the new family was, of course, respectable and powerful. But he had remained a tenant all his life and, despite his considerable economic ambitions, he had apparently been content to be a yeoman. John, his son, had ambitions beyond that. In 1639, five years after he had bought his way into the lordship of Kingston Manor, he obtained a 'grant of arms', and so came to fulfil the social requirements that lifted a man above the yeomanry and turned him into a gentleman. By the time the civil war broke over a troubled England, John Vinall, gent, was well established and could look forward to enjoying his lordship and lands, and the natural deference of his social inferiors living along the street. The Vinalls were becoming rather grand people. Their progress – if that is the correct term – was common enough in their times: all over Tudor England growing wealth had lifted the descendants of simple yeomanry to the new splendours of the English gentleman.

In following the Vinall family's fortunes through the decades from 1589 to the civil war, we have perforce lost sight of life in the rest of the village. We must return to the broader picture, for the intrusion of Dorset into the open fields of Kingston and the tenancy and eventual succession of the Vinalls at Kingston Manor were not the only forces to shape Kingston as Tudor monarchs gave place to Stuarts.

The Dorset intrusion, legal and 'fair' though it may have been, was nonetheless an engrossment and it changed the structure of tenancy and ownership in the village. The lands of Newton and Hardman had provided smaller tenancies before the 1590s. The Coppards and Bowrers were smaller copyholders and they held their lands as independent owner-occupiers. All these lands came together and, along with the demesnes of Kingston Manor, had been occupied in the initial period by the Vinalls. The room for smaller tenancies was sharply reduced at a single stroke, as was the room for independent yeomen.

In the earlier years of Elizabeth's reign there had been other lands for tenants in Kingston. Thomas Michell lived in his renovated and somewhat grand house on the north side of the street, but he leased the lands it pleased him to think of as the demesnes of Hyde Manor, which Thomas Howell had farmed in the 1570s. He and his descendants probably continued to do so through most of the seventeenth century. There were also the 12 yardlands the Eversfields owned ('Alfreye's and Peake's'), which had no doubt given openings to smaller tenants from time to time.

We have already followed the succession to Michell's 'manor of Hyde' in Chapter 6. Michell himself died in 1624. Jane (née de la Chambre) his wife lived on at the house in the street and married that Steven A. Ridge who had engrossed Iford so comprehensively that he was the only man left in the village judged socially capable of exercising the constableship. Jane died in 1630 and the property passed, after a complex succession, out of the de la Chambre family to their cousins the Alchornes. John Alchorne had bought it – probably on rather favourable terms – for £1100 in 1630. It was evidently a less grand holding than Kingston Manor, but by village standards the house and land of a comparatively rich man.

The Alchornes are shadowy figures in the Kingston story. There is barely any record of the family over the next 150 years. All we know is that John Alchorne took up the tenancy of the manor on his own account, lived in Kingston and did not put his 'demesnes' out to lease. There are signs of some commercial success in the early years: in 1647 while the civil war was still unresolved, John Alchorne, described as a gentleman of Kingston, was rich enough to lend money on mortgage against half the value of the manor of Middleton.[31] Beyond that there is very little. It is as if the Alchornes lived out their lives looking inward to their manor house in Kingston Street, and effectively taking their lands 'out of circulation' as far as the village was concerned. Certainly, Hyde was no longer a source of tenancies for a long time after 1630.

There were much more noticeable developments on the Eversfield lands: the six freehold yardlands of Swanborough Manor called Alfreye's, the equal number of freehold yards on Houndean Manor called Peake's, and the one or two yardlands of Kingston Manor. When put together, these of course made a substantial farm; they were equal in area to Kingston Manor demesnes and larger than Hyde. Consequently, until Lord Buckhurst engrossed 15 copyhold yardlands in the village in the 1590s, Eversfield lands were co-equally the largest single holding in the open fields. Though there is no clear record of tenancies, two (or from time to time perhaps three) farmers were accommodated on them in Elizabethan times.

And so the pattern continued in the reign of James I until, in 1617, Sir Thomas Eversfield of Denne died.[32] Then, suddenly and presumably in the process of reordering his father's estate, Herbert Eversfield sold out the lands in Kingston.[33] They were bought by Edmund Bowker, the son of a yeoman family of Southover,[34] and the Bowkers moved into Kingston village forthwith. When Edmund junior, the son of the man who had bought Eversfield's yardlands was married in London, he was described in the licence as a 'gent' of Kingston-near-Lewes.[35] The advent of the Bowkers reduced the availability of tenancies, simply because they came as owner-occupiers where before there had been two or more tenant families. But their impact did not stop there. Within a year or so of his arrival in Kingston, Bowker appeared on the earl of Dorset's rent roll as the duke's farmer on all the lands outside the

Kingston demesne, which the Dorsets had acquired in the 1590s. One of these yardlands was, incidentally, attached to Kingston Manor at the time and was called Diggon's. It was presumably the same land the de Dyghons had held in the distant thirteenth century.[36]

By 1618, then, the Bowkers were a challenge to the pre-eminence of the Vinalls in Kingston. John Vinall was, of course, farming a much larger area than Edmund Bowker, for he occupied the Swanborough and Iford manor demesnes lying outside the village. But, as far as the Kingston open fields were concerned, the Bowkers had achieved a special place. They had built on Eversfield's old engrossment of Alfrey's[37] and Peake's, and had joined their owner occupancy of these substantial freeholds to a tenancy on Dorset's engrossed yardlands – somewhat more than a third of the arable. In these decades before the civil war they were for a while the largest occupiers of village lands proper, and they held a social position in Kingston commensurate with their genteel origins and their control of land. They most probably lived in the old house attached to 'Peake's' – a little distance down the street from Kingston Manor house where Vinalls were ensconced at the time. The old house still stands – perhaps the most venerable dwelling in the modern village. Its transformation from a medieval shape by the addition of chimneys and inglenooks, as well as some splendid stone-built windows, probably dates from the Bowkers' ownership. The fact that until quite recently older Kingston residents believed that it had once been 'a kind of manor house' might well be an echo of the social and economic power the Bowkers once wielded from this place. So the Bowkers followed the Vinalls and, by their joint action of purchasing Eversfield's lands and farming Dorset's, they effectively swept away the opportunities for smaller tenancies in the village – at least for a time. In the eighteenth century this little Kingston land empire, in a slightly changed form, was to be the base of operation for a man who pushed the process of engrossing Kingston even further.

By the 1640s, then, the economic space for smaller tenants was virtually all taken up by the Alchornes' 'closing up' of Hyde Manor as an owner occupied estate, by Dorset's engrossment and by the uses to which Vinall and Bowker had put it. What was left after this?

The smaller owner-occupied lands of Kingston were left. In 1567, these lands, aside from the demesnes of Kingston Manor, amounted to 27 or so yardlands (see Table 6.1) or more than a third of the arable. Dorset's engrossment had taken up five of them, so by the end of the sixteenth century these 'smaller lands' amounted to only 28 per cent of the arable. It is a measure of the Dorset–Vinall–Bowker impact on the village that these lands, which provided a living for a considerable number of families, were less in total area than the lands Vinall had farmed alone in the Kingston fields in the first decade of the seventeenth century, or those that Bowker was farming on his own account by 1618. Kingston peasantry was being squeezed for space, though not by any means as much as in some other villages, Iford for example.

1. Kingston-near-Lewes from Swanborough Hill. The ridge on which Mill Laine is situated can be seen projecting away from the village.

2. Piccombe's cottage, 'Rest Harrow'.

3. The present Hyde Manor House (originally Thomas Rogers's house).

4. A flint barn with the Downs behind.

5. Labourers' cottages in the street.

6. St Pancras Church.

In the late sixteenth and first half of the seventeenth century the succession of ownership of smaller lands was determined to a limited extent by sales and purchases of lands between families and to a greater degree by inheritance. There was a complication in village life here, which must be unravelled to make sense of subsequent events. It consisted in the curious rules of inheritance that had been established by very ancient custom on some of the manors in Kingston – rules that were described as borough English. Borough English inheritance is encountered in a number of parts of England on customary lands (namely on copyholds). It took various forms, but all are distinguished by the succession to copyhold title being passed to the younger son in the first instance. If the younger son died without issue or before his father, the lands would normally go to the next youngest brother, or the youngest daughter. In themselves these rules need not have complicated life more than any other system of inheritance. What made their incidence in Kingston confusing was that they only applied to the copyholds in some of the manors – in fact Swanborough and Houndean. On the others, in Kingston Manor and Iford Manor, the more usual practice of borough French – inheritance passing to the oldest son – was followed.[38] Neighbours holding lands in different manors followed different rules of inheritance. In one household an eldest son could look forward with confidence to his future, while next door the youngest boy in the family might await the arrival of each new baby with anxiety lest his inheritance be usurped by the appearance of a little brother. And then, some families – like the Ades, Barndens or Howells – owned lands in more than one manor, so that lands that had been painfully brought together over long years might be divided into two ownerships at the death of the father.

The coexistence of two systems of inheritance meant that yeomen families that held more than one manor were continually threatened with the possibility that there would be a divided succession. And once succession divided, lands that had once formed a single unit of production might pass, by the failure of a male line for example, into other family ownerships. The incidence of borough English along with borough French made it that much more difficult for Kingston yeomen to engross lands on their own account – harder, that is, to sustain the integrity of the family farm, which is the hallmark of peasant production in all parts of the world. And the intricacies of a particular system of inheritance were not the only problems they had to face. From time to time there were dangers of financial failure, not so much in the profitable early years of the seventeenth century as later on. And there were often temptations to sell out to larger landowners, like the Dorsets for example, perhaps prepared to pay over the odds for one reason or another.

Some were more successful than others in meeting the pressures of the times and the complications of succession. As far as inheritance was concerned, the more successful families were either favoured by fortune (as when there was only one son to succeed on an inter-manorial copyhold farm), or by luck or good judgement built up their holdings in one manor only, or in some cases found ways around the rigours of the succession problems by various arrangements within the family.

The Ades, firmly established in their houses and farmyards at the corner of the street, were among the more successful. Gregory Ade, the patriarch who first appeared in the Kingston record in 1567, lived the whole length of Elizabeth's reign and beyond. He held onto his yardlands, some in Iford Manor and some in Swanborough, until his death in 1610. 'Old Joan Ade', his wife, lived on until 1614.[39]

By virtue of his longevity, Gregory had outlived a number of his sons. However, at his death there were still two brothers in line of succession. John Ade was 45 years old; William his brother was 38.[40] In the normal way of things, John should have succeeded to old Gregory's Iford yardlands – the 'tenement, ban and two virgates called Bishop's' – while William would have taken possession of the Swanborough yardlands called Taylor's. In the event, John the elder brother seems to have inherited the lot.[41] Somehow, Gregory appears to have found a way of avoiding the dismemberment of the lands he had held together for at least 43 years in the Kingston open fields. There is a hint of how this was done in later manorial records. Much later, in 1676, two sons similarly survived a John Ade (who in fact succeeded John the son of Gregory) – another John, the elder of the two, and a younger brother called Stephen. Stephen as the younger should have taken the Swanborough yardland, but did not. In the Swanborough Manor court at the time there was an agreement that John, the elder brother, would have the lands in return for an annuity of £30 to be paid to Stephen.[42] Evidently, in the Ade tradition the integrity of the landholding had become an overriding consideration; a younger son might be required to sacrifice his inheritance, with due recompense, so that it could be sustained.

A similar arrangement within the family must have come into play at the time of Gregory's death. John took over in 1610. His son – also a John – was in possession of the Swanborough yardlands when the steward to the Duke of Dorset drew up a 'new and perfect rentall' of Swanborough manor lands in 1658.[43] William was in effect disinherited. There were ways around manorial custom if it proved irksome to the objectives of a determined family – and the Ades it seems were both determined and tenacious.

What happened to the 'disinherited' William? It is unclear whether he, like his later counterpart, had an annuity to comfort him for what he had lost. It is clear, though, that in 1603, before Gregory's death, he came into possession of the house and grounds belonging to Thomas Michell (at Hyde Manor), which in 1567 had split the Ade properties at the end of the street into two.[44] In one sense, this consolidated the Ade lands at the corner of the street. More important, it gave William Ade a place to live in the Kingston family circle, which nevertheless was separate from the other family houses. William probably lived there most of his life. He did well for himself in various ways. He married well by Kingston measures; in 1615 he wed Joan Vinall, the daughter of the patriarchal John Vinall who was even then building a base for his family by his vast tenancies on Dorset's lands.[45] And William became bailiff to the Duke of Dorset on the demesnes of Kingston Manor,[46] a position that gave him a claim on the rents of assize the manor yielded. His personal and working links with the Dorset–Vinall undertaking were close.

William was not the only Ade to marry into the Vinall family. In 1628 Mary (daughter of the John Ade who succeeded Gregory) married John Vinall the younger,[47] who had by that time succeeded to his father's massive tenancies. The social demarcation between the Ades, who were the largest of the independent copyholders in Kingston, and the genteel Vinalls was not particularly sharp. John Vinall, at the manor house and lord of Kingston Manor from 1634 onwards, acknowledged John Ade the younger, who ran the Ade lands from his farmyards at the other end of the street, as one brother-in-law and William Ade, who had been bailiff to Dorset, as another. And, of course, they had all grown up together in Jacobean Kingston.

They also grew up with little Barndens, for the Barnden family was another stable and steady presence in Kingston. In 1567 John Barnden held three copyhold yardlands of Swanborough Manor (see Table 6.1); 15 or 20 years later he added to them by buying out the lands of Elizabeth Shoesmith of Lewes, also in Swanborough Manor. Whereas the Ades had to struggle with contradictory customs of succession to hold their lands together, the Barndens had the better fortune that all their lands were in one manor and subject, therefore, to one set of rules. This helped them to maintain the integrity of their lands, and the Barndens, in consequence, give us one of the most straightforward examples in Kingston of the workings of borough English.

When John Barnden died in 1594,[48] a string of sons and daughters from two marriages survived him. Two of his children from his first marriage, Edward and Joan, had married Ades, cementing an alliance with that somewhat central peasant family (which married its children 'upwards', 'downwards' and, in this case, 'sideways'). People like the Ades and the Barndens formed a nexus of relationships in the village, which most surely counted in the conduct of everyday affairs.

A striking feature of John Barnden's numerous progeny was that, in succession to lands, the two boys born to Joan Balcombe, his second wife – Thomas in 1575 and young Henry in 1579 – successively displaced the three sons of his first marriage. When John died in 1594, Henry – then 15 years old – inherited.[49] At this point, Henry's mother probably remained in ultimate control of the lands and one of his older half-brothers farmed them on her behalf.

By 1600, or soon after, Henry took over the lands on his own account. He was married soon after and by 1616 had three children: Joan, born in 1610, John in 1612 and Arthur in 1616.

A short year after Arthur's birth Henry died – in 1617. He was only 38 years old. The unweaned Arthur Barnden succeeded to the lands. His brother John was four. Once again the Barnden lands passed to a widow, and once again she looked for an older male in the family to farm them. Thomas Barnden, Arthur's uncle came into occupancy,[50] and stayed on the lands until his death in 1625.

We have no knowledge of how the Barndens dealt with the problem. Arthur, the successor, was still a minor at the time his uncle died: in 1625 he was nine years old. Most probably, one of his 'half-uncles' looked after the lands. At all events, it is clear that when Arthur came of age in 1637 he succeeded to the Barnden yardlands as of right, despite the various vicissitudes of inheritance.

It was not, as it happened, a particularly successful inheritance and that conceivably was to be expected. Poor Arthur had lost a father before he was old enough to know that one might reasonably expect to have one. Then, when his uncle seemed a good enough substitute, he too died and another took over. As events turned out, Arthur lived only two years of his majority: he died at 23 in 1639.[51] But even in that short time there were signs that things had gone wrong on the old Barnden lands. At the time of his death he was beholden to the court of Swanborough Manor for having cut an excessive amount of underwood from his lands in Kingston without the court's assent. It is unclear why Arthur had done this, but there are indications that he was using his lands in various ways for immediate gain without thought for the future. His successor on the lands was obliged to ask the manor court for permission to fell timber in order to rebuild and restore his house.[52]

Arthur's successor was his sister Joan, who had married a member of the Howell family. This John Howell, though doubtless related to the Howells in Kingston, was from Wilmington. His marriage to Joan Barnden gave him occupancy of the lands the Barndens had held for more than a century and from this point forward the Barndens gradually disappeared from the village: references to them in the parish register diminish until by 1680 or so the family name disappears completely. Though they had been one of the steadier yeoman families in Kingston, they were finally forced out of succession by a failure of male line. When Arthur died in 1639, his brother John was recorded in the manor court proceedings as already dead.[53]

The Barnden succession not only demonstrates how land was inherited in borough English. It also gives an example of some of the rationality that attaches to this kind of inheritance system (which had the technical name of ultimogeniture). On two occasions in the early seventeenth century the youngest Barnden son in line of succession was a minor: Henry in 1594 was 15; Arthur in 1617 was only one year old. Borough English was, of course, more likely to lead to such situations than borough French, for if succession passed through the eldest son, the chances were much greater that he would not only have attained majority at the time of his father's death but also that he might have a family of his own.

Succession by a minor child had two possible advantages from the point of view of some family members. For one thing it gave the widowed mother of the inheritor a stronger and more secure position economically. Consider what might have happened to Joan Balcombe, old John Barnden's second wife, if the succession to the Kingston lands had been through the eldest son. In this case, John's eldest son would have taken over the land together with his wife and a substantial family of four children. The calls they could have made on the income from the yardlands would have been considerable and though, following custom, they would have taken responsibility for the widowed Joan Balcombe, the material resources available to look after her would have been restricted. The fact that succession was in fact through the adolescent and obviously unmarried Henry in 1594 gave Joan Balcombe a greater role in making decisions about the family lands and in controlling the income from them. In relation to the rest of the family she moved into a matriarchal role, whereas under the system of borough French she would inevitably have become an old and comparatively powerless addition to a young family. So, also, we must suppose that Henry Barnden's surviving wife in 1617 had a decisive voice in the disposition of the lands that had passed to the infant Arthur, and in the uses of the income from them.

The other aspect of borough English, which is clear from the Barnden story, is that it created circumstances in which older brothers and uncles might naturally obtain the use of lands during the minority of the inheriting child. In 1620, for example, Thomas Barnden, Arthur's uncle occupied the lands in Kingston and no doubt benefited from them until his death in 1625. This accession to family lands not only gave the families of older children like Thomas a greater immediate income. It was also a chance to accumulate a little capital, which might later on be turned to good use in financing a rewarding tenancy on another man's lands. Thomas Barnden was certainly not the only member of the family to benefit from minority succession in this way. When he died in 1625 it is likely that one of his half-brothers took over the land until Arthur attained majority. And, in the preceding generation, Henry Barnden's succession to the lands as a minor had left a chance for one of his half-brothers to use the land in the same way. In short, under borough English there was at least a greater chance that the benefits of a family land-holding might be shared between several siblings than under borough French. It had, in this sense, a somewhat more egalitarian touch than the much more common system of primogeniture. At the same time, as the Barnden history shows, it could preserve a family holding intact as effectively as borough French, or primogeniture, which is widely credited as the reason why English lands were, in general, kept intact as integral parcels and not subdivided between many successors.

In this second aspect also, borough English increased the power of a widowed mother with a minor son. It was she who decided who would work the lands. It was she who, in consequence, might determine how opportunities for wealth were distributed between old members of the family. Under borough English, therefore, the potential power of women was greater than under borough French. From the male standpoint any woman might become powerful provided only that she succeeded as a widow to a minor son. There was, of course, no guarantee that this would happen, but the possibility that it might, must surely have affected the positions that women held in the village. On borough English lands women were *potentially* powerful. A wife, sister or daughter might in the course of events acquire effective control over a large parcel of strips in the open field. Husbands imbued with concern for continuity on the lands would have to make sure that their wives knew enough of their management to ensure it. Brothers and brothers-in-law would take account of the possibility that a widow with a minor son might choose them to work lands under her guardianship. Fathers might look upon their daughters in a slightly different way on borough English lands than on borough French. It would be easy to push the point too far. Of course, the possibilities of an effective female succession in widowhood changed things, but it might never happen. But still it is tempting to speculate that a woman's power and status might be enhanced in such a world, that there were elements of a matriarchy in Kingston more pronounced than in many other villages where primogeniture prevailed.

The Barndens had kept a steady grip on their lands until the family ran out of male succession in 1639. Others also held their lands in a single manor or were able to keep them in the family line for long periods and did not run out of male succession as the Barndens had done. The Towners, for example, held a house, a barn and a farmyard in among the Ade properties on the south side of the street (see Figure 2.4). This family base was a freehold cottage of Houndean Manor[54] and included about two yardlands in the open fields. Peter Towner was installed there in 1567.[55] He was still holding the land in 1580 when the manor court at Swanborough gave his neighbour, old Gregory Ade, permission to 'pull out the posts and rails of a certain customary fence between his property and that of Peter Towner, to remake it'.[56] A son and grandson, both called John, succeeded Peter[57] and the land continued in the peaceful possession of the Towners well into the seventeenth century. The Towners were comparatively poor landowners; senior males in the family are described as 'husbandmen' in the parish register, suggesting a lower status in the social hierarchy than the yeomen Ades and Barndens. But, despite that, they hung on well enough as independent landholders – indeed as freeholders. They had extraordinarily bad fortune as parents: six of the 11 children born to various Towner families between 1600 and 1640 died before the age of five.[58]

The Picombes, on the other hand, were a large, straggling family of many branches, covering all the ranks of rural society from yeoman downwards. By the seventeenth century there were Picombe labourers, Picombe shepherds, servants, husbandmen and even a Picombe tailor.[59] These varieties of Picombe were no doubt descendants of the three Picombe families listed in the 1524 subsidy (see Chapter 5) who had not had access to land. But at the centre of the Picombe world there was a yeoman family. From the 1570s onwards, John Picombe was in possession of a substantial four yardlands of Iford Manor called Hudd's, and lived with his family in a house near Kingston Manor house on the opposite side of the street.[60] His son, also called John, married Sarah Barnden, inherited the land and held it through much of the first half of the seventeenth century. Sarah and he were prolific; they appear to have had at least ten children.[61]

While the Ades, Barndens, Towners and Picombes were content to hold onto their lands, the Howells give quite a different impression. There were as many Howells as Picombes. Indeed, a visitor to Kingston village in the early seventeenth century might have left with the impression that nearly everyone in the village was either a Howell or a Picombe. As with the Picombes, Howells occupied all levels of the social scale. Certainly during Elizabeth's reign, a John Howell was one of the Kingston shepherds.[62] Nevertheless, the descriptions of the Howells who appear in the Kingston parish register in these times leave one with the impression that the differences of wealth within the family – or rather between its various branches – were less than with the Picombes. If so, the reason may be that the lands the Howells held were spread between more family branches than the Picombes.

Unravelling the succession of the various Howells to Kingston lands is one of the less rewarding tasks for an historian of the village. Their multiplicity, their tendencies to use the same names for generation after generation in parallel branches of the family and the paucity of seventeenth-century manorial records all combine to make the undertaking hazardous. What follows represents best guesses at how Howell lands were brought together.

There were two main branches of the family in 1567: Thomas Howell the farmer on Hyde Manor was at the head of one; Robert, his younger brother headed the other. Thomas evidently used his Hyde tenancies to good effect. By 1568 he held two Kingston yardlands – one had been bought from a Moore (see Table 6.1), and the other, probably of Kingston Manor, had come from we know not where (though conceivably by inheritance, since Kingston Manor used borough French and Thomas may well have been an eldest son). These lands passed to Richard, Thomas's only son in the early 1580s.

Richard held them for the next 40. At his death they passed out of the Howell family, for only one child – his daughter Marjory who had married the puritanical Thomas Gower – had apparently survived him, so the lands went to the Gowers.

In 1567 Robert had held only a small amount of land, a barn and half a yardland. He had considerable resources, however, since at some point before 1567 he had owned Hudd's – the four yardlands Picombe purchased as a family base. Perhaps Robert had turned temporarily to tenancy. At all events, during the 1570s he started to acquire land in the village. First, he bought the great barn and yardlands called 'Taberer's' – Iford copyhold land. At this time he went to live with his family in the house associated with Taberer's barn on the south centre of the street (see Figure 6.1). Somewhat later, perhaps in the 1590s, Robert bought out another yeoman family – the Adams. Adam's house – facing down the street from its crossroads with Ashcombe Lane and Well Green Lane – became another Howell house. By this time, say in the 1590s, Robert Howell had turned himself into one of the larger yeomen farmers, for he held four yardlands, albeit in two manors with different rules of succession.

The customs of succession ensured that this large engrossment did not remain intact. Stephen Howell, Robert's eldest son, took over Taberer's on Robert's death and John, his youngest son, took over the Swanborough yardlands. By 1615 or so there were three Howell families of approximately equal wealth in the village: Richard's family, on lands inherited from Thomas; and Stephen and John on lands from Robert.

Only John's lands remained in the Howell family. Stephen's line ran out of males and these lands went to the Harfrey family. John's lands remained in the family, but mysteriously they were divided between John, his eldest son, who should not have inherited under borough English, and Thomas, the younger son, who should have had the lot. How this was done is unclear: perhaps John Howell was able to circumvent the customs of succession in the same way as the Ades managed to do. The outcome, by 1640, was that John, his eldest son, was the dominant Howell in the village – well installed in the house across the road from the Ades – and Robert's substantial acreage of the 1590s was broken down into small bits. The Howells had been less successful than Ades or Picombes in holding their lands together and their position as landholders was quickly eroded. But, at the same time, the forces that made for this erosion – the distribution of lands between family branches whether by design or not – probably had the effect of spreading wealth more evenly between Howells than it was spread within some other families.

By buying up the old a Moore yardland, Taberer's and Adam's, the Howells between them might seem to have made a substantial incursion into the 'small lands' of Kingston. But, as Table 7.1 shows, the subsequent subdivision of Robert Howell's lands meant that little changed in the village. Over the 70 years from 1570 to 1640, the main change on the small lands was a reduction in their acreage because of the Dorset engrossment. As a result of Dorset's policies there were three fewer independent yeomen families in the village in 1640 than in 1570. Despite Howell rearrangements, the average size of holding on these small lands was not much greater than it had been. Kingston peasants were holding their own, but despite forces favouring larger landholdings, they had been unable to accumulate land on a significant scale – at least compared with the larger landlords and capitalist farmers who had come in from outside. Because Kingston's manorial heritage had made it a difficult village to enclose, and because they were a tenacious lot, the village yeomanry had managed to keep their place, but no more than that.

Beneath this yeomanry, from an economic and social point of view there were smaller families – independent cottagers and people who rented cottagers or lived in them at their employer's will and earned their living from labour. By 1640 such people were a good deal poorer than they had been in

Table 7.1: Kingston owner-occupiers on fewer than eight yardlands[63]

1570			1640	
Ade	6		Ade	6
Picombe	4		Picombe	4
Barnden	3		Barnden	3 (plus Shoe-smith)
Towner	c2		Towner	c2
Wolridge	2		via Harfrey	2
Adams	1½	via Robert Howell	John Howell	1½
Robert Howell	½	via	Thos. Howell	½
Thos. Howell	1	both via Richard	Gower	2
A Moore	1	Howell		
Boniface	2½		Boniface	2½
Coppard	3	both these lands		
Bowrer	2	to Dorset		
Total in yardlands	28½			24½
Nos of landholders	12			9
Av. no. yardlands per landholder	2.38			2.72

1570. By the latter half of Elizabeth's reign the parish register and other sources give us a glimpse of who they were. At a guess, there were eight or ten families involved in Elizabethan days. And it is likely that the reduction in small tenancies, which resulted from the activities of Dorset, Vinall and Bowker, increased the number of labouring families as a proportion of the village population.

The 'labouring' families were not all simple labourers. For example, there were shepherds among them. The Picombes provided shepherd families, as did the Howells. There were also less well-connected shepherds like the Baldys.[64] Shepherds obviously played an important part in the life of a downland village where so much production depended on flocks. These men, who spent so much time alone on the solitary slopes above the village looking after their flocks on summer nights, and even sleeping out away from their families, were also a little mysterious.

There were also some craftsmen and a Picombe family of tailors.[65] There was almost certainly a malthouse and a maltster to provide that most essential of all English commodities – beer. A carpenter named William Browne rented accommodation and working space from William Ade and lived among the

Ade family.[66] And it is hard to believe that the village would have been without a blacksmith.

But most were labourers. The Tuppens appeared in Kingston for the first time in 1565.[67] At that time they were simple labourers (though later they produced shepherds). The Tuppens were one of the longest lived worker families in the village – the last Kingston Tuppen died in about 1975, more than 400 years after the first record. And there were many others: Bartletts (1590, 1622), Hills (1593), Coppers (1612), Gills (1612), Moores (1629), and Allens (1679).[68] They tended to describe themselves as yeomen as time went by, but their real role in the village was to provide labour for the lands.

It was, in general, a hard life in Kingston. Infant mortality, for obvious reasons, is a good measure of material welfare. In Table 7.2 there is a summary of infant deaths in Kingston in some of the yeoman families, which gives a measure of things.[69] Compared with peasant societies in today's underdeveloped countries this mortality rate for infants of under a year was not too severe. Slightly less than one baby in five died before its first birthday, whereas in African peasant societies in the twentieth century losing four out of ten was not unheard of – more than twice as many in proportion. At the same time, however, it must be kept in mind that the figures in Table 7.2 relate mainly to yeoman families, who, by virtue of ownership of land, were better off and better nourished. Though comparisons between families in the table are risky because the numbers of births and deaths involved are rather small, it is notable that the Picombes, whose families included a larger proportion of landless wage workers and labourers, had considerably higher mortality rates than the generally richer Ades or the more egalitarian Howells. Possibly the Picombes' experience was more typical of life at the lower end of the social scale than the Ades'. Tuppens, for example, might – like the Picombes – have expected to lose one baby in three or four before the age of one, and somewhere just short of half their children before they were six years old. It was not by modern measures an easy existence and it was, by the look of things, very hard for the poor whose lot had not been helped by the incidence of a century or more of declining real wages.

Let us return to a slightly broader view of the village society in Elizabethan and early Stewart times. It is clear that the main changes in the structure of the community over this period, from 1570 to the civil war, derived from Dorset's engrossment and the closely associated emergence of the Vinall family as a new dominant force in everyday life. In the course of the changes that ensued, there was some reduction in the amount of 'small-lands' in the village. And, because of this, as well as some rearrangements in landholding induced mainly by the Howell family, the number of small owner-occupiers dropped from twelve families in 1570 or so, to nine in 1640. Nevertheless, this independent yeomanry remained in an important way, the core of village society. The nine families formed a network of social relationships around which much of the life in the street revolved. They reinforced their links

Table 7.2: Infant mortality in Kingston, 1560–1670

Family	*Time period*	*No. of births*	*No. of deaths under six years*	*% of births*	*No. of deaths under one year*	*% of births*
Barnden	1560–1660	31	4	12.96	1	3.2
Towner	1600–1640	11	6	54.54	1	9.0
Ade	1560–1680	38	12	31.50	9	23.6
Howell	1560–1660	37	10	27.00	5	13.5
Picombe	1560–1670	45	19	42.00	13	28.8
Totals		162	41	31.00	29	17.90

with one another by marriages. Their extended families included a significant proportion of the wage labour and cottager class. And some, the Ades in particular, married their daughters and sons upwards into the more powerful families above them. The core was somewhat diminished, but in 1640 it remained intact. The changes of the times took place around it. The changes Dorset initiated are summarized in Table 7.3. In effect, Dorset considerably accelerated a process of engrossment that had started long before, particularly on the landlord-tenant lands of Kingston. As we know, Eversfields and Newtons, by 1570, had brought lands together into potentially larger tenancies. Dorset took up the process with a vengeance. Table 7.3 shows the sharp change in the configuration of landholding between 1570 and 1600. By the turn of the century, Dorset lands, which then included Kingston Manor demesnes, were larger in aggregate than all the small lands of the village put together. And, in this initial period, all these lands came under one great tenancy farmed by John Vinall. The overall effect was, of course, to reduce sharply the numbers of small tenancies. Since small tenancies had been characteristic of Kingston, particularly in early Tudor times as the village emerged from the medieval twilight, this was a change of some moment.

Where numbers of comparatively poor families had been able to make a living from the land, there was a single rich tenant family in 1600. The capacity of the village lands to provide directly for the poorer, non-inheriting branches of village families was accordingly greatly diminished. And, at the same time, the need for wage labour, where before family labour had worked, was commensurately greater. The small tenant adjuncts to the independent yeomen families in the village disappeared from view; and the proportion of labouring families increased.

Dorset's retreat from Kingston did not greatly alter the pattern. Though he sold Kingston Manor to Vinall, the concentration of ownership and tenancy on the larger lands in the village was little changed. As it happened, the Bowker family bought up Eversfield's lands and for a while at least farmed these along with the 15 yardlands Dorset retained in the open fields. The sharp reduction in the amount of landlord-tenant land between 1600 and 1640 meant that Vinall's pre-eminence of earlier years was tempered somewhat by the appearance of another rich family: the Bowkers. But its overall effect was simply to increase the number of large owner-occupiers at the expense of large tenants.

As far as life in the street was concerned, the most obvious effect of all this was that it brought the Vinalls into the dominant position in Kingston society and kept them there. They were the richest and most successful family the village had experienced in generations. Kingston had been able to avoid many of the impacts that changing market forces had on other open-field villages. There was no enclosure and no conversion. The fields remained intact. But, nevertheless, the bigger economic changes reflected on the village and, in a clear sense, the seventeenth-century dominance of the Vinalls resulted from them. The forces that made for enclosure, conversion and depopulation elsewhere also made the already enclosed, easily convertible and unpopulated demesnes of Swanborough more profitable than other lands. The economic power of the Vinalls – and their eventual role in the village – was founded on that high profitability. It made them rich. Compared with their predecessors, the Vinalls were at a greater economic distance from ordinary people in the street.

As we have seen, old John Vinall's success as a farmer played its part in inducing the Dorsets to turn their eyes on Kingston lands. Vinall may have had a role in engrossment – the one great impact of the times that was clearly experienced in Kingston. And his achievements clearly provided his family with a solid economic foundation in the village. When John Vinall the younger turned to owner-occupancy at Kingston Manor, the acreages the family controlled may have diminished for a while. But their status in the village and beyond it, as they turned themselves into gentry, did not. And, as we shall see, their presence as lords of the manor was full of portent.

Because it started at Swanborough, the Vinalls' progress reasserted the old importance of the demesnes for life in Kingston and, at the same time, brought together some long strands in the history of the village. One strand stretches back to the very distant Norman past, to the time when Swanborough Manor was created. If Swanborough were available as a great enclosure in 1600, while so many lands around remained in dispersed strips, it was of course because de Warenne had carved it out to attract Cluny to the idea of a priory. Five or more centuries later the consolidated block he had created was still intact, attracting other men for other reasons. De Warenne facilitated changes he could never have foreseen.

Table 7.3: Landholding and social structure: Dorset's impact

		Estimated number of occupants			
c.1575		*c.1600*		*c.1640*	
Hyde-Michel	1	Hyde-Michel	1	Dorset (Bowker) landlord-tenant	1
Eversfield	2–3	Eversfield lands	1–2	Bowker from Eversfield Newton	1 (Vinall)
Hardman	1	Dorset Hyde-Alchorne	1	Coppard/Bowrer	2 including 1
Kingston Manor (Crane)	1	Kingston Manor (Vinall)	1	Kingston Manor	
		owner-occupied 'small-lands'			
Barnden	1	Barnden	1	Barnden	1
Ade	1	Ade	1	Ade	1
		from c.1600 onwards			
Picombe	1	Picombe	1	Picombe	1
		other small lands			
	7		6		6
		number of occupiers			
	18–19		12–13		12
		of which tenants			
	5–6		3–4		1* Bowker
		small owner-occupiers			
	12		9		9 double
		large owner-occupiers			
	1		0		3* counted
		Estimated number of labourer and cottager families			
	8–10		14–18		14–18

But there is another strand too. The Swanborough demesnes had doubtless attracted enterprising and acquisitive men with an eye for good land for many long years. They had, however, been tied firmly to the priory for centuries, until the dissolution in 1538. The dissolution opened the lands to commercially minded landlords and skilled tenants: it had created necessary conditions for Vinall's rise to local power. Indeed, with the appearance of

Vinall, Kingston felt the full effects of the dissolution for the first time – effects the village people could not have anticipated as they stood and watched Portinari's grotesque destruction of the huge priory church, but which in the end were more lasting in their impact than that singular piece of philistinism. The dissolution of the priory opened the way: John Vinall was the first man to exploit the opportunity it created to the full, and so also the first fully to bring home to Kingston village the more material implications of Henry VIII's attack on the monasteries. Vinall was the first, but not the last.

Chapter 8

Hubris and the Vinalls: A Seventeenth-Century Interlude

In the 1640s England was torn apart by civil war. But the struggle between the parliamentary and royalist forces, and the ensuing Commonwealth and Protectorate, do not seem to have made any great impact on life in the village. Kingston lies deep in the southeast of England and that area was uniformly on the parliamentary side and not directly affected by the military campaigns. Indeed, the area around Lewes was traditionally a countryside of Puritan tendency. Its Puritan links dated from well before Mary's reign and they had led that over-zealous queen to the burning of Protestants in the town square. Lewes, she felt, was one of those towns most in need of correction by stern example. Kingston no doubt shared these religious and civil traditions. Though the civil war must have produced some divisions in Kingston Street, the village was not subject to the tensions and violence characteristic of other parts of the country – and at no time was it overrun by the passage of arms.[1]

The most divisive moment came in the course of the civil war itself. By 1645 or so, as it progressed towards the abolition of episcopacy, parliament engaged itself in the further reformation and 'correction' of the Church of England. Among its more radical moves was the setting up of 'committees for plundered ministries'. These were inspired and manned by tougher-minded, more totalitarian Puritans whose purpose was essentially to control the Church Henry VIII had established and to turn it to puritanical objectives. With frightening earnestness and a good deal of self-righteousness the committees directed their attention to the theologically irrelevant problem of the moral conduct of ministers. Men who did not doubt the correctness of their own views of right and wrong sat on them to pass judgement on the behaviour of country vicars, taking depositions – more or less in secret – from individual parishioners and reaching their conclusions without the encumbrance of hearing the case from the other side.[2] Because they were spared the confusions that contrary evidence might introduce and were to all appearances quite certain of their own moral inspiration, the committees reached their conclusions quickly. A vicar might find himself dispossessed without any prior indication that he was under investigation. And, as ever under such obnoxious systems of arbitrary justice, informers had a splendid time satisfying old resentments by informing on the vicar.

There was a Committee for Plundered Ministries in Lewes. Its contribution to the advance of religious and public morality in Kingston was to dispossess the vicar. Henry Shephearde, who had been good enough to baptize, marry and bury many villagers, was simply dismissed in May 1645 – without the benefit of giving evidence on his own behalf – for the rather vague offence of 'drunkenness and other misdemeanours'.[3] John Melvin, 'an orthodox and holy divine' was appointed in his place. For a while after 1645 Kingston had a 'pure' man as vicar.

What had poor Henry done? There is no way of saying with any certainty, but since the righteous had judged him without hearing his story we can at least record the defence made on his behalf in a happier time. Richard Owen, who was vicar in Kingston and Iford from 1692 to 1733 (and as a Restoration cleric not without his own biases), had this to say:

> the offence was only this as I am credibly informed. On Saturday he bought a shoulder of mutton … but came home too late to prepare fewell for the dressing of it. Therefore the next morning he made bold with his axe to give a chop or two to some old fence rails. … This was presently carried to Lewes and on Monday following he was convened and execution done.[4]

The account has some credibility. The Puritan judgement suggests why Henry had come home too late on Saturday to prepare 'fewell' for his Sunday meal. He had probably stayed in the alehouse too long on Saturday night and come home too tired or too drunk to cut wood. So, a little bleary on an early Sunday morning, he had sinned by working on the Sabbath, by cutting down some fencing rails for fuel! Someone conveyed the news of this misdemeanour to Lewes and the pretentious committee reached its conclusions. Kingston was saved from the abyss of sin!

There were people in most English villages with reason to resent the church and its immediate representatives among them. Churchmen were comparatively privileged socially and economically. Tudor attempts to improve the standards of the ministry by increasing the numbers of country rectors and vicars who had been to Oxford or Cambridge – worlds away from the narrow confines of village life – sharpened these distinctions. Also, the moral and economic demands of the church impinged harshly on some people. Men and women were punished insensitively for a variety of peccadilloes and the church demanded tithes from all who held land and from some who did not. So, quite aside from the incidence of genuine doctrinal differences, there were people with scores to settle who might perceive the local priest as a convenient and perhaps appropriate object of resentment.

There were most probably people like this in Kingston: it is a safe assumption that Kingston villagers committed adultery, had illegitimate children from time to time, failed to go to church at Easter and committed minor acts of sacrilege. They would have been punished for these sins and they might well have resented it. They were less likely to have resented the church itself for the tithes they had to pay, for the priory held most of these.[5] After the dissolution they passed to private individuals via the initial grant from Henry VIII to Anne of Cleves,[6] and consequently simply became items of private property. Tithes may have been irksome in Kingston as elsewhere, but they could not have been a source of resentment against the parson himself. The person who ran to Lewes to tell the story of Henry Shephearde's wickedness either had some other reason to resent him or was simply moved by an excess of moral rectitude.

The villagers were surely divided about the consequences. Though the village as a whole was committed to the parliamentary cause, the extent and nature of individual attachments to it varied a good deal, as elsewhere in England. The committees for plundered ministries were the creation of the Long Parliament in one of its more 'radical' moods but, despite their formal legitimacy, it is most unlikely that their activities had the uniform approval of all who supported parliament. Those of more radical inclination may have approved the harshness of the judgement against Shephearde, regardless perhaps of their personal feelings about the vicar. Others surely found it cruelly absurd and wondered perhaps at the direction parliament was taking. Henry in his own small way was a victim in the much greater struggle that was shaping up within the parliamentary ranks between the more radical, puritanical elements seeking to pursue the English revolution to further conclusions, and those whose interests lay in holding together the established order of things. He was ruined because of a momentary parliamentary success by the radical tendency.

There are more general reasons to believe that events during the revolutionary crisis provoked differences of opinion in the village. The civil war meant that rural communities like Kingston, which had in the main preserved a kind of sheltered integrity quite separate from national politics, became more closely concerned with the broader sequence of events. The differences of view that probably surfaced when the Puritan committee found Henry Shephearde wanting were founded on responses to wider divisions in national politics and not only on social alignments or individual likes and dislikes within the village.

In the civil war period, the broader struggle within parliamentary ranks brought two main tendencies into opposition. 'Independents', who eventually won the day, were less concerned with the overthrow of monarchy than with enforcing parliamentary power over the king. The greater part of the parliamentary gentry of Sussex belonged in this camp. Later, once the king had been beheaded and the Commonwealth installed as a political fact, they were divided in their responses to the new order. Men like Henry Morely of Glynde, a cousin of the Morely who had sold Kingston Manor to John Vinall in 1634, and soon to become one of the most powerful of the Sussex members of parliament, reconciled themselves to the Commonwealth even if they had neither sought it nor identified with the regicide. Others were less willing to encompass a revolutionary development they had not wished for and drifted into neutrality,[7] in many cases becoming disillusioned when Cromwell imposed the protectorate.

Against this dominant tendency, more radical elements, usually identifiable by their deeper Puritanism, were in search of more profound change: the abolition of monarchy, certainly, but also extended franchise and, in some cases, profound changes in the laws that protected private property.

Although everyone in Kingston was most likely 'parliamentary', even if only nominally, it would be astonishing if there were not some division of view in the village in the face of the fundamental debates of the late 1640s. The aspirations of the more radical parliamentary supporters must have been threatening to some in the village. The Vinalls, for example, had crossed over from being large tenant farmers to the ownership of demesne lands and manorial lordship. The family had a strong interest in the established social order. Indeed, Vinall had plainly devoted a great part of his energies to secure his own advancement in it. He would hardly have encompassed the wilder sorts of puritanical radicalism that surfaced in the disturbed times. Equally, Edmund Bowker who owned all Kingston freehold lands out of demesnes could have had little interest in the outer reaches of radical reform.

Yet Kingston clearly housed Puritans whose political views were different from those of the aspiring if minor gentry who dominated the village. Much later, 15 years after the Restoration, by which time it demanded great personal courage to be known as a Puritan, a religious census recorded seven Nonconformists in Kingston among 73 conforming members of the established Church.[8] Earlier, while the Church had been disestablished, there were more who had been willing to express more extreme religious and conceivably also political views.

The Wenhams were among them. This family was living in Kingston by the 1640s.[9] In time they came to hold the tenement, barn and yardland that Thomas Gower had acquired by his marriage into the Richard Howell family.[10] It is possible that Wenham had married a daughter of Thomas Gower and inherited the yardland. The Wenhams were Quakers, indeed very early Quakers. George Fox, who started the Society of Friends and founded the Quaker movement, first visited Sussex in 1655. Most Sussex conversions to the movement dated from that visit and the effective and considerable propaganda that followed it.[11] The Wenhams, however, were Quakers before Fox's visit. They are listed in the *Register of Quakers* as early as 1650. Their house in Kingston was one of the earliest Quaker meeting places in the county. In 1668, when life had become much tougher for the religiously and politically radical, it remained one of the recognized gathering places.[12] The Wenhams were indeed punished for being Quakers when the new intolerance of the Restoration years replaced the old. The political, social and religious distances between aspiring Vinalls and radical Wenhams were considerable. Their coexistence in the village through the decades of civil war, Commonwealth, Protectorate and Restoration must have been a strain. In this small way Kingston reflected the larger tensions of the time, for though the Wenhams were the only Quakers in the village, there were no doubt others who were not Friends who nevertheless shared some of their views about the inadequacies of doctrinal reforms in the Church, and perhaps also on political matters. Members of the Ade family held to the sterner sort of Puritanism that eventually led people to break with the Church, albeit at greater personal cost. And perhaps also the Alchornes, despite their well-established interest in land, had a more radical cast of mind than most. After the Restoration members of both families were 'presented' by the Kingston churchwardens (one of whom was John Howell), for persistently failing to attend the village church.[13]

But whatever religious and political tensions lay beneath the surface of village life, events in general seem to have followed much the usual course through the long years of the interregnum. As elsewhere in rural parts of east Sussex, the great changes had little immediate effect on people's lives. Commercially minded men and women got on with their business as they had always done. Labourers struggled for their subsistence at a real wage, which had fallen slowly and steadily for a good deal longer than a century. Once the errant vicar had been chastised there were no more events of note to mark the larger political transformations of the times. Kingston, like so many other Sussex villages that had been devotedly parliamentary in 1640, was happy enough to see the king restored to the throne in 1660, with the probable exception of the Wenhams who had little to hope for from a monarch intent on re-establishing the Church. In 1668, John Wenham died in prison where he had lain for nearly five years for refusing the oath of allegiance. His house in Kingston continued as a Quaker meeting place.[14]

******

The main developments in agriculture in the latter half of the seventeenth century were in many important respects a continuation of the Tudor and Stuart past. The agrarian transformations that had taken place under the preceding monarchies affected them considerably. In particular, landlords, tenants and peasant farmers were learning to take full advantage of the consolidations and enclosures that had affected many villages by that time. The practice of temporary ley became more widespread, for example. Cultivators on enclosed lands became progressively more adept at using them flexibly to respond to changing prices for agricultural outputs and to the requirements for maintaining fertility. The gradual spread of 'up-and-down farming', as the use of temporary leys came to be described, would probably have produced a significant increase in land yields. Old and tired arables that had suffered long centuries of medieval rotation gathered heart again by being left to pasture for two, three or more seasons, where before they were rested as fallows for one season in three.

The use of temporary leys on a wider scale was not the only mark of the times; a good many of the agricultural practices that characterized the 'agricultural revolution' of the early eighteenth century were in fact in the process of gradual introduction long before.[15] The turnip was introduced widely in the late seventeenth century, as were other root crops. Sainfoin, which is nitrogenous, was increasingly cultivated. The main elements of the four-course rotation were present and there were cultivators who had already discovered its advantages. Such experiments were evidently much easier on enclosed land than on open fields, so there was a direct connection between the socially damaging engrossments, consolidations and enclosures of Tudor times and the gradual emergence of a new high yielding agriculture. At all events, whether or not earlier enclosure had facilitated experiments crucial for the future, it is clear that yields *did* improve in the late seventeenth century. Indeed, they improved to such good effect that the price of wheat fell relative to the wage rate, so that in the last decades of the century agricultural labourers enjoyed (if that is an appropriate term), a level of living that remained more or less stable as opposed to the falling standards of the preceding century and a half.[16] English agriculture was not yet in that phase of dramatic yield increase we nowadays call the agricultural revolution, but it was moving in that direction.

Kingston, however, was not enclosed. It remained a 'champion village', irreducibly committed at the time to its open-field system. Since enclosure facilitated many of the improving measures that account for the gradual increase in land yields, one is naturally led to wonder how far the village cultivators were able to take advantage of them.

It is clear, however, that open-field villages were not uniformly prevented from using the newer techniques of cultivation of the late seventeenth century. For example, open-field cultivators were able to agree among themselves to turn groups of abutting strips over to temporary pasture. This was probably done on the basis of the furlong, and required the use of temporary fencing. Though clumsy, it apparently worked.[17] Similarly, some experimentation with traditional rotations was possible provided collective agreements could be obtained.

The problem of such innovation on the open fields was, of course, that it required agreement between the owners of abutting strips in a furlong, which was not always possible to obtain. It was probably easier to achieve if fewer individual cultivators were involved and the total landholdings were larger. In addition, it was probably easier for a group of larger farmers to agree than for smaller peasants. It is true that the system of temporary leys, if judiciously used, could increase the total output of both arable and pastoral products, but at the same time a person probably needed a minimum amount of land to take full advantage of it. The initial effect of turning old arables to pasture was to *reduce* total output, perhaps for a season or two until the new pasture was sufficiently established to support increased animal production. A large landholder might look on the temporary reduction in output as an investment in greater production for the future. But the sacrifice of a given proportion of the year's output, albeit in the interests of getting more later, was much more difficult for a small landowner. The small farmer with a yardland or less was very close to the subsistence level of output at the best of times and so not easily able to encompass any reduction in it whatever the future gains might be. Small farmer reluctance to accept such reductions would be greater when real wage levels were low and, because of the possibilities of compensating for the loss of their own production by wage, labour would be limited. It might therefore be difficult to obtain agreement to turn a furlong over to pasture if the poorer peasantry of the village owned some of the strips in it.

However, after Dorset's incursion into Kingston lands at the end of the sixteenth century, the obstacles in the way of agreed experimentation with the old three-field rotations were considerably reduced. From about 1600 or before, about two-thirds of Kingston land was held or tenant farmed in 'parcels' of more than eight yardlands; and only three or four families of large owner-occupiers or tenants controlled this two-thirds, which comprised the 'large' lands of the village. Moreover, even on the 'small' lands that supported the village's owner-occupier yeomanry, most families held more than two yardlands. At the least, the conditions for a fairly flexible use of the open-field system were a great deal more favourable after 1600 than they had been in the early Tudor years. It is quite likely that dominant families like the Vinalls, Bowkers, Alchornes and perhaps also the Ades were able to sustain the reorganization needed to take advantage of new and improved methods. Indeed, it is all the more likely because one of these families, the Vinalls, by virtue of their long tenancy on the great enclosure at Swanborough and their continued occupancy of its demesnes, knew a good deal about the advantages that could be obtained. It is hard to believe that after 40 years of tenancy on these lands, which were so easily adapted to up-and-down farming, the Vinalls would have sunk so much of their capital into Kingston Manor unless they had some assurance that they could apply similar methods to some of the ancient demesne strips.

There are other indications of possible reorganization of production in the village's open fields. For one thing, a very rough estimate based on Marchant's terrier of 1773 suggests that, by 1630 or so, somewhere between a third and a half of all village arables lay in furlongs where the Vinalls, Bowkers, Alchornes and Ades held more than three-quarters of the strips between them.[18] In these furlongs it would be comparatively easy for large landholders to agree to depart from traditional rotations – perhaps to get the arable put to temporary leys. For another thing, by the Stuart period there are clear signs that rotation by furlongs had decisively displaced rotations by the whole laine or field. The Hyde survey strongly suggests a substantial recovery of arable from 'waste' in the late Elizabethan or Stuart period (see Chapter 2) and that virtually all this assarting took the form of an addition to the arable area of Mill Laine, the open field that ran along the slope between Kingston village and Southover. The assarting accounts for the disproportionate size of Mill Laine compared with Swanborough Laine and the West Laine; Mill Laine is a full 50 per cent larger in area than the others, mainly due to the assarted area (see Table 2.1). The immediate point, however, is that this large difference in the size of Mill Laine strongly suggests that field rotations were a thing of the past in Kingston. Field rotation normally required three laines of approximately equal size – or at least equal productive capacity. That the villagers were ready to extend one of the laines so considerably, unbalancing the system, was an indication that furlongs rather than whole fields had become the basic unit of communal land organization. The practice of furlong rotations enhanced the chances of innovation. The decision to try out new uses for a furlong or two was obviously easier to obtain than a decision on a larger area – and also involved less risk if things went amiss. By 1640 Kingston cultivators had probably found ways of using new methods even though the village was almost completely unenclosed.

Of all Kingston people the Vinall family was the most likely to take advantage of the agricultural improvements of the times. Indeed, one of the main village continuities between the Elizabethan period and the latter half of the seventeenth century was the steady economic and social advancement of Vinalls. Old John Vinall, Dorset's tenant who had come to Kingston in the decade after the Armada, had built well. His son, John the younger, born in the uncertain years before the Armada, took over the great tenancies in 1625 at his father's death, bought his way into Kingston Manor in 1634 and into a gentleman's coat of arms shortly thereafter and, together with his Ade wife, held together the Vinall interests through the long and sometimes threatening periods of civil war, Commonwealth and Protectorate. Those interests were most decidedly intact when he died in 1661 at the considerable age of 77; he had lasted just long enough to see the restoration of the monarchy.[19]

By the time the second John Vinall died the family had lived in the manor house at the head of the street for a full three-quarter of a century; and in his lifetime their position in the village was substantially consolidated. John Vinall, the new manor lord, maintained the tenancy on the Swanborough demesnes on which the family was founded, but he used its surpluses, together with those from his own holdings, to build up the Vinall lands estate. By 1655, in the time of the Protectorate, John had added at least one further manor to family ownership – the manor of Wickam in Clayton, Keymer and Hurstpierpoint, lying to the north of Brighton. This included 300 acres of arable. The Vinalls had become landlords, for they leased out the lands at Wickham rather than cultivate them through a steward.[20]

They had also started on a process of building up their lands in Kingston itself. The Vinalls took a bite into the 'small lands' of the village. At some point before 1658 they bought the three copyhold yardlands of Swanborough Manor, which had belonged to the Barndens earlier and had passed to John Howell of Wilmington by virtue of his marriage to Joan Barnden (see Chapter 7). The 'small lands' were further reduced; the Vinalls were enhanced. Henceforth, Barndens became part of the Kingston Manor estate, although of course John Vinall had to pay homage, as a regular copyholder, to the Duke of Dorset at Swanborough.[21] For Vinall, the formality of paying homage at the manor court of the noble duke was of much less import than that the purchase added a useful 25 per cent to the amount of arable he held in the open fields of the village, and commensurately to his claim on pasture and brooklands.

At the same time the family succession in Kingston was assured. Mary Ade, John's wife, had died in 1641 at the comparatively early age of 34. Nonetheless, in 13 years of marriage she had produced five children of whom four survived her. William, her eldest son, was born in 1633. Benjamin, the youngest, came into the world in 1641 and it may be that his mother died during his birth.[22] There were two daughters – Mary and Margaret. John married again. Elizabeth, his second wife, bore him at least one son: Henry in 1643.[23] When the old man died in 1661 he had secured most of his purposes: a healthy accumulation of wealth and lands for his posterity to enjoy, an indisputable if somewhat recently acquired position as a county gentleman, and a well-founded family to succeed him. The Vinalls had come through the revolutionary decades in a better social and economic state than they had entered them. And, although the interlocking feudal ascriptions of village lands meant that the Vinalls were not the only manor lords to whom villagers paid homage, or even the most imposing, they maintained and increased their status in the street. Their practical power in decisions about the use of village lands was evidently very great. Their social position at the head of the small community was incontestable, even though in relation to the wider world of the county they were but minor gentry.

Social position was evidently a matter of some preoccupation in the succeeding generation of Vinalls. William, who was to inherit the estate from his father John, was as much or more concerned with his social position in the county as with the older family business of accumulating wealth. That much at least is suggested by William's somewhat sad marital history.

William was young when he first married. The lady was Elizabeth Dobell of Streat and William was only 22 when he married her in 1655.[24] The social status of the bride was a more interesting aspect of this marriage than the youthfulness of the groom. The Dobells of Streat were much more decisively gentry than the Vinalls; they had carried arms for longer. Elizabeth's father, Walter Dobell, was no yeoman. He had a distinguished legal career and had been a justice of the peace between 1631 and 1635,[25] at a time when gentlemen aspired and conspired for a position on the 'Commission'. The Dobells were among those leading gentry of the county who could not live confined to their rural manors. They had a town house in Lewes where they frequently stayed to enjoy what the county town had to offer.[26] Young William had found his way into the society life of the county. His marriage was not only a significant social achievement from the Vinall point of view but it was also distinctly advantageous in a more practical way. Elizabeth brought with her a dowry of £800, which measured up fully to her place in the world. In return, old John Vinall settled a generous annuity of £210 on his new daughter-in-law.[27] This was no village marriage such as he had made to Mary Ade.

William brought his lady back to Kingston to the manor house, though they probably spent a good portion of their time in Lewes too. The marriage was not to last long. Regrettably, poor Elizabeth died in 1663[28] after only eight years with William. There were no children.

William's explorations of genteel marriage were not over. In 1665, two years after Elizabeth's death, he was married again to Anne Farrington. This was, if anything, a grander marriage than his first. Sir John Farrington was a leading citizen of Chichester. He had held administrative responsibilities during the Commonwealth, but at this time was acknowledged as a 'loyal' justice of the peace.[29] He was a man who could use his influence in favour of vicars who had lost their benefices at Puritan hands. He could also use it to ensure a suitably grand marriage for his daughter. William Vinall and Anne were married in the cathedral at Chichester, in a service performed by the Lord Bishop himself.[30] This was splendour indeed for the grandson of a tenant farmer. There is no record of the marriage settlement, but in the circumstances we may presume that it was satisfactory.

Once again William, who by this time had inherited the Vinall estate from his father, brought a genteel bride back to the village. Anne Farrington was perhaps the 'highest born' and most elegant lady who had picked her way with due caution through the chalky winter mud of Kingston Street. Could this simple, small village satisfy her after an upbringing amid the sophistication of Chichester? Would Lewes provide enough urban life for her? She may well have wondered herself, for the transition from the glories of Chichester Cathedral to the distinctly rural joys of Kingston and its muddy cattle yards was, to say the least, abrupt.

Sadly, Anne Farrington never had time to put these matters to the test. In two short years she was dead. She was buried in the aisle of the parish church under a gravestone, subsequently covered by a new tile floor in the course of a rather unfortunate Victorian reconstruction.[31] Again, the marriage was childless.

William was now 34 years old, in possession of the estate his father and grandfather had built up, but childless after two short marriages. His brother Richard and half-brother Henry were both dead. Of the males in the family only he and his younger brother Benjamin remained. Benjamin was as yet unwed. In the manner of the times, William and Benjamin must have felt considerable concern at the prospect of a failure in the male line.

In the event, neither brother remained unwed for long. Benjamin married for the first (and only) time in 1668. His bride was Anne Tree (or Attree) from a long established family in Barcombe, just north of Lewes. And William married for the third time. His new lady was Mabilla Davis, who was described in the marriage settlement as a niece of Dame Elizabeth Boys of Lees in Kent. The dowry was large – £1200.[32] William, no doubt, would not have had it otherwise. Mabilla had a happier future than William's earlier wives. She did not die early and she bore children.

Looked at from one point of view, William's marriages were a measure of the Vinall family's achievements over the generations. Kingston was as accustomed as any other village to high birth and nobility in landlords. It was a different matter for a villager to marry into the senior gentry of the county and bring his lady to live among them. Young women from the Dobell family and from the Farringtons must have excited a certain awe among Kingston villagers. The social distance, which had always separated the Vinalls from more ordinary families like the Howells, Picombes or Towners, became greater than before. It is true that in any moderately healthy community social pretension will excite a degree of mockery. William's marriages were pretentious and Kingston was, to all appearances, a healthy enough place, so there was no doubt a certain amount of amusement at his expense. But, in the end, Kingston, like most rural places, was conservative. People were brought up to respect rank. Accordingly, they were probably impressed as well as amused at the Vinall progress. Not for centuries had Kingston aspired to such glitter of social distinction – albeit a level of distinction that was quite minor in the greater society. William's social ascent attested to the economic successes of his forbears.

But these marriages also betokened a change in outlook in the Vinall household. William was unlike his father and grandfather in the purposes to which he put the family wealth. John Vinall, his father, had been rather grand, of course, but grand in village terms. He had social aspirations, but they were secondary to his main preoccupation with the accumulation of lands and wealth. William, on the other hand, aspired to grandeur of a different order. Dobells and Farringtons lived in worlds that were remote from the village, from the world of the ordinary labourers of Kingston, from Baldy the shepherd or the Picombe who tailored smocks and working clothes for others in the village. William had determined to find a place in a higher order of society altogether. And, because of that determination, his priorities were different from his father's or grandfather's. Further accumulation attracted William, but it was not his main preoccupation. It was secondary to his social purpose and of interest mainly because it might help to further that social purpose. He was, most likely, less concerned with getting richer than with using his wealth for social power and pleasure. In this sense, he seems to belong more squarely to the Restoration than to the stricter puritanical times in which he grew up. In this sense too he stood out against the village background. It is an odd reflection that at just the time William was contracting his third society marriage, John Wenham was dying for his Quakerism in Lewes prison. The juxtaposition reflects the wider failure of the radicals of the revolutionary years and the continuity of privilege that landed gentry had been able to preserve. It also reflects a change of purpose in the Vinall family that might have shocked William's acquisitive and earnest grandfather who had resented taking on the office of constable, most probably because it would have taken time and energy he wished to devote to the proper management of his lands.

Something of the priority William's forebears attached to the integrity of their lands in Kingston, and hence to the business of building up and maintaining the estate, showed up in the dispositions John Vinall made at the time he purchased the three copyhold yardlands of Swanborough Manor, which had once belonged to the Barndens. 'Barndens' presented something of a problem. As copyholds of Swanborough these yardlands would normally pass to succeeding generations by borough English, in other words to youngest sons, just as they had through all the long years during which they had been in the Barnden family (see Chapter 7). In the ordinary course of events, therefore, Barndens should have passed, by custom, to Benjamin Vinall, William's younger brother. Since the demesne lands of Kingston Manor were not subject to the same custom, but passed, as did all demesnes, through the eldest son, John Vinall's estate could have been divided into two at the time of his death. John did not wish this. Whatever strength of natural affection he had for Benjamin did not outweigh the threat John perceived in a divided estate. So, when he bought 'Barndens', he somehow arranged with the manor court at Swanborough that the purchase should be in his eldest son William's name as well as his own. When a survey of Swanborough Manor lands was made in 1658, it included among the copyholders: 'John and William Vynall for three yards and a mesne land called Barnde's'.[33] Such joint holding of copy was rare at the time. It worked successfully though to exclude young Benjamin. When John died William was admitted to the land.[34] No doubt some arrangement of a reasonably fair kind was made within the family to take care of Benjamin. At some point after his father's death (when Benjamin was 20 years old) he moved to Iford. But he inherited no property except a cottage held of Hyde Manor, which the Barndens had once owned separately from their Swanborough lands and in which Thomas Barnden had lived as a cottager. When he died in 1676 Benjamin left this small property to his servant Thomas Wilson, a 'husbandman' of Kingston. It stood on the street opposite the Ade properties and became the village malthouse after 1706.[35]

The accumulative instinct that led to Benjamin Vinall's exclusion from a landed inheritance appears weaker in William than it had been in his father. Between his succession in 1661 and his death in 1680 William made virtually no additions to the family lands in Kingston. There were no purchases to compare with that of Barnden's. The sum of William's addition to the estate was a small parcel of four acres of strips he bought in 1677.[36] While he held the lands in Kingston village intact, William did not sustain his father's tenancy on the demesnes of Swanborough Manor. The tenancy passed to

Benjamin instead. In 1673 Benjamin appears in the Duke of Dorset's rent roll as occupier of the 'scite and greater part of the demesnes' at Swanborough.[37] So, in the latter years of Benjamin's life he lived with his wife and only daughter at Swanborough Manor house, while William and Mabilla with their family lived in Kingston Manor. After Benjamin's death William did not take over the tenancy at Swanborough, which passed out of the Vinall family for the first time in a century[38] and indeed forever. William's interests meanwhile broadened. He became a captain of the militia, a post for which minor gentry competed, especially after the Restoration when for a while the militia was the only effective armed force in the country and its control a source of local power.[39] The captaincy was a natural role for a minor but aspiring gentleman like William, who had insufficient status to become a JP but nevertheless sought social recognition. He valued his rank sufficiently to have his gravestone inscribed 'Captain William Vinall'.

Notwithstanding William's captaincy, the striking social purpose to which he put the family wealth and the series of marriages that brought ladies of rank into the Elizabethan manor house at the head of Kingston Street, it is probably true to say that the Vinalls' economic grip on their position in Kingston weakened in his time. In general, landownership became less profitable as agricultural prices fell and income from the land depended more than before on successful increases in yields. Perhaps William achieved this on his open-field strips in Kingston, but he did not keep the tenancy at Swanborough together with his manor lands in Kingston. His opportunities to increase his income were correspondingly fewer than his father's had been. At the same time he had developed a concern with 'society' that was new, expensive and doubtless foreign to his father's frame of mind. In short, the peak of the Vinalls' economic power in Kingston was at the end of John Vinall's time. William held the landed estate together but no more than that. On his death the Vinalls' position in Kingston started to crumble. William's successors failed economically and brought old John Vinall's achievement to an end.

In the first place there were considerable difficulties establishing a succession at all – or at least a male succession. Mabilla Davis bore children but the first three were all girls: Martha, Marion and Mabilla. Little Mabilla died in infancy.[40] Martha and Marion, through their marriages, were to play an important part in the future of the estate. But until the birth of John in 1677 there was no male successor. Then, after the birth of a second son, William, the Vinalls' experienced a disastrous year in 1680. First John died and then William his father followed him. Mabilla was left with her daughters and the infant William who suddenly had become the lineal assessor of the Vinall family at the age of something less than one year. His uncle Benjamin had long since died. There was no Vinall male in Kingston to whom Mabilla, the widow, could turn for support in managing the estate.

Precisely how the estate was managed in the ensuing years is uncertain. The terms of Mabilla's marriage settlement with William gave her the manor demesnes and Barnden's yardlands for the remainder of her life. She was in effect owner of the lands, not simply guardian to the infant William, though in terms of his father's will the estate was to pass to William on his mother's death.[41] In 1684 Mabilla married again, a gentleman of Shoreham called William Blaker.[42] As it happened, her death appears to have coincided more or less with William's majority in 1700, so he only had to wait a few years longer for his inheritance than if Mabilla had held the land in guardianship. She handed the estate to him intact.

Events moved rapidly after young William's accession to Kingston Manor and Barnden's in about 1706. The first step was distinctly promising from a Vinall point of view. In 1706 young William, the new manor lord, took a characteristically Vinall-like 'bite' out of the small lands of the village. He bought four copyhold yardlands of Iford Manor from Thomas Picombe.[43] These lands, which included a tenement, a barn and a close at the head of the street, were called Hudd's and had been the Picombe family base for a century and a half (see Chapter 7). Once again there had been a significant Vinall intrusion into the 'small lands'. The space for smaller yeomen farmers was correspondingly reduced. The Vinall ownership of lands in Kingston had reached its maximum level. The new William Vinall held 19 yardlands in the open fields and Kingston villagers may well have thought they were at the start of a further Vinall ascendancy.

William's next move was also promising. He decided to get married. In 1707 he made a settlement with Richard Gunn, a gentleman of Ringmer, for the hand of his daughter Elizabeth.[44] Elizabeth Gunn came to be lady of the manor in Kingston. William, to all outward appearances, was making quite customary dispositions for an extended future.

But then, in 1710, there was an abrupt change of fortune. William took out a substantial mortgage on Kingston Manor. It was for £700, obtained from Thomas Barret, a gentleman of Lewes.[45] It was followed about nine months later by a second mortgage, this time on the four copyhold yardlands called Hudd's, which William had so recently bought from Thomas Picombe.[46] He raised £315 on Hudd's from Henry Kenward, a cobbler of Lewes.

And matters did not stop there. In 1713 Mary Barret, the widow of Thomas Barret who had lent William £700 on mortgage of Kingston Manor, assigned the mortgage to two other lenders – Thomas Simmonds of Patcham, a blacksmith and Stephen Heaver, a tailor of Lewes. From the subsequent record it seems that these two were willing to lend William further substantial sums from time to time over the years between 1713 and the end of 1716. By 1716 William owed Simmonds £1859 and Heaver £1007 – very large sums of money at the time.[47] On top of these debts William raised a further mortgage on Kingston Manor, this time from his brother-in-law Francis Zouch who had married Martha Vinall. Zouch was a highly successful merchant in London. He lent William an additional £650 in July 1716.[48] William appears to have been in debt to the tune of at least £3800.

This was an unsustainable process. William was not only in debt, but he was in debt on an ascending scale. By 1716 his Kingston estates, which might have been worth about £5000, were mortgaged to the limit. In the end he got out from under the burden. In January 1717 his brother-in-law Francis Zouch took over the estate, paid off the mortgages to Simmonds and Heaver and, in return for a bond of £5000, was admitted as the new lord of the manor.[49] Martha Vinall his wife became the new lady, but the Vinall dynasty was effectively at an end.

What was the reason for this stunning change of fortune, which in seven short years took the young William Vinall from the lordship of Kingston Manor to a condition close to financial ruin? Unfortunately, there is no record to explain what happened. Could the problem have started in Mabilla's time while William was a minor? This seems improbable. Mabilla had remarried four years after her husband's death and, in financial terms, remarried well. William Blaker was the high sheriff of Sussex at the time.[50] Even if she had spendthrift ways, Blaker would have been able to take care of them without any need to diminish her son's patrimony. It is unlikely that she was responsible for the gathering debts at Kingston Manor.

But if that is so the responsibility must have been William's. The puzzle is why and how had he managed to work through practically the whole value of the Vinall estate in such a short while? It is possible, of course, that William was borrowing to invest elsewhere, but this also seems improbable. The pattern of irregularly growing indebtedness, which William's affairs reveal, does not suggest that he was investing in some measured way. It is rather the pattern of a desperate borrower living beyond his means. And that, in the end, is the best guess we can make about this decline. William contrived to live beyond the means his estate could provide – £500 to £600 a year. If that supposition is correct, he must have achieved a level of consumption that was something of a wonder to the villagers who lived around him.

To be fair to William Vinall, there is insufficient evidence to pronounce with certainty on what had happened. However, it is probably quite a good guess. William and Elizabeth left Kingston after the sale to Francis Zouch, and reappeared at a comparatively small manor in Brighton – Erlyes Manor. This came to them as Elizabeth's inheritance from her father Richard Gunn. The Gunn family had purchased it in 1656, and Richard Gunn had willed it to Elizabeth and 'in tail' to her son, also called William Vinall, on his death in 1720. Elizabeth's husband William died in 1733. William, his son, lived on at Erlyes Manor but was afflicted by debt in much the same style, though not on the same scale, as his father. He mortgaged the manor in 1738 to Ralph Thrace of London for £600, and then again for a further £600 in 1743. Then, after a further mortgage in 1745 for £181 (again from Thrace), the manor was sold off for £1600 in 1746. It had been worth much less than Kingston Manor in its time.[51]

This third William Vinall appears to have returned to the Ouse valley after the collapse of his fortunes in Brighton. He became a tenant farmer in Iford and died in 1773,[52] the fifth generation of Vinalls to live in the parish and the last reminder of the family's ascendancy.

Four generations of Vinalls had provided continuity at Kingston Manor from Elizabethan times, through the Stuart reign, the disturbances of the interregnum, the Restoration and the 'revolution' of 1688, right up to the beginning of the Georgian period. They were not the only village family to maintain continuity over this long period of time but they were the most powerful. In Kingston terms they stood for the tenacious domination the English gentry were able to maintain despite momentous political change. Like the Cranes before them, they were after 1634 resident lords of the manor in the village and though Kingston Manor was, in feudal terms, a minor institution compared with Swanborough, the Vinalls gave it a new importance from the point of view of Kingston society. As manorial rights became less important than land ownership, Kingston was more and more dominated in the Vinall period by their large and increasing control over the village arable lands, their consequent weight in fundamental decisions about the communal use of land and their command over wage labour. When Francis Zouch, William's brother-in-law, replaced him at Kingston Manor, an era ended for the village.

For all their accumulation of wealth and position, however, the Vinalls were not 'Kingston' and, in spite of their power, the village had a history that was independent of the whims and wishes of the Vinall family. The second half of the seventeenth century saw other continuities and other changes in the village.

On the manorial front there was not much change. The Dorset family continued in command at Swanborough. One duke followed another and each was served by a succession of stewards. But by this time the manorial powers of the Duke of Dorset were not of great importance to the passage of everyday life – even though most village lands were copyholds of Swanborough and most changes of title to land were recorded in the Swanborough manor court under the jurisdiction of the steward. The dukes of Dorset were, of course, important landlords in the Kingston open fields, but that was quite a different matter.

Hyde Manor, with its demesnes in the open fields, continued in the discreet ownership of the Alchorne family, which to all appearances maintained closer connections with its Buxted relatives[53] than with the village community. In 1653 Richard Alchorne, son of the John Alchorne who had first taken over Hyde Manor, married the daughter of a Buxted yeoman.[54] Anne Olive came to live in the manor house in the street. Richard and Anne plainly spent a good deal of time in Buxted too, for in a mortgage of 1658 he was referred to as Richard Alchorne of Buxted[55] even though the family continued to occupy the lands of Hyde Manor in Kingston and were still there at the end of the seventeenth century.

Outside the demesne lands the Bowker family continued to monopolize the freehold lands in the open fields through their ownership of the six yardlands called Alfrey's and the six called Peake's, which the Eversfields had brought together into a single estate long before in the reign of Henry VIII. The Bowkers were 'genteel' and had many connections in London. When the younger Edmund Bowker married in 1624 he chose a young lady from Kent and the marriage took place in London.[56]

By virtue of their gentility, their large freehold landholding and because in the first part of their residence in Kingston they were tenants on the Duke of Dorset's 15 copyhold yardlands in Kingston, the Bowkers were in a sense the Vinalls' social rivals. However, while the Vinalls built up the area of arable under their control, at least until 1661, the Bowkers were plainly less concerned about such matters. By 1638 the Bowkers had given up a substantial part of their tenancy on the Duke of Dorset's lands. There is an indication of this in the Swanborough court book of the time. Edmund Bowker was fined in the manor court for an encroachment 'on the demesne lands called Hardman's, with posts and pales on the east side of the close ... *late in the tenure of Edmund Bowker, deceased, his father*'.[57] Hardman's lands had consisted of four yardlands (see Table 6.1). It is interesting to note in passing that these copyholds, which the Duke of Dorset himself had purchased, were now plainly regarded as demesnes. More to the point, though, it is clear from the manorial record of the young Edmund's encroachment that he had relinquished a substantial portion of the tenancy his father had held. Indeed, it is a fair guess that the Bowkers no longer farmed any of the duke's lands at this time. The Bowkers had 'retreated' to their freehold strips – the 12 yardlands of Alfrey's and Peake's – and there is no indication that they ever again attempted to extend their Kingston landholdings. In matters of control over arable area, the Vinalls were without rivals after 1638. The Bowkers stayed on in their house in Kingston Street and on their freehold yardlands until late in the seventeenth century. Then, probably in the last decade of the century, there was a failure of the male line. By 1699 the six yardlands of Alfrey's had passed to John and Mary Mackerill, cloth workers of Fletching. Mary Mackerill was born a Bowker.[58] Peake's, the freehold yardlands of Houndean Manor, which together with Alfrey's had formed Eversfield's estate in Kingston, passed to Elizabeth Green,[59] widow of a clergyman of Selmeston, and to her daughter who had married John Bullis, also a clergyman. As the century ended the Bowkers disappeared from the village. In 1699 a tenant farmer called Henry Smether worked Alfrey's, and it is likely that there was another tenant on Peake's.

The Bowkers' decision to give up their tenancy on the Duke of Dorset's yardlands had an importance beyond undisputedly making the Vinalls the largest farmers in the village. It also meant that quite suddenly 15 yardlands in the open fields, which the first Duke of Dorset had engrossed into a single farm and which first the Vinalls and then the Bowkers had worked as such, became available for other tenants. As it happens, the Dorsets were either unable to find a single farmer to take over the whole group of lands or were unimpressed by the advantages of doing so. The lands were divided up in various ways over the years and passed through the occupancies of a number of tenants. To some extent, the Bowkers' decision to give up their tenancy mitigated the initial effect that the large Dorset engrossment in Kingston had on reducing the space for smaller tenant farmers. In the second half of the seventeenth century the general trend towards bigger tenancies was temporarily halted and put into reverse.

Who took advantage of the new opportunities for tenancy that appeared? Incomplete records support the idea that smaller tenancies had once again become possible in Kingston. The first documented tenancy after the Bowkers relinquished the lands was in 1651. In that year the Dorsets leased a barn and six yardlands known as Diggon's to John Titchbourne of Rodmell.[60] The terms of the lease were, as it happened, distinctly disadvantageous to the landlord. Titchbourne got access to the six yardlands for 99 years in return for a capital sum of £45 and a commitment to a yearly payment of only £1. He and his successors enjoyed the six yardlands for a substantial part of the 99 years, probably until the early 1720s.[61] It is a rough measure of the costs of this long lease from the Dorsets' point of view that when the new tenant took over the lands in the second half of the eighteenth century he was willing to pay £25 a year for it on a short lease. For some unknown reason six of Dorset's fifteen yardlands in Kingston were tied up in a most unremunerative way for much of the seventeenth century.

The other nine yardlands were on shorter leases at a much higher annual rent. In 1658 John Walker occupied them at an annual rent of £83, which in proportion was massively greater than Tichbourne's annual payment of £1, even when allowance is made for the down payment of £45 he had made.[62] Subsequently, these lands passed in whole or part to other occupants. In 1673 William Welford held a 'messuage and lands called Coppard's' for £60 a year.[63] In 1677 Welford had departed from the Kingston scene and James Attree, of the Barcombe family of Attrees, held 'a messuage and farm at Kingston' for £30 a year.[64] By 1698 there had been another change of tenant. John Alfrey of Iford, a descendant of the fourteenth-century Alfrey who had given his name to another parcel of Kingston yardlands, leased lands that had acquired the name of Kingston Town Farm for £47.10 a year.[65] The considerable variability in these rents is probably partly because they were only farming parts of the original nine yardlands that were left over after the long lease to John Titchbourne. Another reason was the fall in prices in the latter parts of the seventeenth century. At all events, the Dorset rent rolls indicate that smaller tenants had access to village lands in the second half of the century. By 1698 Dorset's yardlands had been divided into two clearly defined parcels for leasing purposes, Diggon's and the Kingston Town Farm. In 1705, while Titchbourne was still at Diggon's, John Walker appeared as the tenant on Kingston Town Farm at the same rate that John Alfrey had paid.[66]

What happened over this period to the village yeomanry who occupied their own copyhold lands – the families whom we have described as living off the 'small lands of the village'?

While the coincidence of events opened up Kingston lands to smaller *tenant* farmers, the independent yeomanry continued to lose importance as they had done since early Tudor times. The yeoman families of Kingston remained an essential constituent of village life, but they were, as ever, under pressure.

To be more precise, they were under two kinds of pressure. In the first place the total amount of lands available for smaller owner-occupiers was reduced in the second half of the seventeenth century, just as it had been in the first half. The acquisitive Vinalls were responsible for this. The combined effect of Dorset's earlier engrossment and this Vinall acquisition was that the amount of arable available for small landholders fell from about 29 yardlands in 1570 to 25 yardlands in 1640, and perhaps 21 yardlands in 1660. And when William Vinall took a further bite out of the small lands in 1706, the area available fell to 16–17 yardlands. The independent yeomanry may have hung on for longer in Kingston than elsewhere mainly because there was so little Tudor enclosure, but the opportunities for their particular style of landholding were nevertheless eroded.

The second source of pressure on the 'small lands' came from the sales and purchases of land between the owner-occupiers themselves. Its effect was to continue the concentration of ownership that was evident between 1570 and 1640 (see Table 7.1) and that had certainly been an important feature of village life in the earlier Tudor period too. Some yeomen families were more successful than others; most of all, some were consistently successful from generation to generation, while others had periods during which they accumulated lands that were subsequently dispersed.

In the first half of the seventeenth century, before the civil war, the Ades had been notably consistent in the grip they kept on their lands. And, in spite of some complex arrangements within the family in the later 1600s, they were to remain so.

John Ade, old Gregory's grandson, was in possession of all the Ade lands in Kingston in 1658: four Swanborough yardlands called Taylor's and two yardlands of Iford Manor called Bishop's.[67] John died in 1676 and the first complexity arose from the way he organized succession to the lands. John had four children: an elder son also called John; a younger son called Stephen and two daughters called Jane and Joanna who were born between the sons. In the normal course of events the Ade lands would have been split into two at his death. Stephen, the younger son, should have succeeded to Taylor's according to the custom of borough English; John, the eldest son would have had Bishop's because borough French prevailed on Iford Manor. In fact, the eldest son succeeded to both and Stephen was left without land. A special arrangement was made in the Swanborough Manor court to pass Stephen over in favour of John provided he was paid an annuity of £30 a year out of the income from the lands.[68] John Ridge was appointed guardian to John who was still a minor; Stephen was only 15 years old at the time his father died. Perhaps his youthfulness was the reason why he was left out of the inheritance; more likely, though, his father was concerned to keep the Ade estate together.

The estate was kept together but not as old John Ade would have planned. In the first place, the younger John who took over from him was not strikingly successful at running it. In 1689 he fell into debt and was obliged to mortgage Taylor's for £315, which he obtained from Walter Brett, a grocer from Lewes.[69] Shortly afterwards John died. In 1695 his younger brother Stephen, who had married Mary Willard of Chalvington, finally inherited the lands, which the normal working of borough English would have given him from the beginning.[70]

But Stephen did not take over the other group of Ade yardlands – Bishop's. Quite unusually, these went to his sister Joanna who had married Samuel Watts,[71] though with an arrangement that on Joanna's death the property would revert to Stephen and his descendants. Why exactly John followed this procedure is unclear. Perhaps he had become more indebted than his mortgage to Walter Brett would suggest and Sam Watts, his brother-in-law, had helped him out in return for a lifetime loan on the property. More likely, Sam Watts was disadvantaged in some way and the Ade family felt it proper to support the couple. In either event, the departure from custom indicates that manor courts had become flexible to individual requests, even when they were contrary to precedent and that families like the Ades could use this flexibility for their own convenience. John left a divided succession in Kingston, which would probably have shocked and disappointed his father who had gone to considerable pains to keep the family lands intact.

As matters turned out, the Watts occupied Bishop's for a long while. Joanna Watts (née Ade) outlived her brother Stephen. Stephen died in 1721 and Joanna lived on until 1731.[72] Consequently, for 30 years or so from 1690 onwards, Stephen Ade and his brother-in-law Samuel Watts lived as neighbours on the Ade properties at the corner of the street. Eventually, on Joanna's death, the two copyhold yardlands of Bishop's reverted to Stephen's family. They passed to his son William, whose memorial still stands in the Kingston churchyard and who brought together the lands that earlier generations of Ades had striven to keep as a unit.

The Ade estate was not only kept as a unit, it was enhanced. For four generations, the Ade houses, barns and farmyards at the corner of the street had been split into two groups by the Towner family's house and barn. The Towners' property, which had more than a yardland attached to it, was a freehold of Houndean Manor. For the Ades it was probably of more interest because it divided their territorial base into two than for its access to arable land. Acquisition of Towner lands was surely an attractive proposition for them. So, when the Towners decided to sell out in the 1690s it was natural that the Ades should seek to take over.

In fact, the purchase of the Towners' lands came about in a rather unusual way. The Ades did not buy them directly. The purchaser was Stephen Ade's mother-in-law, the widow Willard of Chalvington.[73] She bought the lands in 1699, probably occupied them herself for a couple of years and then passed them on to her daughter Mary Ade in 1703. The Ades had gained two more Kingston yardlands. More important, perhaps, they had unified the group of tenements, barns and cattle yards they held at the corner of the street. The Towners, meanwhile, merely changed one group of Kingston lands for another. They moved across the road from the Ades into the cottage called Adam's, which faced down the street from the other side of Ashcombe Lane. They purchased Adam's and the one-and-a-half yardlands of Swanborough copyhold land that came with it from the Howells in the last years of the seventeenth century.[74]

In the first half of the seventeenth century, the various branches of the Howell family had between them been the next largest peasant landholders in Kingston to the Ades. By 1640, however, the period of 'Howell ascendancy' was over. Howells remained a noticeable presence in Kingston society, partly at least because they were so numerous, but after the breakdown of old Robert Howell's yardlands into separate ownerships they no longer held that particular distinction that comes with having substantial amounts of land. In this regard, John Picombe, head of the yeoman Picombe family, took their place after 1640 (see Table 8.1).

These Picombes stood substantially above their craftsman and labouring relatives in Kingston because they were comparatively wealthy. They were based on the four yardlands called Hudd's, which they had held since the early sixteenth century.

Like the Ades, the Picombes accumulated land in the seventeenth century. At some point in the early 1640s, Thomas Picombe, who by that time had inherited Hudd's, made a substantial addition to the family's holding. He embarked on a bit of engrossing on his own account. He acquired two substantial parcels of land. First, he bought the lands Boniface had held and that had been in that family since at least 1570. Boniface died in about 1640. His lands, which belonged to Swanborough Manor, were 'in the hands of the lord' in 1641,[75] and Thomas Picombe most probably bought them soon after. Second, Picombe bought out a part of the lands Thomas Gower had obtained through his marriage to Marjory Howell. Gower died in 1642 and, though a minor son succeeded him,[76] the family disappeared as Kingston landowners soon after.

By 1658, as a result of these extensions to the Picombe lands, Thomas appeared in the rental of Swanborough Manor as holding 'two and a half yardlands, late Boniface' and 'a yard and a half, late Gower's'.[77] Together with the four yardlands of Hudd's, which were held from Iford Manor, Thomas Picombe had come to hold a full eight yardlands – as much as the Ades and considerably more than any other independent yeoman farmer had held in the village at any time outside the manorial demesnes. The middle decades of the seventeenth century were successful enough for Thomas Picombe in Kingston, even though they brought disaster to so many other people in England!

Table 8.1: 'The small lands': Kingston owner-occupiers on fewer than eight yardlands

1640		1700	
Ade	6	Ade	8
Towner	2		
Picombe	4	Picombe	8
Boniface	2½		
Gower	2 (1 to Picombe Brooks from Howell and 1 to Wenham from Wenham)		
Harfrey	2 (from Howell)		2
John Howell	1½	Towner	1½
Thos Howell	½	Bodle	½
Barnden	4 (sold to Vinall)		
Total yardlands	24½		21
No. of landholders	9		6
Average no. of yardlands per holder	2.72		3.5

The yeoman Picombe family held onto Hudd's and its further acquisition of Swanborough yardlands throughout the second half of the seventeenth century. Though they held lands in two manors with different rules of inheritance, there were no apparent problems of divided succession. When Thomas Picombe the elder died in 1678, his son Thomas took over Hudd's as well as the Swanborough lands, for which he had to pay the Duke of Dorset a substantial heriot of three oxen.[78]

In this period the Picombes almost certainly moved the main family home from the farmyard of Hudd's to the house close to their Swanborough lands. These buildings, most of which still stand and which include a particularly striking barn, are half way down the southern side of the street. The Picombes were next-door neighbours to the Wenhams. To all appearances they lived out their time of comparative good fortune quietly enough. The only sign of difficulty was in 1687 when the Picombes took out a substantial mortgage of £220 from John Elphick, a grocer from Lewes.[79] In the same year John Ade had been obliged to mortgage his Swanborough Manor copyholds, so perhaps it was a poor season for all the village smallholders. At all events, the Picombes cleared their debt successfully the following year. They continued in undisturbed occupancy until in 1706 Thomas Picombe, nearing the end of his life, sold out Hudd's to young William Vinall. Thomas died in 1710.[80] His sale of

Hudd's reduced the family's lands to the four Swanborough yardlands they had acquired before 1658, which made the Ades once again the largest yeoman farmers of the village. By the time of his death Thomas Picombe had taken advantage of the vagaries of spelling to call himself Peckham. Perhaps he was sufficiently affected by the social distinctions of the time to wish to differentiate his family from the numerous more ordinary Picombes in the village.[81]

While the Ades held on with customary tenacity and slowly accumulated, and while the Picombes doubled their holdings of village strips, the Howells lost their grip as independent landholders and yeomen. The Picombes, in particular, benefited because a part of the lands they acquired in the years before 1658 came from the Gowers, who had taken over Howell land.

By 1640 Howell lands in Kingston were already much reduced: essentially, the family held the lands the Elizabethan Robert Howell had passed down through his son John (see Chapter 7) and about a yardland or so of Kingston Manor copyhold. These went in due course to John's sons Thomas and John. John, the elder son, held Adam's, which had a yard and a half of strip lands and included the house on Ashcombe Lane at the end of Kingston Street. This, which the elder member of the family had always held, was the Howell headquarters, the main house of the main Howell family. The older son John had succeeded despite borough English.

Thomas held the 'tenement and half virgate' that had been in the family since at least 1567.[82] Both families were prolific, in the manner of Howells, and it is probable that both sustained their incomes by subtenancies on the rented lands in the village.

This configuration of two yeoman Howell families stayed intact for much of the second half of the seventeenth century. John Howell's lands of 1658 remained in his family until the closing years of the century when they were sold to the Towners.[83] Thomas Howell died in 1666 having held his half virgate for 60 years.[84] It passed to his son John and, in turn in 1687, to his grandson, also John – the Howells showed little originality in their choice of names for male children.[85] Then, in 1693, around the time the elder branch of the family sold Adam's to the Towners, this little bit of Howell land was taken over (by sale or inheritance) by Nicholas Bodle of Kingston, a yeoman.[86] In the meantime, John Howell had also sold his Kingston yardland to the Bayley family, which was accordingly installed in a cottage in the street.

The upshot was that, by the last decade of the century, the Howell family had disappeared as independent yeomen farmers in the village. The agglomeration of Howell lands of the late Elizabethan and early Stuart years was completely gone by 1700. Long before, as early as 1640, the Harfrey family had inherited some Howell lands. They continued to own Taberer's until 1696 when Jane Harfrey, a widow, died and the lands passed to Richard Elphick, a grandson of Stephen Howell.[87] Other Howell possessions of Elizabethan times had gone to the Gower family (Chapter 7). The process was completed in the last decade of the seventeenth century when the main Howell homestead, named after the early Tudor Adam's, was sold off to the Towners, and other erstwhile Howell lands passed to the Bodle family and to the Bayleys. The Howells who had been copyholders in the village for at least two centuries were much diminished, and the yeoman Howells disappeared. The cottager family of Edward Howell, who lived on in the little tenement that is today called 'Shepherd's Rest', survived them. Edward Howell's descendants were still in the village 130 years later when an Act of Parliament enclosed it and they stayed on. They were to be the last remnant of a family that had dominated village society in early Tudor times and maintained a certain kind of dominance – by dint of sheer numbers if in no other way – for a long time after that.

The outcome of the two main forces acting on the independent yeomanry who farmed the 'small lands' of the village is summarized in Table 8.1. In the first place the total area of open-field arables held as small lands was reduced. In 1640, before the interregnum, small independent owner-occupiers still held about a third of village arables. Vinall's purchase of Barnden's lands reduced this proportion significantly. Later, in 1706, a further Vinall purchase of four yardlands from the Picombe family made another cut into the small lands, reducing them to about 16 yardlands, or barely more than a fifth of the village arables.

The other pressure on Kingston yeomanry resulted simply from some families being economically more successful than others. Not only did large landholders like the Vinalls engross the small lands, but the more successful yeoman farmers also converted them into larger family holdings. In this respect, the Ades and Picombes were clearly the outstanding families in the period between 1640 and 1700.[88] Largely because of their engrossments of the lands of other copyholders, the average size of a yeoman holding in the village grew from 2.7 yardlands in 1640 to 3.5 yardlands in 1700 – or by about 40 per cent. It is more to the point, perhaps, that these two families established a distinct economic and social ascendancy among the owner-occupiers of Kingston Street. Between them they held as much of the village arable as had been held by the four largest farmers on the small lands in 1640 (see Table 8.1). Table 8.2 summarizes the process of concentration over the preceding century and a half.

The increasing concentration of small lands in the hands of the two largest village farmers is accounted for by the reduction in the total area of small lands and by the absolutely increasing area held by the largest farmers. By 1700 the social and economic distance between the Ade and Picombe families on the one hand and the rest of the small farmers in Kingston on the other had become more marked than ever before. There was, indeed, a new pattern of differentiation in village society. At the same time, as in the period before 1640, the total number of small owner-occupiers decreased.

But these changes in the role of the smaller yeoman farmers of Kingston should be seen against the broader background of village landholding and

Table 8.2: Gradual concentration of ownership on the small lands of Kingston Village

Year	*No. of landholders*	*Proportion of small lands held by two biggest owners*
1570	12	35%
1640	9	41%
1700	6	76%

social structure. Throughout the century, mainly owner-occupiers held the Kingston arables. The dukes of Dorset, lords of the manor at Swanborough and owners of the Swanborough demesnes remained the only absentee landlords in the village. And, after the first duke's impressive engrossment and subsequent selling off of Kingston Manor, the Dorsets' apparently never sought to extend their holdings of Kingston yardlands.

There were other constancies. The Alchorne family continued at Hyde (which they may from time to time have put out to tenancy) and the Bowkers stayed on as freeholders on the Houndean lands called Peake's. By 1706 the Vinalls had taken over eight yardlands from the small lands. These engrossments by the Vinalls, together with the changes in the pattern of ownership by smaller independent owner-occupiers, were the main shifts in landholding during the latter half of the seventeenth century.

Under ordinary circumstances, the engrossment of land by the Vinalls and the increasing concentration of small lands by the Ades and Picombes might have increased the proportion of families in the village dependent on wage labour in whole or in part. This was the customary result of concentration, for concentration of ownership simultaneously displaced smallholders who relied to a considerable extent on family labour and increased the requirement for wageworkers. Whether accompanied by enclosure or not, engrossment was one factor that turned villages into agricultural proletarian societies in which labourers and their families predominated in numbers though not, of course, in social or any other kind of power.

In Kingston, however, unlike some other areas, seventeenth-century engrossment did not lead directly to an increase in the proportions of working-class families in the village. The reasons for this were largely fortuitous and connected mainly to how the Duke of Dorset's lands in the village were used. It so happened that just as the Vinalls set about acquiring Kingston lands, and the Ades and Picombes took over lands from smaller farmers,

Dorset's lands became free for smaller tenants. Not only did the Bowkers relinquish their tenancies on the Dorset yardlands in the village arable, but also successive Dorsets allowed the 15 yardlands the first duke had purchased to be let out in comparatively small bits to tenants like Tichbourne of Rodmell, John Walker, William Welford and James Attree of Barcombe. Some of these – Walker[89] and Welford perhaps – farmed the lands directly from a family base in the village. Others – Tichbourne and Alfrey – almost certainly sublet to tenants in the village who worked the lands with family labour. It is likely that the Howell and Picombe families took advantage of the opportunities these tenancies offered. And later, in the last decade of the century, the Bowker lands passed to two Bowker daughters married to men who did not live in the village, who let them out in turn to village tenants.[90] As far as the society in Kingston Street was concerned, the disruptive effects of engrossment were to some extent at least set off by the availability of small tenancies. Landless branches of yeoman families and yeomen like the Howells, who for one reason or another were left without land, found corners in the open fields, which they continued to farm.

And so, though the dramatic social ascendancy (and subsequent fall) of the Vinall family was a most noticeable change in the structure of village society, there was much that appeared unaltered. In the second half of the century small tenancy provided space, in economic terms, for less well-capitalized, landless branches of yeoman families, with the result that landless Howells and less advantaged branches of the Picombe family could continue in the village. Just as the complexities of manorial organization held up the process of enclosure in Kingston and left the social yeoman families more intact as an independent peasantry than in many other English villages, so the happenstance of small tenancy allowed others an opportunity to stay on, which they might otherwise have been denied.

The existence of these small tenancies and the effects they had on the balance of village society also partially hid what was perhaps the most significant change in the structure of Kingston. Though the Kingston peasantry survived longer than elsewhere, it was nevertheless severely depleted by 1700. The small group of yeoman families that formed the core of village society throughout the Tudor years and beyond was reduced to six. Two at least (the Bodles and Brooks) were relative newcomers. Moreover, the Brooks, Towners, Elphicks and Bodles were small landholders; only the yeoman Picombes and Ades held positions commensurate with those of the older peasant families that had at one time formed the heart of Kingston. To a discerning eye things were changing. For all the tenant branches of old families in the village, the old nexus of yeomanry had virtually gone. The network of Ades, Barndens, Howells, Picombes, Towners – and yes even Vinalls – that had been at the centre of things in 1600 and for a long while after had disintegrated in the course of the century. William Vinall's three socially ambitious marriages had indicated that the days of easy social equality were gone. When the Howells ceased to number among the village landholders, and Picombes and Ades rose to certain dominance, it became clear that the Vinalls' ascendancy was not a chance event but part of a pattern in which some rose and others did not. The old family names may have stayed on in Kingston – Howells in particular were as numerous as ever – but the nature of social relationships among the central yeoman families had changed.

Though the proportions of cottager and labourer families in the village did not increase significantly over the seventeenth century, there were nevertheless a lot of them. Most probably independent cottagers and labourers living in rented cottages (which in general had too little ground around them to permit subsistence cottage gardening) accounted for more than half the population. At a guess, properly independent copyhold cottages held directly of one or another manor rather than by tenancy at will were mainly taken up by the less privileged branches of yeoman families. There were plenty of such families about, as might be expected of a society in which many families had been settled in the same place for two centuries. Ades, Picombes and Howells were there in number to take up any cottages, gardens and small orchards that were available in the village.

In Kingston, the main landless Ade family descended from old William Ade who had been bailiff to the Duke of Dorset in the early seventeenth century. His son William, born in 1621, was in fact a Vinall grandchild, for old William had married into that rising family. By the 1650s this younger William was head of a considerable family of five. At the same time there were descendants of Richard Ade, probably a grandson of Gregory the patriarch, who had been churchwarden in the parish in the 1630s.[91] The William Ade branch was established in the 'tenement and parcel of land' bought from Thomas Michell in 1603. The house stood in the cluster of Ade properties at the corner of Kingston Street. It is hard to say where or how Richard Ade's descendants found a living, but some members of the family were possibly to be found in the yeoman Ade household, and they no doubt provided a supply of family labour to work the lands of their wealthier cousins. There was a similar grouping of Ades in Iford, where the senior branch of the family held substantial lands in the manor of Northease while Henry Ade, a landless cousin, was a cottager in the village.[92]

Howells, both the landowning ones and others, were prominent in the parish registers throughout the century. George Howell was head of one small Howell family between the 1630s and his death in 1674. It is likely that Edward Howell, who married in 1684 and who in turn had a son called Edward in 1697, was a son of George. This branch of the family were comparatively wealthy cottagers in the 'tenement, close and orchard' standing to the north of the main village on the edge of the great West Laine. It was they who provided a continuity of Howell presence after the yeoman families lost their grip on the land. Young Edward, born in 1697, lost his father at the age of two, but lived on in the cottage and eventually brought up a family of eight girls in the early eighteenth century.[93] Edward, it would seem, worked as a shepherd, as well as cultivating his close and orchard. In 1684 there was also a substantial family headed by a Daniel Howell, who married Joan Copper, probably from Rottingdean.[94]

Various lines of Picombes were also a continuing presence in the seventeenth century. There appear to have been two generations at least of shepherd Picombes: John the shepherd of 1622 and John the shepherd of 1639.[95] It is virtually certain too that at least one family of labourers was present throughout the century, though the complexity of Picombe entries in the parish register makes it hard to distinguish them systematically. There were 'tailor' Picombes; the first sign of the tailor Thomas Picombe appeared in the parish register in 1639 when he was father to a little girl. He does not appear to have had a large family by this first marriage. However, he married again. In 1658 there was a marriage settlement between Thomas Picombe, senior, a tailor, and Mary Bonnicke of Barcombe, a widow, at which point Thomas bequeathed his little cottage in the street with its garden and three-and-a-half acres to Mary and then in turn to their children.[96] There are signs that Thomas passed his trade on to his children, so tailoring Picombes probably lived in the little cottage throughout the century. In 1718 two descendants of old Thomas and Mary Bonnicke sold the property in the street. They were described as Thomas Pickham of Chailey, cordwainer, and William Pickham of Fletching, tailor. The tradition of working with thread lived on in the family it would seem.[97] The cottage was sold to Thomas Penticost a thatcher from Rodmell, who most likely rented it out thereafter.

The yeoman families' poorer cousins took up most of the independent cottages in the village, but there were others who had the good fortune to find access to 'tenement, garden and close'. One such was Thomas Wilson of Iford, the erstwhile servant of Benjamin Vinall to whom Benjamin bequeathed a cottage in 1674 – an unusually generous bequest, presumably in recognition of exceptional service.[98] Two years later Thomas Wilson, now well set up with a barn, garden and orchard, married Alice Mersh, daughter of William Mersh, a shepherd. This William Mersh was most likely a Howell grandchild on the maternal side: in 1623 a Richard Mersh had married Joan Howell, one of the many Joan Howells born in seventeenth-century Kingston.[99] Howell ramifications spread beyond the immediate family. At all events Thomas Wilson settled down with Alice, the distant Howell relative, and they had a single child Mary. The cottage passed to Mary and she and her husband, William Coates, turned it into a malthouse, from which they supplied the needs of Kingston tipplers in the last decade or so of the seventeenth century.

This cottage remained the village malthouse for a long while afterwards. William Coates seems to have used it as the basis for an expanding business. In 1706 he mortgaged it for £40 to Henry Crawley of Piddinghoe; this mortgage was not repaid but assigned from one lender to another for the next 20 years: from Crawley it passed to Francis Gell of South Malling in Lewes; then it was taken up by Elizabeth Bythwood, a widow of Lewes; and finally it was held by Thomas Simmons, also a maltster, in Brighton. None of these saw fit to foreclose, so Coates was probably regarded as a secure and profitable investment. Indeed, he moved up in the world: by 1726 he was an inn holder in Southover, the Lewes parish in which the priory had once stood. In that year he sold the property to Thomas Burtenshaw of Kingston, also described as an inn holder. The malthouse had been elevated in style; it evidently remained the chief drinking place for people in the street.[100]

There were no doubt other tradesmen in the village. Apart from the carpenter William Browne, there was a butcher: when William Godman married Elizabeth Ade in Lewes a person of unknown surname called Nicholas, a butcher from Kingston-near-Lewes, was a witness to the ceremony.[101] But, for the most part, the rest of the village population – perhaps another eight or ten families – were farm labourers and highly dependent on wages. We know little of them but their names: the Beards, Reads, Pages, Tuppens, Stearnes and so on.[102] They were part of that large mass of ordinary people who do not appear in history books and whose function was to provide most of the labour on which other men and women built their fortunes. They contributed, for example, to the fortune young William Vinall dissipated in the first decade or so of the eighteenth century, though their response to his fall was probably simple amazement. As real wages rose in the late seventeenth century, such labouring people were better off in absolute terms than their Tudor counterparts, but they were, however, still the most vulnerable members of any village society. It would not need much in the way of a turn of fortune to put any of them into the poorhouse with which Elizabeth's laws had equipped all parishes and which in Kingston stood on the ridge, well away from the street itself. Though these seventeenth-century labourers were better fed than their forebears, they were also in closer proximity to people of greater wealth than their Tudor counterparts had been. The economic processes of the seventeenth century, in Kingston at least, had almost certainly led to a less equal society from a material point of view.

*****

The main physical features of the village in which this small community lived are still clear in the structures that remain, many of them beautiful, even if quite commonplace, pieces of Sussex downland architecture. There were, in effect, four discernibly different kinds of dwelling in the seventeenth-century street.

First, there were the grander houses, the three main ones in Kingston. The Vinalls were in the rambling Elizabethan house at the head of Kingston Street, above which the ground starts to slope steeply up to the Downs. The Bowkers lived a little way down from them in the medieval house belonging to the freehold yardlands of Peake's. Both houses were special in being separated from the farmyards and barns associated with them, for in each case the farmyards were on the opposite side of the street, but the Kingston Manor house had its stables attached. The Vinalls, Bowkers and Alchornes were probably the only village families with elegant riding horses.

The Alchornes lived in the third of Kingston's grand houses – Hyde Manor, which was perhaps the oldest dwelling in the village. It too stood on the northern side of the street, but further down on the far side of the church. Hyde Manor house, as it is described in Michell's survey of 1567, was surrounded to the north by barns, cattle stalls and stables, so was not separated from its farmyard as the Bowkers' house and Kingston Manor were.

The second main type of dwelling belonged to yeoman owner-occupiers – the Ades, Picombes, Towners, Wenhams and Bodles. These flint-built dwelling houses of comparatively modest size and set in their closes were essentially working places. Storage barns, long cattle 'hovels' set against high flint walls and various structures in which to accommodate small farmyard animals (sties, chicken-runs and hutches) surrounded them. The Ades lived in an extended complex of this kind in 1700. It comprised at least three houses to cope with an extended family, two great barns (which have long since disappeared) and stalls for their oxen, some of which can still be seen on the small but excellent dairy farm called Hambrook's, which occupies part of the site today. The Picombes had two such complexes for much of the seventeenth century: a house, barn and close called Hudd's opposite Kingston Manor at the head of the street (which has now disappeared) and a group of buildings in the centre of the street put together by purchase from Gower and Boniface in the 1640s. The latter is largely intact. The house was given a façade at some point in the eighteenth century, but the barn built in brick and flint and with a charming pigeon loft remains much as it ever was. Elphicks lived in Taberer's and the farmyard, but not the house, is largely intact. It is a classic example of a downland yard. The barn has the proportions of a small cathedral; high flint walls tightly contain the close and the old stalls remain in place. Wenhams, Bodles and Towners held considerably smaller farmyards, particularly the first two families whose arable holdings were among the smallest in the village.

The third and fourth types of dwellings were cottages, but cottages of a different style and purpose. One group housed independent cottagers who could and did reduce their reliance on wage labour for subsistence by intense cultivation of their own plots and orchards, in some cases diversifying their activities into trades and crafts. Edward Howell's cottage with its orchard was a good example. It stood somewhat apart from the street, a little lonely and aloof, beautifully adorned by a Tudor chimney. It remains in place today.

The cottages held by Coates the maltster and Picombe the tailor were also independent properties held directly by copy of court roll. Coates's has gone and has been replaced by a modern house, but Picombe's remains, though its barn has disappeared. Indeed, Picombe's cottage, called 'Rest Harrow' today, is one of the enchanting relics in the street. It is an extremely small one-up, one-down with the proportions of a large doll's house. Its doorways are barely five foot high. Its small front room has southward facing windows; the tailoring Picombes used as much of the light as they could behind these narrow flint walls.

The other class of cottages was really simple rented accommodation for workers. Some, for example, belonged to the Kingston Manor demesnes and these were used to accommodate house servants and farm workers. Two such cottages still stand between Peake's and Kingston Manor house. The people who lived there, as in the small cottages that once stood on the opposite side of the street, had little chance to cultivate their very limited bits of earth and none at all to develop crafts or trades. They were wageworkers and they owed their dwellings to their employments. Most of these humble homes have since disappeared, though the remnant of a wattle and daub structure faced with flint and standing at the entrance to Taberer's yard is probably one of them. It is likely too that in the seventeenth century some farm labourers 'lived-in', in other words shared farmers' houses for the time they were employed. Certainly, the Ades' complex had room to house occasional labour in loft rooms if the need arose, as did the Picombes'.

The community lived among the strips of the open fields, which were ultimately crucial to everyone's well being. They also lived in a countryside privileged by great natural beauty. The street itself sloped gently up a wooded and settled combe, its buildings contained and warmed by flint.

The Downs, rising up 1000 feet to protect the street from the force of westerlies and sweeping southwards towards the sea, provided green pastures throughout the year. Though they might be lowering and dark on bad winter days, there was always the certainty that springtime would come, that the spring light would soften their line and re-enliven that steep turf that fed the village sheep. Away from the Downs, on the other side of the village, the combe opened up. A person working in the West Laine or on the slopes that led to Swanborough, or peering over the hedgerows of Ashcombe Lane, might well pause to take in the majestic sweep of lands that led down to the valley of the Ouse. The light of all seasons played across these lands, presenting them differently from minute to minute, warming them momentarily with sunshine-breaking showers, darkening them with mists, making them glow gold at harvest time. Beyond, the flat brooklands of the Ouse were lit by sun when all else was darkened by cloud – like a Breughel landscape – and beyond the brooklands, where Kingston cows got fat in good years, there was a further line of Downs, peaking in the ancient British hill fortress of Caburn. Lewes was just around the corner of this valley. De Warenne's impregnable castle still towered above it. It rose with a certain magic above the brooklands and could be clearly seen a mile or two away from the Swanborough slopes of Kingston.

Whatever sense of permanence such lovely surroundings might have inspired, Kingston at the end of the century was at the threshold of a transformation more profound, at least in village terms, than any of the changes of the 1600s. The seventeenth century had seen the ascendancy of the Vinalls, an aspiration of social grandeur built on Tudor accumulation by a yeoman family. It had also seen the old peasantry undermined, a process with social consequences that the happy chance of accessible small tenancies had largely obscured. In the eighteenth century, however, the economic and social consequences of the decline of the Kingston peasantry were to come to roost with a vengeance. The changes that ensued were more profound than any the Vinalls' incursion at Kingston Manor had induced.

In 1699 Mabilla Davis, once wife of the first William Vinall and by then married to the man who was about to become high sheriff of Sussex, still owned Kingston Manor. Her son, the ruinous younger William, was still a minor. The Alchornes continued at Hyde Manor. The Ade farm was temporarily divided between the Watts and the Stephen Ade family. The Picombes were well installed. The Bowkers' estate was divided between Edmund Bowker's daughters because there had been a failure of the male line. Bowker lands were tenant farmed.

This last eventuality was, as things turned out, decisive for the future of the village. In 1699 John Mackerill and his wife Mary, who had been born a Bowker and who had inherited Alfrey's, decided to sell out. They also determined to sell the property called Bayley's, a tenant farmer's cottage Mary Mackerill had acquired from a previous marriage.

A tough-minded young man called Thomas Rogers appeared on the scene. He was in his early twenties. He came from Iford and his father purchased the Mackerill lands, which had descended from the Elizabethan Eversfields, on his behalf. He was married to Elizabeth Ade of Iford and he, more than anyone else, was to transform Kingston in the eighteenth century.

Chapter 9

The Rogers in Kingston: The First Phase

The Thomas Rogers who appeared in Kingston in the latter part of 1699 was called a 'yeoman',[1] and that was a precise enough description of his place in society. But the Rogers family of Iford had a singular history, which distinguished them in many ways from the ordinary run of Ouse valley yeomanry and which relates to the part they later played in Kingston village. In an age when many yeoman families, like the Ades and Picombes in Kingston, could trace their local origins back through long centuries, the Rogers were comparative newcomers in Iford, or for that matter in Sussex itself.

The first member of the family who can be traced was Henry Rogers and he was baptized in the wealthy village of Cranbrook in Kent in the early 1570s.[2] Henry was probably a younger son of the Rogers family that held an estate near Biddenden[3] and was enriched by the thriving weaving industry in Biddenden and Cranbrook. Henry spent his childhood in the years when Elizabeth was establishing herself on the English throne. As an adolescent he no doubt shared in the intense excitement when the Armada was defeated. As a young man he was sent to Oxford to be trained for the Church when Elizabeth was still struggling to improve the quality of her clergy in Sussex as elsewhere.[4] He was ordained in 1595.[5] Henry's subsequent career was, to all appearances, quite ordinary for the times. He was at St Michael's in Lewes initially and, in 1609, he was also licensed to practise the art of medicine – not a particularly common accomplishment for a clergyman, but useful to him. Then, a little later, he left Lewes and was given the living at Selmeston, four miles east of Lewes. He lived out the rest of his life there.

Though ordinary enough, Henry left evidence of vigour appropriate to one who had grown up in such stirring times. He kept his parishioners in their places, for example. In 1636, he made accusations against two of them in the archdeaconry court of Lewes. He held Thomas Gower and William Reade responsible for the fact that 'the fences of the churchyard are so ill-kept that hogs doe much annoy it, and for not allowing ... [indecipherable] to the clark for the bells whereby sometimes they cannot have ringing when it ought to be had.'[6] And he left an unselfconsciously assertive epitaph inscribed on a small and rather beautiful brass plate in the church at Selmeston:

> The body of Henry Rogers a painefuil preacher in this church two and thirty years who dyed the sixt of May Ano Dni 1639 and in the year of his age 67 lyeth heere expecting the second coming of our lord Jesus Christ –
>
> I did believe and therefore spake
> Whereof I taught I doe pertake.
> Henry Rogers.

The little tribute is signed with Henry's own signature engraved into the brass, which suggests he had it prepared before his death and left instructions for it to be set up in his memory. Oddly, it is set near the eastern end of the south aisle and faces the wrong way – in other words away from the door of the church. It is consequently difficult to read: one has to lean against the end wall of the aisle to do so. It is unclear how this happened. It is possibly the work of an illiterate craftsman, or just conceivably a farewell gesture from some parishioner like Thomas Gower or William Reade who had his own reasons for remembering Henry Rogers!

Though we may accept that Henry was a 'painefuil' preacher and must take his own word for it that he partook of the lessons he taught his flock, it is plain that he balanced his spiritual dedication with a nice sense of the more material side of life. He had two sons and found the resources to send both to university. Alexander, the younger, matriculated at Magdalen College Oxford in 1627.[7] He later returned to marry a Selmeston woman, was not ordained into the church and appears to have made a career in Crawley.

Thomas, the elder son, was sent to Emmanuel College in Cambridge where he took his MA in 1627.[8] After a period at Chichester Cathedral, he was installed as vicar of Iford in 1632, on the presentation of the Duke of Dorset who held the living. The Rogers had come to Iford and, as it happened, were to stay there for a long while. Though he had no way of knowing it at the time, the young vicar of Iford was to be the first of a whole dynasty of Thomas Rogers – so numerous that the only way to distinguish one from the other is to give them numbers. Thomas, the vicar, will be Thomas I.

The marriage on which this dynasty was founded was curiously appropriate. In 1639, aided by an inheritance from his father Henry who had recently died in Selmeston, the vicar of Iford married Joan Vinall.[9] Joan was the daughter of the first John Vinall of Kingston. Thomas Rogers I became brother-in-law to the second John Vinall, and related by marriage to the Kingston Ades.

There are scant records of Thomas's time as vicar of Iford, even though he held the living for more than 30 years until his death in 1666.[10] He was privileged to preach in one of the loveliest churches in the Ouse valley. The fabric of the church of St Nicholas was virtually unchanged from Norman times. Today it still conveys the simplicity of religious conviction of the people who built it. It is superlatively a village church. There is a small containing nave to hold a village congregation. The chancel, which ends in three slim lancet windows above the altar, is seen as a mystery through a pair of Norman arches, which support the central bell tower. It is hard to believe that any man who preached there Sunday after Sunday could fail to form a deep affection for the place, or be affected by its peacefulness. In the 34 years of his ministry Thomas Rogers the vicar must have had some of this peace.

Yet it would be wrong to imagine that Thomas's ministry was simply a time of peace and religious comfort. It ran from 1632 to 1666 and covered some tortured years in the history of the English Church. He took the living while Charles was still on the throne, but for 20 years of his time at Iford the Church was in varying degrees of turmoil; even country vicars were at risk for their views or behaviour. Rogers was vicar through the civil war, the Commonwealth and the Protectorate. He was at Iford when poor Henry Shephearde, in Kingston, was dispossessed for alleged 'drunkeness and misdemeanour' in 1645. He held on successfully at Iford while the Committee for Plundered Ministries sat in moral judgement on country vicars at Lewes. He continued through the more peaceful latter years of the interregnum. In all these years he evidently made no profound concessions to Nonconformity, or none serious enough to compromise his position when times changed. He continued as vicar after the Restoration in 1660. It is true that many churchmen survived the changes with similar success, but evidently it required skill and discretion about matters of doctrine. Thomas Rogers knew when to keep his head below the level of the trenches; he was a survivor!

The interregnum probably had much more profound implications for the Rogers family than merely inducing Thomas to keep his own counsel when the time was dangerous – and to avoid the alehouse, which had been the downfall of Henry Shephearde. The circumstances of the time certainly changed the course of family history and so in the end had their effect on future events in Kingston.

Thomas the vicar and his wife Joan Vinall had a son in the early years of their marriage. Thomas Rogers II was born in about 1640, just as civil strife was starting. He grew up in the Iford vicarage, no doubt in close contact with his first cousins, the Vinalls in Kingston Manor. The question of his future was a matter of some preoccupation for his parents, since there was no obvious place for him.

In more 'normal' times there would have been a well-charted course for the son of a moderately well off country vicar to follow – precisely the course his father had followed before him. Young Thomas II would have been prepared for the university and ultimately for the ministry.

But when Thomas II was an adolescent – at about the age when such matters would need to be decided – things were definitely not in their accustomed places. His father had every reason to know how complex and risky the life of a churchman had become. Moreover, the universities were in a state of sustained turmoil. The obvious option, which the young man's parents must have entertained since his birth, was closed and that left a puzzle of some seriousness. The vicar may have had a fair amount of wealth but not, as far as can be ascertained, in land; and an Oxford-educated vicar was unlikely to have much agricultural skill or knowledge to pass on to his son.

In the event, despite the lack of land to farm, Thomas Rogers II either elected to stay on in Iford or was obliged to do so – *faute de mieux*. At least in Iford he was near some fairly powerful relatives who might be supportive. However straightforward this decision might appear, it put Thomas Rogers II in a singular position in the long history of Iford and Kingston, for, among the dozens of vicars' children who had grown up in these villages before and have done since, this young man is the only one who can be decisively identified as having decided to stay on. Thomas Rogers II broke with the normal pattern of the clergyman's family and 'went native' in Iford. The rarity of the event is a reflection of the topsy-turviness of the world in which he grew up.

Thomas's early history in Iford is hard to trace, though in the light of subsequent events it gives hints of a certain tenacity of purpose. It is clear that he owned exceedingly little land. In 1660 either he, or more probably his father, purchased a small part of the demesne land of Iford Manor, which had been divided up in a most complex way through the vagaries of inheritance and sales.[11] It is doubtful that these lands amounted to any more than a yardland in the enclosed but much subdivided farm called Stuckles.[12] They passed to Thomas II when his father the vicar died, but there was not enough land to make a man rich.

Despite this limited ownership, Thomas II plainly managed to sustain himself and indeed to accumulate wealth until he met with better times in the mid-1670s. His parents must have left him some money and he probably used it as working capital to finance tenancies, which cannot now be traced. It may be too that in these early years he had a good deal to learn about the land. He had not grown up in an agricultural household and even his Vinall cousins were, by 1666 or so, more concerned to enjoy the social privileges they could derive from manorial lordship than to farm the land itself. In the years between 1655 and 1670, while Thomas II was first growing up, then learning to make his way by tenancy, his cousin William Vinall was engaged in the extraordinary series of marriages that brought him to a place in county society (See Chapter 8). Benjamin Vinall was a tenant on the Swanborough demesnes and may have been of more help.

It is hard to escape the impression that during these years of obscurity Thomas II either knew exactly what route he wished to take or at least was on the lookout for an opportunity. It is at least clear that when events turned his way, from about 1674 onwards, he was ready for them. The precise sequence of these events is not possible to disentangle but their outcome is quite clear.

It is not too cynical to suggest that the most important event of 1674 as far as Thomas II was concerned was the death of Benjamin Vinall, William's younger brother. Whatever his cousin may have meant to him, Thomas must have been impressed by Benjamin's tenancy on the demesnes of Swanborough Manor – a tenancy that had descended to him from the first John Vinall and that brought with it occupancy of the manor house and access to the largest area of enclosed arables on the western side of the Ouse. Though Kingston farmers found ways of dealing with the inflexibility of their champion lands in the open fields, the Swanborough demesnes were still, in 1670, uniquely advantaged over surrounding strip lands. They were still comparatively better adapted to the developing techniques of 'up-and-down' farming and accordingly potentially more productive and profitable. Benjamin's death was Thomas's opportunity – a chance to access a splendid block of lands on a tenancy of decent scale. And though the matter was not without problems, Thomas II was determined to have the land.

The main problem was that Thomas had insufficient capital to cope with the tenancy. He solved this through his association with the Attree family – gentry from the Barcombe area. Thomas knew the Attrees through Benjamin Vinall, who had married into the family. The relationship brought him two things, which were related to one another though it is not clear how. First, to establish himself on the Swanborough tenancy Thomas formed a partnership with William Attree and so resolved the problem of lack of working capital. In the Duke of Dorset's rental for 1677 – the first taken after Benjamin Vinall's death – Thomas II and William Attree paid a rent of £112.10 for the 'scite and part of the demesnes and Stuckles'.[13] This was substantially less than the £200 rent Benjamin Vinall had been paying in the years before his death,[14] which suggests that even with Attree's help Thomas II was stretched by the tenancy and he was thus unable to take on as much as Vinall had been farming.

Second, Thomas's relationship with the Attrees brought him a wife. He married late by the standards of the time, perhaps because of the time and effort it had taken him to build up sufficient resources to make a 'suitable' marriage. In 1675, however, probably *after* he had formed the partnership with William Attree, he married Attree's widowed daughter Mary, who had been married before to William Plumer. She probably brought a substantial settlement to Thomas and, after their marriage, Thomas and Mary settled at Swanborough Manor house to farm the demesnes.

In retrospect, this was a decisive moment in the establishment of the Rogers family. Thomas II was to remain as the Duke of Dorset's tenant for the next 45 years. Once he had acquired the tenancy he held onto it and Swanborough was indeed his main preoccupation as a farmer. The lands he held in ownership were small: a small portion of Iford demesnes he had inherited from his father and a freehold yardland, which he purchased from Arthur Brapple in Iford in 1676.[15] As subsequent events were to show, Thomas II was signally successful as a tenant farmer. Not long after his accession to the lands he was able to dispense with the financial support of William Attree[16] and to increase the size of his tenancy. He established his family at Swanborough and a good deal more than a century after he first took on the lands they were still a Rogers' tenancy.

There was something approaching irony in this situation. Thomas Rogers II, like his cousin William Vinall, was a grandson of the John Vinall who had come from Falmer in the last years of Elizabeth's reign to farm the Duke of Dorset's demesnes. Vinall had built his fortune on the demesne tenancy and here, 80 years on, was a relatively disadvantaged scion of his own family attempting to do the same, and attempting it with the same dedication to accumulation his grandfather had shown. In the meantime though that other grandson, William Vinall, who was lord of the manor in Kingston, was mobilizing the fortune the old man had amassed in the first instance to gain entry to 'county' drawing rooms and establish himself as a 'captain of militia'. If old John Vinall looked down on Kingston in 1676 or so, he might have wondered at the similarities between his own sense of purpose and tenacity and those of Thomas Rogers, and perhaps found it hard to recognize much of himself in the 'gentlemanly' family he had left behind in Kingston.

The Thomas Rogers who was to appear in Kingston in 1699 was the third in line. He was born in 1676 to Mary Attree[17] and was brought up with Swanborough and its demesnes as the centre of his universe, and with considerably greater prospects of economic security than his father had apparently enjoyed. But his childhood was not without event. In 1682, or possibly before, he lost his mother: Mary Attree died. Thomas III was about six years old. His father married again within a short while, this time to Elizabeth Ade of Iford,[18] so creating another link to local yeomanry. Elizabeth bore a son soon after marriage: John Rogers was born in 1683.[19] The subsequent pattern of the Rogers's history in Iford and Kingston was determined by the arrangements Thomas II made for his two boys, though the reasons for these particular arrangements are obscure. Perhaps they merely represented the fairest division of wealth Thomas II could work out, a division he was largely free to determine on his own terms since, as a tenant farmer, he was not bound by customs of inheritance. The arrangements were quite simple. When Thomas III, the elder son, was 23 or 24 years old he was bought lands in Kingston. He married an Elizabeth Ade in 1699 and took her with him to live in the village.

Young John Rogers was 16 at this time. He was kept at home in Swanborough and, presumably, as his father grew older he helped to farm the demesnes. When old Thomas II died at 80 years of age in 1720, John Rogers took over the tenancy the old man had held for so long, and worked it himself until his death in 1766. On his gravestone in the Iford churchyard, which his grandfather had presided over more than a century before, he is described as John Rogers of Swanborough.[20] His son, also a John Rogers, took over the tenancy in turn.

As a consequence, there were two substantial Rogers families in the newly combined parish of Kingston and Iford in the eighteenth century.[21] The Thomas Rogers family was established in Kingston as owner-occupiers and tenants, while the John Rogers family held onto the Swanborough demesnes and lived in the old grange farm the Cluniacs had put up so long before.

From one point of view, the events that led to the appearance of Thomas Rogers III on the Kingston scene were merely a series of historical accidents. It so happened that the young man had a grandfather who, after his ordination, had attained the favour of the Duke of Dorset and so found his way to a living as vicar of Iford. And it so happened also that the young man's father had been caught by a current of larger events, side-tracked from what would have been a more conventional career for a person in his position, and was forced to make his way as a tenant farmer. That Thomas II, his father, had an unusual personal history in no way diminishes the accidental nature of the circumstances.

Yet it is also true that the appearance of Thomas III and the circumstances that led to it were a part of a continuum, for once again the influence of the Swanborough demesnes, created so many centuries before, was making itself felt in the village. Vinall – old John Vinall that is – had accumulated wealth from the surpluses generated off those great, enclosed lands, which allowed his son to enter Kingston as a manor lord. In 1699, after 25 years of tenancy on the same lands, Thomas Rogers II had accumulated enough to provide a curiously similar opportunity for his eldest son, for the lands in Kingston that were bought for the young Thomas Rogers in Kingston were financed out of Swanborough surpluses. The Vinall entry into Kingston produced economic and social changes in the village. It created a larger distance between the 'great' and the 'small'; it squeezed out yeomanry and left less space on the small lands. In his own terms, Thomas Rogers III was to start an even more profound process of change – and once again the initial impetus had come from Swanborough. That Thomas II happened to be a grandson of old John Vinall and can be seen as oddly similar to his grandfather in style and commitment of purpose adds piquancy to the situation. It may be yet another accident of history, but in its own way it sharpens the point about underlying continuity. The general directions of change in Kingston were much the same as elsewhere in Sussex and over much of England for that matter; but the forms it took were interestingly particular. It is not improbable to see the figure of de Warenne, distant in time, but still exerting an influence over village life.

It is highly improbable that such parallels occurred to Thomas Rogers III when he brought his new wife to live in Kingston. If he thought at all about his Vinall cousins, it was probably with a degree of sadness and disapproval. By 1700 William the 'captain of militia' had been dead for 20 years. Mabilla Davis, married to the high sheriff of Sussex, was responsible for the manor. And young William, a distant cousin of Thomas Rogers III, was near the point where he would set in motion the disastrous descent to mortgage and bankruptcy that ended the Vinall ascendancy. It is hardly likely that Mabilla's son, who had been brought up in the higher reaches of county society, had much to share with the young man who called himself a yeoman and who was dedicated to making his way in the world on totally different terms from those that apparently had influenced William Vinall. Thomas Rogers III had more serious business to attend to. And it seems too that he had inherited much of his father's tenacity.

He started out on the six freehold yardlands of Swanborough Manor called Alfrey's, which had been part of the Eversfield and Bowker 'empires', and on a small copyhold of Kingston Manor.[22] His father paid £262.10 for Alfreye's,[23] which was an excellent price for the time, the more particularly because agricultural prices had risen sharply in the 1690s when harvests were poor through much of England. Only a few years later the young William Vinall managed to acquire a mortgage of more than £300 on four yardlands.[24] Some 18 years later Thomas III paid more than £600 for six yardlands, which admittedly included a 'tenement'. By all available comparisons for the price of Kingston land, Thomas III started out with a good deal. He displaced a tenant farmer called Henry Smether from Alfreye's.

The other purchase comprised a tenement and small amount of land customarily described in Kingston deeds as 'Bayley's before Howell's'.[25] The lands were slightly more than those normally attached to a cottage.[26] As far as Thomas and Elizabeth were concerned, they were of less interest than the 'tenement', for it became their home in Kingston.

This house was to play a considerable role in the lives of various members of the Rogers family and, indeed, in the development of the village itself. It is also one of the more mysterious properties in Kingston, for today the imposing house that stands on the site of what was Bayley's cottage is called 'Hyde Manor House'. Earlier, in Chapter 6, we intimated that there is something odd about this because the description of the old Hyde Manor house in Michell's survey of Hyde, done in 1567, does not fit the present 'Hyde Manor' – and nor do the abutments tally. In fact, beyond reasonable doubt, Michell's Hyde Manor house was further down the street and on the other side.

Evidence from the Rogers' early deeds corroborates this, at least to the extent that it shows that the modern 'Hyde Manor House' could not have been called that in 1700. First, there is no doubt that the house on this site was the Rogers family's main residence in Kingston. Thomas III owned it and it was he who was mainly responsible for turning it into the house it is today. Second, Thomas Rogers III did *not* own Hyde Manor and had no reason or right to call the house after it.

The story of the house unfolds a little when one visits it.[27] To the outward eye it is a brick-built early eighteenth-century home of great charm and elegance sited opposite Kingston churchyard. It is in fact one of the more imposing pieces of architecture in Kingston Street.

But there is a touch of *trompe d'oeil* about this. Enter the house through its lovely eighteenth-century front door and you will find yourself, not in the Georgian or Queen Anne hallway you might have expected, in fact not in a hallway at all, but in the main front room of a Sussex cottage of the seventeenth or possibly sixteenth century. It has a timbered interior and there are signs of wattle and daub. The fact is that the central front sections of the house are made up of a straightforward cottage on two floors with parlour extensions on either side of the main structure. The lambent brick exterior is a mere façade added to a simple rural house. Examine it carefully and you will notice that the façade itself has been built in sections as the house behind was extended. The central section corresponds to the original cottage. The eaves have been raised to create grander proportions and there is a line of excellent mathematical tile atop the façade.[28] This is no manor house, but it is a house that tells a story.

When Thomas Rogers III and his wife Elizabeth came to Kingston, it was to take up residence in the charming but unassuming cottage that then stood on the site opposite the entry to St Pancras churchyard. It is unlikely that the parlours had been added on either side of the main structure. It was a simple place. For Thomas, who had lived at Swanborough, it was a mite too simple, as well as too small. Cottage families lived physically crowded lives. It is implausible to imagine that Thomas, who had every reason to expect Elizabeth Ade to bear children to fill the house, would have been satisfied at the prospect of an overcrowded life in three or four rooms. He was not lavish, but he was the son of the Swanborough tenant and, for status as well as practical reasons, he set out to transform the house accordingly.

The first move was to create a façade for the old cottage and perhaps also to raise its eaves. Then, as a second step, the parlour extensions with their grand eighteenth-century bay windows were added and the façade extended to encompass them. Perhaps a small east wing was added at the same time. The outer brickwork of the house suggests that the façade was developed in two stages in this way.

This transformation was not, of course, an original notion. Medieval houses in Lewes were being faced with brickwork and plaster at the time – not always, it must be said, with the happiest results. Thomas Rogers must be given credit for the delicacy of taste and sense of architectural unity that informs the transformation he undertook. It is a splendid and convincing façade. Thomas created a house of distinction from which he could look out on the churchyard with its yew tree and across the closes on the north side of the street to the furlongs of the West Laine. It was turned into a working farmhouse too; there was a barn and close behind it, which became the centre of his farming activities. The house was to experience further extensions, but the basic structure of the Rogers's home in Kingston was created in these early years.

Aside from this striking undertaking, there was not much on the surface to distinguish Thomas and Elizabeth in their first two decades in Kingston from other yeoman families. Thomas worked Alfreye's. He almost certainly held a number of small tenancies whenever they became available and he built up his resources. Presumably there were amiable relationships with the Ades in Iford – his father too had married an Elizabeth Ade in his second marriage –

and the two families, the Rogers and Iford Ades, were closely linked. Presumably also, Thomas III maintained links with his father who, though ageing, continued as the tenant on Swanborough. Old Thomas II lived on till 1720. Thomas III, his son, might well have envied the great tenancy destined to go to his half-brother John, but he could set against that the fact he was already independent, free to build up wealth on his own account, while John was tied to Swanborough and the paterfamilias.

Evidently, Thomas III used this independence to good effect. He built up his wealth quietly and effectively during these first two decades, so that later, when opportunities for further acquisition appeared, he was able to snap them up. In the very years that his cousin William Vinall at Kingston Manor was sinking into awesome debt without hope of recovery, Thomas was laying foundations for the future. The contrast between these Rogers and Vinall great-grandsons of John Vinall was even sharper than between his grandsons – and all the more so because they were neighbours in Kingston Street.

The first two decades were also the years in which Thomas III and Elizabeth established their family. There were four children born some years apart. Mary Rogers was the first in 1702. Then a son, naturally called Thomas, followed. Young Thomas was born in late October 1704, but did not survive long. Seven months later, in May 1705, he was buried in St Pancras churchyard across the street from the Rogers's new home.[29]

Thomas's birth and early death was followed in 1705 by the appearance of another son who was given the Ade name of William; and after William there was a second daughter called Elizabeth (whose dates are uncertain). Then there was a substantial pause, which lasted until 1719. In October of that year Elizabeth Ade bore her last child. It was a boy and he was named after his little brother who had died 15 years before. He was called Thomas Rogers, and grew up to become Thomas IV. If there could not be an elder son called Thomas, then at least there would be a younger one. Sister Mary was already 17 and not many years away from her marriage to John Stanford of Rodmell.[30] Old Thomas II, who had made all this possible, died in the year his grandson was born.

Before the birth of this second son there had been a change of tempo in Thomas III's activities in Kingston. For a number of years he was tenant farmer on the six freehold yardlands called 'Peake's.[31] These, like Alfreye's, had passed from the last Edward Bowker to one of his daughters, and in turn to a granddaughter Catherine who was married to John Bullis, a vicar in Billingshurst. There were probably some financial difficulties, for in 1712 Bullis had been obliged to mortgage the property for £200. In 1718, perhaps as a consequence, Bullis decided to sell out. Thomas III was ready for him and bought Peake's for the considerable sum of £631.1.0.[32]

This purchase once again brought the yardlands of Alfreye's and Peake's into single ownership. It recreated the 'empire' of freehold lands, which the Eversfields had first formed as landlords in the early Tudor period and which had supported the socially distinctive Bowker family through the seventeenth century. More important, though, it changed Thomas Rogers's position in Kingston quite markedly, for it doubled the land he held in ownership from six yardlands to twelve. He now held all the freehold land in Kingston outside the manorial demesnes, and a significantly larger area in total than the Ades or Picombes who lived just down the street. He had been able to mobilize the £631 required, and he put it to the purpose of further accumulation. There was a lull before his next purchases, but in the meantime he was once again building up his resources.

Tenancy, as well as ownership, played an important part in the building up process. Thomas III actively sought tenancies and the best ones in Kingston village were on the 15 yardlands the Dorsets continued to hold as landlords in the village. These, as we have seen, were divided into two farms – Kingston Town Farm and Diggon's. Diggon's, which consisted of six yardlands, was tied up in a long lease until about 1710. The Tichbournes acquired the lease in the mid-seventeenth century and were still in occupancy in 1704.[33] However, a short while after that the Tichbournes relinquished the tenancy and Thomas Rogers III was there to take it up. In Dorset's rentals for 1713–15, Thomas III is shown as paying an annual rent to Mr Medley, the duke's steward, of £21 a year for the six yardlands.[34] In the same rental his father is listed at a rent of £180 for the demesnes of Swanborough. Thomas was on Diggon's farm and there plainly, he intended to stay. He was still tenant to the duke on these lands in 1729,[35] and Diggon's remained a Rogers' tenancy until the end of the century.

With Alfreye's, Peake's and Diggon's under his control, Thomas III had obtained three of the oldest and most distinguished farms in the village. He had also acquired access to at least 18 yardlands, or a quarter of the arable lands in Kingston. And it is likely that he had other unrecorded tenancies. By 1718 Thomas III had carved out a position for himself in the village commensurate with the distinctiveness of the house he had created, so it is doubtful that any villager would have thought of him as pretentious. He owned substantially more land than any other yeoman, more indeed than the Alchornes at Hyde Manor. He worked all the land on Kingston Manor farm, which included 19 yardlands after the acquisitions of Barnden's and Hudd's (see Chapter 8). He was still called a yeoman in 1718,[36] but the day was not far off when it became natural to describe him as 'gentleman of Kingston'. He had in a sense filled the social gap left by the failure of the male line in the Bowker family, but did so very much on his own terms. Whereas the Bowkers had been content to hold onto Alfrey's and Peake's without any apparent motivation to expand their lands, Thomas III was committed to expansion. If the Bowkers had been respected for their gentlemanly distinction, their birth and London connections, Thomas Rogers was respected for his vigour and hard commitment.

During the lull in Thomas Rogers's acquisition of lands after the purchase of

Peake's in 1718, a remarkable transaction took place, which is revealing in many ways about the man and his family. It gives an insight into Thomas's relationship with Francis Zouch, who had taken over the lordship of Kingston Manor from his unfortunate brother-in-law William Vinall. It says something too of Thomas's preoccupation with the house he had created and with the social status he hoped to derive from it. It reveals a dimension of obstinacy in him and it tells us a little about tensions within the Rogers family.

The transaction took place in 1722. The reason for it is quite clear: Thomas III had conceived a great concern about the manorial status of the parcel of lands that included his house. They were copyhold lands of Kingston Manor. Thomas wished them to be given the status of freeholds, and clearly it was very important to him.

Why Thomas should have been so concerned can only be inferred. The annual feudal dues in lieu of labour service cannot have been a serious consideration. They amounted to a mere eight shillings a year[37] and such a small sum would not have bothered Thomas. It is unlikely too that he was concerned about security of tenure. Copyhold tenure in Kingston, as in Iford and generally in the Ouse valley, was highly secure. We have found no instance in the post-Tudor history of the village in which a manor lord asserted rights to withhold customary lands or copyholds from the traditional lines of inheritance. Given the precedents, or lack of them, it is implausible that the lord of Kingston Manor would suddenly take over copyholds of his manor. This cannot have been of serious concern to Thomas. It seems likely that Thomas attached importance to the manorial status of the lands simply because he felt strongly that it was more appropriate that his house should be a freehold rather than a copyhold for mainly social reasons. He wished his newly created home to be independent of feudal dues in the same way as a manor farmhouse might be; he valued the status.

He was able to agree with Francis Zouch on the matter. The centrepiece of the transaction is a copy of the court roll of Kingston Manor for 7 March 1722. It records that the customary 'messuage or tenement' and the virgate of land attached to it called 'Bayley's before Howell's', was 'taken into the lands of the lord' and duly returned to Thomas Rogers III freed of its feudal dues; all that would be demanded in future was an annual quit rent of a penny, a 'fine' (on entry of a successor to the land) of sixpence, and a heriot of the same amount.[38] The property had been 'enfranchised' (in effect turned into a freehold) since the lord had relinquished his rights to dues in lieu of labour service. Thomas Rogers III had his wish.

If matters had stopped at this point the transaction would not have been significant. But, although Francis Zouch agreed to 'enfranchise' the property, he asked for something in return. His terms were that there should be an exchange of various parcels of land between Rogers and himself. He wished Rogers to relinquish the 'barn, close and croft' called Great Barley Croft, which was part of Alfrey's. This amounted to three acres at the head of the village street; it included the great barn, which stands there to this day. In exchange, Zouch would hand over to Rogers two pieces of land – 'Clover Croft', an enclosure of about three acres outside the village on the far side of the road between Lewes and Newhaven, and 'Lattendens', a barn and half an acre of enclosure on the north side of the village street a little way down from the Rogers's house (on the site occupied today by the house called 'Anvil'). Clover Croft had been part of Hudd's, lands William Vinall had obtained from Thomas Picombe. 'Lattendens' belonged to the parcel the Barndens had held in Elizabethan times.

On the surface, this was an equal exchange: Thomas III gave a three-acre croft with a barn on it and got in exchange a three-acre croft and a small enclosure in Kingston Street with a barn. On closer look, though, it is clear that the exchange was more advantageous to Francis Zouch than to Thomas. Obviously, Zouch wished to hold the Great Barley Crofts. They abutted other enclosed lands he already held at the head of the street and they included the largest and most useful barn in the village. The barn Thomas Rogers got in return was almost certainly smaller than the one he had given up, and the close – separated from the barn itself – was out in the 'Lower Ham', in the low-lying lands on the edge of the Ouse valley, subject to flooding and at some distance from the street. The difference must, of course, have been apparent to Thomas III, but he clearly regarded it as a reasonable price to pay for the enfranchisement.

The real measure of Thomas's attachment to the enfranchisement and of his obstinacy about the matter did not lie in his willingness to accept the disadvantage of this exchange.[39] It lay rather in his forcing ahead this complicated transaction in the face of fierce opposition from his wife and eldest son. Thomas IV, the younger son, was only two at the time, so hardly in a position to have an opinion on the matter, but William was 15 and participated. He and Elizabeth, his mother, were very much against the whole undertaking. One can only assume that they were unconvinced of any need for the enfranchisement to which Thomas was so committed. Elizabeth may have reflected that her Ade cousins at the corner of the street had lived for long generations in copyhold houses without being disturbed or notably disadvantaged. She must have wondered at the folly of relinquishing the splendid barn and close of Alfreye's, which she could see from the house and which was so conveniently placed.

Whatever precise considerations weighed on Elizabeth and William, they were deeply angered and publicly so. Francis Zouch was sufficiently disturbed by the dissension in the Rogers household to ask Thomas to provide him with a special bond promising there would be no 'disturbance to the use of the land' by Elizabeth or any heirs of Thomas Rogers. This was duly provided.[40] The bond is the first measure of Thomas's determination. The second, also reflecting a concern to abide by the terms of the agreement with Zouch, comes in a clause in his will.[41] In it he made the following strong stipulation:

> [I]f my said wife Elizabeth and son William or his heirs or assignees … shall at any time after my decease demand or sue for the Upper Barn and Croft which I lately exchanged with the said Mr Zouch for the said Lattenden's Barn and Croft and the said Clover Croft … then the said devise by me … to him or her … shall be void and of none effect.

Elizabeth and William could inherit from him only on condition they accepted the rules he laid down and the agreement he had made. The disagreement in the family was no light affair. Apparently, it remained a major source of resentment and threat for the rest of his life. Young Thomas his son did not become embroiled, for Thomas III found no reason to threaten any sanctions against him. It was a matter between Elizabeth, William and Thomas III. It was never fully resolved and it may account directly or indirectly for the fact that William Rogers was never reconciled to living in Kingston; he left at an early age and never farmed there.

How the family encompassed this lasting division is not clear. Nevertheless, when Thomas III next launched out to buy land in Kingston, in 1734, he involved William, who was then aged about 30, in the transactions. In fact, two of the purchases were made directly in William's name and one in the name of young Thomas IV, who was only 14. The purchases for William may have been part of an effort to reconcile him or induce him to stay on in the village. The first consisted of the excellent farmyard and yardlands of Taberer's, which had been passed down through the Howell family to the Harfreys and then to the Elphicks (see Chapter 8). This was a natural addition to the Rogers' lands. The great barn of Taberer's stood right next door to their house in the street. It was grand enough to stand in considerable measure as compensation for the loss of the 'Upper Barn' of Alfrey's, which had so deeply upset William and his mother.[42] It was perfectly placed to become the centre of the Rogers's farmyard.

The second purchase for William was smaller. It was the barn and yardlands held by the Brooks, who had bought or inherited from the Quaker Wenhams[43] (see Table 8.1). And the purchase for Thomas the younger son was also small: the barn and half yardland, which had been so long in the Howell family and had since passed to the Bodles.[44]

These were the last purchases of land Thomas III made. After 1734 he owned 16 yardlands in Kingston and, when his tenancies are taken into account, he farmed about a third of all Kingston arable. From the point of view of areas, Thomas III had maintained himself as the second largest farmer in the village. Socially, the Rogers stood second only to the Zouches. Thomas III had engrossed more land in 35 years in Kingston than anyone since the first Duke of Dorset. But whereas that Elizabethan magnate had the resources to sweep up copyholds at will, Thomas Rogers III, after the initial impetus of 'Swanborough finance', had been obliged to work doggedly to build up his estate. He was tough and obstinate, dominating and sometimes petty, but consistent in one thing – the drive to accumulate wealth. When he died in 1743[45] he had built a foundation for the Kingston Rogers, which allowed them to further the process he had started. Perhaps in recognition of the rough pre-eminence he had attained in the village, he was buried under a great simple slab of stone, just to the left of the church porch. No one who went to morning song on Sunday could miss the grave of Thomas Rogers – whatever view they had of him while he was alive and in their midst.

At his death the lands passed to Elizabeth for the remainder of her life and were then to be divided between William and Thomas IV.[46] The division of inheritance often went against manorial custom, but apparently raised no questions of legality. Thomas IV, the younger brother, held onto 'Bodle's', the barn and half yardland bought for him in 1734, but he also got 'Peake's', which consisted of six freehold virgates of Houndean Manor land. If custom had been followed it would have gone to the eldest son, as all freehold should. How Thomas III managed to evade the requirements of the manor court at Houndean is unclear. That he did so may reflect a particular affection he felt for his younger son. He also left young Thomas his silver watch – the only really personal bequest in his will apart from one to his wife, 'the use of my bed … five pairs of sheets and linen'.[47]

William got the rest of the land: Alfrey's, which he might have seen as mutilated by the excision of the Upper Barn and Barley Croft; Taberers, which had been bought for him in 1734; Bailey's and the house Thomas III had created out of a cottage; the small barn and yardland of Brook's; and, ironically, the parcel of lands his father had accepted in exchange for Barley Croft and that Thomas had seen as so sadly inadequate. In the final tally, William inherited ten yardlands and Thomas IV got a little over six.

If the purchases for William in 1734 were intended to keep him in Kingston, they failed in their purpose. Before his father's death he had left the village, perhaps as much attracted by the growing charms of Georgian Brighton as discouraged by the conflict with his father. He married Barbara Scrase of Patcham, a member of an important and powerful Brighton family, and went to live in Patcham, a village of great charm lying a few miles north of Brighton.[48] Thereafter, he was always William Rogers, gent. of Patcham.[49] When Elizabeth died in 1750, and was laid in a matching grave next to Thomas III, William did not return to farm his lands. Instead, his younger brother Thomas IV became his tenant. The Rogers's lands were to that extent held together as a unit. William was content to live on his landlord income. Thomas stayed on in the house with the brick façade.

*****

In this first half of the eighteenth century Thomas Rogers III was clearly the most actively acquisitive landowner in Kingston. For the most part, though not entirely, the others were quiescent.

In 1717 Francis Zouch had taken over Kingston Manor from the financially ruined young William Vinall. Through his marriage to Martha Vinall, Zouch was William's brother-in-law. He had been a merchant in London[50] and had lent large sums to William to avert his final collapse, but to no avail. William came tumbling down and Martha, Zouch's wife, must have conceived of the plan to take over Kingston Manor. By that time they had lent William so much money that they may have felt that the outright purchase of Kingston Manor was the only practical way of protecting their 'investment'. More likely though, Martha Zouch foresaw that William had reached the limits of feasible indebtedness, had no way of repaying any of his creditors and so ran the risk of letting the manor slip from Vinall hands. She had grown up there and, aside from wanting to return home, she very probably could not face the prospect of the Vinall manor passing to another family.

Things worked out well for the Zouch family in Kingston. Francis came to live in the house at the head of the street as the new manor lord and Kingston Manor House remained the premier house in the village. Zouch put the manor farm into order and re-established the estate. He restored and extended the house and left a reputation for 'improvement' thoroughly in keeping with the times. There were no dramatic social attainments in his time.

Zouch had no serious wish to extend his lands. His transaction with Thomas Rogers III, however, suggests that he lacked neither astuteness nor concern about his lands. The acquisition of the Great Barley Croft and upper barn in the street was sensible; it meant he held nearly eight acres of enclosed crofts abutting one another and lying right next to his farmyards. It was a good consolidating move, but Zouch's ambitions did not extend to further engrossment in the village. He was prepared to leave the field to young Thomas Rogers down the street.

From the way Martha Zouch ran the estate after Francis's death suggests that, had she been given her way, she may have followed a more active policy. Unfortunately, it is difficult to determine exactly when Francis Zouch died. There is no entry in the parish register, so we presume he was buried elsewhere. From the record of subsequent events, it seems likely that he died in the late 1720s, not very long after his exchange of lands and enfranchisement with Thomas Rogers. In terms of his will, he left the manor and all other Kingston lands to Martha for the rest of her life, and then in default of children the estate was to go to his cousin, the Revd Charles Zouch of Sandal Magna in Yorkshire. In fact, in the years following Francis's death, Charles Zouch appears to have played a supportive role to Martha. He handled a number of small transactions on her behalf in the mid-1730s.

But Martha was by no means inactive on her own account. She took direct responsibility for the manor farm and then, in 1729, launched out on a new enterprise in true Vinall style (or to be more accurate in the older Vinall style of her great-grandfather). That year John Walker of Kingston died. Walker had been the Duke of Dorset's tenant on Kingston Town Farm since the turn of the century and on his death the tenancy fell vacant. Martha Vinall snapped it up, all nine yardlands of it, and so moved onto lands that had been part of early Vinall history. She increased the arable area under her control from the 19 yardlands of the manor estate to 28 yardlands, and for the years after 1729 until her death in 1750 she was the largest farmer in Kingston,[51] certainly more of a match for her Rogers cousin down the street than her brother William had been. Martha had not engrossed lands, but she had allied a substantial tenancy to her manor farm and so contributed in her own way to reducing the space available for smaller landholders.

Matters were different at Hyde Manor. A succession of Alchornes had persevered on the lands of Hyde, but few of them had much interest. The deeds for the manor become quite obscure in the eighteenth century and it is likely that, through lack of concern or interest, the property was allowed to decay. Certainly by the latter quarter of the eighteenth century the medieval part of Thomas Michell's manor house had been demolished, and it is likely that the process took place earlier.[52] The Alchornes were in no mood to add to their Kingston lands.

Though the other large landowners in Kingston had been content to hold onto what lands they had and not to extend, the incursion of Thomas III by itself was sufficient to produce some marked changes in landowning and in village society. Thomas's engrossments had two main effects. First, they cut into the lands that were available for smaller tenancies. At the end of the seventeenth century both Alfrey's and Peake's were sources of small tenancy as they passed into the ownership of Bowker daughters who married men from outside the village. Indeed, in 1699, when Rogers purchased Alfrey's, it was in the occupancy of Henry Smether.[53] Indeed, quite aside from the engrossment of land into ownership, Thomas III followed an active policy of tenancy on his own account, which in itself reduced the amount of land on which smaller tenants might establish themselves. As he became established in the village and built up his working capital he cut into that ready supply of small tenancies that had so influenced the social 'shape' of Kingston in the previous half century and, in particular, had delayed its transformation into a village of agricultural labourers.

The second effect of Thomas III's engrossments was that they cut into the small lands of the village, just as earlier engrossments had done. This was not true of his first two major purchases: larger landowners had always held Alfrey's and Peake's as landlords or owner-occupiers. It was true, however, of his later purchases, or of purchases he made on behalf of his sons during 1734. These look over the lands of three small owner-occupiers – the Brooks, Bodles and Elphicks. The Brooks had taken over the yardland the Gowers had owned in the mid-seventeenth century and which had subsequently passed to the Wenhams. It is possible that the Brooks came into possession through marriage to a Wenham daughter and that there was a failure in the male line of the Wenham family. Bodle had taken over a small amount of Howell land in 1693 (Chapter 8) and it remained in the family for three generations.[54] Then, soon after the admission of a third Nicholas Bodle in 1728, the lands appeared in the possession of Thomas Upton, who sold them to the Rogers family.[55] The Elphicks' lands had come down to them from the Harfrey family who had inherited Stephen Howell's lands in about 1625 (Chapter 7). When Jane Harfrey died a widow in 1696, Richard Elphick's 'youngest grandson' Stephen Howell was admitted. Taberer's remained in Elphick ownership for two generations. Then, in 1733, William Elphick died. Sarah his widow was left with a young son William and evidently decided to leave the village, probably to marry again. She and her son sold out to Thomas III.[56]

The impact of these three purchases was considerable. In a single year the number of independent yeoman families on small lands was reduced from six to three and lands that had for long been the preserve of small copyholders effectively lost their separate identity. At the same time, along with William Vinall's purchase of four yardlands of Hudd's from Thomas Picombe in 1704, Thomas III's incursion reduced the total area of arable farmed by owners of eight or less yardlands from 21 yardlands in 1700 to a paltry 13½ by 1735. The decay of the village's smallholder peasantry, which had started long before but been delayed in various ways, was now clearly revealed. Indeed, by 1735 the old owner-occupier 'core' of village society was virtually gone. Only three families belonging to the old tradition remained.

The circumstances in which this change came about are worth a little consideration. Dorset was a manor lord who took copyholds 'back into demesne', but there is no evidence that he used manorial powers to force people to sell or to intervene in inheritance and successions. He simply bought his way into the copyholds that became available. Vinall's more gradual accumulation of village lands was quite obviously a straightforward outcome of various members of the family seizing commercial opportunities as they arose when family resources were available to finance a purchase. Similarly, the quite rapid and determined intrusion of Thomas Rogers III was a commercial process. He acquired resources to buy other people's land as it came onto the market. It does not indicate that Thomas III had exceptional commercial powers he could mobilize to induce people to sell. His engrossments in the first 35 years of the eighteenth century greatly reduced the space available for smaller owner-occupiers on village arables and he certainly played a central role in the final dissolution of the 'yeoman' village of earlier years. It does not follow though that he ousted anyone from the land to achieve this.

It is true that smaller farmers were under various kinds of pressure in the early decades of the eighteenth century. In Kingston some of the economic pressure on them came from the active way in which Thomas Rogers III sought tenancies and presumably competed for them. Small tenancies were often important to the livelihood of small farmers and as they diminished in availability life become harder. It is also probable that small farmers in Kingston suffered from the disabilities that encumbered small farmers elsewhere.

Prices were generally weak in the first half of the century and profitability was depressed. The 1730s, during which Thomas III was able to pick up three small units, were particularly arduous times. Larger farmers responded to these adverse circumstances with the various 'improvement' measures so characteristic of this period of 'agricultural revolution'. Small farmers may either have been less knowledgeable about new techniques, so less able to keep themselves afloat, or disadvantaged in applying them.[57] Chapter 8 highlighted some of the difficulties that smallholders on the Kingston open fields experienced in adapting strip farming practice to the use of temporary leys. Similar obstacles limited the use they could make of the other great improving measures of the times. It is certainly likely that men like Thomas III's father and John Rogers, his half brother who farmed the enclosed demesnes of Swanborough, were better placed to experiment with new methods and rotations than most. And it is possible that Thomas III was able to learn from Swanborough and to apply the lessons to good effect in Kingston, while smaller farmers were in difficulty.

Economic pressures therefore played a part in reducing Kingston smallholdings in this period. However, another feature of Thomas III's acquisitions also played a role. Failures in the male line of landholding families generally led to sales and purchases of farms in Kingston. This is to be expected in a male dominated society in which women move to their husband's home on marriage, which usually meant that newly wed women would leave the village. Consequently, when a woman inherited village land by virtue of a failure in the male line, there was a high probability that she would be living elsewhere in a family economy centred on her husband's lands. And, moreover, in most cases her husband would take over her inheritance. These circumstances attendant upon a woman's succession to village lands considerably increased the chances that sooner or later the land would be sold. As far as the woman and her husband were concerned, their inherited Kingston lands were 'outliers' – not part of their main estate – and valuable mainly as an asset to be sold to buy land in their home area. The pattern is not inevitable by any means, but there are a number of instances in Kingston history. A particularly notable case is the Barnden inheritance, which passed to Joan Barnden in 1639 (see Chapter 7). Joan was married to a John Howell of Wilmington, and it was not long before they sold their inherited lands to the second John Vinall, who added them to the estate of Kingston Manor.

Thomas Rogers III benefited considerably from failures in the male lines of Kingston families. He acquired Alfrey's from John Mackerill of Fletching because he had married a Bowker and she, in turn, inherited the lands because Edmund Bowker had no son. Thomas III also obtained Bailey's, the property on which he built his splendid new house, from the Mackerills. Later he bought Peake's, which had also descended through the female line of the Bowker family. In fact, lands that had become available in this way formed the very heart of his Kingston empire.

Similar circumstances surrounded some of his later land purchases. When he bought Taberer's from the Elphicks, there was a male successor in possession of the lands but he was a very small boy in his mother's guardianship. Sarah Elphick had her own reasons for wishing to leave Kingston and sold out. In the case of Bodle's land, there is a high probability that there had been a failure in the male line. Nicholas Bodle had been admitted to the lands at the Swanborough Manor court in 1728. There is no record of a sale by the Bodles, but when Thomas III bought the lands a few years later they were in the hands of Thomas Upton, who was not 'of Kingston' and who would have been unlikely to have acquired this obscure parcel in the open field in any way other than inheritance through his wife. So Thomas III's engrossment owed as much to such particular family circumstances as to any greater economic process. Failure in the male line played a considerable part in the subsequent history of Kingston.

Failures in the male line had begun to 'afflict' the remaining yeoman families of Kingston too and, in the light of the consequences that often flowed from such happenings, their grip on their lands had weakened. The Picombes, or Peckhams as they had become by 1700, were more directly affected than the Ades and the Ades more so than the Towners.

Thomas Peckham, who sold Hudd's four yardlands to the Vinalls, died in 1710. It is unclear who succeeded to the four virgates he held or to the house and barn quite close to Thomas Rogers's house in Kingston Street. It is likely that he had no male heir because by the early 1730s the Bradford family held these lands. In 1734 they passed from the first to a second John Bradford.[58] Then, the family petered out. In 1742 the second John Bradford died and the lands passed to John Paine, his nephew.[59] Thenceforth they were known as Paine's Farm. The old yeoman Picombes, or Peckhams, were no longer part of Kingston. John Paine held the lands an earlier John Picombe had brought together from the Gowers' and Bonifaces' yardlands. He became Rogers's near neighbour in the year Thomas III died.

The Ades – so long guardians of the corner of the street and so tenacious in their hold on land – lasted a little longer. At the beginning of the century the vagaries of John's succession divided the Ade estate in two. Stephen Ade held the lands called Taylor's and some land that had belonged to the Towner family in the previous century. His sister and brother-in-law Sam Watts held Bishop's, the other group of yardlands that had been part of Gregory Ade's Elizabethan estate in Kingston. When Stephen died in 1721 his 22-year-old son William Ade succeeded him. Eventually, in 1731, Joanna Watts died too and the lands called Bishop's reverted to William. So, by 1730, William Ade had once again brought the old estate together into a single unit and, indeed, the Ade holding had increased in size to eight yardlands.

But this new coherence did not last long. When William died in 1742, he was the last of the yeoman Ades to be buried in the churchyard.[60] And he died without a male heir. The main part of the Ade lands – Taylor's and Bishop's –

were left to his nine-year-old daughter Mary, under the guardianship of her mother Ann Ade. The yardland called Towner's, which Stephen Ade's wife Mary Willard had inherited much earlier, was left to William's other daughter Ann who died young, whereupon the land reverted to her sister Mary.

On her coming of age Mary Ade was a lady of considerable wealth. She did not have immediate access to all the Ade lands – her mother was to hold Bishop's directly until her death in 1762 – but she had every expectation that she finally would and, from the beginning, she had a fair-sized holding in her own name. She did not have to wait long for marriage. Sometime before 1759, while in her early twenties, Mary married James Glover.[61] A few years later, in 1765, the lands her mother had held reverted to her.[62] The whole Ade estate had been brought together again, but it was no longer called Ades. It was now Glover's Farm – rechristened after many centuries of Ade ownership – for James Glover found the attractions of the Ade lands sufficient to induce him to settle down in Kingston. And the Ades, like the Picombes, had disappeared from the list of Kingston landowners.

The Towners, on the other hand, held out. Despite the extraordinarily high mortality rate among Towner children (see Chapter 7), they managed to maintain a male succession. In 1742, Stephen Towner was recorded in the court roll at Swanborough as holding the house and one-and-a-half virgates that had belonged to Adams in the reign of Henry VII.[63] They stayed on at Adam's and in the house at the end of the street where Robert Howell had once lived as head of his family through the first half of the eighteenth century and beyond. His son, also called Stephen, succeeded the Stephen Howell of 1742. The lands of this second Stephen – the yardland and a half of Adam's – are catalogued in Marchant's terrier of 1773 (as seen in Chapter 2).

In short, though Thomas Rogers III made inroads on the old yeoman lands of Kingston and took up 'economic space' that smaller farmers had occupied before, his intrusion was not the only factor in the decline of the village yeomanry over the first part of the century. In addition, the older families of Ade and Picombe had broken successions. Their names, which had had a certain prestige in social terms in the seventeenth-century village, simply disappeared from among the landowners. Their successors were never able to establish the same sense of continuity they had achieved and, to that extent, Kingston society was very much changed. There were still Ades and Picombes about in Kingston in the 1720s, but they were members of the economically weaker families who had always clustered about their more fortunate yeoman relatives. The old core of the village was gone. William Ade's death in 1742 was the signal of its going. The main continuity in village life during this time of change came from the continuing presence of a number of independent cottagers. By and large the cottager class in the village was maintained intact to a greater degree than the yeomanry.

The most steadfast cottager family (and unfortunately also the least recorded) was the Edward Howell family living in the lonely cottage called

'Shepherd's Rest' on the edge of the West Laine. Edward's children, who were all girls, grew up quietly in this cottage through the early years of the eighteenth century (see Chapter 8). He was to live on there to a great age. He was still in the cottage when Marchant made his terrier of Kingston in 1773.[64] He died in 1779 at 83 when his youngest grandson, called Thomas Wise, inherited the property.[65] He, more than most people in the village, had a sense of how much it had been changed.

A second important cottager family became established at the old malt-house William Coates had owned in Kingston Street. In 1726 the Lewes innkeeper William Burtenshaw sold this house with its close and orchard to John Ridley, a carpenter from Iford.[66] It passed from Ridley to his wife and then, probably in 1740 or so, to his daughter Jane. Jane married William Tuppen, who came from a long-established Kingston family. The Tuppens were mainly labourers and shepherds, but their antecedents in the village go back to at least 1565, and almost certainly before. They had married into the poorer branches of the yeoman families: in 1582, a Richard Tuppen had married Joan Howell; in 1634 Joan Gower married another Richard Tuppen. In the late 1650s and 1660s, John and Katherine Tuppen had a particularly large family from whom many subsequent Tuppens in Kingston and Iford were descended.[67] William Tuppen, by virtue of his marriage to Jane Ridley, was probably the first of the family to establish himself as a cottager.

Jane and William became the senior branch of the family in Kingston. They had at least six children, of whom five survived. Among them was Jane, the eldest daughter, William the eldest son and a youngest son called Henry, born when Jane was comparatively advanced in years, who later became a shepherd.[68] In fact Jane bore children over an extraordinarily long period, from 1750 until 1773; the cottage in Kingston Street became a busy noisy place. There was a second Tuppen family in the village contemporary with William and Jane Ridley. Another William Tuppen married Elizabeth Harriss who bore seven children between 1762 and 1773.

On the opposite corner of the street from the Ade houses and barns there stood another cottage. This is still a place of charm, though horribly diminished by tasteless transformation into a 'country pub'. Its early history is impossible to trace, but in 1742 James Baker, a shepherd from Iford, owned it. Baker leased it at an annual rent of 40 shillings to his parents – John Baker of Kingston, also a shepherd, and his wife Elizabeth.[69] Then in 1756 the cottage passed to Benjamin Ridge and John Rogers Jnr, the nephew of Thomas Rogers III, both from Iford. While they owned it, it was rented out to the Pollard family,[70] who were agricultural labourers. In 1767 it was sold to George Cuttress, a husbandman from Kingston, who lived in it as an owner-occupier. Later it was to pass to another Kingston husbandman, or labourer, called Samuel Alcorn[71] who leased it to the Richardson family in 1784.

And there were others. James Read occupied a small cottage in the street as an independent owner around the middle of the century,[72] and there is evidence that his family had held it for a century at least.[73] The cottage stands today. James and his wife Ann had a substantial family of three boys and three girls between 1756 and 1770. In 1768 they evidently fell on hard times and James was obliged to convey the cottage to the churchwarden and overseers of the poor for £15. In exchange he obtained a lease for 40 years at £1.10s a year, as well as an assurance that if he could repay the £15 he would be allowed to redeem his cottage.[74] This he appears to have done, for when he came to sell it in 1774 to a Brighton plumber called John Penticost, there was no mention of the somewhat unusual transaction he had made with the churchwarden. After 1774 the Reads became tenants in the cottage they had once owned – an indication perhaps that they had not recovered from the difficulties they first encountered in 1768.

The Wenhams' cottage, which was next to Thomas Rogers III's new house on the east side, passed through various occupancies: by the middle of the eighteenth century it was owned in two halves by the Smith and Geering families.[75] Both these were established Kingston families. John Geering who died in 1763 passed the cottage on to his son Richard. In the 1770s he and his wife Jane had a family of five, which must have been hard put to find space in what was a 'half-cottage'. In the earlier decades of the century the Smiths were a smaller family, to judge from the parish register, but in the 1770s Henry and Ann Smith, who had moved into the cottage, filled their half of it with nine children of whom eight survived. So, in that decade at least, this little corner of Kingston had a striking density of population. At any time in the 1770s there might have been 15 people or more inhabiting the two halves of the cottage.[76]

Finally, there was the tiny cottage in which Thomas Picombe had plied his trade as a tailor in the seventeenth century. This had passed in the early years of the eighteenth century to Picombe relatives who no longer lived in the village, and who sold it to Thomas Penticost of Rodmell, a thatcher (see Chapter 8). The cottage remained in the Penticost family whose members became tradesmen in Brighton. John Penticost, who bought out James Read in 1774, almost certainly owned the old Picombe cottage too and was on his way to becoming a landlord. The Picombe cottage was rented out, probably to the Pollard family, which had formerly lived in the cottage and which Cuttress came to own.[77]

In short, the decline of the yeoman class had not been paralleled by any notable decline in the cottagers. They were a vigorous group in Kingston in the middle of the eighteenth century. Howells, Cutresses, Tuppens, Reads, Smiths and Geerings were independent landowners, albeit on a small scale. They had enough land for gardens and orchards, which provided them with a substantial proportion of their needs, though they no doubt supplemented their incomes by wage labour on the village farms. The cottager community was concentrated to a large degree in one part of the village. On the corner of the street opposite the Ades' farmyards there were three cottages in a row – the Cuttresses', the Tuppens' and the Picombes' cottage, which was rented out. The Howell's cottage stood somewhat on its own across the way. They were connected by orchards and gardens, and delineated from one another by a complex of flint walls. This was cottager country. Cottager children from the Tuppen, Howell and Pollard families – of which there were plenty – must have played together in the stretch of orchards that lay between their homes. The equally prolific Reads, Smiths and Geerings were not part of this little geographic unit – though they evidently were part of the same community.

In fact, it is hard to escape the impression that the decline in numbers of independent yeoman families had given a new prominence to this cottager community. As the numbers of family farms decreased and the proportion of villagers who depended on wage labour increased, the cottagers became a more clearly defined level of village society. By the middle of the eighteenth century it was they who 'divided' the large occupiers and tenant farmers at the top of village life from the wageworkers at the bottom. The disappearance of so many yeoman farms over the centuries brought the cottagers into a new prominence, however modest it might be.

A decisive change in the pattern of village life – the natural result of the engrossment of farms and smaller tenancies – was the increase in the proportion of families dependent virtually entirely on wage labour for their livings. It is hard to find out much about this majority of Kingston villagers who lived in the smaller landless cottages attached to the farms. From the parish register it is possible to discern at least three groups among them.

First, it is clear that offshoots of cottager families worked as wage labour, the most notable being the Tuppens and Reads. The 'other' William Tuppen family of the 1760s and 1770s was prolific and settled. Alongside the James Read cottager family of the 1750s there was at least one labouring family. In the period from 1769–79 John and Elizabeth Read raised a substantial family in the village. They were cousins of James Read's children. In the later years of the century, when the Reads had ceased to be cottagers, three of James Read's sons, John, Henry and James, also headed labouring families in the village.

In addition to these, there were a number of families who established themselves in a permanent way in the village, raised lots of children and supplied the farms with the core of their labour force. Such were the Harrisses who were present in the seventeenth century and were especially numerous in the years between 1730 and 1750 when John and Sussanah Harriss were having children. An Elizabeth Harriss later married the labourer William Tuppen. The Richs were similar. They were present in the village in the early years of the century. In the 1740s Stephen and Mary Rich had a large family; and the Richs were still present in Kingston 120 years later when the census of 1861 was taken. The Pollards first appear as tenants in the cottage George Cuttress later came to own and occupy. In the 1750s James Pollard and Anne Baker lived with their two boys, John and James, in Thomas Picombe's cottage in Kingston Street. Later, John raised three boys in the same house. Then, in the late eighteenth century, from about 1770 onwards, a number of new and similarly established working-class families appeared on the scene: the Smiths who had eight children between 1771 and 1787; successive families of Richardsons after 1777; the Bartholomews who bore ten children between 1773 and 1792; the Mockfords who formed a family of ten between 1773 and the end of the century; the Wises and, towards the end of the century, the Colemans. This increase of settled working families in the village after 1770 or so attests to the growing need for labour on the expanding farms of the later eighteenth century.[79]

These were settled families, many of whom were still part of Kingston in the nineteenth century. In addition there are glimpses of a much more transitory population of workers in the village, for throughout the eighteenth century there were families who appeared on the scene for a few years and then left. In the first part of the century the Stokers, Riggles, Reckels, Humphreys, Smarts, Willards, Becks, Mantles and others arrived in Kingston, married perhaps, had a child or two, and then went. One suspects they were among the poorest and least supported members of the community. They were not able to establish themselves with the same continuity and permanence as the settled families of working-class Kingston.

*****

By 1750 older inhabitants of Kingston may have looked back with surprise – perhaps regret – at the changes the new century had brought, for Georgian Kingston was a different place indeed from the little Restoration village where Vinalls and Bowkers had ruled the social roost. The simple numerical facts about the change were straightforward enough. In 1700 (see Chapter 8) there were 11 or 12 separate landholders, excluding cottagers. By 1750, by virtue of the Rogers engrossments and the consolidation of tenancies by Rogers and Martha Zouch (née Vinall), there were only six. Indeed, the parish register suggests there was only one tenant in addition to the Rogers and Vinalls. This was Richard Relf.[80]

Then, in 1700 there had been six small owner-occupiers – the yeoman group. Only three were left in 1750 and their grip on the land was less secure. The old yeomanry was virtually gone. The necessary counterpart of the decline in small peasant family farms and the consolidation of tenancies and larger owner-occupied lands into bigger parcels was an increase in the need for wage labour. As the yeomanry left, agricultural labourers took up their places in the village community, with cottagers providing some of the wage labour. In 1700 there were an estimated 14 to 18 families in this position. In 1750 there were more than 20, seven of whom were independent cottagers.

In short, there had been a decisive change in the complexion of Kingston society over the half century. It was, of course, a change many other English villages had experienced. The circumstances of the late seventeenth century delayed it in Kingston, but after 1700 it could be held back no longer. Significantly, change when it came was facilitated by the surpluses a serious tenant farmer could garner from the favoured demesnes of Swanborough.

Obviously, Thomas Rogers III was not the only cause of this transformation. Martha Zouch had also done her bit to reduce areas for smallholders. Even William Vinall, in the brief years before things started to go wrong for him, had taken up four yardlands of 'yeoman land' from Thomas Picombe. And, on top of that, failures of succession, which brought lands onto the market that might otherwise not have come and also resulted in the quite rapid disappearance of the old families, compounded the decline in the social and economic role of yeomen. But for all this, Thomas III was a prime mover. It was he who used the situation and tipped the balance in the direction of increasing concentration of landholding. This was because Thomas, for reasons of his own, was committed to becoming richer and more powerful in a way and to a degree his peers were not.

In this, Thomas III, like his father at Swanborough, had much in common with his Vinall forebears; he perhaps owed something too to the vigour and assertiveness of the Elizabethan and Stuart vicar of Selmeston. But, for all these parallels, there was a sense in which Thomas III's attack on Kingston lands was unlike earlier engrossments. In the past major incursions into the village arable had centred on the acquisition of manorial demesnes. Dorset's engrossment had started with the purchase of Kingston Manor, and the 15 yardlands he eventually bought from erstwhile copyholders had been a complement to the demesnes. Vinall had started from the manor demesnes and built outwards. Rogers started much less grandly on less distinguished lands. It is a measure of his determination that from the bits and pieces that came onto the market in the village he cobbled together a parcel of lands that rivalled the manor estate in area. He had to build his estate in spaces others left, and he did so successfully. There are signs that he cared deeply about the less grand status of his patchwork of freeholds and copyholds compared with the lands of Kingston Manor. They show in his aggrandizement of the house on the street and in the fuss about the enfranchisement of the property on which it stood. In the end he took what he could get and turned it to good account, which in the main meant profit. One might think of young William Vinall, resplendent at Kingston Manor for a short but presumably dramatic period of consumption, as the product of a Restoration childhood, and Thomas Rogers III as the first representative of Georgian capitalism in the village. The contrast is not far fetched.

When Thomas III died in 1742, Thomas IV his younger son was 23; when Elizabeth died he was 31. He had farmed the family land with and for his mother during her widowhood; he was certainly to take them on in earnest after her death. William, his elder brother and landlord, was settled with Mary Scrase in Patcham and had no intention of coming back to Kingston. The last record of William in the village – apart from wills and deeds to land – was in 1751 when there is a sad note in the parish register recording the burial of Mary, the daughter of William and Mary Rogers of Patcham. Presumably the little girl had died in the village.

Thomas IV was to take effective control of the lands his father had brought together and to live out his time in the village his father had done so much to alter. He happened to come into this mixed and complex legacy when it must have seemed to Kingston villagers that the old stable and predictable times had gone for good. William Ade had died in 1742 and Ann Ade ran the farm as guardian to a little girl (Mary) who was still too young to marry. But what would happen when she did? Would the Ade farm be gobbled up and engrossed when Mary went to live with a husband who had lands elsewhere? John Paine, who had inherited the lands Thomas Picombe once farmed from his house just down the street from the Rogers family, was showing signs of leaving the village and leaving his lands to a tenant. Above all, in the year Thomas IV took over, Martha Zouch (née Vinall) died and Charles Zouch, a Yorkshire clergyman, inherited Kingston Manor, which he had no intention of keeping. This last circumstance, more than the others, was to determine the shape of the village society in which young Thomas had to operate. Ensuing events at Kingston Manor are an important part of village history in the second half of the eighteenth century, and provide the framework in which the second phase of the Rogers's ascendancy was worked out.

It was indeed true that Charles Zouch had no intention of holding onto the manor. That much may have been known in the village before Martha's death. At all events, very soon after she died the manor, together with the various copyholds the Vinalls had accreted, came onto the market and found a ready buyer, who by the look of things had been prepared for some time for this eventuality. The man was John Crouch, a grocer from Southwark in Surrey.[81] He was a rather rich grocer and paid £4210 for Kingston Manor,[82] which, though less than Francis Zouch had paid 35 years before, was a large amount of money for the times.

How had this unlikely personage come into the Kingston picture? By what means did a Southwark grocer come to hear of the sale of an obscure and not especially well-endowed manor in a downland village? And, having heard of it, why should he wish to buy it? The answer seems to lie in the rather particular circumstances of succession in the Crouch family. John Crouch was unmarried. He had inherited his business from his father and his successor was his aunt, a lady by the name of Elizabeth Cockle (née Crouch). Ralph and Elizabeth Cockle in turn had a single child – a daughter called Elizabeth who was first cousin to John Crouch. This young cousin played a central part in the sequence of events that brought the Southwark grocer to manorial lordship.

Young Elizabeth married a man called John Ridge,[83] who was almost certainly a junior member of the large Ridge family that had held land in Iford since Elizabethan days.[84] In 1750 John Ridge lived at Stoneham – a hamlet on the northern outskirts of Lewes – with his wife Elizabeth, who was John

Crouch's cousin and would eventually succeed to Crouch's fortune. Ridge was probably a small tenant farmer who had his way to make in the world. It was he who made the connection between Kingston Manor and the Southwark grocer. As far as Ridge was concerned, Kingston Manor represented an admirable opportunity for tenancy. With John Crouch's help he could establish himself and his family there. It was Ridge and his wife who drew Crouch's attention to the forthcoming sale of Kingston Manor and put into his mind the idea of buying it and leasing it out to them.

John Crouch accepted the idea. Perhaps in default of children or family of his own, he favoured his cousin Elizabeth and wished her to enjoy the advantages of the wealth she would one day inherit without having to wait for his death. Perhaps he saw the matter also as a sound business proposition, a partnership between himself as landlord and Ridge as tenant at a time when the profitability of agriculture showed signs of rising because of the pressure of demand from rapidly growing cities. As a grocer in Southwark, Crouch had direct knowledge of the growing demand for food and rising prices. That may have produced a general inclination in his mind towards an investment in agriculture. He would also have recognized that he would require a trustworthy and knowledgeable tenant, for he himself had no knowledge of farming and would be unusually dependent as a landlord on the skills and honesty of his farmer. Who better in this case than John Ridge? John Ridge could certainly be trusted to handle the tenancy with proper care and attention because it was strongly in his interests to do so. John Ridge was in the unusual position that he could expect to inherit the manor farm on which he was to be tenant; the capital resources Crouch sank into the purchase would one day pass to Ridge himself. He had every reason to treat his tenancy with care and attention, for he would be the ultimate loser if he did not! Plainly, Crouch had strong guarantees and an unusually solid basis for an agricultural investment. Plainly too, he trusted Ridge who handled the actual purchase on Crouch's behalf as he did not even come to Sussex to sign the papers.[85] So it came about that the Southwark grocer became lord of Kingston Manor, and John and Elizabeth Ridge moved into the house in Kingston where Martha Zouch had recently died.

John Crouch's 'lordship' was not the first instance of capital accumulated outside agriculture being put into village lands. After all, Francis Zouch was a London merchant in his day and his mercantile money had been poured out, first to rescue Vinall and then to buy the manor so that his wife could come home. In addition, there had been the string of tradesmen who mortgaged William Vinall. There were other examples. In 1735 Charles Zouch, with Martha's legal approval, sold some small parcels of land to a Captain William Scutt. Scutt was a mariner and made his money trading at sea.[86] He purchased some pieces of brookland and a property at the end of Mill Lane, virtually on the outskirts of Southover, for use as a timberyard.[87] He evidently went into the timber business in Lewes and later established a wheelwright at the yard.

In 1728 Scutt had married Ann Ade, a daughter of Stephen Ade, which accounted for his interest in the village.[88] Then also, Francis Zouch had given a long lease on the village windmill to a Lewes tradesman. In 1722 Walter Brett Jnr, a grocer, took over the mill on top of the ridge running from Kingston to Lewes in return for £1 a year.[89]

Zouch's connections with Kingston had been rather particular and the other instances of merchant capital in the village were minor. Crouch, though not the first, was the clearest example of a new kind of landlord – the kind Daniel Defoe had spotted in his travels about the country:

> It is observable that ... there are several very considerable estates purchase'd, and now enjoyed by citizens of London, merchants and tradesmen. ... I mention this to observe how the present encrease of wealth in the City of London, spreads itself into the country, and plants families and fortunes, who in another age will equal the families of the ancient gentry, who perhaps were bought out.[90]

To describe Kingston Manor as a 'very considerable estate' would be to stretch the point, but in all other respects the description fits John Crouch rather well.

The partnership between Crouch and John Ridge worked out well. For the next 25 years Ridge farmed the manor and lived with Elizabeth his wife in the village. There was no attempt to add to the manor lands, but there were signs that the farm was carefully run. It was John Crouch and John Ridge who, in 1773, decided to call in Marchant, the surveyor, to draw up a terrier of Kingston parish in which Crouch's strips were carefully specified and every morsel of land in the parish measured and designated. It is perhaps a sign that the landlord was anxious for a precise and total record of his possessions – the rural equivalent of a grocer's stocktaking! John Ridge paid Marchant £29.19.6 for the invaluable record he made of Kingston lands. In his hand-written marginal notes on one copy of the terrier, Marchant noted that John Ridge was tenant occupier of Crouch's lands,[91] and indeed he had been since 1750.

This land and prosperous undertaking ended in 1774–75, for John Crouch died in 1775.[92] John Ridge was still alive but his wife Elizabeth, Crouch's heiress, was already dead. Like her mother and grandmother before her, Elizabeth had only one child and, as in earlier generations, the child was called Elizabeth. This lady was named in Crouch's will as his heiress.[93]

Elizabeth, who had been born Ridge, was already married when she came into the estate. Her husband was Robert Maitland, the son of a London merchant and a merchant himself. In the manner of the times, Maitland took charge of the estate – the 'mercantile tradition' at Kingston Manor was to be maintained. Robert and Elizabeth Maitland had three sons at the time they came into the manor lands, and Crouch's will specified that John Maitland, the eldest, should inherit from Elizabeth with 'remainders' going to Alexander the second son and Robert the youngest.[94] The manor was firmly settled in

Maitland's hands in 1775. Because of his wife's untimely death, John Ridge never came to be lord of Kingston Manor, but he had the pleasure of seeing his daughter and Maitland son-in-law installed in that role.

The Maitlands were no more interested in living in their new manor than John Crouch had been before them. They stayed on in London where Robert Maitland continued in his business. John Ridge, his wife's father, was left in occupancy in Kingston as his son-in-law's tenant.[95] When he died in 1778 or 1779, he left some additional parcels of land in South Malling to his daughter, and Robert Maitland immediately signed a lease for the vacant tenancy. John Wood took it up for 14 years, at an annual rent of £260, and held the tenancy of the manor until the end of the century and well into the 1800s.[96] It is a measure of the growing profitability of the land that the annual rent for the farm rose from £260 in 1779 to £420 in 1808.

The main outcome of these acquisitions and successions was that there was never again a time when the lord of Kingston Manor lived in the village. After Martha Vinall's death the manor house became the home of tenant farmers. John Ridge was the first. He had a special position because his relationship with Crouch was not the usual one between landlord and tenant. Ridge had reasonable expectations, until the death of his wife, that he would one day own the property himself. After his death, however, the manor passed to more conventional tenant farmers.

This was all very much in keeping with the times. Over much of England the accretion of larger and larger landed estates had created a much-enlarged role for capitalist tenant farmers. Though John Ridge and later John Wood were less wealthy than many other English farmers, they were representative enough of their type. The time was not far off when men like these would be called gentlemen rather than yeomen – not that they were ever yeomen in the older tradition.

The death of Martha Zouch and advent of tenant farmers at the manor had implications for the Rogers. Henceforth, they were to be the only large owner-occupiers in the village and, as time passed, they came to hold first position in the social ordering of the village. At 31, when he took over the family farm, Thomas Rogers IV must have realized that he had a new position in Kingston that was more prominent than the one his father had held. Perhaps he felt that, as the last lineal descendant of John Vinall left in Kingston, it was a position he could claim of right.

Chapter 10

The Rogers: Culmination and the Transformation of Kingston

The second half of the eighteenth century is usually identified as the time of 'agricultural revolution' in England. So much has been written about it that there is no need to go into detail here.[1] A few points about this rapidly transforming background to events in Kingston are, however, crucial. They set the backdrop against which the history of the village must be viewed.

The agricultural revolution was more a process of acceleration in the use of cultivation techniques that had been known for a long while than a discontinuity.[2] The main principle of many of these techniques was that they opened the way to a closer integration of arable farming and animal husbandry. That had been the purpose and great technical advantage of 'ley farming' in Tudor times; indeed, more widespread use of temporary leys was a feature of the late eighteenth century too, especially on heavy clay lands. The distinctive feature of the period of 'revolution', however, was the increasingly widespread use of new crop rotations. Four-course rotations that included root crops or legumes considerably increased the food supplies available for animals. More animals meant more manure on lands that were tired for lack of it, and so increases in yield. And, as yields rose, the level of stock could be further increased. New rotations brought pastoral and arable production together to the advantage of both and, as the potential for animal production increased and the advantages attached to it were more fully perceived, attendant improvements followed. Animal breeding became a new preoccupation; new feeding systems were developed; and meadows were floated to facilitate the early production of spring grass. The new rotations opened the way to more profitable cultivation of lighter soils and to the use of lands that had been unsuited to arable under the older three-course systems.

We may doubt how quickly yields and output responded during the last 50 years of the century, but there is no real disagreement that they ultimately did and that the supply of food to rapidly growing cities expanded accordingly. There could be no quarrel with the technical virtues of the new systems. But these changes in technique came upon village societies that, though they had undergone many profound changes, were still in varying degrees adapted to older modes. There had been much enclosure in English villages since Tudor times, but in many parts of the country open-field organization predominated on the arable, just as it did in Kingston. The open-field system, flexible to a point, was not naturally adapted to the new rotations or to the new approaches to animal production. Four-course rotation did away with fallow and if it were to be applied on open fields it required the simultaneous agreement of numbers of individual strip owners, not all of whom were as informed or advanced in their approach to cultivation as they might be. The newer methods had another implication: in many areas they made it profitable to extend arable at the expense of pasture, 'waste', or 'commons' that had been overgrazed but still provided sustenance for poorer villages. The advent of the new methods meant that there was a crisis in rural England that could only be resolved by reorganization. Reorganization took the form it always had – enclosure.

From 1760 until the end of the century, and indeed well beyond, there was a long sequence of enclosures 'by private act' in one English parish after another. The process reached a peak between 1790 and 1812 during the years of war against the French. It had died down to a comparatively low level by 1820 or so, although various measures of enclosure continued into the nineteenth century.[3] Enclosures by private act covered reorganization of open fields, the extension of ownership over 'waste' and the apportionment of commons. They were carried out on the principle of prior agreement between manorial lords, owners of the tithes and landholders in a parish. This agreement might then lead to a petition to the House of Commons, which usually specified that the lands in question 'are intermixed and dispersed in small parcels and in their present situation are incapable of any considerable improvement, but if ... [they] ... were divided inclosed and allotted it would be very much to the advantage of the ... petitioners and the public.'[4] The petition customarily led to a bill being placed before the House of Commons, which at its second reading was normally referred to a committee consisting of members for the county whose approval was required before the bill passed into law. Thereafter, the process of apportionment of lands in the parish became the business of commissioners, who at least informally came to represent three interests: the manor lands, those who held the tithes in the parish, and the landowners.

Each stage of this process was the subject of deep political disagreement among contemporaries and continues to be the subject of controversy among historians today. Much as in the case of the Tudor enclosures, the centre point of controversy concerns the equity of the process and the extent to which it bore most heavily on the poorest. For some, the enclosure movement was primarily responsible for turning English villages into communities of wage labourers and for dispossessing the weakest members of rural society of their vestigial rights in the interests of landlord profits.[5] Others, like the great agricultural 'improver' Arthur Young, might concede that there had been social costs in the process but were deeply convinced of its merits in opening the way to better practices.[6]

Various developments in farming practice and in the controversial reorganization of the countryside coincided with (and may well have been stimulated by) an important evolution of the economy. First, by 1750 English cities were already growing rapidly and this process was accelerated later in the century as industrial growth began to get under way. At the same time, from about 1740 there was appreciable growth in the population as a whole. The market demand for agricultural output expanded and, though productivity was rising in the rural economy, this increased demand was sufficient to exert a general upward pressure on agricultural prices and profitability from 1760 onwards. Second, on top of this growing need for food and supplies there was a sharp increase in demand for rural outputs after the outbreak of the Napoleonic wars in the 1790s. The results were predictable. Agricultural profits were high for most of the latter half of the century. They provided the capital resources 'improvement' required and the promise of greater profits brought more enclosure and more improvement. Throughout this period there is a close relationship between the movements of wheat prices and the numbers of private acts for enclosure. At the same time, rising prices reduced the real wages of the poor in the rural economy. The agricultural revolution took place against a background of deepening poverty and destitution.

These developments in the second half of the century reflect the widespread and deepening influence of market forces on rural life. It is true, of course, that English agriculture and pastoral production had been 'market-oriented' for a very long time, but in the eighteenth century, with the emergence of fast-growing demand in the cities, the market for agricultural outputs became less regional and more 'national' than before. Its influence was felt uniformly throughout rural England. It is no surprise then that many of these greater movements are in Kingston history. We can trace the enrichment of larger farmers in the years of prosperity (which were customarily years of dearth for the poor), and we can note the influence their growing wealth had on life in the village.

Kingston is distinguished from other English parishes in one respect. During the scramble to enclose the English countryside, the village remained irreducibly committed to its open-field system. It was largely unaffected by enclosure in Tudor times and remained so right through the eighteenth century. Only in 1831 was a private act passed to enclose the combined parishes of Iford and Kingston, which is why Marchant's map of 1773 shows a village whose main lines of organization had not changed for centuries – an open field virtually unchanged by rearrangement apart from a small amount of assarting in later Tudor times (see Chapter 7).

Kingston was not unique in resisting the current of the times. There were other villages with intact open fields as late as 1831, but they were a small minority. The enclosures of the later nineteenth century were more about apportioning commons and waste than about splitting up open fields, which were by and large a thing of the past when Iford and Kingston came to be enclosed. There is evidence to show that Kingston was among very few parishes in Sussex to escape enclosure even before the upsurge of private acts in the eighteenth century.[7] Why had the village withstood enclosure for so long?

It is likely that enclosure in Kingston was sustained in the eighteenth century, as in Tudor times, partly by the complexity of the manorial system in the village. In 1750, as before and afterwards, Kingston landholders owed allegiance to a considerable cluster of lands. The Dukes of Dorset held Swanborough, as they had from Elizabethan times; from 1750 John Crouch, and after him the Maitlands, held Kingston Manor; the Alchornes held Hyde Manor, in so far as it was a manor at all. All three of these manor lords had landholdings of their own in the village. Crouch and the Maitlands at Kingston Manor and the Alchornes at Hyde were on the ancient demesnes de Warenne had usurped from Queen Eddid after the Conquest. Dorset held the 15 yardlands the first duke had 'taken back into demesne' before 1600. These three at least had direct interests in the future disposition of village lands. In addition, Abergavenny, as lord of Houndean Manor, and a group of people who had come to share the Iford lordship between them would have a voice in any attempt to enclose by agreement.[8]

The 'manorial interest' in Kingston involved a considerable number of people, any one of whose individual interests would have interfered with the possibility of an agreement on enclosure. Indeed, for the manor lords, enclosure presented considerable complications. The normal basis of allocation in an enclosure agreement was an assessment of individual landholdings. In Kingston individual holdings included lands of more than one manor, and each landholder had a variety of feudal dues to more than one lord. A reallocation of land between landholders would not correspond in any simple way to a reallocation of these feudal dues in a manner that would satisfy the various lords involved. Though the dues any individual landholder might owe were small, the sum of feudal payments for heriots, fines and in lieu of labour service on Kingston arables nevertheless amounted to a considerable amount. While this was so there would be difficulties convincing the manor lords of the desirability of an enclosure. Once again, the ambitious undertakings of her early Norman lords affected Kingston many centuries later, for it had been de Warenne who carved the village into a manorial patchwork to meet the labour needs of his cherished priory.

In addition to the manorial problem there was also the fact that enclosure required agreement between landholders and, though the smaller interests of cottagers might not have weighed in the balance, there were still a number of individual interests to be satisfied. In 1750 there were six landholders in Kingston who could have raised objections to enclosure, including of course the manorial lords. All in all the chances of a disagreement, which would throw any enclosure arrangement into the melting pot, were quite high. Despite the concentration of landownership and social power in the village, too many people had to be satisfied and we must assume that differences of interest among them caused the long delay in the advent of an enclosure act.

In consequence, improvements in farming practice, which certainly took place on village arables, were put into practice on an almost intact open-field system. This in turn required adapting to the way fields were used to cope with the more complex rotations that were required, and to escape from the use of fallows. This adaptation could only have been accomplished by rotation of individual furlongs, certainly not whole fields, and it required village landholders in any furlong to reach agreement between themselves on the uses to which the land was put, not just in any particular year but over a cycle of seasons. The reduction of individual landholders in the open fields in the first half of the century, though insufficient to facilitate agreement on the larger question of enclosure, surely helped the way to agreements on year-to-year matters of land use. Thomas Rogers III may have contributed to the disappearance of the old yeomanry, but in doing so he also eased the way towards a more flexible use of the arables – albeit mainly in his own interests.

In the last decade of the century the Revd Arthur Young[9] toured Sussex to examine the progress of 'improvement' in the county. In general, he found little to approve of apart from the experimental activities of a few great landholders who, like the Earl of Egremont at Petworth in the west part of the county, had brought in and adapted some East Anglian techniques. Young liked the farmhouses well enough, admired the housing for ordinary labourers and was enthusiastic about the habit of 'stacking … corn on circular stone piers', which protected the harvest from rodents.[10] He was less than impressed by the cultivation practices of the generality of Sussex farmers – especially those on the Weald. He found the turn-wrest plough to be overrated, 'clumsy and unmechanical'.[11] He was constrained to start his chapter on tillage with these remarks: 'the more improved tillage of land, as at present practised, is confined to individuals. Little is there that deserves commendation. The ploughmen are not remarkably adroit in handling their implements which for the most part are clumsily constructed.'[12]

Young's strongest criticisms were directed in the main to the Wealden farmers, not the downland ones. He was appalled at the continued use of fallow on the heavy soils of the Weald.[13] He was better disposed to downland farmers who had largely moved over to the use of four- and five-course rotations, and his observations made it clear that in the region around Lewes, where most farming was along the edges of the Downs, the new rotations were well implanted. Over 20 years from 1773 he gives details of rotations on an 'extensive and highly cultivated farm in the neighbourhood of Lewes', which show the flexible use of new methods.[14] From the acreages involved and the listing of fields, it is likely that this is the farm at Swanborough on which the second John Rogers of Iford was tenant over the period. Closer at home to Kingston, Young remarked on the 'miserable rotations' practised on the open fields around Lewes, but makes it clear that the open-field farmers in question, who must indeed have included Kingston farmers, were at least practising the new methods and had dispensed with the use of fallows, to which their less advanced colleagues in the Weald remained committed.[15] Their rotations were 'miserable', mainly because they made inadequate use of root crops and because they tended to plant turnips in rotation before wheat. This led to an under-utilization of the turnip for fodder, for it meant that they had to be removed from the soil at a time of year when there were alternative animal feeds in relative abundance. It seems that by the 1790s Kingston farmers on the open fields were lagging behind the more advanced improvers in East Anglia and, indeed, in Sussex too, but they had plainly turned over to the new systems and, despite the persistence of the 'tenantry laines', were by no means backward compared with the generality of Sussex cultivators.

Such was the context in which Thomas Rogers IV started his career as a Kingston farmer in 1750 after his mother's death. Thomas Rogers IV was in many ways in a privileged position in 1750. Whereas his father and grandfather had started with limited access to lands and had been obliged to build up their holdings, Thomas IV occupied all the lands his father had accumulated. He was in a situation many younger sons of landowning families would have envied. Since his brother William had no interest in the Kingston estate, save as a source of rents, Thomas IV could farm it all. He continued occupancy of his father's façaded house opposite St Pancras churchyard and after Martha Zouch's death in 1750 he farmed a larger area of village arables than anyone else. Accordingly, at the comparatively early age of 31, Thomas IV had an unusually prominent position in village society. His nearest competitor in lands, and hence in immediate power over the organization of Kingston cultivation, was John Ridge at Kingston Manor, but he was a comparative newcomer. Thomas IV was part of Kingston from birth. His grandfather had achieved economic distinction at Swanborough Manor. His half uncle John Rogers still farmed the demesnes there and lived at the grange. And, above all, Thomas IV was his father's son – a son that is to a man who had done more than most to make his presence felt in Kingston. While Ridge was purely a tenant farmer, the Rogers family owned a substantial part of the village and, though tenants like old Thomas II at Swanborough might well achieve recognition as 'gentlemen', ownership still counted for much.

Despite this privileged opportunity, there were ambiguities and uncertainties about the world of Thomas Rogers IV in 1750 that were different from any his father and grandfather had faced. In the first place he *was* a younger son and, though he had more to thank his father for than the silver watch he had so affectionately left to him, he was nevertheless a comparatively small *landowner*. He held the six yardlands of Peake's, more than he expected to inherit but not enough to alter the fact that his base of operation in Kingston was very different from his father's. Thomas III had started out from lands he owned; he appended tenancies and bought more land from the proceeds, but it was always his enterprise. Young Thomas IV was predominantly a tenant farmer to his brother. And, though the land remained within the immediate family, this led to some differences.

This curious state of affairs meant that Thomas IV faced uncertainties. William was a good deal older than Thomas IV and the question of who would inherit the Kingston estate from him and what they would wish to do with it created a problem for Thomas. This must have increased as it became clear in the 1760s that William was likely to be survived by two daughters who could be expected to marry and whose ambitions for the future uses of the Kingston lands were hard to predict.[16]

Thomas IV's unavoidable commitment to tenancies rather than ownership had a more immediate implication for him. It meant that compared with his father he had fewer resources to play with. However generous William might have been in setting the terms of the tenancy, indeed however close the brothers were to a business partnership, the lands were supporting more people in the 1760s than they had in the time of Thomas III. The possibilities of accumulation were thereby constrained. Although Thomas IV farmed Kingston at a time when prices were more favourable to landholders and the possibilities of reducing costs greater than when Thomas III had ruled the roost, he had to contend with the fact that his brother William could claim a substantial part of the surplus the land yielded.

In the end there was little to be done about these circumstances. Thomas IV settled down in the house opposite the church and made his way in Kingston. Whatever his problems, they were hardly cause for great regret. There was plenty of land to farm. He started a family soon after his mother's death. Thomas IV's grandmother had been an Attree from Barcombe. Sometime before 1753 he too married an Attree – Elizabeth Attree of Newick – and reinforced the bond with a family that had had a good deal to do with his grandfather's eventual and startling success as tenant at Swanborough.[17] Thomas IV and Elizabeth had a first child in 1753, a girl called Elizabeth who died at the age of two. A son was born in 1754. He was inevitably named Thomas and was followed by a second daughter in 1757. There do not appear to have been more children.[18] Thomas and his wife Elizabeth established themselves and their children, Thomas and Mary, in the family home.

The first long period of his time in Kingston is scantily documented. Thomas benefited from the rising prices of the late 1750s and 1760s and, though he found it harder to accumulate than he would have done had he owned the whole farm, he succeeded. The main thrust of his policy in these first two decades was to extend tenancy. Tenancy demanded working capital, but nothing like as much as land purchase, so it was a natural choice for Thomas IV. What is more, these were good times for tenants, especially if they had a reasonably long lease. Rents were set in function of prices and profitability at the time a lease was signed and if prices rose subsequently, the gains in surplus obtained from the land would accrue mainly to the tenant. Prices moved favourably throughout the 1750s and 1760s. Thomas IV took advantage of them. By the early 1770s no one in Kingston could have doubted that Thomas IV had inherited his father's instinct for farming as a business.

Marginal annotations on a copy of the Marchant terrier indicate the extent of Thomas's success.[19] These show that William Rogers still owned the house in the street and that Thomas occupied it. They also show that in terms of ownership there had been comparatively little change in the village between 1750 and 1773, but that in terms of occupancy there had been important changes. Table 10.1 is a summary of information from the terrier. The changes in occupancy are striking. A William Vinall had appeared as occupier of the Duke of Dorset's Kingston Town Farm, which Martha Zouch had leased until her death in 1750. This was the son of the last William Vinall of Kingston Manor who had mortgaged himself out of village life in 1716.

But Vinall's appearance was a comparatively minor event. The terrier makes it plain there had been other important changes. Stephen Towner soldiered on in his yardland and a half, but John Paine, who succeeded to Picombe's lands, had left the village and put the lands to tenancy. James Glover and Mary still lived in the village but did not farm their lands (still called 'Ades'). The weakening grip on yeoman lands was manifest by 1773. At Hyde Manor, a Mrs Norton had inherited and put the nine ancient demesne yardlands out to tenancy with Richard Relf (see Chapter 9). A striking outcome of all this was that tenants held the vast majority of village strips. For the moment Kingston was a village of tenants: Thomas Rogers with his six freehold yardlands was the largest owner-occupier. The only other apart from cottagers was Stephen Towner on the old parcel of Adam's lands. The number of occupiers was one fewer, at five, than it had been in 1750 (see Chapter 9).

More remarkable was the progress Thomas Rogers IV had made in his policy of tenancy. By 1773 it is clear that he farmed 34 yardlands in the arable. Though he only owned six yardlands, this was probably the largest proportion of village arable that had ever been farmed as a unit by a single individual. It amounted to about 47 per cent of the whole parish. Clearly, Thomas had more than compensated for the disadvantages he had faced on taking over his father's lands. He had taken leases on the old Ade farm as well as on Paine's and these, added to the lands his father had farmed, made up his new empire. Tenancy, in times of rising prices, could make a farmer very rich and in Kingston Thomas IV, in dogged Rogers style, was on his way to being so!

And this was not the end of his progress as a tenant. Very shortly after Marchant had drawn up the terrier, William Vinall (who lived at Iford) died. The Duke of Dorset's farm fell vacant and Thomas IV stepped in at this moment to extend his lands yet again.[20] This meant that by 1775 Thomas had a grip on well over half the village land. It was the high point of his first phase in Kingston. He was 56 years old and the dominant economic and social presence in the street. His family prospered in the house old Thomas III had built. It is plain that Thomas IV had plenty of energy left and much he yet wished to do. In a sense it was the beginning rather than the end of things.

In this process of expanding tenancy Thomas Rogers IV had created the basis for considerable wealth. By the mid-1770s he had become rich and held

Table 10.1: Ownership and occupancy in Kingston open fields, 1773

Owner	*Farms*	*No. of yardlands*	*Occupier*
Dorset	Kingston Town Farm	9	William Vinall
	Diggon's	6	Thomas Rogers
William Rogers	Alfrey's, Bailey's, Taberer's, Brook's	10	Thomas Rogers
Thomas Rogers	Peake's, Bodle's	6½	Thomas Rogers
Glover's	Ade's Farm	8½	Thomas Rogers
Paine's Farm	ex-Picombe's	4	Thomas Rogers
Stephen Towner		1½	Stephen Towner
John Crouch	Kingston Manor Farm	18	John Ridge
Mrs Norton	Hyde Manor Farm	9	Richard Relf
Total		72½	

large sums of fairly accessible money. During this time he is on record in *Brighton Manors* as lending money on mortgage to various speculators involved in the development of that town as its popularity grew.[21] Though he was constrained to put money to work in this way, Thomas's objectives went beyond the extension of mortgages. Once he had established himself as the dominant Kingston tenant, he was ready to start on a new phase of accumulation in the village. It was a much shorter phase than the first. He had toiled away to good effect as a tenant farmer for 20 years. In five years from about 1778 he turned his mind to ownership and mobilized the resources he had carefully assembled in a rapid and dramatic onslaught on village lands.

The first sign of this change came in the late 1770s, probably between 1777 and 1779. Around that time John Paine sold out his group of copyhold yardlands. This was the first substantial transaction in Kingston lands in more than 25 years and Thomas IV was at hand as the buyer.[22] He made the purchase in the name of his son, whom we must now call Thomas V and who was about 25 years old at the time.[23] This purchase, which increased the land in Thomas IV's ownership to 17 yardlands, did not, however, add to the area he farmed. He had been occupying Paine's Farm before the purchase. Indeed, it is quite likely that at about this time, there was a slight reduction in the area Thomas IV farmed. By 1780 he had relinquished the tenancy on Ade's farm to Samuel Ridge of Iford. The purchase of Paine's was a signal to the way in which Thomas's mind had started to work.

The big opportunities came soon enough, but not without prior anguish and uncertainty. In the 1770s Thomas IV was still at risk in that he had no way of knowing what would follow from the death of his brother William. William Rogers of Patcham died in 1776.[24] He was 71 years old. His gravestone in Patcham lies to the left of the porch entrance to the church, just like his father's in Kingston. William had claimed equivalent prominence. But William's is a grand eighteenth-century monument suited to a gentleman in Brighton, in contrast to the stark solidity of the stone slab that lies over Thomas III, the Kingston patriarch.

His will[25] stipulated that his lands in Kingston should pass to his wife in the customary way for the remainder of her life; then they were to go to his two daughters equally. One of these, Barbara, had married Nicholas Willard and the other, Elizabeth, had wed Nathaniel Blaker[26] of Shoreham. Both were attached to the new urbanity of Brighton. There was no mention in the will of William's younger brother Thomas IV who had farmed the Kingston lands for so long, nor indeed was there any reason why he should be recognized. These new circumstances must have brought home to Thomas IV the uncertainties that had so long attached to his grip on the Rogers family lands in Kingston. Barbara, William's wife, lived on till 1779.[27] After her death, effective power of decision over the disposal of the lands passed jointly to Nicholas Willard and Nathaniel Blaker.

It is reasonable to suppose that Thomas was put in an uncomfortable position. It was unclear, at least for a while, what Blaker or Willard intended to do with the Kingston lands. The uncertainty was resolved two years later. In late April and early June of 1782, Thomas IV purchased the lands – or the bulk of them – from Nicholas Willard and Nathaniel Blaker. He paid Willard and Blaker £2400 for Alfrey's[28] – lands for which his father had paid £262 in 1699 (see Chapter 9); and he paid £2000 in total for the barn and yardland called Brook's and the house and yardland called Bayley's – the house his father had turned into a kind of family mansion.[29] These latter properties were bought in the name of his son, Thomas Rogers V. In addition, he reached an agreement on the other lands his brother William had inherited: in the land tax returns from 1783 Thomas IV is shown as owner of all the Willard–Blaker lands. The deeds show that he (or rather Thomas Jnr, his son) was admitted to Taberer's, Lattenden's and the Clover Croft in 1786.[30] The reason for this delay in the formal transference of these smaller parcels of land is unclear. However, in this springtime transaction of 1782, Thomas IV took over all the lands he had farmed as tenant to his brother for the previous 32 years.

In doing so, Thomas IV brought together again the whole estate his father had created in Kingston and added to it Paine's Farm, which he had bought a few years before. The Rogers's farm was once again a single unit in single ownership. The time of doubt about the future disposition of the lands was over. Thomas had been obliged to wait a long time. In May 1782 he could for the first time claim as his own the house in which he had been born and lived his whole life. He was 63 years old. Thomas had been obliged to pay dearly for the property and family relationships had not prevented Willard and Blaker from driving a hard bargain. As later purchases showed, £2400 was a great deal to pay for the six yardlands of Alfrey's. The £2000 he paid for Bayley's and Brook's included the value of the family house, but it was nevertheless a lot. There were only two yardlands attached, indeed there may have been less. Thomas IV paid for his triumphant reintegration of the farm, but no doubt felt it was worthwhile.

This was not the only transaction in which Thomas Rogers was involved at the time. All through the time he had been negotiating with the Willards and Blakers he was busy on other matters too.[31] Over the years the Hyde Manor demesnes had passed down from Alchorne to Alchorne and then, through failure in the male line, to John and Elizabeth Norton in the 1770s. John Norton was a county magistrate; he did not live in Kingston but rented his lands to Richard Relf. Norton died in the 1770s and his wife held the land. They were apparently childless. Over the preceding two centuries there had been considerable decay at Hyde Manor. By the early 1780s the medieval and Tudor splendours of the manor house Michell had so proudly described in his 'survey' of 1567 were long since gone. Only Michell's 'newly builded' wing of 1567 remained, full of stone from the old priory and Tudor timberwork; it probably housed Richard Relf the tenant farmer in the 1770s. Even the ascription of manorial status to the lands seems to have fallen into disuse. For all that, the lands were considerable. There were nine perfectly good yardlands in the Kingston open fields. When Elizabeth Norton died in 1781,[32] the lands passed to her Alchorne cousins[33] and for a short while a Mrs Alchorne owned them, but it was clear that they were in effect on the market.

The prospect of nine Kingston yardlands was enough to excite the attention of Thomas Rogers IV. Throughout the time he was negotiating with his nieces and their husbands for William Rogers's lands, he was also engaged with the Alchornes. He purchased the old demesne lands of Hyde Manor in May 1782 at virtually the same time as he was admitted to the old Rogers's estate! Whereas he had paid £2400 for the six yardlands of Alfrey's, he obtained the nine yardlands of Hyde for less, £2100.[34]

Taken together, these were remarkable purchases. It is a true measure of Thomas IV's success as a tenant farmer in his first three decades in Kingston that he was able to pay out at least £6500 for land in May 1782, without any need to borrow. Indeed, this is almost certainly an underestimate because it leaves out payments he made for Taberer's, Lattenden's and the Clover Croft. In total, he paid out substantially more than £8000, and all the evidence indicates that he was a 'cash buyer'. This was of course a considerable sum of money for a tenant farmer to find. It suggests strongly that Thomas had been saving against the day when he might pull off just such a coup as he eventually managed in 1782.

In the five short years since his purchase of Paine's Farm, Thomas IV had transformed his position in the village. After 30 years of careful accumulative tenancy, he had suddenly become owner-occupier on 30 yardlands in the open fields. For a long time he had established himself as the largest single farmer; now he became the largest single owner as well. Since he continued to farm the Duke of Dorset's 15 yardlands, he was occupier on a total of 45 yardlands, or substantially more than 60 per cent of the open-field arable. Kingston had been engrossed to a new degree.

In accreting Kingston yardlands in this way – partly by engrossment and partly by his large tenancy – Thomas IV had made it easier to organize the open fields in new ways. The lands that lay outside his ownerships or effective control were held either by Robert Maitland, who had taken over Kingston Manor in 1775 and leased it out to John Wood in 1779, or by James and Mary Glover, heirs to the Ade family who leased their yardlands to Sam Ridge of Iford. Stephen Towner held a very small part as well. This meant that by 1782 the reorganization of land use in the open fields, so as to exploit the new rotations (which was probably done by basing rotations of the furlong), only required agreement between three farmers for the most part. And, as the map shows, the predominance of Thomas IV's holdings in many furlongs meant that his decisions were bound to count heavily.

These two large purchases were the culmination of Thomas IV's second and dramatic phase in Kingston. They brought him to a unique position of economic and social dominance in Kingston as an owner-occupier. Each of his purchases meant more to him than a simple accretion of land in ownership. For the Willard–Blaker lands he had been willing to pay 'above the odds' because their acquisition recreated the family estate on which he had founded himself. In the case of the lands of Hyde there was also an aspect to the transaction that went beyond the mere fact of the exchange.

When Thomas IV bought the lands of Hyde, he acquired a 'manor' too and it is plain that this was significant to him. In fact, the claim to manorial status for Hyde had always been dubious. As we know, the lands were never described as manorial demesnes until Michell made that claim in 1567. It is likely Hyde had been merely a knight's fee. Thomas Rogers IV revived the manorial status of Hyde with the same vigour and assertiveness as old Michell had shown three centuries before. Indeed, he followed directly in the Michell tradition since he appears to have been responsible for having a copy made of Michell's survey of 1567.[35] This was to be part of a newly established court book. The court book is mainly a record of very small quit rents received from a number of landholders elsewhere in East Sussex. How these rents came to be associated with the lands of Hyde is unclear, but that they should have been paid to Thomas IV in 1783 and after implies that the claim to them had been sustained over past centuries. Pelham at Falmer paid sixpence a year on 100 acres; William Newton of Lewes paid 4/8 a year on 60 acres near Lindfield; a John Paine in Chailey paid one shilling a year on 40 acres; and Joseph Martin paid five shillings a year for 50 acres near Kymer. The only claims in Kingston were on two cottages that had been part of Thomas Michell's demesnes in 1567, which he had subsequently sold: William Tuppen paid fourpence a year; the Glovers appear to have paid a similar amount. No manor court appears to have been held and the court book is simply an account.

Thomas IV and his successors were in no way deterred by any doubts about the status of Hyde. Hereafter all descriptions of their estate in Kingston start with 'Manor of Hide with appurtenances', or 'The Manor or reputed Manor of Hyde' if the lawyer drawing up the document was duly cautious and a little doubtful.[36] There is little doubt that at this time the family house opposite the church had the name Hyde or Hide attached to it. The mystery of the wandering manor house in the village street is accounted for by Thomas IV's purchase of the lands of Hyde and his subsequent assertion of manorial status. So the old manor house, which incidentally was never given the name Hyde Manor House even by Michell, was forgotten and the name became attached to the house Thomas III, the Kingston patriarch, had created. It was a surprising elevation in rank for a dwelling that had started out as a small copyhold cottage, even if it had been converted to a kind of eighteenth-century grandeur and enfranchized by the obstinate insistence of old Thomas III. For Thomas IV, in 1782, the claim to feudal grandeur as lord of Hyde Manor may have seemed fitting in view of his new access to a major part of village lands. It gave him equality with the Maitlands at the head of the street, which probably mattered to him.

At about this time the house was extended and renovated. The east wing Thomas III had built was either demolished and replaced or extended. At the back of the original cottage the building was pushed outwards to produce a new set of rooms and increase its area. As he approached the age of 70 – the year France burst into revolution and left the English middle classes wondering if something similar might happen to them – Thomas IV might have looked across from his enlarged and beautiful house to the church and fields and felt satisfaction at what he had accomplished as a younger son. He had decisively followed in his father's footsteps. He was, however, increasingly willing to hand over responsibility for the lands in Kingston to his son Thomas V, who by 1790 was 36 and no doubt impatient for a larger role in the world – albeit the small world of Kingston. In fact, in 1790 Thomas IV, though ageing, still had some years to live and more to do in Kingston. To continue the account of his life into its third phase in Kingston without considering other aspects of village experience would, however, lack balance. Thomas IV was a massively dominant figure in eighteenth-century village history but he was not the only influential force acting on Kingston.

By the 1780s the only representatives of the old yeoman farmers left in Kingston were the Towners and Glovers. The Glovers soldiered on as best they could on their yardland and a half. They steadfastly followed borough English where so many others had found ways of subverting the ancient rules of succession. In the 1770s Stephen Towner held the lands called Adam's and John, his elder brother, lived on in the village, unmarried and partly supported by the family lands.[37] John died in 1781 before Thomas IV made the great purchases that turned him into a manor lord. Stephen lived on until 1786. He left a widow and small daughter. The Towners had run out of male descendants after many centuries, but the Towner widow continued as owner-occupier for the time being. She was helped no doubt by her son-in-law, for the Towner daughter married around this time.

The Glovers continued too, but not as farmers on their own lands. By 1773 the old Ade farm was leased out. Thomas IV farmed it for a while and then, in the later 1770s, Sam Ridge took it over. The Glovers' retreat from active farming was probably influenced by the tragic ill fortune they encountered in their efforts to raise a family. The Glover family memorials in Kingston churchyard are inscribed on the sides of old William Ade's grave of 1743 under the great yew tree. They tell the sad tale. Four children had died in infancy, and since they are unnamed they must have been stillborn or died too quickly to be baptized. A fifth, fittingly called William Ade Glover, died in 1772 at four years of age; by 1773 the Glovers had one surviving child, Mary Ade Glover, who had been born in 1771. She lived on and later married a man called George Willmott from Kent.[38] It is hard to escape the feeling that James and Mary Glover were weighed down by these events and never quite came to terms with the loss of five children out of the six born to them.

At all events, in 1786 the Glovers decided to sell out in Kingston. Lands that one family had held continuously for at least two centuries came onto the market. The yardlands called Bishops' and Taylor's, which Gregory Ade had acquired to found his family in Kingston before Elizabeth's reign, were relinquished. The freehold 'tenement' with some scattered strips, which Thomas Michell had sold to William Ade in 1600, was the only portion of Ade property that was kept. This solitary parcel passed to Mary Glover, the surviving daughter, and she held onto it for a long time. She kept the cottage on the corner of the street until 1801, and also held onto some small bits of brookland after her marriage to George Wilmott in 1811, leasing them out to a succession of small tenants.[39] But in 1786 the rest of the Ade farm was relinquished. Once again successive failures in the male line had weakened a family's grip on lands: first William Ade had died without a son and then James and Mary Glover.

The land that came onto the market was about eight yardlands and included the old Ade farmhouses, barns and closes at the southern corner of the street. It was in fact the last substantial bit of Kingston land still outside the control and ownership of the large landowners, who had been eyeing the

Glover fortunes for a while. Thomas Rogers IV, with his history of acquisition, must have been interested, but as it happened Robert Maitland, the absentee lord of Kingston Manor, purchased the land. Perhaps by 1786 Thomas IV had reached the limits of his capacity to purchase without borrowing. Perhaps Robert Maitland was sufficiently encouraged by the rents he obtained from the lease he had given John Wood to see the advantage in extending their mutual undertaking. He bought the lands and John Wood was installed as tenant on them.[40] Kingston Manor had swallowed up Ade's farm. When Maitland renewed a 14-year lease to John Wood in 1794[41] he increased the rent on Kingston Manor farm from £260 to £285 and charged John Wood a further £85 a year for Glover's – 'two tenements with barns, buildings and eight yards of land in … Kingston'. The manor estate had increased to 27 yardlands, but despite the increase it was still a little smaller than the total of Rogers's lands.

With Maitland's engrossment of Ade's farm, the configuration of ownerships and tenancies on the Kingston open fields changed to a pattern that was to remain, with minor changes, until the Enclosure Act of 1832. As far as the open fields were concerned, the changes of the eighteenth century had been more profound than any the village had experienced. The combined effects of two generations of engrossment through the efforts of the Rogers and Maitland families towards the end of the eighteenth century had in effect turned the open fields into two large farms – Kingston Manor farm and the Hyde Manor farm Rogers had cobbled together from virtually all the remaining freeholds and copyholds. The Dorsets continued to hold the 15 yardlands but Thomas Rogers IV farmed them integrally with his own lands. Thomas Rogers ruled the roost in Kingston.

The small lands – the open-field holdings of fewer than eight yardlands on which the village yeomanry had been based – were virtually wiped out by 1790. The Towners were the only yeoman owner-occupiers of significance and their lands were very small. John Wood at Kingston Manor and the Rogers family in their newfound manor house determined the uses of Kingston arable between them.

These changes in the control of open fields had predictable consequences for the structure of the village society. They simply meant that, aside from the Rogers, Wood and Towner families, the rest of the village was made up almost entirely of cottagers and those who depended on wage labour for their livings. By 1790 there were probably 19 or 20 families in the latter category. Because the independent cottagers were still there Kingston was not entirely a village of agriculture labourers, but it was nearly so, and the economic and social distance between the gentleman farmers, Wood and Rogers, and the rest of the street was greater than any that had existed since medieval times. The village was forming the pattern of relationships so characteristic throughout England in the nineteenth century that so deeply conditions our modern image of rural life.

In the 1790s times were hard for Kingston wage labourers. In Chapter 9 we traced their presence in the village and the large families they established in tiny tenements. The Smiths, Mockfords, Richardsons, Bartholomews and Colemans, as well as more established and older labouring families like the Tuppens, Harrisses and Pollards faced economic difficulties in the latter part of the century that were probably as severe as anything Kingston workers had dealt with since the late seventeenth century. The problem was an old and familiar one. The movement of agricultural prices, which had so enriched Thomas Rogers and Robert Maitland and was to favour their fortunes even more in the 1790s, meant that the real cost of food and subsistence for the labourers rose sharply. Population was growing in the late eighteenth century, labour was abundant and money wages did not increase by much. Since agricultural production then depended so much more on labour and so much less on machines than it does now, the accumulation and enrichment of the Rogers family was founded on this progressive destitution of farm workers. It was not of course a destitution for which Thomas Rogers IV could be held responsible. He did not cause it. The market caused it, but the market, in which we must presume he believed, worked to his advantage and against the material interests of his workers. The dramatic price increases of the 1790s, when disastrous crops coincided with a wartime inflation of prices, did nothing to relieve them.

Arthur Young's estimates of earnings and expenditures of six labouring families in Glynde in 1793 give some inkling of the implications of price movements for the labouring class. Glynde is close enough to Lewes to be taken as a reasonable guide to circumstances in the neighbourhood. The figures Young collected are summarized in Table 10.2. Not one of the six families he studied could make ends meet and in some cases the shortfall of earnings below necessary expenditures was dramatic.[42]

After the introduction of the Speenhamland system, the gap between earnings and expenditure was made up by support from the parish poor box under the Elizabethan poor laws. The Speenhamland system formalized a procedure whereby such support was adjusted to the estimated subsistence needs of families of various sizes. Consequently, individual farmers had an interest in holding down the wages they paid in the expectation that the rates others paid to the parish would support their workers. This was only sustainable because the labour market had driven the real wage down so far and workers were abundantly available. Glynde was a comparatively rich parish and, though Iford and Kingston farmers were less disposed to pass wage costs on to their neighbours, so paid higher wages than most, there is no reason to believe that people in Kingston in 1793 were much better off than those Arthur Young had interviewed.

The change in the composition of the population had turned Kingston into a village of mainly impoverished people by the last decade of the eighteenth century. The process had, however, depended crucially on the changing structure of land ownership in the open fields, the disappearance of small owner-occupiers and their replacement by labouring families; it had not come from the destitution of erstwhile smallholders. The majority of people in Kingston were almost certainly poorer at the end than at the beginning of the eighteenth century, but this was because labourers everywhere in England were poor, especially in the 1790s, and the force of new circumstances had turned the village into a community of labourers.

Table 10.2: Earnings and expenditures by six families in Glynde in 1793 (from Young)

Family	*No. of persons*	*Income*	*Expenditure*
No. 1	8	£28.12s	£42.14s
No. 2	3	£13.0s	£18.2s
No. 3	6	£36.8s	£36.14s
No. 4	6	£31.4s	£37.8s
No. 5	7	£36.8s	£40.10s
No. 6	3	£22.2s	£23.8s

Kingston cottagers escaped some of the rigors of the time because they held a little land. To that extent they were hedged against the rising costs of provisions, and in the 1780s and 1790s the cottager class remained a noticeable group in the village, their relative independence marking them out all the more as Kingston turned progressively into a labouring community. But even cottagers showed signs of diminishing independence. By 1780 or so they fell into two distinct groups. The first consisted of the Tuppens and the Edward Howells and their descendants. The Tuppens held onto their cottage after the death of William and in 1795, when his widow Jane died, it passed on to her son William.[43] He continued in possession as an owner-occupier for the next 20 years. William and his brother Henry, a shepherd in Kingston, built up a new generation of Tuppens at this time. In a similar way, continuity was maintained at the old Howell cottage on the edge of the West Laine. Here, Edward Howell's youngest grandson Thomas Wise took possession and stayed.

Elsewhere there were changes. A second group of cottages passed into the hands of people who subsequently leased them out to Kingston families. By the 1780s this had already happened to two cottages – the Picombe's, where the seventeenth-century tailor had lived, and James Read's, who was probably obliged to sell for financial reasons (see Chapter 9). John Penticost, a Brighton plumber and glazier bought both and rented both to Kingston families, but in 1792 he sold the Picombe cottage to his business associate, a glazier from Lewes called Thomas Standley.[44] As time passed a further cottage slipped into this category. In 1781 George Cuttress, who had lived with his wife and family in the cottage across the street from the Ade properties, sold to a Samuel Alcorn. Samuel Alcorn came from a cottager family in Hamsey, two or three miles north of Lewes.[45] He leased his Kingston cottage to the Richardsons from 1784 and it became their home until the end of the century.[46]

Cottagers like the Richardsons, the Pollards (who leased Picombe's cottage from Penticost until about 1785) and the Reads (who leased the cottage they had once owned) were in a less protected position than traditional owner-occupiers like the Tuppens and Howells. They were subject to rising rents when prices rose and at all times they had to bear higher costs. They were comparatively better off than farm labourers who rented cottages that were virtually landless, but not always by very much. So, for example, the Richardsons found it impossible to maintain their lease and drifted back to the status of ordinary labourers; and the same thing appears to have happened to the Pollards in the 1780s.[47]

This then was the shape of Kingston in 1790 – a shape established largely by successive engrossments, in the main determined by the Rogers family. It was on the face of it a harsher social environment than it had been for centuries. It is true there had always been labouring poor in the village, but in the late eighteenth century they were not only more numerous but probably more vulnerable. When yeomen were at the centre of village society, their labourer relatives could turn to them for help when times were harsh, but the possibility of such support from an extended family no longer existed in 1790 because, though a community of rural labourers might have developed patterns of mutual assistance, nearly everyone was equally poor. When bad times came there was no one with extra resources to help out poorer relatives. Thomas Rogers IV and his father cannot be held solely responsible for this profound change in circumstances, for much the same pattern could be found over England as a whole, in enclosed and unenclosed villages. But the Rogers family was the agent of the change in Kingston. One wonders whether they ever acknowledged the fact.

Thomas IV's predominance is obvious from his control over the open field. In a curious way his meticulous acquisitiveness stands out with special clarity in the care with which he picked up whatever portions of Kingston property he could. For example, he 'farmed' the village tithes; ownership of the tithes was vested in two people who had obtained them by a complex succession – a Mrs Nonk and a Mrs Blunt.[48] Thomas IV paid these two a fixed annual rent in return for the tithes he could collect. Many of these accrued on land he farmed, but some were due on Maitland's yardlands too. In addition, Thomas had acquired some of the village tithes for himself as a part of this property. He held the tithes on the yardlands called Diggon's – in short, on the farm he leased from the Duke of Dorset.[49]

Over and above the tithes, Thomas IV had been quick to take advantage of the fact that from 1765 the vicar of the combined parishes of Iford and Kingston had little interest in living in either village and so leased out the glebe lands. The Reverend John Delap was among the more remarkable of Kingston vicars. He had had a distinguished academic career at Magdalene College in

Cambridge where he held a fellowship and became a doctor of divinity in 1762. Subsequently, he was granted the living of Iford and Kingston in 1765 and also of Woolavington, another East Sussex Village, in 1774. But his interests in pastoral work were not extensive. He lived most of his life in Lewes and devoted his time to writing. Delap was prolific. He started with a number of lengthy elegies, which were marred, however, by being mainly about his own ill health. He was undeterred. The hypochondriacal elegies were followed by a major onslaught on the West End. He poured forth dramatic poems, used his extensive connections to get them published, and on two memorable occasions actually prevailed on Garrick to present his work on stage. *Hecuba* ran for ten days in 1761; it was 'not without merit but cannot by any means be called a good play'. *The Captives* ran for three days some years later. It failed as drama; the critics noted that the audience left the theatre in tears of laughter. Delap met Johnson and Miss Burney, who said of him, 'when he has anything to say he works it threadbare'. He was evidently a bore and lacked judgement, but he had his merits. He wrote a play against slavery, which, though exceedingly poor quality, was quite radical for his time.[50]

A man like Delap evidently had more to do than farm his glebe lands. Thomas IV accordingly leased them and was tenant to Delap for much of the vicar's life. It was an improbable partnership but it brought another morsel of income-yielding property to the Rogers family, which from its viewpoint was enough to hold it together for years. While Delap successfully solicited Lord Palmerston and his family to subscribe to the long volumes of poor poetry, Rogers farmed the vicarage lands and the labouring parishioners struggled through the dreadful years of the mid-1790s.

After the dramatic acquisitions of 1782, Thomas IV entered a third phase of his farming life in Kingston. It was less striking than the first two had been, for it was devoted to what might be called 'mopping up operations'. These consisted of a series of minor purchases essentially designed to 'rearrange' the village to the greater convenience of the Rogers family. Thomas IV initiated this process, but did not execute it alone. He was advancing in years – by 1790 he had reached 71 – and the mopping up business was done in partnership with Thomas V his son. Thomas V carried it forward after the death of his father at 85 in 1805.[51]

By 1785, about the time the first signs of a partnership between father and son became evident, Thomas V was a little over 30. In that year, against the background of the substantial transformation in family fortune his father had affected, Thomas V married a lady called Elisabeth Ridge. Very soon he and Elisabeth started a family, which was to be the largest brood of Rogers for many generations. A son was born in 1785. Inevitably, he was baptized Thomas. Perhaps because of the confusion that would arise from three generations of Thomas Rogers being alive at the same time, this new young Thomas was differentiated from his grandfather and father by being given a middle name – he was called Thomas Attree Rogers. It was a natural middle name to give him. His grandfather had married an Attree; his great grandmother had been an Attree and, at the time young Thomas was born, his aunt, Mary Rogers, the daughter of Thomas IV, was courting an Attree. In 1788 she married a Richard Attree of Laughton. The Attree connection was extended to a third generation.[52]

Thomas Attree Rogers was followed by a succession of brothers and sisters – Elisabeth (1786), Mary (1788), John (1790), Ruth (1792), Henry (1796), Anne (1798), and Charlot (1800). It appears that all these children survived. Thomas V and Elisabeth his wife soon filled the house, which had become a 'manor house' and which, fortunately, had been extended in the early 1780s. Of these eight children, four were to play rather particular roles: Thomas Attree was of course in line of succession; Elisabeth and Mary, the elder girls, were staunchly concerned about family fortunes; and Henry was to play a rather unexpected role. But all this lay in the future. In the 1780s and 1790s Thomas IV entered the last phase of his life surrounded by his grandchildren and no doubt enjoyed them.

The elements of partnership between Thomas IV and his son were present in the big transactions of 1782. Bayley's, the yardlands attached to the family house and indeed the house itself, were purchased in the name of the younger Thomas V. Later, Taberer's, Lattenden's and the Clover Croft were made over in his name and Paine's Farm, acquired in the last years of the 1770s, was purchased for him.[53] As the years passed more and more of the family lands came to be listed in his name.

In 1785 he appears as proprietor of the demesnes of Hyde, which had been Norton's Farm; by 1790 nearly half the estate was his; in 1798 Thomas IV made over the whole farm except for a small field, which for some reason he kept as his own.[54] In the meantime, in 1791, the second John Rogers at Swanborough, grandson of Thomas II from his marriage to Elisabeth Ade, died at Swanborough. The Rogers's succession on the Swanborough demesnes came to an end after more than a century, for John Rogers died childless. But the lands old Thomas II had started with in the seventeenth century, plus lands the succeeding John Rogers had added – all in Iford – passed to Thomas Rogers's family in Kingston. From 1792 onwards they were in Thomas V's possession – and they were a substantial addition to his landed wealth, for they amounted to at least 70 acres and possibly more.[55]

As Thomas V's increasing role in his father's affairs would indicate, it is right to regard the mopping up operations that ensued, and that marked out the last part of Thomas IV's life, as a joint undertaking. Mopping up started early on with a remarkable bit of reorganization. Throughout the 1770s two cottager families lived in the house next door to the Rogers's on the west side. The Smiths and Geerings were prolific (see Chapter 9) and the Rogers family may have frowned on the teeming children who played about the street in their immediate vicinity. More to the point, though, the northern part of this old cottage, where the Smiths lived, abutted Kingston Street itself and constricted the entrance to the yard and barn, which lay behind the Rogers's house. It was an encumbrance. In 1782, as Thomas IV became a 'manor lord', he took the opportunity to buy it from the Smiths.[56] The Geerings appear to have continued in possession of the 'southern half' of the cottage, while Thomas IV demolished a substantial part of the northern part to widen the access to his yard. An independent cottage had disappeared from Kingston, but the Rogers had opened up their yard so that guests in pony traps or coaches could drive in without bother. In 1792, Thomas IV appointed Geering, his neighbour, as trustee to this small piece of land and permission was obtained to demolish whatever parts of the old structure continued in existence.[57] The access to Hyde Manor House attained its modern form.

This preoccupation with the grandeur of the house was so characteristic of the Rogers as to be almost a family tradition. Fully as characteristic was their vigorous opportunism in gaining access to any bits of income-bearing property that became available. By the mid-1780s there was not a great deal of land outside the ownership of large landowners, but such scraps as became available were of interest to Thomas IV and Thomas V as they tidied up the 'loose ends'.

In 1780 the heirs of William Scutt, the 'mariner' who lived in Lewes and who married an Ade woman from Kingston, still owned a small parcel of lands bought from the Zouches in 1735 (Chapter 9). They consisted of 12 acres of 'brooklands', called Belson's and Bormer's brooks, and a timber yard and garden on the road to Lewes beneath the slopes of Hill Laine. The brooklands, though small in area, were important because these marshy meadows produced a lush crop of grass and, as the number of animals in the village grew, they became increasingly valuable.

William Scutt died in or about 1754 and his bits of land passed to his Ade widow. In terms of his will they were subsequently to go to two of his nephews, Richard Tidy of Brighton and Dighton Elgate.[58] Tidy and Elgate took over in 1786 on trust to sell out William Scutt's lands. The timber yard and garden were sold in 1787 to John Kennard, a miller in Lewes, who in turn sold out in 1790 to Thomas Swaysland, a carpenter and wheelwright who set himself up in business on the property where he remained for the next 40 or so years. The brooklands, though, were to be auctioned and, in November 1786, Thomas V was the highest bidder for them at a sale held in the ancient White Hart Hotel in Lewes. He rode back to Kingston owning yet another morsel of Kingston land.

Eleven years later, in 1797, the two Thomas Rogers picked up another parcel, or at least a share of it. For many years the Earl of Thanet, a relative of the Dorset family, had owned about 33 acres of strips in the open fields known as the priory lands.[59] This parcel came into the ownership of a Mr Edward Jeremiah Curteis who sold it in 1797. Robert Maitland and Thomas Rogers IV and V shared the pickings. The Rogers father and son's part consisted of about eight acres of arable together with 40 sheep leazes, for which they paid the rather large sum of £532.10s, a measure of the increase in land prices at the time.

More interesting than these small acquisitions of arable, which only added marginally to the Rogers's already established position as landowners, was that both Thomas IV and Thomas V appear to have become preoccupied with acquiring *cottages* in Kingston. The reasons are not entirely clear, but one can make some reasonable guesses at them. First, this interest in cottages was unlikely to have been occasioned by the lands attached to them. Most cottage land in Kingston lay within flint-walled closes in Kingston Street and consisted of intensively cultivated small orchards and gardens. They no doubt looked neat and tidy, but they were of little commercial interest to farmers on the Rogers' scale.

A better guess is that Thomas IV and his son were concerned about the availability of labour for their estate. By the 1790s they employed as much as two-thirds of the agricultural labour force in the village and, though workers were available at the time, it was in their interest to ensure that a ready supply of labour was sustained. They may have seen the Kingston cottages as an encumbrance to this purpose. Cottagers, even those who rented their homes and gardens, were partly independent of wage labour. They could, with careful husbandry, provide a substantial part of their subsistence from their own bits of land. They might still have to make up by working for wages and no doubt they did, but unpredictably. And being semi-independent, they may not have been the most docile workers in the village! For the Rogers family there was a reason to buy out cottagers and replace them with waged workers whose tenure in the cottage was linked to their employment on the Rogers's estate. That at least is what Thomas IV and his son appear to have set about doing in the 1790s. After his father's death Thomas V continued the policy.

The first cottage to be taken up was the one in which the Geerings had continued to live after Thomas IV removed its northern half to accommodate the driveway into his yard. The Geerings surrendered the cottage in the Kingston Manor court in 1790. It appears that they continued to occupy it as tenants to Thomas IV. This purchase was followed a little later, in 1791, by the acquisition of the cottage in which the Read family had lived. James Read had been obliged to sell this to John Penticost in the 1770s (see Chapter 9). In 1779 he in turn sold it to Thomas Virgoe, a husbandman from Southease. The Read family probably continued to occupy during this time. In 1791, Virgoe sold out to Thomas Rogers IV.[60]

After this there was a delay of about ten years before the Rogers family was again able to access cottages. The next occasion arose in connection with some slightly mysterious transactions made by Henry Tuppen, who was a shepherd in Kingston. Henry appears to have purchased two cottages himself in quite rapid succession, but was unable to hold onto either. In 1802 Mary Glover, the daughter of James and Mary who had sold the Ade farm to Robert Maitland, sold the small tenement, which she had inherited and which stood among the old Ade properties on the corner of the street. Henry Tuppen acquired it.[61] Since it was separated from the small parcels of land formerly associated with it, it had the status of a cottage. Henry owned this property for two short months before selling it to Robert Maitland. Maitland evidently was not averse to pocketing a cottage or two, probably for the same reasons as the Rogers.

Then, two years later, Henry Tuppen bought a second cottage. This was the house and orchard in which the Cuttresses had lived. The Alcorns of Hamsey sold it to Henry in 1804, apparently on the basis of a mortgage of £100. This time Henry held onto his property for about nine months before choosing or being obliged to sell.[62] Thomas Rogers IV bought it from him. He now held three cottages that had once been independent copyholds.

Thomas Rogers IV died in 1805[63] but, after his death, Thomas V continued to buy up cottages as they became available for purchase. In 1813 Thomas Standley of Lewes, who had come into the possession of the old Picombe cottage, sold to Thomas V.[64] Then, in 1817, William Tuppen, who had continued as an independent owner-occupier for many years in succession to his parents, sold out too, also to Thomas V.[65] This was the most important direct sale by an occupying cottager. It may well have been enforced by financial circumstances. In 1802 Tuppen had been mortgaged for £50. Thomas V paid him £400 for the cottage.

With this sale the independent cottagers as a group virtually disappeared from Kingston. Only Thomas Wise, living on in the old Howell cottage, was left. Nearly all the dwellings in the street were now in the ownership of Rogers or the Maitlands and, in the main, they housed the labouring families who worked for the two large farmers in Kingston.

When Thomas IV died in 1805 he was 87 years old. He had handed over control of the farm to his son in 1800, but Thomas IV and his father between them had controlled the growing Kingston estate for exactly a century. At his death Thomas IV could look back at a life, which, in his terms, had been profoundly successful. He had taken over his father's substantial lands as a tenant farmer and, though privileged in having access to such a large tenancy, being a younger son had also disadvantaged him. It had required great patience and a large amount of accumulated money to overcome the disadvantage, but with persistence Thomas IV had done so. He was over 60 before he accomplished the great engrossment, which had no doubt been an objective throughout his life. Like his grandfather who had started the family on the road to wealth at Swanborough, Thomas IV had been forced to wait for many years for the opportunities he wanted. And he shows many of the qualities of his forbears in the tenacity of purpose with which he appears to have conducted himself. Thomas IV was a Rogers, but also a Vinall and indeed an Ade as well. He drew on yeoman traditions, which accounted for his singular dedication to maintaining and building the family lands, and he also drew on traditions of vigorous capitalist tenant farming. He had been greatly helped in his purposes by the increasing profitability of farming in the last half of the century, but he had the acumen to exploit the opportunities of the times. By the end he had brought the Rogers family – well represented in his cluster of grandchildren – to an economic and social peak. At no point in the history of the village had a single person farmed such a large part of its lands or owned so many of its houses and cottages. Not for many centuries had the village community as a whole been so dependant on the will of a single individual – not indeed since the feudal organization of Kingston had fallen apart in the times after the Black Death.

The whole Rogers undertaking had profound effects on the structure of village society. Already weakened by 1700, the independent yeomanry had disappeared by 1800, as indeed it had from most English villages. In Kingston, the Rogers incursion was the predominant agency of change. The process of disintegration of village society was pushed further in the last phase of Thomas IV's life when he and his son bought their way into cottages, probably to increase their access to wage labour. By 1805 there was a huge gap in wealth and social status between the two farmer families (Rogers and Woods, who continued to farm Kingston Manor) and all the rest. 'All the rest' – essentially the population of Kingston – were hardly differentiated from one another at all in terms of social class and wealth. They were wage labourers. Only the Towner widow, on Adam's land, and the Tuppens and Wises in their cottages, remained to represent the older more differentiated and complex social order of Tudor times; and the Tuppens were soon to relinquish their independent cottage. Kingston had been vastly simplified as a social system. It was also a much poorer community than it had been for many centuries, partly because of the impoverishment of labour resulting from falling real wages but just as much because of the drastic change in the composition of society. That change had been much accelerated after 1700 when Thomas III as a young man appeared in Kingston with his pockets full of the money his father had made out of Swanborough and with his mind set on tenancy and engrossment. It had been driven home finally after 1782 when Thomas IV achieved engrossments on a scale his father had neither accomplished nor probably foreseen.

It is interesting that all this had taken place in a village that was 'unenclosed', a village that indeed had experienced less by way of enclosure over preceding ages than the vast majority of Sussex villages. Some historians ascribe the kinds of changes Kingston experienced in the eighteenth century (and happening elsewhere in other ways) mainly to the process of enclosure. Kingston's experience shows that the disappearance of small farmers and yeomen, and the disintegration of cottagers as a class could come about without enclosure. The Rogers family accomplished these changes in Kingston through engrossment. When enclosure came, the village had already been changed into the rural proletarian community it was to remain throughout the nineteenth and into the early twentieth centuries.

Thomas V naturally took over the whole estate on his father's death. In

1805 he was already fifty years old. He had been in effective control since 1800 but, like his father, had been obliged to wait a long time for ownership of Kingston lands. However, the terms under which he had waited were very different from those his father had faced. All his life he had been assured that he would one day control the greater part of Kingston arable. His father may have sought and achieved that as an objective, but had not been certain of his place in the way his son could be. Thomas V had no need to struggle. He simply took over the estate as a going concern. He and Elisabeth lived on with their family in the grand house, the façade, extensions and renovations of which told the story of the family's increasing matter and success. In 1805 his heir, Thomas Attree Rogers, was 20. Elisabeth, the eldest daughter was 19 and her sister Mary 18. Young Henry was a mere 9. The future of the Rogers lands was to lie with these young people, though not perhaps on terms they could have foreseen at the time.

Thomas IV was buried in an altogether grander tomb than this father's. It stands on the grassy hummock beneath the yew tree in St Pancras churchyard. It is appropriately prominent and inscribed with memorials to various members of the Rogers family who were to follow. Next to Thomas IV, on the grassy hummock, lie the Towner brothers – the last yeoman farmers of Kingston and a little further off there is the family grave of William Ade, whose death in 1743 had been the beginning of the end for Kingston yeomanry.

Chapter 11

The Nineteenth-Century Village

Throughout its long history, economic and social relationships between people in Kingston had depended very much on the pattern of landownership and occupancy. Changes in that pattern, like the long drawn out reduction of the small lands on which the yeomanry had made their living, were ultimately reflected in changes in social organization. While the yeomanry held firm they formed a middle level in the social order of Kingston Street with close family links in many cases to labouring families 'beneath' them. Consequently, they were at the centre of a tightly knit community with families, through kinship or friendship, able to rely on a degree of support when times were bad. As yeoman lands were progressively engrossed and yeoman families put their small amounts of capital to new uses, sometimes to trade in Lewes, the polarization between rich and poor in the street became more pronounced. When, on top of this, the independence of the remaining cottagers in the street was finally undermined, the polarization was largely completed. No one stood between a Rogers and his tenant, or between a farming Wood and an ordinary worker. The distance between them became even greater in the war years at the end of the eighteenth and beginning of the nineteenth centuries. Prices rose, sometimes quite dramatically, because of weak harvests and war demands; money wages hardly changed. The rich, here represented by the Rogers family, got distinctly richer. The real wage fell, with results that Arthur Young recorded in Glynde nearby to Kingston: the poor, in short, got poorer as they did everywhere in England.[1]

The poor were not only poorer than they had been for a long time, but they were also more vulnerable. No doubt the old instincts for mutual support remained, but since everyone was poor, with links to families of middling wealth gone because most of them had left the land, mutual support could not be as effective in simple material terms as it had once been. The role of the yeomanry as redistributors of wealth had been considerable. Once they and the cottagers had gone there was nothing to protect the poor from poverty except the poor law itself.

Consequently, the nineteenth-century village has as it were two histories: a history of the poor and a history of the rich. They are not separate, of course, but they appear more so than at any earlier time, or at least more so than at any time since the feudal period. By 1800 the humble of the village were so humble in relation to the great that arrangements between the large landowners and changes in their fortunes hardly impinged on the ordinary business of living for the majority. Kingston was a village of wage labourers; wage labourers simply had to get on with their work to stay alive. Changes in regime hardly mattered to people living at or near the breadline so long as they did not actually threaten to push them below it. In feudal times the continuity of manorial custom meant that, by and large, one lord was as good or as bad as another; the capitalist markets of the nineteenth century produced much the same results. One master was not that different from another unless one had the good fortune to work on the estate of an enlightened landlord or the bad luck to encounter an exploitative sadist. Kingston had neither. The history of village workers is simple and hard: a continuum of toil and poverty. That is one 'history' of the nineteenth century village to which we shall return.

The more obvious history, better documented and therefore easier to uncover, is the history of the rich. It played itself out against the backdrop of poverty. By 1805, when Thomas Rogers IV died, the arable lands in the ancient open fields were to all intents and purposes engrossed by three landowners. The Duke of Dorset held the 15 yardlands his ancestor had taken into demesnes. Robert Maitland, whose wife Elizabeth had inherited from John Crouch, held the 27 yardlands that made up the Kingston Manor estate. Thomas Rogers V held nearly all the rest: a large estate cobbled together from freeholds and copyhold crowned by the acquisition of the Hyde demesnes and manorial status of a kind. In 1805 there was no need to anticipate that any of these landholders would sell out. Prices of grain and arable products varied greatly in the last decade of the Napoleonic wars up until 1815, but they were always high and often very high compared with their prewar levels. It was thoroughly profitable to hold land and foolish to think of exchanging such an asset for any other.

Accordingly, the landowners held on. Dorset was satisfied to allow Thomas Rogers V to take over the tenancy his father had held for so long. The Maitlands stayed on too, despite the ill luck of a sharp succession of deaths in the family. Robert Maitland and Elizabeth both died in 1811.[2] They left a family of three sons: Robert, Alexander and Henry. An older son had died in 1801.[3] Robert, the oldest of the surviving brothers, inherited the major part of the Kingston estate. His youngest brother Henry, however, succeeded to the copyhold yardlands of Hudd's (which the Vinalls had added to the estate) and to Glover's farm, which Robert Maitland, senior, had purchased in 1787 (see Chapter 10). Borough English was still at work, but Henry relinquished his inheritance immediately to his elder brother, presumably in return for an appropriate payment, and the Kingston estate remained intact in Robert's hands.[4] All seemed settled for another period of Maitland landlordship. Then, in 1812, one year after his parents, Robert Maitland died himself. Most of the estate passed directly to his infant son, also Robert, the third in a row. It was managed for him by John Maitland his guardian, who was a member of the

Royal College of Surgeons. At the same time a part of the estate went to Ebenezer Maitland who continued to hold it until the 1830s. These were the copyhold yardlands of Barden's and Bishop's, which had once belonged to Gregory Ade. Young Robert eventually took over the landownership of the manorial desmense,[5] but since he became a busy barrister in Middle Temple in London he probably never exercised his manorial lordship in person, but always through his steward. The lands remained firmly in the Maitland family. John Wood farmed them alone until 1808, then subsequently in partnership with James Flint.[6]

With the Dorsets and Maitlands well ensconced and happily in receipt of substantial Kingston rents, the Rogers' policy of engrossing Kingston lands came to an end. Thomas Rogers V had no serious prospects of accessing more of the arable than his father. From 1805 there was not much left for him to do but get on with farming his land and the 15 yardlands he had rented from the duke of Dorset. Though the great days of major acquisition had passed, Thomas V had little cause for complaint in the decade that followed. Farming had never been so profitable. As a substantial owner-occupier, he had a very limited burden of rents and splendid opportunities to enrich himself and his family. This we must assume he did. At about this time a new west wing was added to the family house. It was a drawing room, higher and grander than any other room in the house, and appropriate for the style of entertainment then in vogue in the English countryside.

In the meantime, the Rogers family had grown up. In 1809 there were three marriages. Thomas Attree, the eldest son, married Mary Elizabeth Fuller, a young lady of reasonable fortune from Lewes. She brought the young man a dowry of £2000. In return, Thomas V his father made over to Mary an annuity of £250 to be paid out of a part of his Kingston lands in the event that she outlived her husband.[7]

Elizabeth Rogers, his eldest sister, also married in 1809. She became the wife of James Hodson of Eastdean, a downland village some way to the east between Lewes and Eastbourne. Mary, the middle child, was wed at the same time. She married John King of Wilmington. Hodson and King were both gentlemen and farmed on their own accounts.[8] James Hodson was also a surveyor.[9]

Thomas Attree and his wife stayed on in Kingston, sharing the now enlarged and grander house with old Thomas V and his wife. There were no children in the early years of the marriage but, aside from this, which might have caused concern to Thomas V, all seemed well. The family was firmly established, as it had been for more than a hundred years. That at least was how it may have appeared. In fact, as subsequent events were to show, some profound changes were afoot in the position of the Rogers family in Kingston.

The first sign that all was not well came in 1817 and took the dramatic form of a £4000 mortgage. Thomas V borrowed this money from William Madgwick, a grocer from Lewes.[10] This loan was followed shortly after by a second. In 1825 Thomas V approached Thomas Usborne of London for a loan of

£8000 and mortgaged his entire Kingston estate. Of this, £4000 was required to extinguish the debt to William Madgwick, which had not been reduced in the intervening seven years.[11] These were very large sums of money. At a guess the Usborne mortgage for £8000 amounted to half the value of Thomas Rogers's lands in Kingston.[12] It was certainly greater than the whole of his working capital in the form of flocks, herds, equipment and stocks, probably three times as much, and it was perhaps four times the size of the annual wage bill for all the labour done on the Kingston estate.[13] The interest charge on the mortgage was £400 a year. This was at least a third of the annual income the family enjoyed in a normal year, so must have cut into their living standards somewhat abruptly.

The reasons for this drastic slide into debt are unclear. Thomas Rogers did not advertise them and the great legal documents, which record the mortgage and allied transactions, are the only evidence that remain of this tragic turn of events. However, there are some signs of what may have happened. First, under the best circumstances the Rogers family, like other landowners and tenants, would have had more difficult times financially from about 1815 forwards. The long war with the French ended with Napoleon's defeat at Waterloo and the pressure of demand generally slackened. But more important, from 1813 until the end of the decade, harvests were good. For the first time the new productivity of 'improved' English agriculture was strongly felt in a large expansion of output. Accordingly, grain prices fell. By 1815 or so they were back to prewar levels, thirty years of unstable but generally very high prices had come to an end. The times of spectacular profitability were over[14] and many farmers, owner-occupiers or tenants, had to adjust to the new circumstances. It was a sign of the times that when James Flint renewed his lease with the Maitlands in 1826, it was for one year only; until then leases on Kingston Manor had always been for 14 years.[15] When prices were weak, tenants tended to prefer short leases, for they left more opportunity for reductions in rent in response to falling profitability. And there had indeed been a fall in rents: in 1808 John Wood and James Flint paid £634 a year for the Kingston Manor estate; in 1826 Flint alone, on his one year lease, paid £477. This was a symptom of falling profitability and incomes and it must have weighed on the Rogers family, just as it weighed on the tenant farmer at Kingston Manor and on the young Robert Maitland as landlord.

But it is hard to believe that indebtedness on the scale Thomas Rogers V experienced was simply the outcome of agricultural depression. In the main, farmers who got into financial difficulties during these leaner years had over-extended themselves in the first decade of the century, had borrowed and mortgaged to buy their way into land when it was at its most profitable. The Rogers family was not like this: it was, on the contrary, extremely well founded. In comparative terms, they were not large landowners and until 1817 there had been no debt outstanding. All their lands were paid up without borrowing and they had not over-extended their tenancies. Thomas V remained a tenant to the duke of Dorset, but the tenancy was restricted to 15 yardlands, which the family had farmed for a century. There can be no doubt that Thomas V felt the impact of falling prices like everyone else, but was better protected than most to meet the problem. Painful though the loss of income must have been, it is important to keep its effects in perspective. In the hard times of 1815–17, prices were still higher than they had been in the 1780s and a good deal higher than in the 1760s and 1770s. In those years old Thomas IV, as a tenant in the main and occupying a good deal less land than the family held in 1817, had not only made enough to extend the house and live comfortably, but had also been able to accumulate to extraordinary effect.

Consequently, it is hard to escape the impression that when Thomas Rogers went to William Madgwick for £4000 in 1817, he had more to deal with than simply the effects of agricultural depression on his income. The family had discovered a considerable capacity for expenditure, a capacity that fitted ill with the times through which they were passing and yet somehow could not be contained. Subsequent events point in the same direction. Seven years later, after a period when grain prices had recovered well from their low point in 1815–17, they were even more deeply in debt. They needed a further £4000 and incurred the crippling mortgage of £8000 from which, by virtue of the interest payments they had to meet, it was practically impossible to recover. The additional debt they had built up suggests they had been spending £350 to £400 a year over and above their normal annual income. At a rough guess this meant that their outgoings had been 50 per cent higher than their income. At this time Thomas V retreated from Kingston to live in a house, which he probably leased, in Southover.[16] Thomas Attree, his son, presided over the lands in Kingston and occupied the family house.

The large mortgage to Thomas Usborne was signed along with a number of other formidable documents on 31 March 1825. The old man at Southover, now in his seventieth year, had a sad and heavy day. The terms of the mortgage and other arrangements Thomas V was obliged to make throw a little light on the events that had brought him to this disastrous point: the centrepiece of the day's concerns was the mortgage document itself. It consisted of nine large pages of vellum and it shows the necessary thoroughness with which Thomas Usborne approached the business of obtaining security.

The loan was secured with all Thomas Rogers's Kingston lands, which are duly listed starting with the 'manor or reputed Manor of Hide'.[17] Usborne was meticulous about having the titles to the various pieces of Rogers land properly tested. His lawyer, Charles Richmond of Middle Temple, accordingly examined all deeds to freeholds held by Thomas Rogers and gave his opinion on their validity.[18] No such documents accompanied the Madgwick loan in 1817. Even Thomas's title to small cottages was explored. The mortgage paper is a long list of a century's accumulation: a record of success that had suddenly turned to failure. It is complete: even a small piece of land on the Clover Croft, which had passed to Thomas Attree's ownership for some reason, was surrendered to the mortgage. Usborne was not inclined to overlook anything, not even three acres near the edge of the brooklands!

The terms must have been especially painful for Thomas. Perhaps the worst was that Usborne required Thomas Attree and his wife, Mary Elizabeth, to relinquish their claim to the annuity of £250 a year to be paid to Mary Elizabeth should she outlive her husband. This must have cut deep, for that annuity was made out in return for Mary Elizabeth's marriage settlement. Its dissolution left her more or less unprotected. It is perhaps a measure of the circumstances that Thomas V could be brought to agree to such an extreme action.

Perhaps it was just as painful that Usborne demanded and obtained agreement that a receiver should be appointed. A gentleman called Anthony Sheppey Greene was to take control of the rents and profits from the mortgaged estates, and to pay Usborne his interest (at 4 per cent) as a priority. This was for 'the better securing of the punctual payment of the interest on the said sum of £8000'.

On the same day he signed this painful document, Thomas V handed the estate over to two trustees – his sons-in-law James Hodson of Eastdean and John King of Wilmington. The terms of the trust made it clear that Thomas had in fact given up.[19] Hodson and King were to take over all the lands in Kingston, then in the occupancy of Thomas Attree, as part of a family arrangement designed to recompense Mary Elizabeth, née Fuller, for the annuity of which she had been deprived. The trustees were required to sell the land in Kingston, subject to Thomas V's agreement while he remained alive but subsequently upon their own best judgement. They were to dispose of the proceeds after the mortgage had been paid off in a manner agreed on and described in a separate 'indenture', which has not survived. These arrangements were clearly made to take care of Mary Elizabeth, Thomas Attree's wife. The trustees also had the right to raise money in any way they may think necessary to meet interest payments on the mortgage. They were obliged in this matter too to obtain written consent from Thomas himself for any transactions done in his lifetime, but otherwise were free to make their own decisions. In particular, it was agreed that 'the concurrence of the Heirs of … Thomas Rogers in any sales … shall not be deemed in anywise essential to the validity thereof.'

This trust and the particular terms on which it was established give the clearest clue to the Rogers problem. It is clear that Thomas V was unwilling to leave the management of the disastrous family affairs to his son and heir, Thomas Attree. His solid and reliable sons-in-law were brought into the picture in a manner that in effect took all decision-making power out of Thomas Attree's hands. Indeed, Thomas Attree was to all intents and purposes disinherited. The trustees were obliged to sell the lands, and Thomas Attree was explicitly precluded from having any say at all. The money realized from the sale was particularly intended to look after Thomas Attree's wife in the event she survived him, but Thomas Attree himself was not given a hand in the matter. The trust was set up to protect the family's remaining resources from Thomas Attree; it is a reasonable guess therefore that Thomas Attree had shown himself incapable of handling those resources and was indeed the main cause of the collapse. That, most likely, is why Thomas Usborne, the tough and careful mortgager, had wished to have a receiver appointed to guarantee that he would obtain his interest payments. Though Usborne's demands might seem unduly harsh taken by themselves, they are clearly justified by the fact of the trust: plainly Thomas V himself had no confidence in the financial reliability of his son. What had Thomas Attree done?

On this matter, all is silence. There are no clues worth the name. It seems that in a comparatively short time Thomas Attree had managed to spend a large amount of money. It was a time when a great deal of money could be easily spent. Brighton, which had been a shabby fishing village in the early eighteenth century, became an increasingly fashionable resort in its last decade. By 1800, the Prince Regent had determined upon the town as a favoured watering place. He came each year, surrounded by fashionable society to conduct his mainly uninteresting affairs. He brought not only the 'fashionable' but also the habit of lavish receptions, gaming tables, horse races and a hundred excuses for conspicuous expenditure.

It is possible that Thomas Attree was caught up in all this, but if so he would have been a small fish in a rather large ocean. In the Prince Regent's time, an estate like his in Kingston could change hands in the course of an ill-conducted evening's card play; it could be lost on a bad run at the races. It was a large matter for Kingston, but of trifling value in the society that followed the whim of the prince and invaded Sussex. Thomas Attree would not have been alone in seeking the salons and gaming tables; much of county society was there too. Indeed, if he gambled in Brighton circles it is a wonder he did not run up even larger debts.

These can only be speculations, but there are matters that are not speculative. The Rogers family was ruined in 1825 and Thomas Attree's role in the sad tale meant that he could not be left with any power of decision-making over the remnant of their fortune. Thomas Attree continued to occupy the lands in Kingston and lived on in the village under the trustees' control and Anthony Sheppey Greene's watchful eye. He did not last long. Exactly three years after the signature of the mortgage, his death was announced in the *Sussex Advertiser*: 'On Tuesday morning, the 25th of March 1828, at his house at Kingston … Thomas Attree Rogers, gentleman, aged 43 years, deeply lamented by his family and friends.' Then, on 7 April 1828, one of those telling little announcements to creditors appeared in the same newspaper: 'All persons who have any claims upon the estate of Thomas Attree Rogers … deceased, are desired forthwith to send in the particulars thereof to Messrs King and Gell, solicitors, Lewes.'

In 20 years from the death of Thomas Rogers IV, the Kingston estate had fallen apart. A century of careful accumulation was dissipated in two decades.

The Rogers family had toppled from its pinnacle in Kingston. After Thomas Attree's death, his younger brother Henry took over occupancy with the trustees, his brothers-in-law James Hodson and John King. Henry did the farming. Mary Elizabeth, Thomas Attree's wife, stayed on with her two sons George, born in 1818, and William, who had arrived some while later.[20] Thomas V lived on in Southover until 1833, but the long Rogers line the vicar of Iford had established was weakened, and the Rogers ascendancy in the affairs of Kingston village effectively ended.

There is an interesting parallel between the decline of the Rogers family in the second decade of the nineteenth century and the collapse of the Vinalls a century before. The Vinalls had handed lands on to a son whose ambitions were social rather than economic and he, in turn, had passed them on to a son who ruined the estate. Thomas Rogers IV, like all the Kingston Rogers, was a lineal descendant of the first John Vinall as well as of the Iford vicar and before him the Elizabethan vicar of Selmeston. Thomas IV had the characteristic acquisitiveness of his forebears and their patience. Thomas V, on the other hand, stands in a position rather like that of the first William Vinall. He, like William Vinall, simply inherited family lands without any need to accumulate on his own account. Like the first William Vinall he did not dissipate the estate, though he added little to it and sanctioned some levels of expenditure that might have distressed earlier generations. Thomas Attree Rogers, who followed Thomas V but never came into his inheritance, was to the Rogers family as the second William had been to the Vinalls. Both were a second generation away from the last great accumulators in their respective families. Both had found the means to end the wealth and prosperity of their families by destroying large estates. There may well have been some in the village who remembered from their fathers and grandfathers something of the folly of expenditure that had ended the Vinalls' position. Kingston had been invaded twice by engrossing farmers. On each occasion they had founded themselves initially on the great desmense of Swanborough, and each of those families had been ultimately undermined, just as surely as Portinari had undermined the priory church. And, in each case, female members of the family did what they could to rescue the remains. Martha Zouch induced her husband to buy out the lands of the ruined William Vinall and come home to Kingston. Elizabeth Hodson and Mary King, sisters of Thomas Attree, stood behind the two men Thomas V appointed his trustees. And Elizabeth's role was not over; she had a long Kingston future ahead of her, though she probably did not realize that in 1825.

*****

After this dramatic turn of fortune, events in Kingston moved ahead rapidly. In 1830 the trustees occupied Thomas V's lands; Thomas's youngest son Henry farmed these lands and bore the burden of interest payments to

Thomas Usborne as best he could. Robert Maitland, grandson of the Robert Maitland who had taken over Kingston Manor estate from John Crouch, rented his lands to James Flint on short leases. The 15 yardlands long held by the Dukes of Dorset had, through a failure of succession, passed to Lord de la Warr; and, in the course of the retrenchment now forced upon them, the Rogers family had relinquished the tenancy. Verrall and Lancy of Southover now farmed them, probably on a subtenancy.[21] The village lands, still unenclosed, were comprehensively engrossed and, indeed, in 1830 the process of concentration went forward a further small step: widow New, who held onto Stephen Towner's yardland and a half, died and the last bit of yeoman land was taken up and divided between Robert Maitland and Thomas Rogers's trustees.[22] Aside from Thomas Swaysland, who had a wheelwright's yard on the road to Southover, and John Maxfield, who held the windmill that stood on the hillside leading to Lewes, there were only three landholders in Kingston.

At this juncture, after long delays, agreement was reached on enclosure. Why it should have been accomplished at this point is unclear. The Dorsets may have held it up and the de la Warrs changed policy at Swanborough Manor. Or, perhaps, the Rogers family now sought enclosure because Thomas and his trustees had every intention of selling out and may have believed that a comprehensive enclosure of the village would increase the value of their lands. At all events, agreement was reached and the process of enclosure started in 1831.[23]

The process involved the total dismemberment of the system of open fields and furlongs, which had been a central aspect of village life for many centuries. The Rogers, de la Warr and Maitland lands were to be exchanged against one another to produce a few unified blocks. The downland pastures and brooklands were included. By the time the enclosure commissioners had finished their work, the whole area of the parish had been allocated between the three landholders. A new landscape was in the process of formation.

The allotments the commissioners made were as follows: 253 acres to de la Warr; 641 acres to Maitland; and 674 acres to the Rogers trustees. These areas included pasture, meadows and brooklands as well as arable. They tell the story of three waves of engrossment in the village starting in Elizabeth's reign. De la Warr's acres were the remnant of the first serious engrossment in Kingston by the earliest Duke of Dorset. Maitland's were the product of the Vinall engrossment, which the first Robert Maitland had supplemented by his acquisition of Ade's farm in 1787. The trustees' acres were founded on the onslaughts Thomas Rogers III and IV had made on village freeholds and small lands. In each case less than half the area allotted was arable.

The allotments changed the face of the village. The old 'laines' were simply obliterated. West Laine, Mill Laine and Swanborough Laine became irrelevancies and their names lost all force in the geography of the village. Virtually the whole of the West Laine was allocated to Maitland together with a long section of downland pasture lying along the whole northern boundary of the parish. The larger part of Swanborough Laine went to Thomas Rogers V and his trustees along with another section of downland stretching the whole length of the parish. Lord de la Warr got the rest of Swanborough Laine, which abutted his demesnes at Swanborough farm. Mill Laine, lying along the sweep of hills leading to Lewes, was divided into three sections. Lord de la Warr was awarded the bit lying nearest to Southover; Thomas Rogers got the middle section; and Maitland had the part lying nearest to the village. The Latchetts and Well Green went to Thomas Rogers.

Enclosure dispensed with any need to distinguish furlongs and, accordingly, furlong names disappeared. The multitude of strips whose boundaries and locations had preoccupied generations of farmers simply vanished under the plough or under encroaching pasture. The nomenclature and vocabulary of the village was simplified because its surface geography had been simplified. Hardly any of the old names survive today. Within a few years of the enclosure, Kingston land was brought together into vast hedged fields, which still characterize the village. The distinction between pasture and arable was blurred. For example, James Flint, Maitland's tenant, might turn his large enclosures in the West Laine to ley for long periods, returning them to rotational cultivation depending on the soil and on the market. The flexibility with which he could use the land was greatly increased. And, of course, the same was true for Henry Rogers, tenant on his father's lands, as for Verrall and Lancy who farmed de la Warr's.

There were, of course considerable costs involved in this transformation of the lands. Hedges and ditches became boundaries between individual landholdings and crucial to controlling the use of lands within any one of the large farms. The old boundaries that demarcated the 'laines' and separated arable from pasture were no longer sufficient or particularly useful for the organization of farming. On top of the costs of transforming and subdividing the land, the enclosure also involved administrative expenses. Robert Maitland incurred expenses of £1215 in the course of enclosure.[24] He was obliged to seek his brother's help to defray the costs. No doubt Hodson and King as trustees to old Thomas Rogers had similar costs.

Enclosure did not affect the disposition of lands within Kingston Street itself. These old enclosures remained almost entirely untouched, so that the net effect was to leave the street as it had always been, but as a kind of island of habitation in the midst of sweeping expanses of hedged land. The cosier complexity of the old strips and furlongs that had clustered around the village was gone. For a while at least, as the new organization of lands took shape and the old strips disappeared, Kingston villagers must have felt curiously exposed, even dominated, in this new environment. The sheer economic dominance of Rogers, Maitland and de la Warr, was underlined by throwing their individual holdings into great unified blocks.

Beyond this and the modifications in the daily pattern of work and movement attendant on the new disposition of lands, the enclosure did not affect the welfare of the ordinary workers of the village. By the time it came, all the small farmers of the village had been displaced anyway and the Rogers family had effectively bought out the cottagers. The labourers who lived in the street had hardly any rights to land and, such as they had as small tenants, were preserved because the old enclosures in Kingston Street, where all the small gardens and orchards lay, were excluded from the allocation. Kingston was a poor community in the 1830s, but the conditions that accounted for that poverty had been created long before when men started engrossing bigger holdings. They had little to do with enclosure itself. Indeed, it is reasonable to suppose, in the case of this village, that the circumstances that had turned it into a community of rural wage labourers also facilitated the eventual enclosure, rather than that enclosure was a cause of poverty or of social change.

It must be supposed that enclosure in Kingston, as elsewhere, increased the efficiency with which the land could be used, so eventually increased profitability and rents.[25] In the 1830s, when prices were comparatively weak, enclosure may have seemed a necessary defence against the incipient tendency for rents and profits to fall. At all events, the advantages of the Kingston enclosure, whatever they were, did not accrue to Thomas Rogers V or Robert Maitland, at least not in any long-term way. In 1832 and 1833 there were further sharp changes in the ordering of village lands. To people who had observed the financial collapse of Thomas Rogers in 1825, his appointment of James Hodson and John King 'on trust to sell', the early death of Thomas Attree and the sweeping enclosure of the parish, it might have seemed that change and disruption in the ordering of life was to be a continuing feature of Kingston. In fact, the events of 1832 and 1833 were no more than the logical extension of the engrossment that the Dorset, Vinall and Rogers families had been about for a long time. A new and formidable buyer appeared on the Kingston scene. The trustees of the estate of Charles Goring of Wiston came to Kingston to buy lands.

The Gorings were engrossers of entire estates and landlords on a scale Kingston had not experienced before. The family had been long established in Sussex; their name has been traced back at least to the time of Henry III[26] and there had been various titled branches. In 1745 Charles Matthew Goring married a Miss Elizabeth Fagg, who stood in line to inherit the old Shirley estate of Wiston in the western part of Sussex. The Gorings established them selves at Wiston thereafter. The first Charles Goring of Wiston was succeeded by a second, who died in 1829. His eldest son, also Charles Goring, in turn succeeded him. He was a minor at the time and Mary Goring his mother was appointed his guardian. The trustees who came looking for land in Kingston had been appointed under his father's will. This young man of 14 was heir to one of the largest estates in Sussex. Gorings owned land in literally dozens of villages in West and East Sussex.[27] Kingston was a mere speck in their vast list of possessions.

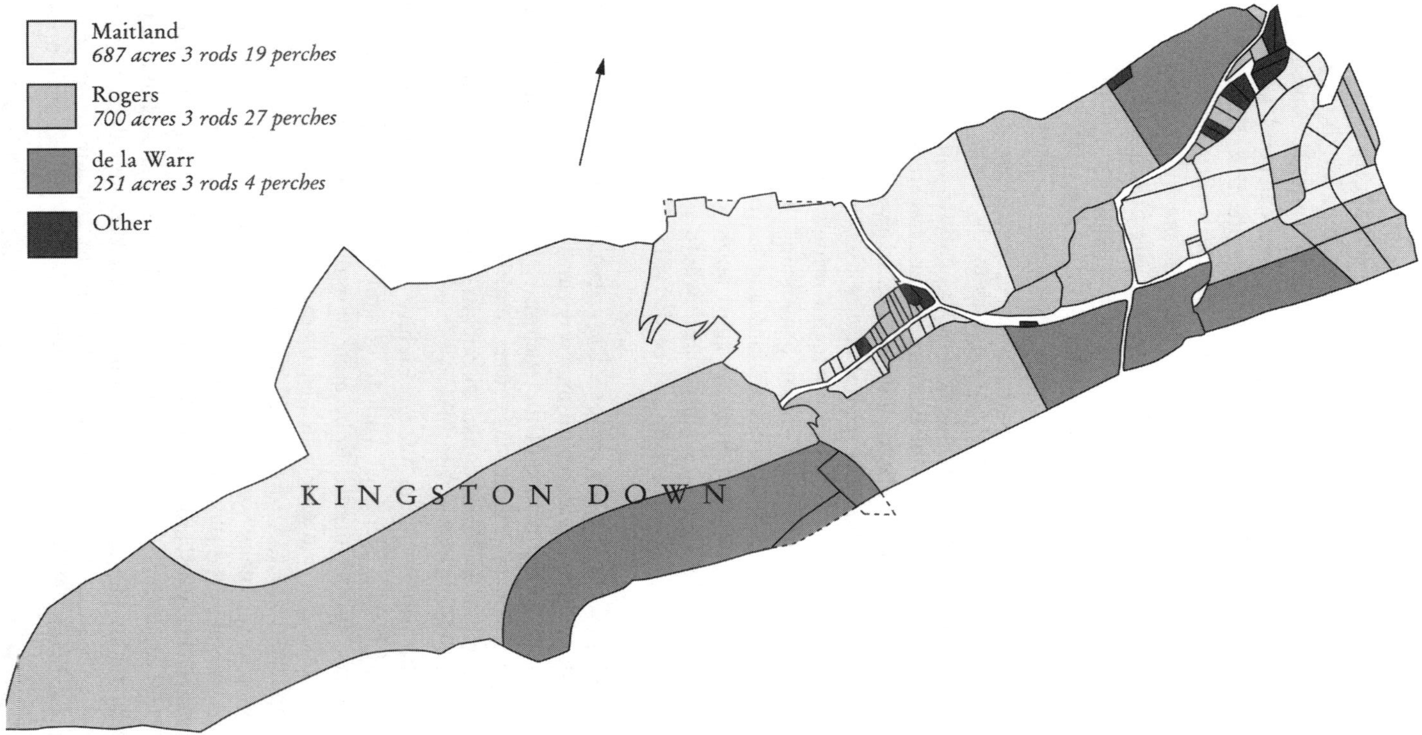

Figure 11.1: The Enclosure Apportionments, 1833

Charles Goring's trustees made offers for Robert Maitland's and Thomas Rogers's land. They may also have made an offer to the Lord de la Warr, but if so he did not accept it. Maitland accepted and so did Rogers. Old Thomas V, now nearly 78 years old and no doubt weighed down by the sequence of heavy misfortunes he had been obliged to bear, gave James Hodson and John King his permission to sell the family lands. It was the end of a long history of landownership in Kingston, and it is hard to imagine that Thomas, in his house in Southover, was insensitive to that. He may well have wondered at the turn of fortune that had brought him from his pre-eminence in 1800 to the sad and final moment of sale. For him the sale in Kingston must have meant a great deal more than it did to Robert Maitland who, established as a London barrister, had no deep connections with his land. He organized the affairs of the estate carefully, appointed good tenants, worried about his returns but never lived in Kingston.

The sales of these two large Kingston estates to the Goring trustees were unavoidably complicated, taking a long time to organize and complete. Both properties were agglomerations of desmense lands, freeholds and copyhold, the latter of course held of the various manors of the village. The Wiston archive contains 500 documents relating to the long history of titles to the village lands. These were the basis on which Goring's lawyers tested Robert Maitland's and Thomas Rogers's rights to ownership.[28] They were required to follow through the successions of 'admissions' and surrenders of village lands over long periods of time, consulting the court books of the various manors and sometimes, in the case of small cottages where successions sometimes were vague, seeking out old inhabitants of the village to confirm particular transactions.

All this followed very closely on the enclosure of village arable. Enclosure probably facilitated legal searches in some ways and hindered them in others. It helped in that, in the course of the enclosure, the commissioners had to confirm legal titles to ensure they were entitled to give allotments in exchange. Kingston landowners had to put their family papers in order in their own interests.

Even so, the papers in the Wiston archive make it clear that Goring's lawyers were left with plenty of work to do and it seems that the enclosure commissioners had not needed to be quite so punctilious about the precise legalities of title. Enclosure only helped them a bit in their labours. It may have complicated life too, for in 1832 the titles Maitland and Rogers held referred first to the many yardlands they had once held in the village open fields, and second to the allotments the commissioners had made in respect of these 'parcels'. The yardlands, of course, no longer existed. The titles referred to an ancient organization of village lands, which had now ceased to be a part of material reality. To establish the claims of Maitland and Rogers to their great new enclosures, the lawyers were required to examine rights to non-existent yardlands. William Figg, the surveyor who had drawn up the enclosure map for Kingston, was called in to attest to the commissioners' intentions in granting allotments to the various Kingston landowners.[29]

It is no wonder in the circumstances that the transaction took time. The first to be completed was the sale of Kingston Manor and its estate by the Maitlands. In November 1832, Robert Maitland handed over the manor and a total area of 688 acres in exchange for £17,020 specifying that henceforth the rents of £625 on the estate should be paid to the Gorings.[30] A month later, Ebenezer Maitland, Robert's uncle and a director of the Bank of England,[31] sold off a small area of the family lands, which had passed to him.[32] In total the lands fetched over £18,000.

A full year passed before the transaction with Thomas Rogers was completed. In October 1833 the lands of Hyde Manor, which had now become the description for the Rogers estate, were sold to Goring. They included more than 600 acres.[33] There followed some smaller sales from Thomas Rogers and his trustees to the Gorings: in January 1834 a small piece of ground not included in the original transaction was added,[34] and in August 1834 an unidentified cottage and garden was sold off.[35]

Goring's trustees may have been unable to convince the Lord de la Warr to sell out his Kingston lands along with those of Robert Maitland and Thomas Rogers, but they were plainly intent on 'tidying up' as much of the land of the parish as they could. One such property had belonged to Captain William Scutt, who had married a member of the family in the eighteenth century.

Captain William Scutt had died a long time before in Brighton.[36] On his death he left a number of small properties to his wife. Among these was a wheeler's yard in Kingston, at the very end of the parish where Kingston abuts the Southover part of Lewes. Scutt's will required that, on his wife's death, Dighton Elgate and another nephew Richard Tidy, who were appointed his trustees, should sell this property, along with some others. Mrs Scutt lived on until 1786, by which time the carpenter Thomas Swaysland had taken on the lease of the wheeler's yard.[37] It was sold as William Scutt had directed. John Kennard, a miller from Lewes, purchased it.[38] Thomas Swaysland continued as 'occupier'. Then, in 1790, Kennard sold out to Thomas Swaysland[39] who was to hold it for more than 30 years. By the 1830s, however, Thomas Swaysland had died after a long career as a wheelwright in Kingston village and there was much dispute between his five children over their rights of inheritance. Once these had been resolved, the property was sold and, of course, Goring's trustees were on hand to buy it.[40] This was in November 1833, while they were involved in their far larger purchase from Thomas Rogers.

The full impact of the Goring purchases shows up in the pattern of ownership of property in the village in 1835. It was as follows. Young Charles Goring, far away at Wiston Park to the north of Shoreham, had come to own 84 per cent of the village lands, together with virtually all the cottages and houses. Lord de la Warr owned the only appreciable land area out of his control. The engrossment of Kingston, which had been built progressively on the increasing areas brought together over centuries, was now about as comprehensive as it could be. The remaining small properties in the village

Table 11.1: Ownership of property in Kingston, c.1835

Owner	*Land in acres*	*Other property*
Charles Goring	1390	4 houses, 17 cottages
Lord de la Warr	206	
Davey*	–	mill
George Rogers	3	
Fuller	1	
Verrall	1	
Willmott	1 1/3	
Thomas Wise	1	cottage

* On long lease from Goring.

were of no particular interest in economic terms, though some were notable as reminders of the past. George Rogers, who held three acres in a small field, was the son of Thomas Attree Rogers, who had been cut out of an inheritance by the terms of the trust his father set up. George was admitted to these lands on the death of his father and under the guardianship of his uncle, Henry Rogers.[41] He died in 1838[42] at the age of 20 and the land passed to his younger brother William. Though William was very young, perhaps 18 years old, he was far from home at the time. In 1838 he was in Bahia in Brazil. He continued to travel because in 1849, when he eventually sold the three acres to Charles Goring, he was in Bombay. This morsel of land was the only part of Kingston Thomas Attree Rogers actually owned on his death in 1828. It had been a part of the old Clover Croft, which in 1835 had vanished along with the other open-field divisions. It was the last Rogers ownership in Kingston.

Similarly, the acre and a half George Willmott owned had a link with the past. Willmott had married Mary Ade Glover, daughter of James Glover and Mary Ade. For some reason, possibly sentiment, the Willmotts held onto their tiny piece of Kingston for many years. Not until 1866, when Charles Goring was dead, did they finally sell to his executors.[43] The acre and a half was the last reminder of the Ade estate, a connection, albeit very tenuous, with the Elizabethan yeomanry.

Finally, there was the cottage and land of Thomas Wise. Wise had succeeded to the cottage on the death of his uncle Edward Howell many years before (see Chapter 9) when he had been an infant. The cottage had been in the ownership of Howells for centuries and in 1835 it was the last truly independent cottage left in the village. Thomas Wise withstood all temptations to sell to the Rogers family and he was to resist the Gorings in the same way. In the 1840s, by virtue of his ownership of the old Howell cottage, he, along with Charles Goring and his tenant farmer, was one of only three people in Kingston entitled to vote in parliamentary elections. He lived until 1858 and, on his death, his widow Phoebe agreed to sell to the Gorings.[44] He was the last representative of the older social order in Kingston, a reminder of the times before the village had been reduced to a society of labourers and had a more distinctive social structure of its own.

The Goring purchase produced a structure of ownership and organization in Kingston that was entirely characteristic of nineteenth-century rural England. When the great nineteenth-century English economist David Ricardo described and analysed the relationships in the agricultural sector of the economy, he simplified the picture, but his description fitted Kingston perfectly. There were just three discernable classes in Ricardo's rural world: large landowners who held lands they did not in general farm; farmers who were large tenants and who stocked up the lands by laying out their own capital; and the mass of wage labourers working at rates that were primarily fixed at the level of subsistence. This indeed was to be the pattern of the Kingston economy in the nineteenth century.

*****

As far as Kingston people were concerned, the landowners, the Goring family, remained a distant power. Even the tenant farmer of the Goring estate in the village, which after 1832 came to be known simply as Kingston Farm, dealt with the Gorings mainly through their agents.[45] Charles Goring, who had been a mere 14 when he came to own Kingston estate, died in 1849 at the early age of 31. He had no children. His Kingston lands were held in trust for a number of years after his death.[46] In 1865 the Revd John Goring was admitted to the various lands in the village. The family remained distant landlords throughout the century, though on one occasion in the 1870s they took a lively interest when St Pancras church was struck by lightning and badly damaged; and the Reverend John Goring paid for its restoration. For the rest, however, the Gorings were not part of the village society, even though they evidently had a major claim to the surpluses produced from Kingston lands. Others exercised the immediate social ascendancy in Kingston.

By the time the Goring trustees had completed the purchase of lands in Kingston, old Thomas Rogers V was dead. His death marked the end of Rogers landownership in the village. But, though the Rogers family was down, it was by no means out and its story in Kingston was far from over. Whatever problems Thomas Attree had in dealing with the world, there were other family members with all those qualities of toughness that had created the empire in the first place. For example, when successive blows fell on their father, Elizabeth and Mary Rogers rallied to stand behind Thomas V's trustees, Hodson and King. And, in these critical years, their younger brother

Henry Rogers was a continual presence. He had taken on the family farm, mortgaged as it was up to the hilt, when Thomas Attree died in 1828. He had become guardian to Thomas Attree's children and had stayed on in Kingston.

A surprising twist in Kingston history came in 1834, the year after Thomas V's death and the sale to Charles Goring. Amid all these changes of fortune, indeed despite them, Henry emerged as the tenant farmer on the huge new Goring farm in Kingston. It was a resurgence one might have expected in the Rogers family. Henry had, in fact, taken on the largest tenancy the village had ever known, 1390 acres.

This tenancy demanded considerable resources. First, Henry had to meet a rent bill of £1170 a year. To cover this and to make an acceptable living for himself and his family, he required a fully stocked farm. In 1833, as in later years, Kingston had pasture for well over 1000 sheep. In the 1850s, for example, the flock was normally between 1400 and 1500 ewes and ewe lambs, along with a few (rather busy) rams.[47] In addition, there was other livestock: customarily Kingston Farm supported about 20 to 30 head of dairy cattle, two to four plough teams of oxen and some horse teams, as well as smaller animals, notably rather a large number of pigs. All this, together with seed corn and equipment, required Henry Rogers to make a capital outlay of about £4000.[48] Henry also required a large labour force. Most of the 25 families in the village worked for him and this necessitated an outlay on wages of possibly £1500 to £2000 a year, also part of his working capital. In all, he probably had to find somewhere near £6000.

Henry Rogers had a good start towards stocking the farm because up until the sale to Goring he had been farming, under the trustees, an estate that was fully half the size of the new Kingston Farm. The not insubstantial remnant of the family capital was once again sunk into Kingston lands, as it had been for more than a century. Henry, as the major tenant farmer and the only large farmer living in the village, was the dominant personage of Kingston.

The power wielded by a man in the position Henry Rogers had come to occupy is hard to envisage today. Henry was, for example, churchwarden and overseer of the poor in the parish. He collected the poor rates from all residents; he determined on payments out of the poor rates to support paupers; he could send a man and all his family to the new workhouse for the 'able bodied poor' at Newhaven. He also collected the highway rate, again from all residents. It was Henry's right to organize the repair of the lanes that ran through Kingston and of Kingston Street. Above all, Henry was employer to virtually everyone in Kingston and collected cottage rents from nearly every family. He never used his power over the poor of the village unscrupulously, but it is a measure of his predominance that he possessed it[49] – all this despite the collapse of the Rogers family fortunes in 1825.

Indeed, Henry's position in Kingston after 1832 was in many ways comparable with that of his great-grandfather Thomas II in the seventeenth century, when he acquired the tenancy of the Swanborough demesnes and laid the foundations of Rogers supremacy. Henry's tenancy in enclosed Kingston was considerably larger than Thomas II's had been at Swanborough, and was potentially highly profitable. With a bit of luck, he could have re-established the family in a permanent way.

But Henry did not have a great deal of luck. He and his wife were slow to have children and lost a son in infancy. Then, after the birth of a second son, Henry died at the early age of 45 in 1842 because of a chronic infection of the liver.[50] There was no Rogers to take over the tenancy. Kingston may have thought that, after five generations, the family had finally disappeared from the local scene. Yet even that was not to be. Henry Rogers was dead but Elizabeth Hodson, née Rogers, his elder sister and wife of old Thomas V's trustee James Hodson was still very much alive. James and Elizabeth, probably at Elizabeth's behest, turned their eyes towards the Kingston tenancy.

Indeed, a good deal had happened to the Hodson family in the years between the trusteeship (around 1825) and the death of Henry Rogers. James and Elizabeth had started their married life as tenant farmers on Birling Farm, near Eastdean, a village lying 15 miles east of Lewes.[51] They sold out in Eastdean in 1837, by which time James was well on the way to becoming a farmer of substance. The Eastdean farm held nearly 900 ewes and ewe lambs. It also had two threshing machines – the new steam-driven devices agricultural labourers so resented in the early 1830s because they led to destruction, violence and rick burning.

From Eastdean, the Hodson family moved to Falmer village in the parish neighbouring Kingston. By this time James was 57 years old and Elizabeth was 51. They had been married 28 years and had produced a large family. There were five girls – Elizabeth, Anna, Harriet, Sarah and Catherine – and two sons. The older son, Anthony William, was born in 1821 and the younger, James, in 1822. Anthony William was 16 when the family moved to Falmer and James Jnr 15.

The move to Falmer brought the Hodsons a big step nearer Kingston, where Elizabeth had been born and which James knew intimately from the years he had looked after Thomas Rogers's interests in the village. When Henry Rogers died in 1842 and the tenancy fell vacant, James and Elizabeth took over the farm in Kingston; they moved from Falmer to live in the old Rogers house in the street, which had become the centre of the new farm. The Rogers family as such may have gone, but a Rogers lady lived on at the family house and it was full of old Thomas V's grandchildren. Elizabeth's position strangely echoed that of her forebear Martha Vinall, who married Francis Zouch and returned to Kingston Manor in the early eighteenth century after the collapse of the Vinall fortunes in Kingston. In the same way, Elizabeth brought her family back to the home in which she was born and which had been the centrepiece of Rogers family life and fortune for so long before the financial collapse in 1825. It is as if, in true Rogers fashion, Elizabeth were unwilling to release the family grip on Kingston. As we shall see later, she was always sharply conscious of being a Rogers, just as Martha Zouch held to her Vinall ancestry and sought to restore the family position.

By any normal measure, James Hodson had reached a good age by the time he moved to Kingston; he was 62 in 1842. Yet, as it turned out, he was just starting a long and singular tenancy that was to last another 30 years until his death at 91 in 1871. James Hodson farmed in Kingston from the earliest years of Victoria's reign, the hungry 1840s as they were called, through the long period of heavy industrialization when so much changed all over England, and on until the second great Reform Bill opened the way to universal male suffrage. When he came to the village in 1842 Kingston, like the rest of rural England, was gripped by poverty. At his death 'high farming' was entrenched and, for the first time in decades, the agricultural real wage was slowly rising as the productivity of the land increased steadily and ordinary Englishmen began to reap a small part of the benefits of industrialization, largely through their own exertions in the face of an implacable capitalism.

In 1842 Hodson could not have foreseen that he was merely at the outset of a new career as a farmer. It is true that he was still highly active. When the family moved to the house in Kingston, James kept on the farm at Falmer.[52] He also kept up a high level of activity and earned a substantial amount as a surveyor.[53] At the same time, he was inclined to hand over the work of farming to his son, Anthony William. The poor rate books for Kingston in the 1840s list James and A. W. Hodson as the tenant-occupiers of Kingston Farm, so presumably both men farmed Falmer in similar partnership.[54] In Kingston, Anthony William took over as overseer of the poor law and became churchwarden, roles the Rogers family had filled as senior farmers in past decades. Anthony William, grandson of Thomas Rogers V, was 21 at the time of the move to Kingston. In the late 1840s he married Frances Ellis and had four children,[55] including an elder son called John and a younger called James. The intention was plain. As James senior grew older Anthony would take over the tenancies and, by 1850, he had in fact taken them over already.

But things did not work out as the Hodsons had planned. In 1851, at the age of 30, Anthony William was thrown by a mare and killed,[56] leaving his four small children to be brought up by their mother, grandparents and Hodson aunts in Kingston. Anthony William was buried in Kingston churchyard. His gravestone is unusual, for it describes him not simply as the son of James and Elizabeth Hodson, as would have been conventional, but also as 'grandson of Thomas Rogers'.[57] This was a measure of the force a Rogers background continued to exert in Kingston and was most likely the work of Elizabeth, James's wife. It stands for her identification with her family and a certain pride in the face of adversity: old Thomas Rogers may have been ruined by forces he failed to control, but it was still to the point that the up-and-coming young farmer of Kingston who had died so tragically should be recognized on his tomb as part of the long Rogers dynasty.

After Anthony William's death, old James Hodson had no alternative but to take over the whole farming operation on his own. His second son, also James Hodson, did not enter the picture. He lived on in Kingston, together with his sister Sarah,[58] but had no part in the farming. He died in 1864, childless and unmarried, and his death certificate is a sad indication of the problems he, and his father, had to encompass. Young James Hodson died of delirium tremens at the age of 42. He had been incapable of taking the place Anthony William had left vacant.[59] So, at the age of 70, James Hodson faced the prospect of farming in the village with which he had such long associations on his own, without the help and support of his son Anthony William. Not unnaturally, James retrenched somewhat. In 1852, the year after Anthony William's death, he sold out the stock at Falmer Court Farm and gave up the tenancy. It was a large farm and more than 900 ewes and lambs were put up for sale. Taken together with the Kingston Farm, where James had a flock of 1400 sheep in 1852, it was too much for him to manage.[60] Indeed, James Hodson may have contemplated quitting Kingston, for he had a detailed survey of Kingston Farm made at the time, a quite expensive procedure often done prior to a sale. Whatever the reason for the survey, he decided to stay on and occupied that pre-eminent position as Goring's tenant farmer for a further 20 years.

By and large, they were probably good years apart from the tensions and pain the family experienced through the incapacity of Anthony William's younger brother. From the 1850s onwards, increases in agricultural productivity and a recovery in agricultural prices, largely due to the massive growth in urban demand for food, opened the way for renewed profitability for tenant farmers. James Hodson, with his long farming experience and intimate knowledge of his Kingston lands, benefited from the times. For most of his last years he supported a substantial family in the village: his errant son James lived in a house in the street with Sarah, the older daughter, who seems to have remained a spinster; his grandchildren and their mother, Anthony William's family, stayed on at Kingston Farm. There were eight members of the Hodson family in Kingston when the 1861 census was taken.[61] One of them, Anthony William's son John, set up as a tenant farmer in Iford, probably in the latter 1860s when he was in his early twenties.

For the last 20 years of James Hodson's long life the farm at Kingston was kept intact and thriving. Each year he entered up his account book with the Goring family; he paid an annual rent for his Kingston land, which rose slowly from £1300 in 1848 to £1450 in 1871. Against this rent, Hodson could enter a number of costs on the landlord's account: the great tithes on village lands, costs of lime for the land, costs of repair on the larger houses in his tenancy, and the regular costs of keeping up the fabric of the farmhouse the Rogers had once owned. The account appears year after year in Hodson's handwriting, though it became scrawled as the years passed and in the last years of his life some other member of the family drew it up for him: his wife perhaps or his daughter Sarah.[62] However, he remained an active farmer and, indeed, active also in the other functions associated with his powerful position in the village. He collected the poor rate, the highway rate and the property tax. He remained churchwarden until his very last years. When he died in 1871 the stock and farm implements were sold off. Kingston was more intensively farmed than it had ever been before. There were nearly 1700 Southdown sheep, where earlier in the century the flock had never been much more than 1400. There was heavy farm equipment, especially threshing machinery. There were the customary 12 pairs of oxen, the three horse teams for ploughing (named after the ploughmen who looked after them), and there were dairy cattle and riding horses. The sale of all this realized nearly £7700. Even allowing for increases in agricultural prices over the years, the tenant's property at Kingston Farm was substantially more valuable at the end of James Hodson's life than it had been in 1852 when it was valued at about £4500.[63] The Kingston venture had plainly worked out well.

On James's death in 1871, no Hodson was around to take over the tenancy. James's own sons were dead and two of his grandsons appear to have moved elsewhere. The third, young John Hodson, was farming at Iford on what was a comparatively small tenancy. Elizabeth Hodson, née Rogers, the woman responsible for bringing the family to Kingston, died at or about the same time as her husband. The tenancy of Kingston Farm passed to a Mr James Stacey.[64]

But the Hodsons' days at Kingston were not over. Stacey farmed the estate until 1895. Then John Hodson, James's grandson, took it over from him and became the Gorings' new tenant. He was to stay on in Kingston until 1980, seeing out the Victorian era and the nineteenth century in the village.

It is fitting in many ways that this John Hodson should be the last of the Kingston tenant farmers to have a place in our account of the village. He was, by virtue of his grandmother, as much a Rogers by lineal descent as a Hodson and that made him especially part of Kingston. As a Rogers, he was a lineal descendant of the grand Vinalls, who had taken such an important part in engrossing the village many years before and who, like the Rogers, had come to financial grief. On top of that, John Hodson could claim descent from the Ades too, the last and strongest of the Tudor yeomanry of Kingston. Two centuries after his distant Rogers forbears had first come into Kingston to change it irrevocably John Hodson was the dominant person in the village. The Rogers family had a way of sticking to Kingston, despite the vigorous changes of the times! John Hodson was their last representative.

*****

The process that brought first Henry Rogers and later James Hodson and his successors to their extraordinary positions of pre-eminence in Kingston society had started long before. Its origins lay in the extrusion of yeomanry from the 'small lands' that had resulted from engrossment and, particularly in the eighteenth century, from the extensions of ownership by the successive members of the Rogers dynasty. The counterpart of that process, as we have seen, was the transformation of the rest of Kingston society into a community of wage labourers. That too had become a reality by the end of the eighteenth century, especially as the last cottagers left the scene. In 1831, a year before the enclosure of village lands and subsequent purchase by the Gorings, we get a clear picture for the first time of the structure of the 'new' village. It comes from the census taken in that year, the first national census in England. Though the Kingston census does not provide names, addresses and all the detail that later censuses were to include, it does give a detailed picture of the occupations and livelihoods of the people who lived in the village. Its main conclusions are shown in Table 11.2.

In 1831, the village was much the same size it had always been, or at least the size it had been over most of the period covered in this book. There were 160 inhabitants in 31 families, so slightly more than five people per family on average. Kingston families then were a little larger than the modern average. The remarkable discrepancy in numbers of males and females is at present inexplicable. The overwhelming majority of the families in the village were employed in agriculture, as one might expect. The single family engaged in trade was most probably the Swayslands, who by this time had an established wheelwright yard on the road between Kingston and Southover. The people in 'other employment' are hard to trace.

The most telling data in the census return concern patterns of individual employment. There were three 'first-class occupiers', farmers who held land and employed wage labour. These were Henry Rogers, farming his father's mortgaged estate under the trusteeship of Hodson and King, John Wood and James Flint who shared the tenancy of the old Kingston Manor farm between them and paid their rents to Robert Maitland in London. There were no 'second-class occupiers', such as the old yeomanry who made substantial use of family labour would have been. Virtually everyone else in the village, apart from the craftsman Swaysland, was a wage labourer. Indeed, by a simple piece of subtraction, it is clear that 24 of the 27 families engaged in agriculture were wage labourers. A few years later, when Goring merged the two great estates into one, there would be only one first-class occupier and everyone else was a waged worker. In 1831 there are signs of a considerable amount of unemployment in the village. With 47 males over the age of 20, even allowing for a proportion of very old men no longer fit for work, at a guess there must have been at least 55 males available for work and seeking it. There were also 69 women, strikingly fewer than the number of men. It is reasonable to suppose that a good proportion of these sought work, perhaps about 30. In total, this makes an estimated 85 people seeking employment. Against this, the census records only 49 people in regular employment. Times were bad in 1831 and it may be that these figures reflect the impact of a general recession on the village.

Except for a small but interesting qualification, the pattern the 1831 census revealed persisted throughout the nineteenth century. Kingston was composed of lowly people. Even after the Parliamentary Reform of 1832 extended the franchise throughout England, very few Kingston villagers could meet the

Table 11.2: Data from the official census of 1831[65]

Total inhabited houses	29
Total families	31
of which	
Families employed in agriculture	27
Families employed in trade	1
Other occupations	3
Total population	160
Male	91
Female	69
Male population over 20 years old	47
Main employments	
First-class 'occupiers' (employing labour)	3
Second-class 'occupiers' (no wage labour employed)	0
Labourers	40
Craftsmen	1
Female servants	5

property requirements for qualification as a voter. In 1842, for example, Charles Goring had the right to vote, as did his tenant Henry Rogers. The only other voter was old Thomas Wise, who hung on as the last independent cottager. The remaining villagers were politically mute and economically subject. The qualification to this pattern of simple social dominance by a tiny number of large tenants was minor and, though it had significance for the future, it was of little importance at the time. It is reflected in the occasional appearance in the village of residents, usually retired middle-class people, who rented one or another of the larger houses (such as Kingston Manor).

As early as 1839 a Mrs Windus appears to have rented Kingston Manor House from the Gorings. She remained there until at least 1845 when the Reverend T. Scott, who was not the vicar of Kingston, seems to have been taken it over. At the same time a Mrs Figg rented another of the larger houses, probably the old Ade farmhouse on the corner of the street. People like this paid rents of £20 to £25 for their houses, five or six times the rent cottagers paid. By the end of the century they had increased considerably in number. They were, in fact, the advance guard of the urban bourgeoisie who turned to the English villages in the twentieth century and made expensive residential areas out of parishes that had been in the depths of poverty in the 1830s. But in the nineteenth century such people were a small minority in Kingston. The pattern of tenant farmer and subject wage labourers was to be the central characteristic throughout.

Who were these Kingston villagers and how did they live? First, there were elements of considerable stability in village society. Table 11.3, which is an incomplete account of the village population over the century, reflects some of this. In the left-hand column there is a list of family names that can be traced back to before 1750 (see Chapter 9). Of these families, all except two (Bartholomews and Harriss) were still present in 1840. What is more, these older families were numerous in the 1840s. In 1848, for example, three Reads were renting cottages; a year or two before there had been five.

These were not all family units; older Reads tended to live alone or with another old person, so rented separate cottages from the more numerous younger families. The frequency of separate cottage tenancies by the family is a rough measure of their relative importance in the labouring society of the village. In the same way, there were two separate Rich families in tenant cottages and two separate lots of Colemans. These 'pre-1750' families continued to be important presences in the village for much of the rest of the century. Of those present in the 1840s, all except the Ades (a labouring offshoot of the old yeoman family), Wises and Richardsons were still in the village when the 1861 census was taken.[66] Only after 1875 or so did these older families diminish in importance in the village population. It is an indication of the stability of the working population of Kingston that in 1840 the new families, namely families that were not traced back to the 1750s, were less than a third of the village. In the mid-1800s, the substantial majority of labouring families had been present for at least a century.

But the stability of the village population can be exaggerated. It seems to have been a more prominent feature in the first half or three-quarters of the century than later. For example, the 'new' families of the 1840s, some of whom may well have been present for several decades, were more mobile than the older ones. Moppets, Wickhams, Weavers and Riddles were mostly gone by the 1860s. Gorringe was the village blacksmith in the 1840s but there were no Gorringes left after 1850. The Hylands were butchers but no butchers appear in the 1861 census. This impression of greater mobility is heightened in families that first appear in the 1860–70 period. The Nyes and Davies made Kingston their home for 15 to 20 years, not much longer. Thomas Diplock, a journeyman who regularly appeared in James Hodson's account as having received payment for repairs to the farmhouse (claimed against the landlord, Goring), was gone by 1864. The Earls took over the wheelwright business Swaysland had once owned, but stayed for only one generation. Of this group only the Backs and Parsons were still present at the end of the century.[67]

It is a fair guess that by the end of the century only a minority of village families had been present for longer than 50 years. Though there were some remarkable residents like the Tuppens, who had been in Kingston for 200 years and in Iford for considerably longer, there was a great deal more change in the village population in the last quarter of the nineteenth century than in the preceding century. The greater mobility of workers in a rapidly industrial-

Table 11.3: Kingston labouring families 1750–1900

Earliest record of family name				
1750 and before	*1840s*	*1860–70*	*Subsequent*	*Last date in register*
Reads (3)			1878	
Tuppens				1899
Ades		1850		
Rich (2)				1891
Pollard				1893
Smith				1887
Richardson (1)				1853
Coleman (2)				1872
Wise				1845
Mockford				1873
Harriss	pre-1830			
Bartholomew	pre-1830			
Moppet		1860		
Wickham (2)		1860		
Weaver		1870		
Riddles		1860		
Gorringe		1860		
Hylands				1850
Nye				1890
Diplock		1864		
Davies				1886
Earl		1870		
Back				1900
Parsons				1900
Hoather				1892
Pope				1900
Pradger				1900
Green			1880	
Ward				1890
Turner				1890

izing country was working its way. On top of that, the relaxation of poor law requirements, which had greatly restricted the movement of labourers in the eighteenth century, probably played a part as well.

How did they live? From the mid-eighteenth century onwards the population of Kingston became progressively more subject to wider economic forces. In part this was a natural outcome of the changing structure of the village, its transformation into a proletarian community. In part it reflected the development of the whole British economy into a unit under the pervasive influence of industrialization. In the early eighteenth century, while the remnant yeomanry were still important in Kingston and the cottagers still a distinctive independent group, the village economy had been largely oriented towards providing its own food. Access to land, even little bits of it, was an elemental security against the vagaries of the market. From 1750 onwards, the number of people in Kingston who could enjoy that degree of security diminished fast. Increasingly, the welfare of the community came to depend on forces outside the control of the individuals who made it up. In a village of wage labourers, welfare depended on the level of wages compared with the prices of life's necessities and on the availability of wage work, not just for the male of the family but also for his wife and children. The 'objective' force of the larger economy determined wages, prices and the amount of employment available.

The vulnerability of rural workers had become sharply manifest in the years of the French wars. In the 1790s the price of wheat and other essentials rose dramatically and money wages were by and large static in the whole of English agriculture. Prices varied a great deal between 1790 and the end of the war in 1815, but they were much higher than they had been in the relatively palmy days of the mid-1700s. The early nineteenth century was, generally speaking, a dreadful time for agricultural workers. The real value of their wages was forced down to the very limits of subsistence. G. M. Trevelyan speaks with good reason of 'the pauperization of rural England, the long drawn-out disaster with which the nineteenth century opened'.[68] It was a disaster, which continued after the conclusion of the war with France. Prices fell sharply at the end of the war, making the years around 1820 very difficult for large tenant farmers like Thomas Rogers, but the lower prices brought little comfort to the rural labourer, for in many places money wages fell too and, more important, the amount of employment fell off in the period of post-war depression. The destitution of rural workers was a continuing reality; after a brief respite in the mid-1820s, there were severe times again in the 1830s. This indeed was a period of acute unrest. In southeast England, including the area around Lewes, the distress of the agricultural population found harsh expression in a wave of rick burning and destruction of equipment, particularly of threshing machines, which were held responsible for the shortage of work.[69] In 1832, when old Thomas Rogers sold out to the Gorings, Sussex was in uproar.

The wave of violent unrest passed but the problem of rural poverty persisted. There was some recovery in the early 1840s, but then another depression, with unemployment and extreme hardship again in the middle of the decade. The 1850s were hard too. Only in the 1860s did real wages in agriculture begin to increase a little and village people share modestly in the massive expansion of production the industrial revolution made possible.

The effects of these long hard decades are manifest in Kingston in various ways, but mainly through the experience of the village workers with the poor laws of the time and through glimpses of their family histories. The poor laws were a central aspect of village life throughout the century. In the early 1800s the old poor law, based on Elizabethan legislation, was still in force. The much-abused 'Act of Elizabeth' was, in a modified form, to keep rural families alive through the time of fearsome price increases during the French wars. In its original conception it had distinguished between the 'impotent' and 'able-bodied' poor. The impotent, widows, orphans and the chronically sick, had a natural claim on society. Parish landowners contributed to a parish fund, which the poor law overseer disbursed to maintain them. The position of the 'able-bodied' was more ambiguous. Ideally, they should be put to work. In practice, in most parishes it was clear to magistrates and overseers that this was not always possible. A system of 'outdoor relief' grew up: in all English parishes the able-bodied poor were eligible, in varying degrees, for support from parish funds – at the cost of farmers and landowners. Then, in the 1790s, 'outdoor relief' was systematized in response to desperate conditions in rural parishes. The Speenhamland magistrates accepted as a principle that the able-bodied, when unable to earn the means of subsistence, were entitled to parish relief on a sliding scale determined by the prevailing price of wheat and on the amounts they needed to keep themselves and their families alive.

The application of the new principle varied greatly across England, but in general it had two consequences. First, it created incentives for farmers to keep money wages down, for they could rely on the parish to provide their workers with extra resources should their ordinary earnings prove insufficient to live on. This had the effect of driving up the poor law rates in most parishes and to that extent was self-defeating because farmers paid the rate. Second, though the Speenhamland interpretation of the law meant that many more people were driven to take relief, in other words were pauperized, it also preserved the vulnerable wage earners in agriculture from the worst effects of inflation and depression. It kept people alive, even though it also guaranteed that the rural workers would be kept at the level of bare subsistence and had little chance of rising above that level.

Speenhamland scandalized that increasing proportion of the British political leadership that had come to believe in free markets. A poor law commission in 1834 castigated the working of the old poor law. It led to low money wages and contradictory increases in the poor rates. It pauperized labour and accustomed the labourer to the idea that he or she had a 'right' to relief; hence, it demoralized the working population. The commission clearly believed it had established a close relationship between debauchery, promiscuity, drunkenness and sundry other inadequacies and the system of 'outdoor relief'. A new poor law was brought in. It accepted the needs of the impotent but it attempted to transform the position of the able-bodied. Its ultimate objective was that all able-bodied poor should be 'put to work': if they persistently failed to find jobs, they were to be sent to workhouses financed by the 'unions' of several parishes, where every endeavour would be made to ensure that inmates received less than the poorest people in employment outside. Outdoor relief was not strictly abolished, but the conditions under which it might be given were circumscribed and overseers were encouraged to reduce the amount they made available to the able-bodied.[70]

How did the poor law affect life in Kingston? First, there is unfortunately very little evidence on the incidence of the old poor law in its 'Speenhamland' form. Such as there is suggests that Kingston landowners in the bad years at the turn of the century were, if anything, less rapacious in their exploitation of the law to keep down the wages they individually paid to their workers. Horsfield remarked in the late 1820s that farmers paid reasonable wages in the area, so the poor-law rates were kept down.[71] This would have made sense in a parish as highly engrossed as Kingston was by 1820. There were two large farms at that time. The poor-law rate fell more heavily on large farmers – Rogers and Maitland's tenant John Wood – than on anyone else. The incentive for either to force wages below subsistence was minimal, for in the end they would simply be obliged to pay out the difference in the form of a higher poor rate. Very few farmers in the parish sought opportunities to reduce the wage in the hope that their neighbours' poor-law contributions would support the destitute villagers. Kingston farmers behaved well in the wage policies because it made sense for them to do so.

Accordingly, the shreds of evidence about the old poor law suggest that the use of outdoor relief in the village was limited. In the bad years of 1814 George Pescodd, the village miller, was overseer of the poor. There were 'impotent poor' to whom he made regular payments over the whole year: the Smith, Tuppen, Read and Geering widows and aged men like James Smith. In this year, outdoor relief to the 'able-bodied' was paid out in the first quarter, between January and March, bad months at the end of the winter. The recipients were John Rich (£12 in total), John Smith (£1), James Read (£11), Samuel Moxford (£6), Nathaniel Wise (6s), Henry Read (14s) and George Coleman (18s). In short, at a time when real wages were in general very low, only three able-bodied workers – John Rich, James Read and Samuel Moxford – received enough relief to suggest that the parishes were supporting their families. Other recipients of outdoor relief were given only small amounts and these may well have been as support during periods of illness. At this time the village does not appear pauperized, though it would be wrong to infer that people were especially well off. The level of support no doubt kept them alive and active as workers, but no more. If they achieved this without recourse to the parish, it was probably because Kingston wages were not pushed down as in some other Sussex villages.[72] But even under these conditions, it is clear that some families were vulnerable and sustained largely by the outdoor relief they could get.

The picture of village poverty becomes clearer as records of the new poor law of the 1830s become available. Henry Rogers was, as we have seen, overseer of the poor until 1843; James Hodson and his son Anthony William took over when Henry died. Once again, there are signs of a certain liberality in relation to the poor. The most marked is the extensive use both Henry Rogers and James Hodson and his son made of 'out-relief'.[73] In the 1835–40 period Henry Rogers sometimes paid out quite large amounts as out-relief, almost certainly more than was required for the 'impotent' poor alone. Similarly, in the 1845–48 period, the Hodsons administered large out-relief payments. Times were very bad. The interesting point is that in neither of these periods did the overseers send people to the Newhaven workhouse (except for a few isolated cases). Despite the theoretically stricter rules discouraging out-relief after 1835, Roger's and the Hodsons found the means to avoid committing their workers to the 'bastille', as the workhouses had come to be called. They extended out-relief instead.

The partial records available for Kingston poor-law payments between 1835 and 1866 are shown in Table 11.4. There were comparatively small outlays of out-relief in the latter 1830s, followed by sharp increases in the period around 1845 when Kingston, like the rest of the country, was suffering an acute depression. Subsequently, in the 1850s there was less need for out-relief, but conditions were still a good deal worse than they had been in the 1837–38 period. Also, in the 1850s James Hodson made significantly more use of the Newhaven workhouse than in the 1840s. It was only in the 1860s that the need for out-relief fell off, probably more or less to the level required by the 'impotent' poor,[74] though there continued to be a number of Kingston villagers in the workhouse.

Table 11.4 adds further information. In the 1835–38 period, Henry Rogers had supported comparatively few people out of the rates; nearly all the payments he made were regular disbursements to the 'impotent'. But in the 1840s it was not uncommon for 16 to 18 people to receive out-relief. Notwithstanding the stricter regime of the new poor law, James and Anthony William Hodson remained attached to the old ways of Speenhamland and gave out-relief where they could. Many such payments were no doubt made to particular individuals, but some were to heads of households so that, overall, a high proportion of the village depended on relief in these bad years. Then, though there were probably smaller numbers on out-relief in the 1850s, James Hodson was obliged to use the workhouse much more than before. As we shall see, this was partly the consequence of special circumstances.

But, though these figures document the progress of village poverty, they are a very detached measure of the circumstances. Behind the figures there are people, and some of them at least can be traced.

The pattern of the late 1830s becomes clear from a valuable record in Henry Rogers's *Churchwarden and Overseer's Account Book*.[75] In the first years of his overseership, Henry kept unusually detailed accounts of payments under the poor law. From March 1834 to June 1835 he listed all payments. These were comparatively good years prior to the depressed 1840s. Henry made regular payments, week in and week out, to three people: John Mockford, Samuel Mockford and John Packham. These were all for comparatively small amounts and it is a reasonable guess that they were 'impotent' poor. In addition, from time to time other payments appear. In June 1834 Richard Smith received support at 12 shillings a week. William Smith, described as 'a pauper from India', was helped in September. In June and October 1834 the Bartholomews' rent was paid – a practice the commission of 1834 had particularly deplored. In March 1835, James Read's rent was paid. Earlier, in August 1834, James Read and William Moppet had both received payments because of illness. This evidently was the normal pattern of parish support in good times. The impotent poor were always there. On top of that, there were a few particularly vulnerable people who took assistance in the form of rent payments. And there were occasional illnesses that obliged villagers to turn to the parish because they could not earn their daily bread.

Henry Rogers's overseer's book includes an exceptional payment. In April 1834 he paid a large sum of £85 to finance the emigration to America of nine villagers – George Coleman with his wife and three children and Henry Harwood with his three sons left Kingston for good. They were duly conveyed to Portsmouth to embark and the Coleman family was given a sum of £5 to help them on their way. Other Colemans remained in Kingston.

This overseer's book is the only detailed record of out-relief payments in Kingston. For further details of the poor in the village, we have to turn to the Newhaven workhouse admission and discharge book.[76] It is a distinctly chilling record of the disasters that could befall the most vulnerable.

In the early years, as Table 11.4 suggests, comparatively few Kingston people were admitted to the workhouse. Mark Ditch, a single labourer, was committed in 1836. Also in 1836 Henry Smith with his wife and daughter spent six weeks in the workhouse. The Mockford family, father, mother and five children, had two spells in 1843 when times were harder. In total they spent 13 weeks in Newhaven. They were described as 'extremely good' and were let out when John Mockford found further work as a labourer in Kingston. These families were committed when Henry Rogers was overseer. In 1851 Anthony William Hodson admitted the Rich family, Alfred, his wife Susan and their son George. They were found work a month later and came back to the village. Though the Smiths, Mockfords and Richs were plainly among the more vulnerable people in the village, they at least avoided the long entanglements with the workhouse in which some others got involved.

The Moppet family was profoundly unfortunate. There were at least two branches in Kingston in the 1840s and 1850s, both sprung from William

Moppet, the labourer who died at the age of 81 in 1847. Four years after this, in April 1851, one branch, the John Moppets, were committed to Newhaven.

Table 11.4: Numbers of people supported out of poor rates in Kingston

Period	*Number on out-relief*	*Number of person days in workhouse*
Quarterly data		
December 1835–March 1838	maximum 4 per quarter	mainly 1–2 very little
March–June 1838	7	–
June–September 1838	7	–
September–December 1838	13	–
January–March 1839	8	–
March–December 1839	4 per quarter	–
July–September 1844	5	–
September–December 1844	7	–
January 1845–March 1845	7	–
March–June 1845	16	–
June–September 1845	18	26 days
September–December 1845	18	–
January–March 1846	19	26 days
March–June 1846	18	12 days
June–September 1846	17	–
Biannual data		
September 1854–March 1855	n.a.	460 days
March–September 1855	n.a.	396 days
September 1855–March 1856	n.a.	422 days
March–September 1856	n.a.	187 days
September 1856–March 1857	n.a.	297 days
March–September 1857	n.a.	254 days
September 1857–March 1858	n.a.	175 days
March–September 1858	n.a.	189 days
September 1858–March 1859	n.a.	303 days
March 1863–September 1866	n.a.	189–306 days

John's wife had died and his four children William, John, Thomas and Samuel were taken in with him. The Hodsons had sent John Moppet away because he was insane, or judged to be. In July 1851 the workhouse master reached the conclusion that Moppet was unsuitable as an ordinary inmate and sent him off to a lunatic asylum in London 'by order'. His four sons stayed on in the workhouse. Their subsequent history shows how hard it could be to break out of the clutches of the poor-law system. William Moppet, the oldest boy, had the least difficulties. He appears to have been released soon after his father's tragic departure and was recommitted in September 1851 because he was 'ill'. He left again in January 1852 but before the month was out he was in again, this time because he had no work. Then, in March 1852, after three months at Newhaven, he was released to take up a job. He seems to have left Kingston, for there is no further record of him.

William's brothers remained for varying lengths of time in the workhouse. John was discharged at a very early age and presumably found service. Thomas spent at least five years in the workhouse. He was released and soon found himself back in again in December 1856. By May 1857 he had solved his problem. He went to sea and we hear no more of him. Young Samuel Moppet remained in the workhouse until November 1860. He had grown up in the place for nine years. Within a week or two he was recommitted. He had gone into 'service' and had apparently not done well at it. After three more months Samuel followed the path his brother had taken. He too went to sea, never to reappear as a Kingston resident.

While this Moppet family was being brought up in the workhouse and eventually dispersed from it and from its native parish, another Moppet appeared. James Moppet from Kingston 'lost his place' in January 1852 and was committed by James Hodson. He left in April to return in May, once again out of work. It was the beginning of a long saga. In the ensuing 15 months James Moppet entered the workhouse four times. After the initial commitment in January 1851, he was released in April. A month later, in May, he was again out of work and again sent to Newhaven. He stayed on until 5 July. During this period the workhouse overseer described his behaviour as 'indifferent'. His departure on 5 July was for an extremely brief period. Three days later he was again unable to find work and was again committed. This time he remained at Newhaven for a month. In August work was obtained for him, probably on the harvest, and for a while all appeared to be in order. Then, in November 1852, the poor man fell ill and was readmitted to the workhouse, though this time, it was hoped, on the slightly better terms applicable to the 'impotent' poor, which he had become. He was sick for a long time. He only left Newhaven the following spring of March 1853. There followed a long spell in which Moppet was able to keep himself out of the 'bastille', but in October 1858 it came to an end. He fell ill again and found himself back in what must have been sadly familiar surroundings. He died in Newhaven in February 1859 after four months of illness; he left the workhouse for the last time for a pauper's grave.

Just as the Moppet family had been peculiarly vulnerable to poverty and were frequently in the workhouse in the 1850s, so also the Read family, or branches of it, fell on hard times in the 1860s. The Reads were descended from the eighteenth-century cottager family that had run into poverty nearly 100 years before. Between 1862 and 1867, a James Read who suffered from chronic epilepsy was in and out of the workhouse on nine different occasions, almost always on grounds of illness. On three occasions over the same period a relative called Walter John Read was taken to Newhaven because he was out of work. All in all, comparatively few Kingston families were committed for in-relief under the new poor law. Those who were showed that life in the village could be harsh for economically or physically weak members of the community. Some became lost in a cycle of illness and poverty from which they could not escape; some became regular inmates at Newhaven, which was as harsh and degrading a place as any average English workhouse of the time. Despite the apparently liberal implementation of the poor law by Henry Rogers and later James Hodson, some people became caught up in the system and could not find their way out of it.

It is possible that the liberal implementation of the poor law in Kingston hides the real impact of poverty in the village. Kingston villagers may have been spared the workhouse more than people from other parishes around, but that does not mean that they escaped poverty. Other data about the village give an indication of living conditions. Table 11.5, for example, shows the average age of death in Kingston between 1837 and 1900.[77]

Over the whole period from 1837 to the end of the century, the average life span of a Kingston villager was just under 40 years. This, of course, is very low by modern British standards. If, as some people argue, life expectancy measures are particularly revealing about people's material welfare, it would seem that the nineteenth-century Kingston workers were exposed to generally harsh conditions. It is noticeable, though, that there is a good deal of variation in the average age at death over the course of the century. The low average for the period as a whole is largely the outcome of exceptionally low figures in the 1850s and 1860s (though at no time during the century was life expectancy anywhere near modern standards). The 1850s and 1860s were periods of recurrent recession and the low average age at death in these decades is due to the large number of infantile deaths. Indeed, as in all poor communities, the infantile mortality rate in Kingston was tragically high. For example, between 1837 and 1865 there were 97 births in the village. Of these, 29 children died before the age of five and 26 of them before the age of one year. This is a rate of mortality among children we would identify with a very poor community today, living under extremely severe material conditions.

Deaths in infancy (before five years) account for 37 of the total 123, or 30 per cent of all deaths, a high proportion and indicative of a vulnerable community. Children died of a wide variety of causes (11 are listed as 'infantile diseases'), though today many of them would be related to the poor health of mothers or more generally to diseases of poverty. Diseases associated with poverty (tuberculosis in particular) were the main causes of death for people who died in their middle years (say between 15 and 50). The high incidence of tubercular disease might be explained by the fact that villagers relied heavily on local supplies of milk, which were doubtless infected from time to time. Gastric and bronchial diseases, also associated with poverty, were mainly child-killers. Some people, though by present-day standards compara

Table 11.5: Average age at death in Kingston village, 1837–1900

Period	*Average age at death*	*Number of deaths*
1837–1850	45.8	40
1851–1860	24.0	22
1861–1870	27.0	23
1871–1880	49.2	14
1881–1890	31.8	16
1891–1900	36.9	8
1837–1900	39.3	123

tively few, lived to old age. Only about 15 per cent of those alive in 1837 lived past the age of 70, which is roughly the present average life expectancy in Britain, but one or two, like James Hodson, the tenant farmer or Thomas Diplock, the village journeyman, lived into their nineties.

The record of Kingston deaths shows a more general kind of poverty than appears from workhouse registers – a poverty by and large spread uniformly through the village community. Certainly, some families managed to achieve a certain economic vigour in a limited and comparative sense. They were mainly those with minor advantages of one form or another. The Gorringes were blacksmiths in the 1850s and their lot was better than most. Gorringe was able to afford a more expensive cottage than any village labourer.[78] In the birth registers for the 1850s he is described as being a bailiff, a function he must have added to his role as village smith. In the earlier years of the century Thomas Wise and his family stubbornly held onto their copyhold cottage, maintained a certain level of economic independence and benefited correspondingly. The Tuppens, though never able to rise above the ranks of wage labour, were a 'strong' family. In the 1861 census Tuppen was recorded as a shepherd. He lived with his wife and a large brood of 11 children in a single cottage. The Tuppens, still shepherds and sometimes cowmen, were still present in force in the last decade of the nineteenth century. Old Jane Tuppen, mother of the large family of 1861, appears to have played a major role as midwife in the village. She was witness to many of the births in the village. Thomas Diplock, the journeyman who was repeatedly called on to conduct repairs on James Hodson's house and farm buildings, died at a ripe old age and in good health.

The differentiation between these slightly more fortunate families and the rest was not really very great. It was a differentiation between shepherds, cowmen and minor craftsmen on the one hand and ordinary field labourers, servants and dairymaids on the other. There was a little, but not much, to choose between them. Their children died with about the same frequency in the bad times and of the same kinds of diseases. The majority were illiterate: about 67 of the 123 death certificates for the village were witnessed by people who could not write, a situation that changed only gradually with the development of a school in the latter part of the century. By and large they were all vulnerable to the smallest turn of fortune, which might drive them below the level of subsistence. Accordingly, though mutual support must surely have remained strong in so small a community and generally helped to make a hard life more bearable, mutual support in itself could not do much in material terms. Even those who were modestly better off could do little to help when a family fell below the survival line, as the Rich family did in the 1860s. In 1861 John and Ann Rich lived in a labourer's cottage at Newmarket Farm on the outskirts of the parish. They had seven children. There had been eight but one had died of rickets before 1861. Three more children died in 1862 and 1863; all were infected with scrofula, a tubercular disease of the skin. In 1864 Ann Rich died of consumption. Her husband lived for a little longer and then died of debility and general exhaustion. There was not much to be done for the Richs. Though they escaped the long entanglements with the Newhaven 'bastille' that ruined other lives, they were not much better off than those who were sent to the workhouse.

It is natural to speculate whether nineteenth-century poverty in Kingston was more or less severe than the poverty of the past, but hard of course to reach any clear conclusion about the matter. In one sense there is a risk of exaggerating the harshness of the nineteenth-century experience in comparison with earlier times simply because there is more information about it. Also, Kingston's poverty in the 1800s was a reflection of the profound change in the structure of village society that had marked the eighteenth century, its transformation into a village of landless labourers. Consequently, to compare nineteenth-century conditions in the village with earlier epochs is in the main to compare the incidence of poverty in very different forms of social organization. In the later Tudor period, for example, and in the early seventeenth century there had been hard times because money wages failed to follow the price increases in basic foodstuffs. But then far more people in Kingston had access to land than in the nineteenth century, so a larger proportion shared in the rising profitability of agricultural production, or at least could protect themselves from the vagaries of rising food prices by producing some of the food they needed for their own consumption. Even comparisons between the condition of nineteenth-century wage labourers and the wage labourers of the seventeenth century are hard to make, not just because the data are extremely scanty but also because the Kingston wage labourers of the earlier time were often connected to yeoman or cottager families who might extend support to them in times of dearth. This possibility did not exist for Kingston workers in the nineteenth century.

Comparisons with even earlier times are more hazardous still. In the medieval period before the Black Death while a good deal of the manorial organization was still extant, there had been some dreadful times. The pressure of population on the land was increasing intolerably and harvests were poor in the decade before the plague struck. Yet, though conditions were doubtless extremely harsh, the majority of those medieval villagers had had access to copyhold land as villeins. No doubt, the land in our village, as in many others, had lost its heart through excessive tillage, but it is still possible that it provided a degree of security.

In the end, however, such comparisons, however tempting they may be, are really beside the point. The basic facts about the village in the nineteenth century are clear enough. For the majority of villagers the period from 1790 to 1870 was hard and, even thereafter, as the real wage rose slowly there was little relief. In the middle of the twentieth century there were still old men who could remember life in the last decade of the nineteenth. They had started farm labour at the age of eleven. Work started at 6.30 in the morning. Lads who had just started their jobs on John Hodson's farm harnessed the animals to the ploughs in the dark, at least in spring and autumn. Good Friday and Christmas Day were holidays but there was not much else besides. The working day stopped at around five. At this time a lad who had just started work earned four shillings a week. Farm labourers got a wage of 12 shillings plus their cottages, a cowman or carter got 15 shillings and shepherds a little more. There was good bread. Meat was only fair and consisted mainly of table rabbits raised in the cottage gardens. Beer was good, with hops floating in it and there were a number of 'good beer drinkers' in the village. Life was better than it had been in the middle of the century but it was no bed of roses. One old man recalled that 'whatever your politics, it was better to say you were Conservative if you wanted to keep your job'. The reforms of the nineteenth century, the growing pressure of union organization among agricultural workers and the increasing productivity of the land had improved matters, but as the century ended, Kingston was still a politically and economically subject community as it had been at its beginning.

*****

John Hodson, the last representative of the Hodson–Rogers–Vinall line, left the tenancy of Kingston Farm in 1908. By that time life was better for the ordinary villager than it had been in earlier years, though the reforms that would eventually produce a real improvement in the material welfare of agricultural workers still lay in the future. At the same time there were aspects in which village life had plainly changed drastically. People were moving out of agricultural jobs. John Hodson's farm had been far more mechanized than his grandfather's, and the future lay in the direction of even greater displacement of farm labour. This one aspect of 'modernization' was already apparent.

Another was the steady improvement of transport throughout the nineteenth century. Since the late eighteenth-century there had been great improvements to the appalling Sussex roads, not least to the road along the northern perimeter of Kingston parish, which linked Lewes, the county town, to rapidly expanding Brighton. By the late nineteenth century, this and the road from Lewes to Newhaven had become reliable and comparatively comfortable highways for all seasons. Then, after 1842, the railway came. The Lewes–Brighton line was opened in that year and ran parallel to the main highway, along the northern strip of the parish. Kingston Halt was a small station set on the railway embankment where villagers could catch the train to Lewes or Brighton. The immediate effects of these advances in transport on village life are hard to discern. They were probably not great. Kingston had always had unusually privileged access to Lewes, lying a mile or two away, and from the farmers' as from the villagers' points of view it is likely that the new roads and railways were comparatively minor advances. But there were others who saw them differently.

The new accessibility of the village was probably more important to outsiders than to villagers. It made it possible for people with resources to come and live in Kingston without feeling they were sacrificing themselves to a rural backwater. Retired clergymen, genteel widows and members of the new professional and trading classes in Lewes took a different view of accessibility from that of farmers and villagers. What might have seemed a minor advance to people in the village looked different to outsiders. It brought them to Kingston. By the time John Hodson had relinquished his tenancy these new middle-class inhabitants were more numerous than they had been before. They were a sign of the future because eventually they, and others like them, would take over the village as the need for labour diminished and cottages in which families had struggled through the impoverished decades of the nineteenth century were transformed into housing for a new bourgeoisie.

In the early years of the twentieth century they mainly occupied the larger houses of the old yeoman families – houses where the yeoman Picombes and Ades had lived and Kingston Manor House, now quite separate from the farm, where once the tenant farmers of Robert Maitland lived and before them the Vinalls. These new arrivals lived in style among the workers in the street. They may have seen their labouring neighbours as representatives of an old rural order, of that 'unchanging' rural world that is so dear to the idealizations of people whose main life and business is in towns. Of course the villagers of Kingston were not like that at all. They were at that time the remnant population of the economically oppressed nineteenth-century village. Their lines of connection with the more remote yeoman past were non-existent. The old rural world had finally gone. As the new inhabitants from surrounding towns turned towards Kingston, Kingston village society in John Hodson's days was as much a product of industrialization and a century of industrial capitalism as they were.

Notes

Chapter 1: Introduction

1. See the map in Figure 1.1.
2. Right up to the nineteenth century the village was referred to as Kingston juxta Lewes.
3. In Chapter 2 I give a full description of the Kingston open field system and discuss these points in detail.

Chapter 2: Open Fields and Manors

1. *Walter of Henley's husbandry*, translated by Elizabeth Lamond (New York: Longmans Green, 1890), pp. 13–15.
2. D. M. Stenton, *English Society in the Early Middle Ages* (Harmondsworth: Penguin, fourth edition, 1965), p. 123.
3. Max Weber, *General Economic History*, translated by Frank H. Knight (New York: Collier Books, 1961), Chapter 1, 'Agricultural organisation and the problem of agrarian communism'.
4. Sussex Fines III, no. 1867, p. 92, SR XXIII.
5. Wiston Arch. 1648.
6. P. F. Brandon, 'The origin of Newhaven and the drainage of the Lewes and Laughton levels', *SAC*, CIX (1971), pp. 96–8.
7. Wiston Arch. 5593–5. Wiston Arch. 1714 and 1715 are copies of the terrier Marchant drew up to accompany the map.
8. Copied by W. M. Figg, the surveyor in 1851. The document has not been recovered. W. M. Figg, *Tenantry Customs in Sussex: The Drinkers Acres*, *SAC*, IV (1851), p. 20.
9. ESRO, Adams Mss. 51. The Dorset map is in large part a copy of the Marchant, though there are differences in detail. The Marchant map was drawn for John Crouch, a grocer of Southwark who owned Kingston Manor at the time. Wiston Arch. 5651 is a copy of a receipt for payment from John Ridge to Marchant. Ridge was tenant farmer to Crouch at the time. The map and terrier cost £29.19*s*.6*d*, of which £26.5s.0*d*. was for 'surveying and planning the parish'.
10. ESRO, Enclosure Award and Map. See reference to abutments to property no. 24.
11. The track is shown clearly in the Yeabell and Gardner map in Chichester Cathedral, although on a much smaller scale (*c*. 1780).
12. Marchant's terrier (Wiston Arch. 1714 and 1715) lists each strip in the tenantry laines, together with its customary statutory acreages.
13. The classifications into steep, medium and gentle were done by comparing Marchant's map of the furlongs with the actual terrain in Kingston. In the absence of a detailed contour map this act of judgement was unavoidable. The following is the classification of furlongs, using the Marchant notation: Mill Laine (steep) D, H, J, P, Q, R, S, X, Y, Z; (medium) A, B, C, E, F, G, I, A_1, B_1; (gentle) K, L, M, N, O, T, U, V,

W, C_1. West Laine (steep) E, F, G, M, Q, K, O, P, R; (medium) D, I, L, N, S; (gentle) A, B, C, H, T, U, W. The notation corresponds to that used in the Dorset maps.

14. *Henley's Husbandry*, p. 9.
15. W. Budgen, 'Wists and virgates of land', *SNQ*, X, no. 4, Nov. 1944.
16. W. Hudson, 'On a series of rolls of the Manor of Wiston', *SAC*, LIII (1910), pp 149–55.
17. W. Budgen, 'The acreages of the Sussex hide of land', *SNQ*, IX, no. 4, November 1946.
18. Wiston Arch. 1714. Towner's land can be traced back to the middle of Elizabeth's reign in Sw. Ct. Bk 1578/83 WSRO. Add. Mss. 524.
19. Wiston Arch. 1904–20.
20. Wiston Arch. 1975 and ESRO Land Tax Assessments, 1780.
21. See for example, Stenton, *English Society*, p. 125.
22. For more detailed accounts of open field organization see, for example, W. E. Tate, *The English village community and the enclosure movements* (London: Gollancz, 1967), particularly Chapter 2. There is a particularly enjoyable account in Warren O. Ault, *Open Field Farming in Medieval England* (London: Allen & Unwin, 1972).
23. Ault, *Open Field Farming.*
24. P. F. Brandon, 'Arable farming in a Sussex scarp-foot parish', *SAC*, C (1962), p. 60, on Alciston.
25. Wiston Arch. 5205.
26. Wiston Arch. 1931 is a copy.
27. Wiston Arch. 1703 and 1945–53; also Hyde survey in Wiston Arch. 5205 and *Book of John Rowe*, *SRS*, XXIX. Also 'Sussex lay subsidy rolls', *SRS*, LVI.
28. Wiston Arch. 1601–08 for eighteenth century; also *Book of John Rowe*; Wiston Arch. 5205 and WSRO. Add. Mss 524, Sw. Ct. Bk 1578/83.
29. Wiston Arch. 1925–31; also *Book of John Rowe*. The latter shows John Eversfield as owner of 'Peakes' in 1600. Eversfield had held this land since 1567 at least, so that 'Peake' himself, who is lost in a more distant past, was certainly pre-Elizabethan.
30. Wiston Arch. 1940–43; also Iford Manor Rental, 1685.
31. Wiston Arch. 1859–66; 1703–23 and 1972. 'Sussex Fines III', *SRS*, XXIII, no. 2702, 1 Hen IV and no. 2709, I Hen IV.
32. Chartulary; *SRS*, XL, pp. 45 and 35, 36. The trace of Diggons Land is not possible to follow in any detail. Edmund Bowker held 'one yardland called Diggons' of Kingston Manor in 1619 (Adams, 45), which it is plausible to argue were the original lands.
33. This line of connection is traced later in the text. See *Book of John Rowe*, pp. 195, 206. For later history Wiston Arch. 1904–20, and for early evidence on the atte Hyde family in Kingston, 'Sussex subsidies', *SRS*, VIII, pp. 48, 168, 282; 'Chartulary', *SRS*, XL, pp. 34, 38, 105 (2), 126.
34. Adams, 45 as in (32) above. To trace the shift in the name to the 13 yardlands, note that Thos. Rogers Jnr appears as tenant to Dorset for 'Diggons farm', which was to all appearances a substantial holding in 1720. See C. Leeson Price, 'A rent roll of his Grace the Duke of Dorset', *SAC*, XXXIX, pp. 134ff. Also in the Enclosure Award, loc. cit., de la Warr is credited with 13 yards called Diggons Land.
35. Wiston Arch. 1972.
36. Cf. Wiston Arch. 1972 and 1703–23.
37. Wiston Arch. 5205.

38. See M. M. Postan, *The Medieval Economy and Society* (Harmondsworth: Pelican Books, 1975), especially Chapters 2 and 3. Also, Colin Platt, *Medieval England* (London: Routledge & Kegan Paul, 1978), Chap. 2, especially pp. 42ff.
39. Postan, *The Medieval Economy and Society*, particularly Chapter 2.
40. ESRO Adams Mss 51. See Figs 1.1 (p. 1) and 2.1 (p. 9).
41. ESRO Adams Mss 51. Also, for acreages, see *Book of John Rowe*.
42. C. Platt, *The Monastic Grange in Medieval England* (London: Macmillan, 1969). See p. 57 and, on Swanborough lands, p. 70.
43. Ibid. p. 57.
44. ESRO, Tithe Commissioners, Parish of Iford, Sussex.
45. ESRO, Tithe Commissioners, quoted by Platt, *The Monastic Grange*, p. 10.
46. ESRO, Tithe Commissioners; also ESRO, Enclosure Map for Iford and Kingston.
47. For example Ault, *Open Field Farming*.
48. *Book of John Rowe*, p. 141.
49. See, for example, D. M. Stenton, *English Society*, pp. 138–9 and M. M. Postan, *Medieval Economy*, Chapter 5.
50. Postan, *Medieval Economy*, Chapter 6.
51. Postan, *Medieval Economy*, p. 98.
52. See Ault, *Open Field Farming*, p. 75. Ault suggests that as many as a third of English 'vills' may have had divided lordship.
53. See *VCH*, vol. 7, sections on Iford, Rodmell, Piddinghoe and Newhaven. Iford, the sister village to Kingston, had Swanborough lands (though not in the open fields), Iford Manor, Northease Manor and the Manor of Withdean-Cayliffe (see *Book of John Rowe*). The latter is particularly curious, for Withdean (which was presumably the site of the desmesnes), is 12 miles off. It is now a suburb of Brighton. There are many other examples; an interesting one is discussed in P. S. Godman, 'The Manors of Cowfold', *SAC*, LXII, pp. 153ff. There were six manors in Cowfold.
54. See sections on Kingston juxta Lewes in WSRO, Catalogue of the Wiston Arch. (1974).
55. References to properties in Table 2.2. These are primary sources that indicate the manor to which the properties belonged and provide a trace of their titles to the late sixteenth century. (1) Alfreyes (Wiston nos 1859/66; 1703/23, 1972; Swan. Ct. Bk 1578/83); (2) Alfreyes (Wiston nos 1973/4; 1639/41; Sw. Ct. Bk 1578/83); (3) Adams (Terr. 1773; Wiston nos 1887/96; LTA, 1780–1800; Sw. Ct. Bk 1578/ 83); (4) Boniface and Howells (Sw. Rental 1658; Wiston no. 1975; Terr. 1773); (5) Barndens (Sw. Ct. Bk 1578/80; Wiston nos 1601/8; Sw. Rental 1658. Also Wiston no. 1623/6); (6) Priory Lands (Wiston nos 1832/4; 1835/41); (7) Taylors (of 1603) (Sw. Ct. Bk 1578/80; Wiston nos 1609/20, *SAC*, XXIX, pp. 119ff.); (8) Dorset's lands in tenantry laines (*SAC*, XXIX, pp. 119ff; Terr. 1773; LTA 1780–1830); (9) Taberers (Wiston nos 1940/3; Sw. Ct. Bk 1578/83); (10) Hudds (*SAC*, XXIX, pp. 119ff; Wiston nos 1955/68); (11) Towners (*SAC*, XXIX, pp. 119ff; Wiston nos 1724/39; Enclosure Act); (12) Bishops (Wiston nos 1955/68; *SAC*, XXIX, pp. 119ff.); (13) Kingston Manor Desmesnes Manor Farm (Wiston nos 1648/1702, 1713, 1723, 1755/58); (14) Bayleys (Wiston nos 1945/53); (15) Peakes (*SAC*, XXIX, pp. 119ff.; Wiston nos 1925–31, Kingston Rental 1779); (16) Bayleys (Wiston nos 1945/53); (17) Hyde Manor Desmesnes/Nortons Farm (Wiston nos 5205; Surrey 1567, Rental 1783; Wiston

nos 1904/20); (18) Houndean-Dorset/ Peakes (Houndean Rental, *c*.1600, *Book of John Rowe*). Note that (3) became New's Farm in the eighteenth century and (4) became Paine's.

56. Manorial ascriptions of strips in Mill Furlong and Horselong Furlong (and furlongs adjacent to them) were obtained (a) by tracing ownership of strips from the Elizabethan survey of Hyde Manor (Wiston Arch. 5205) and Marchant's terrier (Wiston Arch. 1714/5); (b) by linking a strip-owner's names to properties, using the 'traces' given in note 55 above. This exercise can only be done for some furlongs because some owners of 1567 and 1773 held lands of more than one manor. The 1799 Dorset map (ESRO, Adams Ms. 51) was used to draw the sketch maps.
57. The origins of Swanborough Manor are the main subject of Chapter 3.
58. Wiston Arch. 5205. In 1567 Skinner's and Culpeper's yardlands were held by Newton, from whom the Dorset family eventually purchased them. See *Book of John Rowe*, pp. 139–40.
59. See, for example, the 'new and perfect rentall' of Swanborough for 1 January 1658 (ESRO Adams Mss. 46). There were two small Swanborough properties in Iford: (i) messuage, barn, gardens, orchard and yardland of ten acres (which became the Iford family home of the Rogers); (ii) a tenement or cottage and garden.
60. *Book of John Rowe*, pp. 3ff.
61. The various holdings in the street have been traced partly through the references (in note 55) above, partly through the Hyde survey, and the Marchant terrier, partly through abutments extracted by L. S. Cole from an early Iford Manor survey (University of Sussex Library, Documents Section, SW 3), and partly from ESRO; Enclosure Act for Iford and Kingston.
62. Joseph Cooper, 'The hundred of Swanborough', *SAC*, XXIX, p. 143. Cooper lived at Kingston Manor in the early twentieth century.

Chapter 3: The Norman Transformation

1. The Domesday entry is given later in the text. On Niworde = Iford, see A. Mawer and F. M. Stenton, *The Place Names of Sussex*, vol. I, The English Place Name Society, vol. VII (Cambridge: Cambridge University Press, 1930), pp. 517–18.
2. See for example, D. M. Stenton, *English Society in the Early Middle Ages*, pp. 138ff.
3. Both appear in the Charter of 'the second founder' of the priory of St Pancras as having given their lands to the priory at an earlier date. 'Chartulary of the priory of St Pancras of Lewes', vol. 1, *SRS*, XXXVIII, p. 12. Since their names do not appear in the Domesday Record, it is plausible to suppose they had given up their lands before 1086.
4. J. Cradock, 'The Anglo-Saxon cemetery at Saxonbury, Lewes, East Sussex, *SAC*, CXVII (1979), pp. 85–102.
5. See Charles H. Lemmon, 'The campaign of 1066', in Whitelock et al., *The Norman Conquest* (London: Eyre & Spottiswoode, 1966), pp. 86ff. for a brief discussion of the disbanding of the fyrd in the south.
6. See David Douglas, 'William the Conqueror: duke and king', in Whitelock et al., *The Norman Conquest*, p. 50.
7. The following paragraphs drew on D. Douglas, ibid.
8. Douglas, ibid., p.54.

9. '"Seneschancie", unknown thirteenth century author', in E. Lamond (translator), *Walter of Henley's Husbandry* (London: Longmans Green, 1890), p. 105.
10. See, for example, Colin Platt, *Medieval England* (London: Rontledge & Kegan Paul, 1978), pp. 4ff.
11. 'Chartulary of the priory of St Pancras of Lewes', translated by L. F. Salzman, *SRS*, XXXVIII (Part I), p. 2.
12. The following account comes from the 'first Charter of William de Warenne, the first founder of the monastery or priory of Lewes', 'Chartulary (1)', *SRS*, XXXVIII, pp. 1ff. Robert Auncall, a later prior, brought the chartulary together in 1444. It is acknowledged that the first charter is a late copy, probably fifteenth-century (see L. F. Salzman, 'Chartulary (2)', *SRS*, XL, 'Introduction'). However, as Salzman argues, there is no reason to doubt the authenticity of the text itself.
13. 'Chartulary (1)', *SRS*, XXXVIII, p. 3.
14. See Noreen Hunt, *Cluny under St Hugh, 1049–1109* (London: Edward Arnold, 1969). On Cluniac expansionism, see pp. 124ff.
15. Ibid., pp. 132ff. on the European religious revival.
16. Ibid., p. 130. See later in text.
17. 'Chartulary (1)', *SRS*, XXXVIII, pp. 7ff.
18. Hunt, *Cluny under St Hugh*, p. 173 with reference to William of Malmesbury, 'De Grestis Pontificum Anglorum'.
19. Ibid., p. 174.
20. Hunt suggests that the architecture of the new church was greatly influenced by the large basilica at Cluny and, in turn, that the double transept at St Pancras informed the concept of Canterbury Cathedral. The priory is now a rather undistinguished ruin. However, the splendid remains at Castle Acre – a subsidiary house – convey something of the architectural splendour of de Warenne's foundations (*Cluny under St Hugh*, p. 182).
21. 'Chartulary (1)' *SRS*, XXXVIII, p. 25. Charter of William de Warenne, 'the second founder'. It is plain that this was a new church, not the first stone structure, since the first deed to Cluny of some 20 years before had granted 'the church of St Pancras and its appurtenances', the church mentioned in the foundation charter. Since the initial grant was about 1077 (and certainly before Domesday), it is a reasonable guess that the new church of c.1097 had taken more than ten years to build.
22. 'Chartulary (1)', *SRS*, XXXVIII, pp. 10ff.; the 'Second Charter'.
23. Hunt, *Cluny under St Hugh*, p. 174.
24. Colin Platt, *The Monastic Grange*, pp. 68–70 certainly interprets the evidence of a consolidated area of tithe-free land in this way: 'the circumstances of the foundation at Swanborough virtually guaranteed that the estate should be placed on the fringes of marginal land' (p. 10). However, the Swanborough lands were marginal only in a spatial sense, being situated at the edges of existing cultivation. They were not marginal in terms of fertility, as Platt seems to suggest. That 'nearly half of … the farm was downland, of value only for sheep' proves nothing. Sheep were perceived as 'a moving dunghill' and a higher proportion of pasture to arable would provide more fertilizing dung per cultivated acre. If anything, local evidence points to a contrary conclusion to Platt's. On Swanborough Court Farm there were 0.96 acres of downland pasture to each acre of arable in 1799 (from Adams, 51); in Kingston vill there were 1.46 acres per arable acre – in spite of the much greater population pressure to extension of arable in the village than on the Court Farm.

A plausible conclusion is that Swanborough arables were better in natural fertility than Kingston's, and *needed* less sheep dung to keep up their yields.

25. 'Chartulary (1)', *SRS*, XXXVIII, pp. 10ff.
26. Salzman suggests the unnamed place was Balmer (then Burgamere), which is today a farm on the northwestern fringe of Kingston parish. See 'Chartulary (2)', *SRS*, XL, Introduction, p. xix. The account of the first deed is based on Salzman's summary.
27. 'Chartulary (1)', *SRS*, XXXVIII, p. 4.
28. *Domesday Book, vol. 2, Sussex*, ed. J. Morris (Chichester, 1976), p. 12,7.
29. It is mostly agreed that Domesday 'ploughs' are a safer guide to arable areas than Domesday 'hides'. (M. Postan, *Medieval Economy*) The Domesday hide was a Geldhide – or a device for tax assessment. It differs from the 'field-hide', which was by custom an area made up of four yardlands. Note, however, that in Niworde, the Domesday Geldhide seems to have corresponded quite closely to the field hide.
30. Colin Platt, *The Monastic Grange*, for an analysis of the conditions for grange farming sought by the Cistercians.
31 For an account of the eleventh-century structure, see Platt, *The Monastic Grange*, pp. 20ff.
32. On the 16 yardlands of Swanborough Court Farm, see *The Book of John Rowe*, p. 140. Precisely how these 16 yardlands relate to the '2 ploughs' of the original deed – and later of Domesday – is unclear. Postan argues that a Domesday ploughland amounted to a hide, but that does not seem to fit local facts in Swanborough.
33. 'Chartulary (1)', *SRS*, XXXVIII, p. 12, the charter of William, the second founder.
34. This follows from the dating of the charters by Salzman.
35. *Domesday Book, Sussex*, p. 12,3.
36. 'Chartulary (1)', *SRS*, XXXVIII, pp. 35/6.
37. Ibid.
38. For William, son of Godwin, see ibid., p. 31. Salzman dated this gift 1145, but it was almost certainly earlier. The gift of three hides is recorded on p. 29.
39. 'Chartulary (1)', p. 21. This first appears in a charter described as 'the general charter of William the second founder'. This would place it at about 1095 or so. There are, however, problems about the dating, since if it is correct – and if the charter is in fact of the second earl, it must antedate the grants of '3 hides in Kingston' of the third earl. In this case the quotation in the text would underestimate the hidage of Swanborough in Kingston. This sequencing is in fact improbable: the words quoted in the text are repeated in later de Warenne charters – especially in 1140 (p. 29) and much later in 1331 (p. 29). In neither of these later charters is an adjustment made for a putative additional three hides. It must be assumed that the three hides are included in the passage quoted in the text and that there is an error in the ascription of the charter in which it first appears to the second earl (possible because the chartulary was copied in 1440), or a mistaken date applied to the three Kingston hides (less likely).
40. *Seneschaucie*, p. 91. So that there was as much land for desmesne as the lord could obtain labour to cultivate.
41. From 'Ceo est Hosbanderie' in *Walter of Henley*, p. 63.
42. 'Chartulary (1)', *SRS*, XXXVIII, p. 152.
43. Ibid., p. 134.
44. 'Chartulary (2)', *SRS*, XL, p. 50.

45. Ibid.
46. Ibid., p. 51.
47. PRO Cal. Inq. p.m., I, 711, translated in 'Records of the Barony and Honour of the Rape of Lewes', *SRS*, XIV.
48. Ibid.
49. Ibid.
50. See L. F. Salzman; 'The property of the Earl of Arundel, 1397', *SAC*, XCI, p. 32 (1957).
51. Ibid. See *Calendar of Patent Rolls, Richard II, 1396–99*, pp. 209, 220.
52. T. H. Noyes, 'Roll of a subsidy levied 13 Henry IV, 1411–12', *SAC*, X, pp. 129ff.
53. 'Chartulary (1)', *SRS*, XXXVIII, 'I, Earl William de Warenne had granted and given to the church of Kingestone one acre of land which Pater the Sheriff gave there for making of a church.' This makes it appear that the church was a comparatively new foundation – and is consistent with the interpretation that the single church in Niworde mentioned in Domesday, was the church of Iford.
54. See 'Chartulary of Chichester Cathedral', *SRS*, XLVI.
55. It may seem that there is little doubt that the de Warennes held Kingston manor directly from the post-Norman Conquest settlement until the family ran out of a male line. This, I believe, was the case. However, apart from some of the complexities noted later, there are two possible reasons for questioning the simple view. One is that there is no subsidy levied on de Warenne's moveable goods in Kingston in 1296, 1327 and 1332 ('Sussex subsidies', *SRS*, X, pp. 48, 168, 282), nor is the manor of Kingston mentioned in the subsidy rolls. On the other hand, in 1296 the 'Comit' Warrenn' was taxed in 'Westute' (for Houndean Manor); in 1327 the 'Manerie de Hundeden' was taxed and de Warennes were taxed for 'Manerie de Northese' and 'Rademelde'; in 1332 de Warenne was again taxed for these two manors (though not for Houndean). Does this indicate there was no manor of Kingston held by them? Not necessarily. For one thing, the subsidy rolls are hardly consistent in the manorial descriptions (Houndean, though mentioned in 1296 and 1327 is not specified in 1332); for another, the desmesnes of Kingston Manor were probably leased out (as seems to have been the case in Houndean in 1332 where Wilmo de Achescombes's tax rose significantly from 1327, the manor is no longer mentioned as it had been in 1327, and de Warenne is not taxed for it) in which case the lessor would have been liable for the subsidy as the owner of 'moveable goods'. The second problem about Kingston Manor is raised in the *Victoria County History* (*VCH*, vol VII, pp. 51ff.). There are two indications of a manor of Kingston held by the *Prior of Lewes*, in 1316 (in 'Feud, Aids V, 135) and at the dissolution when priory lands passed to the king ('Sussex Feet of Fines', *SRS*, XX, no. 426 – note Horsfield has a similar interpretation, *History of the County of Sussex*, pp. 138ff). I am not convinced these refer to the manor of Kingston or that there is any need to postulate a 'second manor' – as the *VCH* for Sussex does. I suspect that the references to the *prior*'s manor in Kingston are really references to Swanborough yardlands in the village and that as commutation of villeins had gone a long way by 1316, the clerks describe these as a separate holding to the grange itself. Note that in 1331, (namely after the reference in 1316), the de Warenne confirmation of grants to the priory ('Chartulary (1) …', *SRS*, XXXVIII, p. 69), mentions the manor of Swanborough (for the first time), but no manor of Kingston. I do not believe, therefore, that there was 'a second manor'.

56. See note 54 above.
57. 'Chartulary (2) ...', *SRS*, XL, pp. 42, 43, 64, 70.
58. 'Testa. de Nevil', quoted by J. Cooper, 'The hundred of Swanborough', *SAC*, XXIX, p. 143.
59. S. Harvey, 'The knight and the knight's fee in England', *Past and Present*, no. 49, November 1970.
60. Wiston Arch. 1593.
61. Wiston Arch. 1904.
62. *Book of John Rowe*, p. 195.
63. Oddly enough, under the manor of Portslade, although Portslade is many miles west of Kingston along the south coast. In the early years of James I, the lord of Portslade claimed that he held these lands as a knight's fee. Accordingly, they are entered in the survey of his Manor (*Book of John Rowe*, p. 206), and ascribed to Thomas Michell. The entry recognizes that there were feudal dues to the Manor of Kingston ('et rato-abile auxil' iiij.s Manerium de Kingston'). There is record of a quitclaim in return for £4 from Abraham Edwardes (who was lord of Portslade) to John Alchome, who inherited the land (1630), in respect of all tenure by knights service heriots and suits of court to the Manor of Portslade. See Wiston Archive, no. 1904. The link with Portslade may have originated through the de la Hyde family from whom the knight's fee took its name. In 1332, 'a Simon de la Hyde owned "moveables" in Kingston (and probably land too); a person of the same name was taxed in Portslade too.' 'Sussex subsidies', *SRS*, X, pp. 283, 288. It is of some relevance perhaps that the entry in the Portslade survey specifies one-fifth of a knight's fee (only part of the total perhaps?) and also speaks of the lands as having been held by de la Hyde – not just *called* Hyde (as in other references). The quitclaim demonstrates that the Court of the Barony had accepted the Portslade claim.
64. *Book of John Rowe*, pp. 189, 192.
65. Mawer and Stenton, *The place names of Sussex*, Part II, p. 322.
66. 'Record of the Barony ... of Lewes', *SRS*, XLIV.
67. Ibid., p. 74.
68. John Gardner, *The life and times of Chaucer* (London: Paladin, 1979).
69. See note 64 above.
70. Ibid.

Chapter 4: Medieval Glimpses

1. This is based on inference from the lists of 'villani' of the Prior of Lewes in the subsidy roll for 1332. 'Sussex subsidies', *SRS*, X, p. 282.
2. From an Inquisition Post Mortem. PRO Cal. Inq. p.m. I, 813, quoted in 'Records of the Barony and Honour of the Rape of Lewes', *SRS*, XLIV, pp 69–70. The Inquisition is for 1271.
3. The following is drawn from 'Records of the Barony', *SRS*, XLIV, pp. 12, 30. Snelling is listed in the Subsidy of 1297 for Kingston – see 'Sussex subsidies', *SRS*, X, p. 48.
4. 'Records of the Barony', p. 72.
5. A. E. Wilson; 'Farming in Sussex in the Middle Ages', *SAC*, XCVII (1959), p. 106.
6. William Hudson, 'On a series of rolls of the Manor of Wiston', *SAC*, LIII (1910), pp. 149–55.

7. See M. M. Postan, *The Medieval Economy*, pp. 139–40 for a discussion of the weight of such feudal incidents.
8. Ibid., pp. 79, 139.
9. Ibid., p. 264.
10. See 'Records of the Barony', p. 72 for le Byke's ploughing obligations.
11. From 'Records of the Barony'. The Hamsey Inquisition, p. 72.
12. For a discussion of Anglo-Saxon developments, see D. Whitelock, *The Beginnings of English Society*, Pelican History, vol. 2, pp. 115ff. On later developments, see D. M. Stenton, *English Society in the Early Middle Ages*, Pelican History, vol. 3, pp. 160ff.
13. See *Walter of Henley*, pp. 61–3.
14. 'Chartulary (1) ...', *SRS*, XXXVIII, p. 9.
15. See, for example, M. Postan, *The Medieval Economy*, pp. 110ff.
16. See P. D. A. Harvey, 'The English inflation of 1180–1220', *Past and Present*, no. 61, November 1973.
17. The subsidy rolls for Sussex are published in 'Sussex subsidies', *SRS*, X; see pp. 48, 168, 282 for the 'vill at de Kyngeston' in 1296, 1327 and 1332.
18. Ibid., 'Introduction', where some of the vagaries of the tax in Sussex are discussed.
19. 'Chartulary (1) ...', *SRS*, XXXVIII, p. 9.
20. L. P, *Henry VIII*, vol. XI, 94, 149, 181, 237.
21. M. Postan, *The Medieval Economy*, pp. 169ff. See also E. Miller, *The Abbey and Bishopric of Ely* (Cambridge, 1951).
22. Harvey, 'English Inflation, *Past and Present*, no. 61, p. 74.
23. M. Dobb, *Studies in the Development of Capitalism* (London: Routledge, 1963).
24. 'Sussex subsidies', *SRS*, X, p. 289. The continuance of labour service at this time was not exceptional – villeinage at Wiston Manor was only partially commuted in the years after 1300. See W. Hudson, 'On a series of rolls of the Manor of Wiston', *SAC*, LIII (1910), pp. 149–55. The Wiston custumals give an unusually clear picture of the commutation process: 'ferlingers' (who held a quarter virgate) who had no week-work obligations, paid an extra amount of money rent exactly equal to the value of those 'works' priced at the daily valuations applied to those who had full uncommuted week-works.
25. 'Chartulary (1) ...', *SRS*, XXVIII, and 'Chartulary (2) ...', *SRS*, XL.
26. 'Sussex Fines II', *SRS*, VII (1908), no. 848.
27. Ibid., no. 668.
28. Ibid., no. 247.
29. 'Chartulary (2) ...', p. 35.
30. 'Sussex Fines III', *SRS*, XXIII (1916), no. 2290.
31. Ibid., nos 2702, 2709.
32. For example, a comparison of the Wiston Custumal for *c*.1300 with the subsidy rolls shows the following: (i) nearly all the freemen of Wiston Manor are listed in the subsidy; (ii) only 6 out of 19 'full villein' families were taxed in either 1296 or 1327 – most of these appear in 1327 when the tax appears to have covered more poorer families; (iii) 3 out of 5 villein families who had had their labour services commuted appear in one or other of the subsidies; (iv) more of the 'smaller' villeins or cottars were taxed in the Subsidy. Cf. W. Hudson, *SAC*, LIII, with 'Sussex subsidies ...' *SRS*, X, pp. 55, 155, 270.
33. 'Records of the Barony', *SRS*, XLIV, p. 72.

34. There is a fairly consistent pattern in thirteenth-century East Sussex custumals and extents, showing that 'virgators' were obliged to a total of 2½ days a week from 'Michaelmas to St Peter ad Vincula' (29 September to 1 August). A. E. Wilson, 'Farming in Sussex in the Middle Ages', *SAC*, XCVII (1959), p. 106.
35. Extent for Manor of Willingdon, 1296; PRO. SC. 11/675; quoted in A. E. Wilson, 'Farming in Sussex', p 110.
36. See R. H. Hilton, *The Decline of Serfdom in Medieval England* (London: Macmillan, 1969), p. 39. Also Warren O. Ault, *Open Field Farming* (London: Allen & Unwin, 1972), p 32, gives thirteenth-century wage rates for harvest time as 1d a day with food and 2d a day without.
37. From 'Records of the Barony', *SRS*, X, p. 72. These valuations are quite well in line with the estimates of a villein's gross income before payment of rent of assize made in Table 4.1 – remembering that the villein estimates in Table 4.1 suppose that a substantial amount of barley was sown, and so do not apply to wheat alone.
38. A. E. Wilson, *SAC*, XLVII, in reference to the Manor of Cakeham. Also, in the Manor of Chittyngton, *c*.1300, 'John le Wolf holds … freely 18 acres … and he renders yearly … £5.' See W. Hudson, *SAC*, LIII, p. 157.
39. 'Chartulary (2)', *SRS*, XL, pp. 42, 43, 63, 64.
40. Ibid., p. 23.
41. See Chapter 3.
42. 'Chartulary (2)', *SRS*, XL, pp. 47, 67.
43. *Rotuli Hundredorum* (Record Commission, 2 vols, 1818), II, pp. 201–19.
44. 'Chartulary (1)', *SRS*, XXXVIII, p. 41.
45. 'Sussex Fines I', *SRS*, II, p. 6, no. 22.
46. Ibid., p. 15.
47 'Sussex Fines II', *SRS*, VII, p. 52, no. 700.
48. Ibid.
49. Based on evidence from the subsidies: the de Rademelds were not taxed in Ovingdean and Hamsey, even though they had substantial holdings there at the time of the subsidies. The inference is that their lands were 'farmed out'.
50. 'Sussex Fines', *SRS*, XXIII, p. 136, no. 2140.
51. 'Chartulary (2)', *SRS*, XL, p. 8.
52. Ibid., pp. 34, 38, 105(2), 138.
53. Ibid., pp. 35, 36, 44(2), 45, 67.
54. See note 32 above.
55. There were after all 41 copyhold yardlands in Kingston in 1600 and probably about the same number in 1300. The subsidy returns for 1332 list only 18 tax-paying families. (Cf. Chapter 2 and Table 4.3).
56. 'Chartulary (2)' *SRS*, XL, p. 35.
57. The old manor house is described in the 'Survey of Hyde Manor' commissioned by Michell in 1567 (see Wiston Arch. 5205). We discuss the house in Chapter 5.
58. The de Rademeld's were almost certainly *not* freemen of Swanborough – else they would have appeared in the priory record. If so, they must by exclusion have belonged to Houndean, the only other manor with 'free' lands in Kingston.

Chapter 5: New Lords for Old

1. See, for example, M. M. Postan, *The Medieval Economy*, Chapter 2; and A. R. Myers, *England in the late Middle Ages* (London: Pelican, 1976), pp. 60–1.

2. From the levy of taxes 14, Edward III, Novarum Inquisitiones, Royal Commission, folio, 1807, quoted by W. H. Blaauw, 'On the Novae of 1340', *SAC*, 1, p. 58.
3. Using John Rowe's statement that 64 yardlands existed in Iford *c.*1600 (*Book of John Rowe*) and supposing that each accounted for 12 acres.
4. Postan, *The Medieval Economy*, pp. 136–9.
5. There are several accounts of the plagues and a good deal of debate about their effect on population; see, for example, Philip Ziegler, *The Black Death* (London: Penguin, 1969).
6. See A. R. Myers (ed.), *English historical documents*, vol. IV *(1327–1485)* (London: Eyre & Spottiswoode, 1969), pp. 993–4.
7. See *VCH* Sussex, VII, p. 70.
8. 'Sussex Fines', *SRS*, XXIII, no. 2140, p. 136.
9. See Chapter 4.
10. Weyville still held Rodmell in 1411. See T. H. Noyes, 'Roll of a subsidy levied, 13 Henry IV', *SAC*, X, pp. 129ff.
11. See Chapter 3.
12. As early as 1339, William 'Drasey' bequeathed ten acres in Kingston (together with a pasture for 25 sheep) to his daughter Lucy. This land was leased to the de Rademelds ('Sussex fines', *SRS*, XXIII, no. 1867).
13. It is clear that de Rosey held a knight's fee in Kingston (and Smithwycke, a locality that is no longer identifiable but probably lay between Ashcombe and Balmer abutting Kingston parish on the north) in 1440 when the Rape and Barony of Lewes, as part of the inheritance of the Earls de Warenne, was divided between the Duke of Norfolk and Lord Abergavenny. The knight's fee was ascribed, inter alia, to Norfolk (Chan. Inq. p.m. Hen VI no 28). The succession through Hilder and Garton is quoted in an extent for the manor of Portslade; see *Book of John Rowe*, p. 206. Garton held it in 30 Henry VIII, namely 1539; in 1494 Hilder, following de Rosey, apparently held it.
14. The de Warenne succession is discussed in L. F. Salzman, 'The property of the Earl of Arundel, 1397', *SAC*, XCI (1951), p. 32.
15. See Salzman, ibid., quoting PRO, C 145, no. 269.
16. Wiston Arch. nos 1648–1702.
17. Salzman, ibid.; *Calendar of Patent Rolls* 1396–9, pp. 209, 220 (see *VCH*); T. H. Noyes, 'Roll of a subsidy levied 13 Henry IV', *SAC*, X, pp. 129ff. At this time Thomas, Earl of Arundel and Surrey held Lewes Castle and the barony, and all the de Warenne manors, including 'Kyngiston … with Swambergh hundred'; and *VCH Sussex*, II, p. 97.
18. See *VCH Sussex*, VII, p. 67.
19. See *Book of John Rowe*, p. 195. In the list of jurors at the court the name of John de la Chambre appears 'pro terris in Kingston … voc' le Hide … feod. mil'.
20. See R. B. Dobson (ed.), *The Peasant Revolt of 1381* (London: Macmillan, 1970), p. 93.
21. J. Gardner, *The Life and Times of Chaucer*, pp. 233–4.
22. On Cade see E. F. Jacob, *The Fifteenth Century, 1933–1485* (Oxford: Clarendon Press, 1961), pp. 496–502.
23. See 'Cade's adherents in 1450', *SAC*, XVIII, p. 27.
24. Ibid. In addition to the 'men' raised by the prior, some of whom must have come from the village, the list for Swanborough hundred includes at its end the clause: 'together with many others of the hundred aforesaid'. The hundred included only Iford, Kingston and Westout.

25. The first record of Alfreys is in fact in 1296, in 'Dene' in the hundred of 'Ristondene' ('Sussex subsidies', *SRS*, X, p. 32). However, from the mid-fourteenth century onwards they appear to have been substantial landholders around East Grinstead (with smaller holdings in Worth). See 'Sussex fines III', *SRS*, XXIII, nos 2015 (1347), 2607 (1390), 2777 (1407), 2782 (1408), 2787 (1408) and 3169 (1429). In 1524 there was still an Alfrey family in East Grinstead; see 'Lay subsidy rolls 1524–5', *SRS*, LVI.
26. 'Lay subsidy rolls', *SRS*, LVI, pp. 93–4. The taxes paid are for 1524 only; the subsidy was also levied in 1525. For a fuller account of this and other Tudor taxes, see Penry Williams, *The Tudor Regime* (Oxford: Oxford University Press, 1979), Ch. 2.
27. 'Lay subsidy rolls', *SRS*, LVI, 'Introduction'. The basis was (a) a tax of one shilling in the pound of annual income from land; (b) a tax of one shilling in the pound for goods worth more than £20 and of 6d per pound for goods valued between £2 and £20; (c) a tax of 4d per persons in receipt of wages above £1 a year.
28. See Wiston Arch., no. 5205.
29. See 'Lay subsidy rolls', *SRS*, LVI, p. 94, entry for 'Iford' in Swanborough hundred.
30. Wills PCC, More Fo. 25. See L. F. Salzman, 'The last prior of Lewes', *SAC*, LXXVI, pp. 178–9.
31. See P. Bowden, 'Agricultural prices, farm profits and rents', in J. Thirsk (ed.), *The Agrarian History of England and Wales*, vol. IV, p. 865.
32. 'Sussex subsidies', *SRS*, X, entries for Hamsey.
33. Comber, *Sussex Genealogies*, 'Lewes Centre' (Cambridge: Heffer, 1933), p. 6 for Awood of Hamsey. Also 'Lay subsidy rolls', *SRS*, LVI, for Hamsey.
34. Comber, ibid., for John a Wood, 'Sussex wills II', *SRS*, XLII, p. 254 for Elizabeth Wood. Will, PCC Spert. fo. 5. Comber gives 'issue'.
35. For Eastbourne, 'Sussex wills II', *SRS*, XLII; for Willingdon, 'Sussex wills IV', *SRS*, XLV. Wills, John Howell (d.1559), ACL, vol. AV Fo. 520; Simon Howell (d.1545) ACL, vol. AI Fo 826; William Howell (d.1546) ACL, vol. AI Fo. 144b all at Eastbourne; and Richard Howell (d.1541), ACL, vol. AI, Fo. 966 at Willingdon.
36. 'Sussex subsidies', *SRS*, X. See Malling and Cliffe for 1296, Cliffe for 1327, Barcombe for 1332.
37. 'Sussex wills III', *SRS*, XLIII, for Iford. John Pecham died 1542; Will, ACL, vol AI Fo. 2.
38. Ibid., ACL, vol AI Fo 2, Kingston; Wills, ACL, AI Fo. 162; ACL, A IV Fo 3246.
39. 'Sussex P.M. Inq.' *SRS*, XIV, nos 3 and 4 (given as Chan. Inq. p.m. vol. 31, no 66; and vol. 41, no. 22). Also 'Sussex wills II', for Fletching. Wills, PCC Adeane Fo. 12; P.C.C. Porch, Fo. 2.
40. For William Adam who left money to the poor of Wilmington, see 'Sussex wills IV', *SRS*, XLV, p. 356. For John of Tarring Nevill, 'Sussex wills IV', and ACL, vol. A IV, Fo. 318; and John of Battle, 'Sussex wills I', and PJDB Book I, p. 56.
41. 'Sussex wills II', *SRS*, XLII, ACL, vol. A I Fo. 158.
42. 'Sussex wills II', for John Alkecocke (d.1558), Nicholas Awcock (d.1558), William Awcock (d.1558) and Rychhard Awcoke (d.1557), in Fletching. Refs given to wills.
43. 'Sussex wills III', *SRS*, XLIII, for Kingston, ACL, vol. A IV Fo. 88.
44. 'Sussex wills III' for Little Horsted; Wills PCC Bennet, Fo. 16 and ACL, vol. A I Fo 52. For Buxted 'Sussex wills I', PCC Maynwaryng, Fo. 4.
45. 'Sussex wills III', p. 164 for extract from John Thatcher's will.
46. L. F. Salzman, 'The Last Prior', *SAC*, LXXXVI.

47. 'Sussex wills III', pp. 8 and 60.
48. 'Sussex wills III', Laughton.
49. 'Sussex wills III', Andrew Ellis died there in 1518. PCC Ayloffe Fo. 16.
50. 'Sussex wills II', for Chiddingly and Hailsham.
51. 'Sussex wills III', for Westmeston.
52. 'Sussex wills IV', *SRS*, XLV, PCC Blamyr Fo. 16 and PCC Fetiplace Fo. 17. See Comber, *Genealogies*, p. 285 for genealogy.
53. 'Sussex wills IV', for Willingdon.
54. 'Sussex wills IV', for Thomas, PCC Dyngely Fo. 25; for John, PCC Porch, Fo. 15.
55. 'Sussex PM Inq.', *SRS*, III; no. 65 for 16 EL.
56. 'Sussex wills III' for Kingston, ACL, vol. A IV Fo 330.
57. Comber, *Sussex Genealogies*, p. 175. See 'Sussex wills I' for Barcombe.
58. Comber, pp. 175ff.
59. Comber, p. 145.
60. See *VCH Sussex*, Vol. II, pp. 66ff.
61. See L. F. Salzman, 'The Last Prior of Lewes', *SAC*, LXXVI, p. 178.
62. *LP Henry VIII*, Add. 1217.
63. Ibid., p. 17.
64. *LP Henry VIII*, vol. 9 (1), no. 42.
65. *LP Henry VIII*, vol. 9 (1), no. 632.
66. For an account of the laws of treason, see P. Williams, *Tudor Regime*, p. 375.
67. The letters are discussed by Colin Platt, *The Monastic Grange in Medieval England*, pp. 127ff.
68. *LP Henry VIII*, vol. 2, no. 583.
69. *LP Henry VIII*, vol. 2, no. 214.
70. See, for example, Eric Kerridge, *Agrarian Problems in the Sixteenth Century and After* (London: George Allen & Unwin, 1969), p. 86; and reference to A. Savine, *English Monasteries on the Eve of the Dissolution* (Oxford, 1909), p. 54.
71. See Platt, *Monastic Grange*, p. 128 and *LP Henry VIII*, vol. 2, nos 373, 448, 583 for the following.
72. *LP Henry VIII*, vol. 13 (1), no. 384.
73. *LP Henry VIII*, vol. 13 (1), no. 574.
74. Letter from Polsted to Cromwell, *LP Henry VIII*, vol. 13 (1) no. 293.
75. *LP Henry VIII*, vol. 16, no. 305.
76. 'Sussex wills III', *SRS*, XLIII, p. 146; PCC Coode Fo. 6.
77. *LP Henry VIII*; vol. 13 (1), no. 734.
78. Ibid. no. 1059.
79. *LP Henry VIII*, vol. 16, no. 305.
80. *LP Henry VIII*, vol. 13(1), no. 554.
81. Ibid. no. 590.
82. *LP Henry VIII*, vol. 16, no. 503 (32).
83. Ibid., no. 878 (93).
84. *LP Henry VIII*, vol. 19, no. 11.
85. Wiston Arch. nos 1648–9.

Chapter 6: Yeomen and Gentry: New Ascendancies

1. Discussed in most economic history texts. See, for example, Brian Murphy, *A History of the British Economy* (London: Longman, 1973), p. 100–1.

2. For a summary, see J. D. Chambers and G. E. Mingay, *The Agricultural Revolution* (London: Batsford, 1966), Chapter 1.
3. W. G. Hoskins, 'The Rebuilding of rural England', *Past and Present*, vol. IV, 1954.
4. Murphy, *History of the British Economy*, pp. 220–1.
5. Murphy, *History of the British Economy*, pp. 177–83 summarizes the issues.
6. For an assessment of the effectiveness of such legislation and a valuable account of the condition of the poor, see Penry Williams, *The Tudor Regime* (Oxford: Clarendon Press, 1979), especially pp. 175–215.
7. Sir Thomas More, *Utopia*, Book 1.
8. Wiston Arch., nos 1714, 1715.
9. For Swanborough, see the tables on the Dorset map of 1799, ESRO, Adams Mss. 51.
10. See Chapter 5, p. 134.
11. The early post-dissolution deed for Kingston Manor (Wiston Arch. no. 1648) shows that there were 400 sheep-leazes associated with the 15 desmesne yardlands. Assuming that rights to pasturage were proportional to arable holding, which is reasonable, this would give a total of 2000 downland sheep-leazes in the parish.
12. 'Chartulary (1)', *SRS*, XXXVIII, pp. 1ff.
13. This was L. E. Salzman's view, see Chapter 3, note 26.
14. 'Sussex subsidies', *SRS*, VIII.
15. G. R. Burleigh, 'An introduction to deserted medieval villages in East Sussex', *SAC*, vol. III, pp. 45ff.
16. Ibid.
17. See *SAC*, LX, pp. 36ff.
18. Wiston Arch. no. 1648.
19. A. Norris and E. Hoskins, 'Excavations at Balsdean Chapel', *SAC*, XCI, pp. 53ff.
20. Wiston Arch. no. 5593–5.
21. Wiston Arch. no. 1648.
22. *LP Henry VIII*, vol. 16, no. 305.
23. ESRO, Adams Mss. no. 51.
24. The evidence for severalty comes from the Dorset map (ESRO, ibid.), which shows that the Duke of Dorset's claim to eight yardlands out of the 32 took the physical form of a claim to one-fourth part of each area. The linking up of 'Stuckles' – the Duke's farm – to Swanborough, where the Dorsets were manor lords – was very likely the result of de Warenne grants of Iford yardlands to the priory in much earlier times. See Chapter 3.
25. Wiston Arch. no. 1714.
26. Chapter 2.
27. Murphy, *History of the British Economy*, pp. 184ff.
28. P. Brandon, *The Sussex Landscape: The Making of the English Landscape* (London: Hodder & Staunton, 1974), p. 149, fig. 19.
29. M. Dobb, *Studies in the Development of Capitalism* (London: Routledge, 1963), p. 65.
30. R. H. Tawney, *The Agrarian Problem in the Sixteenth Century* (London, 1912).
31. 'Post-mortem Inquisitions', *SRS*, III, no. 30.
32. Ibid. See also WSRO, Add. Mss. 524, which is a court book containing records of courts of manors held by the Caryll family c.1580. Among these are the earliest manor court records for Swanborough.
33. 'Post-mortem Inquisitions', loc. cit.

34. See M. A. Lower, 'Sussex Gentry in 1588', *SAC*, 1, p. 32.
35. 'Post-mortem Inquisitions, 1485–1645', *SRS*, XIV, no. 215.
36. See *VCH Sussex*, vol. VII, p. 55.
37. Penry Williams, *Tudor Regime*, pp. 435–6.
38. Translations from Swanborough court rolls by L. S. Cole, in University of Sussex, Swanborough Boxes, SW1, from WSRO Add. Mss. 524. The ability of the manor court to give instructions to the lord of the manor is an interesting example of its legal status. Kerridge, *Agrarian Problem*, discusses a number of examples.
39. Wiston Arch. no. 1648. Kingston Manor had 50s of feudal rents attached.
40. 'Lay subsidies', *SRS*, LVI, p. 101.
41. 'Sussex wills', *SRS*, XLII, Piddinghoe. See ACL, vol. A III, Fo. 39.
42. Ibid., 'Kingston'; also ACL, vol. A III, Fo. 1636.
43. 'Post-mortem Inquisitions, 1485–1649', *SRS*, XIV, no. 306.
44. Wiston Arch. no. 1651.
45. T. H. Noyes, 'Some notices of the family of Newton', *SAC*, IX, p. 312.
46. Wiston Arch. no. 1652.
47. *The Book of John Rowe*, *SRS*, XXXIV, p. 3.
48. See *VCH Sussex*, vol. VII, pp. 51ff.
49. Above, p. 103.
50. *Book of John Rowe*, p. 195.
51. J. Comber, *Sussex Genealogies* (Lewes Centre) (Cambridge: Heffer, 1933), pp. 91–2.
52. *Book of John Rowe*, p. 195.
53. Wiston Arch. no. 1904. See also Comber, *Genealogies*, p. 92.
54. F. W. T. Attree, 'Cuckfield families: the Michells', *SAC*, LIII, pp. 107ff.
55. *Book of John Rowe*, p. 18. It appears that Lord Bergavenny demised 'a moeity of Cuckfield Park' to Michell in 1567. In Comber, *Genealogies*, p. 92, Michell is described as 'of Kingston and Cuckfield'.
56. Wiston Arch. no. 5205. On the Manor of Hyde see Margaret Thorburn, *An account of the Manor of Hyde* (Lewes, 2001), *passim*.
57. A. Rathbone, *The Surveyor* (London, 1616), quoted in Kerridge, *Agrarian Problems*, p. 17.
58. Wiston Arch. no. 5205.
59. See the Marchant Map, Wiston Arch. nos 5593–5, and the accompanying 'terrier', Wiston Arch. nos 1714 and 1715, the section on the village.
60. Wiston Arch. nos 1911–20.
61. The evidence shows independently that the house called Hyde Manor House today could *not* have had that name in 1773. The 'modern' Hyde Manor, which has its own story, was owned by William Rogers in 1773 – see Marchant's terrier (Wiston Arch. no. 1714) and the Rogers did not hold the manor at that time, although they came to do so later on. There is also architectural evidence, but it will be discussed later on.
62. Comber, *Genealogies*, p. 92.
63. For the complicated (and rather partial) history of the Alchorne succession, see Wiston Arch., nos 1904–20.
64. Wiston Arch. no. 5205.
65. See 'Post-mortem Inquisitions', *SRS*, XIV, nos 383, 384.
66. E. Straker, *Wealden Iron* (London, 1931), *passim*.
67. 'Post-mortem Inquisitions', *SRS*, XIV.

68. *The Book of John Rowe*, p. 5, under 'Houndene', shows Thomas Ersild as a freeholder of lands once owned by Bannesters.
69. See University of Sussex Swanborough Boxes, SWI, WSRO Add. Mss. 524.
70. Wiston Arch. no. 1972, suggests that two of the yardlands had been held by Budd and four by Richard Aboove before the Eversfield family bought them.
71. This is a slightly risky conclusion based on using the ascriptions of abutments to Thomas Michell's strips as a random sample of the pattern of ownership. The ascriptions are given in the Survey. Wiston Arch. no. 5205.
72. *The Book of John Rowe*, pp. 139–40. Rowe appears to have misspelt Alfreyes as 'Awfords'.
73. 'Post-mortem Inquisitions', *SRS*, III. See also W. S. Ellis, 'On the origins of some Sussex families', *SAC*, XXIV, p. 25.
74. *The Book of John Rowe*, loc. cit.
75. Ibid. Culpepper's land remained in that family's ownership in 1565. See 'Post-mortem Inquisitions', ibid. However, the Survey of Hyde (Wiston Arch., 5205) shows that two years later, in 1567, the Newtons had taken them over.
76. T. H. Noyes, 'Some notices of the family of Newton', *SAC*, IX, p. 312.
77. M. A. Lower, 'Sussex Gentry', *SAC*, I, p. 32.
78. 'Abstracts of Sussex Deeds and Documents', *SRS*, XXIX.
79. 'Lay subsidy rolls, 1524–5', *SRS*, X, for 'Balmer'.
80. See Wm. Figg, 'Tenantry customs in Sussex: the Drinker acres', *SAC*, IV, p. 20 (1851), where Elizabeth Shoesmith is shown as 'having the Drinker for ij yard wishes' in 24 Eliz.
81. Comber, *Genealogies*, p. 265.
82. Landholding patterns in table are based mainly on sources quoted for Table 2.5. (5) Shoesmith's two yardlands became Howell's later in the sixteenth century; and (8) Ade held Bishop's of Iford and Taylor's of Swanborough (*Book of John Rowe*).
83. 'Sussex subsidies', *SRS*, X, pp. 168, 282.
84. 'Lay subsidy rolls, 1524–5', *SRS*, LVI, p. 101.
85. M. A. Lower, 'Notes on old Sussex families', *SAC*, XXV, p. 101.
86. Ibid.
87. The position of Ade property located in Figure 2.4 mainly by inference from the Hyde survey of 1567, the Marchant terrier and map (from which Figure 2.4 is a tracing), and the enclosure award of 1833. The Hyde survey abutments suggest the position of Peter Towner's house and barn of 1567, adjacent to the Ade barn and close. These Towner properties, with one yardland attached later passed to the Ades and on to the Glovers. They are shown, consistently, as 'of Iford Manor' in the enclosure award. Ade's house is also given as of Iford Manor in the enclosure award. Michell's house of 1561 later passed to Ades (Wiston Arch. nos 1740–44; 1755–58).
88. 'Sussex subsidies', *SRS*, X, pp. 44, 168–73, 284, 286.
89. 'Lay subsidy rolls', *SRS*, LVI, p. 102.
90. 'Sussex wills IV', *SRS*, XLV, for 'Southease'.
91. 'Sussex wills III', *SRS*, XLIII, Kingston; ACL, vol. AIV, Fo. 277.
92. WSRO, Add. Mss. 524.
93. 'Abstract of Sussex Deeds', *SRS*, XXIX, p. 75.
94. 'Lay subsidy rolls', *SRS*, LVI, p. 102 for Rodmell. For Barnden wills in Rodmell, see 'Sussex wills IV', *SRS*, XLV, Rodmell.

95. Hyde survey, Wiston Arch. no 5205, for abutments.
96. *Book of John Rowe*, pp. 139–40.
97. Cf. Wiston Arch. no 5205 and the Marchant terrier. Adams owned the lands that became Stephen Towner's in the eighteenth century.
98. Wiston Arch. no. 1975. The Swanborough yardlands Grower owned in the seventeenth century were almost certainly Thomas Howell's in 1567. Michell's Hyde survey when compared with Marchant's terrier shows that Thomas Howell's lands of 1567 passed to Thomas Paine in 1773. A part of Paine's lands had been owned by Gower before. The Gowers married into the Howell family (Thos. Gower married Mary Howell in 1610), and this is the most likely succession of the Swanborough lands.
99. WSRO, Add. Mss. no. 524. Wiston Arch. no.5205.
100. Wiston Arch. 5205; the Hyde survey.
101. See *Book of John Rowe*, pp. 139–40.
102. Rowe describes these lands, held by 'Barrenden', as '3 yards called Pierce's, late Pickombes' (*Book of John Rowe*, pp. 139–40).
103. A search through the Wiston deeds suggests that the following refer to independent copyhold cottages: (i) Wiston Arch. no. 1991 – referred to as a 'half-cottage', probably next to the 'modern' Hyde Manor House; (ii) Wiston Arch. no. 1933/8 – a small double cottage opposite the old Hyde Manor House, namely on the south of the street; (iii) Wiston Arch. no. 1977/9 – by 1834 described as a 'toft upon which a cottage lately stood'; (iv) Wiston Arch. nos 1570–89 – a cottage that stood opposite the Ade's properties, namely on the northern corner of the street and today a public house; (v) Wiston Arch. no. 1542–68 – next door to (iv) above. This became a malthouse in the seventeenth century; and (vi) Wiston Arch. no. 4409 – the tiny cottage called Rest Harrow.
104. Richard Howell held an orchard in the street – but no arable land in 1567 (Wiston Arch. no. 5205); the tiny cottage in Wiston Arch. no. 4409, was apparently held by Picombes in the seventeenth century.
105. Wiston Arch. no. 1648.
106. In the 1658 'Rental' for Swanborough Manor (ESRO, Adams Mss. no. 46), the lands called 'Alfreyes' had three tenements attached to them. At the time, as for at least a century before, Eversfield or his inheritance held 'Peake's' as well, which also had tenements attached.
107. See Williams, *Tudor Regime*, pp. 196ff. for a review of Tudor poor laws.

Chapter 7: Engrossment: Comings and Goings at Kingston Manor

1. See Chapter 4.
2. ESRO, Adams Mss. 51; the Swanborough Map includes details of all field sizes on the desmesnes and in Stuckles Farm.
3. *VCH Sussex*, vol. VII, on Swanborough hundred.
4. R. B. Manning, *Religion and Society in Elizabethan Sussex* (Leicester, 1969), *passim*.
5. The appearance of John Vinall is a little difficult to pin down. However, his son – also John – was recorded many years later in 1639 as a witness in an Ecclesiastical Deposition Book, as 'John Vinall of Kingston-near-Lewes, yeoman' having lived in the village fifty years, and coming to it from Falmer. This, the son of the first John Vinall, was fifty-five years old at the time (namely he had

been brought to the village when he was five), and had been born in Falmer. See W. Renshaw, 'Witnesses from Ecclesiastical Deposition Books, 1580–1640', *SAC*, LVI, pp. 1ff.

6. Notice of the family in BL Harl. Mss. 144.
7. Ibid.
8. See J. Cooper, 'The vicars and parish of Cuckfield in the seventeenth century', *SAC*, XLV, pp. 1ff. Also W. S. Ellis, 'On the origins of the arms of some Sussex families', *SAC*, XXXVII, p. 37. Ellis suggests that Fynehagh of Battle Abbey in 1383 may be an ancestor. Also 'Lay subsidy rolls', *SRS*, LVI, for Wivelsfield shows a wealthy Vinall in 1524, and F. W. Attree, 'Wivelsfield', *SAC*, XXXVI, p. 38 and XXXV, p. 47 discusses the family.
9. Joseph Cooper was distressed by this. See J. Cooper 'The hundred of Swanborough', *SAC*, XXIX.
10. Wiston Arch. nos 1652–7.
11. Crane had been given seisin at 21 in 1576 (Wiston Arch. no. 1651).
12. T. H. Noyes, 'Some notices of the family of Newton', *SAC*, IX, p. 312.
13. W. S. Ellis, 'Subsidy roll, Rape of Lewes, 19 Jas. I, 1621', *SAC*, IX, p. 71.
14. *Book of John Rowe*, p. 140.
15. Wiston Arch. no. 1655.
16. Data on the general price level are from Brian Murphy, *A History of the British Economy, 1086–1740* (London: Longman, 1973), p. 225. It would be better to use local Sussex prices, of course, but these are unavailable.
17. Wiston Arch. no. 1659.
18. The term 'champion' – as in 'champion country' – derives in this case from the French *champs*. It was applied to open-field villages in post-Tudor centuries to distinguish them from villages in which enclosure had transformed the strip farming system.
19. We take some licence here. The first certain record of Vinall occupancy of house and lands comes from 1603, nine years after Dorset's purchase. See *Book of John Rowe*, p. 139.
20. At this time and later, Vinall was probably one of the largest tenant farmers in the Ouse valley and the neighbourhood of Lewes as a whole. Colin Brent has commented on his pre-eminence in 1615. See C. E. Brent, 'Rural employment and population in Sussex between 1550 and 1640', *SAC*, CXIV, p. 35.
21. *Book of John Rowe*.
22. Kingston parish register.
23. Loc. cit. That Rowe only mentions Vinall's Iford tenancies is from the context of the remark. It was not intended to give an exclusive list of Vinall's tenancies.
24. ESRO. Adams, 54.
25. *Book of John Rowe*, p. 139.
26. For data on landholding in Iford, see ibid., p. 62 on Northease Manor. Also, on Iford lands held of the manor of Withdean Cayliffe, see *SNQ*, II, 1929.
27. As Rowe, *Book of John Rowe*, p. 138, indicates, he owned a small amount of land in Barcombe.
28. Wiston Arch. no. 1659.
29. See 'Sussex marriage licences', *SRS*, I, for 1628. This was John Vinall's second marriage. The first (1612) was to Ursula Ockenden, daughter of a Telescombe gentleman.

30. Wiston Arch. no. 1660.
31. See 'Abstracts of Sussex Deeds', *SRS*, nos 615–16.
32. See Comber, *Horsham Centre*, under Eversfield. Incidentally, Sir Thomas had married into the Morley family of Glynde.
33. Wiston Arch. no. 1972 for Alfreye's. The time of sale of Peake's is less certain, but it is most likely that it followed the same pattern and was bought at the same time by Edmund Bowker. In a Houndean Manor Rental of 1825, these lands are described as Peake's, formerly Bowkers and before Eversfield's, *ESRO*, Adams 239.
34. There is some uncertainty about this. In 1613, a John Bowker, yeoman of Southover, stood surety at a wedding there. See 'Sussex marriage licences', *SRS*, I for 1613. A John Booker (an accepted alternative spelling for the family name) still lived as a landowner in Lewes in 1621, by which time Mr Edmund Bowker was one of the largest landowners in Kingston. See W. S. Ellis, 'Subsidy Roll, Rape of Lewes, 19 Jas 2, 1621', *SAC*, IX, no. 71.
35. 'Sussex marriage licences', *SRS*, I, for 1625.
36. ESRO; Adams 45 for the so-called 'composite rental' of Swanborough and Kingston manors for 1619, which is in fact a rent-roll, not a manorial document as such.
37. As far as Alfreye's is concerned, Bowker was a Swanborough freeholder on 'three tenements and 6 yards late Eversfield's in 1658' (ESRO, Adams 46), and Wiston deeds confirm their descendants held the land in 1699 (Wiston Arch. nos 1703–5; see also Wiston Arch. no. 1945).
38. On borough English and its incidence in Sussex, see G. Corner, 'On the custom of borough English', *SAC*, VI, p. 164.
39. Kingston parish register.
40. Ibid.
41. The succession cannot be proved, but is virtually certain. In 1621, after Gregory's death, John Ade was taxed for lands in Kingston; William was taxed only for 'goods', implying that he owned no arable but was a tenant farmer (see W. S. Ellis, 'Subsidy roll', deeds from Wiston Arch. nos 1609–20 and 1955).
42. ESRO, Adams 43.
43. ESRO, Adams 46.
44. Wiston Arch. no. 1740.
45. Kingston parish register.
46. ESRO, Adams 45.
47. Kingston parish register.
48. Dates of births and deaths of members of the Barnden family in the following are from the Kingston parish register.
49. See *Book of John Rowe*, loc. cit. Rowe ascribes 'Shoesmith's' to Henry Barnden in 1603, and the original three yardlands to the widow Barnden.
50. W. S. Ellis, 'Subsidy roll, 1621', *SAC*, IX.
51. ESRO, Adams 42.
52. Ibid.
53. Ibid.
54. See *Book of John Rowe*, p. 5, which records that in 1594, John Towner was a freehold tenant with 'one tenement and lands in Kingston-near-Lewes' – formerly John A. Bowers. Also ESRO Adams 239, a rental of Houndean Dorset in 1825, shows 'John Flint for a tenement and lands in Kingston, late Glovers, before Ades, before Wenhams and formerly Towners'.

55. Wiston Arch. no. 5205.
56. WSRO, Ad. Mss. no. 524.
57. *Book of John Rowe*, p. 139; W. S. Ellis, 'Subsidy roll, 1621', *SAC*, IX.
58. From Kingston parish register.
59. From Kingston parish register.
60. *Book of John Rowe*, p. 139 shows John Picombe in possession of Hudd's.
61. Kingston parish register. Only one son, Thomas, appears to have survived his father John, who died in 1656.
62. He died in 1597. See Kingston parish register.
63. Successions to: (1) *A Moore's*, Sw. Ct. Bk 1583, WSRO Add. Mss 524; ESRO, Adams 40, Sw. Ct. Bk 1642; *Book of John Rowe*, p. 139; (2) Tenement, barn and one yardland. By inference, Wiston Arch. no. 5205 suggests Thomas owned a yardland in 1568. This is confirmed by *Book of John Rowe*, p. 139. There is no reference to a Swanborough yardland fitting this description, but Wiston Arch. no. 1945–53, shows a yardland in *Gower* succession that was probably inherited from Richard Howell; (3) *Taberer's*, Wiston Arch. no. 5205 shows Wolridge in possession of the barn and tenement and, by inference, the yardlands. Then see *Book of John Rowe*, p. 139. For Harfrey's, Wiston Arch. nos 1940–3; (4) *Adams*', Adams retained possession in 1567 (see Wiston Arch. no. 5205). He was present at 1575 (see Figg, *SAC*, IV). However, by 1603, land is ascribed to Robert Howell (see *Book of John Rowe*, p. 139). John was Robert's youngest son in 1597, died in 1617 and was in turn succeeded apparently by his eldest son (see ESRO, Adams no. 46); (5) By inference. This half-yardland was held by Thomas in 1658 (ESRO, Adams no 46) and is the only Howell land that Robert might have owned in 1567, when it is known he had land (Wiston no 5205).
64. 'Sussex marriage licences', *SRS*, I, 1639, p. 241.
65. See pp. 194–5. Also Wiston Arch. no. 4409, which mentions a Thomas Picombe of Kingston who was a tailor.
66. Wiston Arch. no. 1741 for William Browne of 1657–58. Also 'Sussex marriage licences', *SRS*, I, 1632, p. 200.
67. Kingston parish register, 1565, for the first reference to the family.
68. Dates refer to entries in 'Sussex marriage licences', *SRS*, I.
69. These data were compiled from the Kingston parish register.

Chapter 8: Hubris and the Vinalls: A Seventeenth-Century Interlude

1. An invaluable history of Sussex for the period, is A. Fletcher, *A County Community in Peace and War* (London: Longman, 1975).
2. E. Sawyer, 'Proceedings of the Committee of Plundered Ministries relating to Sussex', *SAC*, XXX.
3. Ibid.
4. British Library, Add. MS. 5698: the Burrell Mss.
5. See Chapter 3. Kingston church, along with Iford church, had been a de Warenne gift to the priory, and so had all de Warenne 'tithes of Kingston'. In addition, de Warenne had granted all the tithes of Hugh, son of Golde, to the priory. These were attached to the lands of Iford Manor in Kingston, which were not held directly by de Warenne. The vicarage directly held only a small portion of Kingston tithes.

In 1180, Seffrid II, Bishop of Chichester, confirmed these impropriations, noting exceptions: 'And in Kingston, saving to the vicar a messuage to the same church belonging with two acres of land ... and all obventions to the altar, except of the land of de Warren, and 12 semes of corn yearly to be received out of the barn of the monks.' See 'Chartulary of Chichester Cathedral', *SRS*, XLVI.

6. See Wiston Arch. no. 1774 for a transaction of 1559 in which the tithes and advowson passed to the Sackvilles, having been held by Anne of Cleves. Subsequently, the tithes were divided into a quarter part, which passed to the Blunt family (Wiston Arch. no. 1774) and eventually was divided between the Rogers and Maitlands in the nineteenth century; and three-quarters, held by the Knight family at that time (Wiston Arch. no. 4472).
7. See A. Fletcher, *County Community*, Chapters 13 and 14.
8. See J. H. Cooper, 'A religious census of Sussex in 1676', *SAC*, XLV, p. 142. Iford had 64 Conformists and 9 Nonconformists at the time.
9. This is an inference. The Wenhams succeeded to lands that Thomas Gower, who died in 1642, had held. See 'Calendar of wills and administrations'; Archives Court of Lewes in the Bishopric of Chichester, 'Henry VIII–Commonwealth', *British Record Society*, vol. 24, 1901.
10. Wiston Arch. nos 1945–53. These deeds cite only a 'barn and yardland'. The tenement later passed into separate ownership and was eventually pulled down, probably to make an access to the Rogers' house – see later. Wiston Arch. nos 1977–79.
11. Fletcher, *County Community*, pp. 120–2.
12. P. Lucas, 'Some notes on the early Sussex Quaker registers', *SAC*, LV, pp. 74ff., see in particular p. 90.
13. 'Churchwardens presentments', *SRS*, L, Part II.
14. William Figg, 'Sufferings of the Quakers in Lewes', *SAC*, XVI, p. 80.
15. See, for example, Christopher Hill, *Reformation to Industrial Revolution* (London: Penguin, 1967), pp. 150–1; also J. D. Chambers and G. E. Mingay, *The Agricultural Revolution* (London: Batsford, 1966), p. 4.
16. Hill, loc. cit.
17. See Joan Thirsk (ed.), *The Agrarian History of England and Wales* (Cambridge: Cambridge University Press, 1967), pp. 177–8.
18. This is a rough estimate based on the following: (i) Strips of 1773 are allocated as follows: Rogers to Bowker, Norton to Alchorne, Cronch to Vinall, Glover to Ade. (ii) The strip ownership in each furlong was then adjusted in the case of Rogers (Bowker) and Cronch (Vinall), to allow for the small lands acquired by each over and above the 1635 holdings of Bowker and Vinall.
19. Kingston parish register.
20. Wiston Arch. no. 1663.
21. ESRO Adams Mss. no. 46.
22. Kingston parish register.
23. Ibid.
24. See Kingston parish register. Also Wiston Arch. no 1663 for an account of the marriage settlement.
25. Fletcher, *County Community*, p. 352.
26. Ibid. p. 9.
27. Wiston Arch. no. 1663.

28. Coffin inscriptions in Burre Mss. British Library Add. Mss 5698.
29. Fletcher, *County Community*, p. 123.
30. Extract Kingston parish register by L. S. Cole. There is some controversy about whether William in fact married Anne Farrington, but this and Joseph Cooper's evidence on the buried tombstones in Kingston (see below) seem conclusive.
31. Joseph Cooper, 'The hundred of Swanborough', *SAC*, XXIX, records the inscription, 'Anne Vinall wife of William died in 1667'. It is found in the Burrell Mss. There is no record of Anne's death in the parish register but this is easily explained by the substantial gaps in it. In the nineteenth century Joseph Cooper found the church caretaker using sections of the old register to kindle the heating system. He rescued most of it but substantial damage was done.
32. Wiston Arch. no. 1666.
33. ESRO, Adams Mss. no. 46.
34. ESRO, Adams Mss. no. 43, shows that William's wife Mabilla and their infant son (also William) were admitted in 1680. See later.
35. Wiston Arch. no. 1538. For the ascription to Hyde Manor, see Hyde Manor 'Court Baron' of 1785, which, however, mistakenly leaves out Vynall's ownership. Wiston Arch. no. 5205. The so-called court baron records the Barnden ownership.
36. Wiston Arch.
37. Copy of the rent roll by L. S. Cole, University of Sussex, Swanborough Boxes, Sw.2.
38. Ibid. for 1677 shows Thomas Rogers as farmer of part of the desmesnes.
39. Joseph Cooper, 'hundred of Swanborough'. The gravestone beneath the floor of Kingston church is inscribed 'Captain William Vinall'.
40. The deficiencies in the Kingston parish register make some guesswork unavoidable. It is clear that the Vinalls had these daughters (see Wiston Arch. for Marion and Martha; Mabilla was buried in the same grave as William in the church aisle). It is not certain that these were the first three children, though extremely likely.
41. Wiston Arch. no. 1666.
42. Wiston Arch. no. 1668.
43. Wiston Arch. no. 1955.
44. Wiston Arch. no. 1673.
45. Wiston Arch. no. 1668–70.
46. Wiston Arch. no. 1958.
47. These are the amounts Francis Zouch had to pay Simmonds and Heaver to release the property (Wiston Arch. no. 1664). It is unclear how these additional debts were incurred. It could be that Simmonds and Heaver had been assigned other mortgages that William had taken out, like the loan of £315 from Kenward, but this seems improbable.
48. Wiston Arch. no. 1690.
49. Wiston Arch. no. 1664.
50. See Comber, *Genealogies*, 'Lewes Centre', p. 101.
51. *VCH Sussex*, VII, p. 256, and abstracts of title in SAS BRI 166 and 145. I am much indebted to John Farrant for these references.
52. W. S. Ellis, 'Subsidy roll, Rape of Lewes, 1621, *SAC*, IX, p. 75n.
53. John Alchorne who bought the manor in 1630 had come from Buxted (Wiston Arch. no. 1904).

54. Wiston Arch. no. 1910.
55. Wiston Arch. no. 1922.
56. 'Sussex marriage licences', *SRS*, I, p. 150.
57. ESRO, Adams Mss. no. 42.
58. Wiston Arch. no. 1703.
59. Wiston Arch. no. 1925.
60. See 'Sussex deeds in private hands', *SAC*, LXIV, p. 72.
61. Dorset's rent roll for 1713 shows Thomas Rogers of Kingston as occupier; in 1704–5 Titchbourne was still in possession. ESRO, U269/A133/2/pp. 1–20; Adams Mss. and U269/A133/4 pp. 1–17.
62. ESRO Adams Mss. no. 46.
63. L. S. Cole's notes in University of Sussex, Swanborough Boxes, SW2.
64. Ibid.
65. ESRO; Adams Mss. U269/A133/2/pp. 1–20.
66. ESRO; Adams Mss. U269/A133/3/pp.1–23.
67. ESRO; Adams Mss. no. 46; Wiston Arch. no. 1955.
68. ESRO; Adams Mss. no. 43.
69. ESRO; Adams Mss. no. 43.
70. Wiston Arch. no. 1609.
71. Iford Court Book, copied by L. S. Cole, Wiston Arch. no. 1955–68.
72. Kingston parish register.
73. Wiston Arch. no. 1724.
74. Wiston Arch. no. 1887. The exact date of purchase is uncertain. L. S. Cole's notes suggest it was in the 1690s and the continuance of the Towner family in Kingston after their sale to the Ades in 1699 supports the idea that they purchased Adams' either before or at the same time as they sold their old lands.
75. ESRO, Adams Mss. no. 42.
76. ESRO, Adams Mss. no. 43.
77. ESRO, Adams Mss. no. 46.
78. ESRO, Adams Mss. no. 43, and L. S. Cole's transcription from Iford Court Book, University of Sussex, Swanborough Boxes, SW15.
79. ESRO, Adams Mss. no. 43.
80. Kingston parish register.
81. Wiston Arch. no. 1958.
82. ESRO, Adams Mss. no. 46.
83. From University of Sussex, Swanborough Boxes: from Swanborough Court Rolls.
84. ESRO, Adams Mss. no. 43.
85. Ibid.
86. University of Sussex, Swanborough Boxes: from Swanborough Court Rolls.
87. Wiston Arch., nos 1940–3.
88. In 1700 Ade lands were in fact divided between two branches of the family. However, since this was quite clearly a temporary and special situation (see earlier in the chapter), it is no great distortion to group them together.
89. John Walker held a tithe-paying cottage in the village in 1654 or so (Kingston parish register).
90. For example, when Thomas Rogers bought Alfreye's from John Mackerill and his wife Mary (who was born Bowker), it was occupied by Henry Smether, a tenant farmer (Wiston Arch. no. 1703).

91. Kingston parish register.
92. From Iford Court Book, extracts by L. S. Cole, University of Sussex, Swanborough Boxes.
93. Kingston parish register.
94. Bob Copper, grandson of a nineteenth-century farm foreman in Rottingdean village, has given a splendid account of his childhood and youth.
95. Kingston parish register.
96. Wiston Arch. no. 4409.
97. Ibid.
98. Wiston Arch. no. 1538.
99. Kingston parish register.
100. Wiston Arch. nos 1542–53.
101. 'Sussex marriage licences', *SRS*, I.
102. Kingston parish register.

Chapter 9: The Rogers in Kingston: The First Phase

1. Wiston Arch. no. 1703.
2. By inference, Henry took his MA at Oxford in 1595. See W. Renshaw, 'Some Clergy of the Archdeaconry of Lewes, *SAC*, LV, p. 261.
3. See Hasted (ed.), *History of the County of Kent*, vol. VII, p. 134, in *Classical County History Series*, 1972, EP Publishing Ltd/Kent County Library.
4. See R. B. Manning, *Religion and society in Elizabethan Sussex*, *passim*.
5. Renshaw, loc. cit.
6. *SAC*, LV, p. 261.
7. *SAC*, IX, p. 364.
8. Renshaw, *SAC*, LV.
9. 'Sussex marriage licences', *SRS*, I.
10. Renshaw, *SAC*, LV.
11. *SRS*, XIX, p. 241; *SRS*, XX, p. 461.
12. See above, Chapter 6, on enclosure in Iford.
13. From L. S. Coles transcripts, University of Sussex, Swanborough boxes, SWZ.
14. J. Comber, *Sussex Genealogies*, 'Lewes Centre' (Cambridge: Heffer, 1933), p. 219.
15. ESRO; Adams Mss. no. 43.
16. ESRO, Adams Mss. U269/A133–2, shows Thomas Rogers as sole tenant in 1698, paying a rent of £180.0.0. Since other rents had not risen since 1677, the increased payment probably indicates a substantial increase in the size of his tenancy.
17. Kingston gravestone evidence.
18. 'Sussex marriage licences', *SRS*, VI.
19. Iford gravestone.
20. Iford gravestone.
21. The two parishes were brought under a single vicar on Thomas Rogers's death in 1666.
22. Wiston Arch. nos 1859 and 1945.
23. Wiston Arch. no. 1859.
24. Wiston Arch. no. 1955.
25. The tenement called 'Bailey's before Howell's' was plainly among the third Thomas Rogers's first purchases in Kingston (Wiston Arch. no. 1945). It was shown as the

main Rogers house in Kingston in the Marchant terrier of 1773 (Wiston Arch. no. 5649) when William Rogers owned it. The Kingston Manor rental of 1779 confirms that this house was 'Bayley's before Howell's' (Wiston Arch. no. 5210). Willard and Blaker, who inherited from William Rogers, owned it in 1779.

26. See Wiston Arch. no. 5210, Rental of Kingston Manor 1779. Here the house was owned in moeities by Willard and Blacker and had 20 acres attached to it.
27. I am indebted to the owner, the late Mr Andrew Thorburn, for his knowledgeable help in 'interpreting' the house.
28. Wiston Arch. no. 1867 gives the genealogy on which this is based, but contains no dates. Dates from Kingston parish register.
29. Kingston graveyard evidence.
30. Wiston Arch. no. 1867.
31. Wiston Arch. nos 1925–31 indicate that he was in occupancy on a substantial part of Peake's in 1718.
32. Wiston Arch. nos 1925–31.
33. ESRO, Adams Mss. no. 25, A133/3.
34. ESRO, Adams Mss. no. 25 A 133/4.
35. ESRO, Adams Mss. no. 25 A 133/2.
36. Wiston Arch. no. 1930.
37. Copy of court roll in Wiston Arch. no. 1946.
38. Ibid.
39. For the various elements in the exchange, see Wiston Arch. nos 1702, 1710–11, 1706–9, 1623–6, 1940–3.
40. Wiston Arch. no. 1708.
41. Wiston Arch. no. 1931.
42. Wiston Arch. nos 1940–53.
43. Wiston Arch. nos 1945–53.
44. Wiston Arch. no. 1973–4.
45. Kingston graveyard.
46. Wiston Arch. no. 1931.
47. Ibid.
48. Wiston Arch. no. 1961.
49. For example Wiston Arch. no. 1719.
50. Wiston Arch. no. 1676.
51. See Wiston Arch. nos 1703–23 for the succession and Charles Zouch's transactions of 1735. On Martha Zouch's tenancy, see ESRO, Adams Mss U 269/A 133/2.
52. The Marchant terrier of 1773 indicates that the older sections of the building described in the Hyde survey of 1567 had disappeared (Wiston Arch. no. 5649).
53. Wiston Arch. no. 1859.
54. Admissions of a second and third Nicholas Bodle are found in the Swanborough Manor court books for 1722 and 1723.
55. Wiston Arch. no. 1973–4.
56. Transcriptions from Iford Manor Court Books by L. S. Cole, University of Sussex, Swanborough Boxes, SW15.
57. For example, J. D. Chambers and G. E. Mingay, *The Agricultural Revolution, 1750–1880* (London: Batsford, 1966), pp. 41ff.
58. ESRO Adams Mss. no. 20.
59. Ibid.

60. Wiston Arch. no. 1609–19.
61. Wiston Arch. no. 1612 shows her married to him in 1759.
62. Wiston Arch. no. 1962.
63. ESRO, Adams Mss. no. 20.
64. Wiston Arch. no. 5594–5.
65. Wiston Arch. nos 4417–21.
66. Wiston Arch. nos 1555–6.
67. Kingston parish register.
68. Kingston parish register and Wiston Arch. no. 1743.
69. Wiston Arch. no. 1570.
70. Wiston Arch. no. 1593.
71. T. W. Horsfield, *History and Antiquity of the County of Sussex* (2 vols, Lewes, 1835), I, p. 27.
72. Wiston Arch. nos 1933–8 and Marchant terrier 1773 Wiston Arch. no. 5594–5.
73. The list of 'tithe paying cottages' in the Kingston parish register shows a James Read as owning one in 1651–54.
74. Kingston parish register.
75. Wiston Arch. nos 1933–8.
76. They still held it jointly in 1773 (Wiston Arch. no. 5584–5).
77. Kingston parish register.
78. Land tax assessment for 1780 shows an Edward Pollard occupying about four acres owned by John Penticost. This acreage is more likely to have been associated with the Picombe than the Read cottage, which Penticost also owned at this time.
79. Data on families from Kingston parish register.
80. Kingston parish register. All other families can be accounted for as cottagers or wage-workers. It is conceivable that there were some very small tenancies.
81. Wiston Arch. no. 1604.
82. Wiston Arch. nos 1713–15.
83. Wiston Arch. no. 1605.
84. *Book of John Rowe*.
85. Wiston Arch. nos 1713–15.
86. Wiston Arch. nos 1710–11.
87. Wiston Arch. nos 1801–9.
88. Kingston parish register.
89. Wiston Arch. no. 1697.
90. Daniel Defoe, *A Tour Through England and Wales*, quoted by J. D. Chambers and G. E. Mingay, *The Agricultural Revolution, 1750–1880*, p. 19.
91. Wiston Arch. nos 5650–1.
92. Wiston Arch. no. 1605.
93. Ibid.
94. Wiston Arch. no. 1723.
95. The leases of Kingston Manor for 1779 describe it as having been in Ridge's occupancy up to that date (Wiston Arch. no. 1844).
96. Wiston Arch. nos 1844–7.

Chapter 10: The Rogers: Culmination and the Transformation of Kingston

1. For example, J. D. Chambers and G. E. Mingay, *The Agricultural Revolution 1750–1880* contains a fairly comprehensive bibliography.
2. Ibid., Chapter 4.
3. Ibid., p. 83.
4. See W. E. Tate, *The English Village Community and the Enclosure Moments* (London: Gollancz, 1967).
5. J. L. and B. Hammond's *The Village Labourer* perhaps remains the most influential text on destitution caused by enclosure.
6. See, for example, Arthur Young, *Political Arithmetic* (1774).
7. Peter Brandon, *The Sussex Landscape* (London: Hodder & Stoughton, 1974), p. 147.
8. By the eighteenth century, Iford Manor was not only held in moieties, but each moiety was divided, as a manorial holding, between a number of 'lords', among them Thomas Rogers II (see *VCH Sussex*, vol. VII).
9. Arthur Young, *A General View of the Agriculture of the County of Sussex* (London: Sherwood, Neely & Jones, 1813).
10. Ibid., pp. 20ff.
11. Ibid., p. 56.
12. Ibid., p. 66.
13. Ibid., p. 67.
14. Ibid., pp. 76–7.
15. Ibid., p. 74.
16. Wiston Arch. no. 1867 includes William's will.
17. Ibid., for the marriage to Elizabeth Attree.
18. Kingston parish register.
19. Wiston Arch. no. 5650.
20. ESRO, LTA, 1780 shows Thomas IV as occupier on all Dorset's Kingston lands.
21. SAS, BRI, 58, Brighton-Lewes.
22. There is no manorial record of this or, oddly, any tithe deeds. But there can be no doubt about the purchase. See the conditional surrender in Wiston Arch. nos 1596–8.
23. ESRO, LTA, 1780 shows Thos. Rogers Jnr as owner.
24. Wiston Arch. nos 1959–67 and Patcham graveyard.
25. Wiston Arch. nos 1959–67.
26. Wiston Arch. no. 5210, New Rental for Kingston Manor 1779. Also Wiston Arch. nos 1959–67.
27. Wiston Arch. nos 1959–67.
28. Wiston Arch. nos 1862–7.
29. Wiston Arch. nos1951–2.
30. Wiston Arch. nos 1940–3, 1623–6.
31. *SAC*, XXXIX, p. 132
32. Inference from ESRO, LTA 1782.
33. Wiston Arch. nos 1911–20.
34. Wiston Arch. nos 1911–20.
35. Wiston Arch. no. 5205.

36. Wiston Arch. nos 1897, 1633–4 for examples.
37. Kingston parish register and gravestone evidence.
38. Kingston graveyard.
39. ESRO, land tax assessments 1786–1832.
40. Wiston Arch. nos 1609–19, 1728, 1964.
41. Wiston Arch. no. 1844.
42. Arthur Young, *General View*, pp. 439–40.
43. Wiston Arch., no. 1561.
44. Wiston Arch. nos 4410–15.
45. Wiston Arch. nos 1515–16.
46. Wiston Arch. no. 1577.
47. ESRO, LTA, 1783. Edward Pollard gave up his lease of the three to four acres to Penticost.
48. Wiston Arch. nos 1777–87; ESRO, LTA, 1780 onwards.
49. ESRO, LTA, 1780 onwards.
50. *Dictionary of National Biography* (London, 1908), vol. v., p. 761.
51. Kingston parish register.
52. Kingston parish register.
53. The deeds to Paine's Farm are obscure, but ESRO (LTA 1780) shows Thomas Rogers Jr as proprietor of lands that were almost certainly John Paine's before.
54. From data in ESRO, *LTA*, 1780, 1785, 1798.
55. ESRO, Land Tax assessments for Iford.
56. Wiston Arch. no. 1981.
57. Wiston Arch. no. 1977–9.
58. Wiston Arch. nos 1820–8, 1878–85.
59. Wiston Arch. nos 1628–32, 1832–41.
60. Wiston Arch. no. 5120, Kingston Manor Court Book, 1790; also Wiston Arch. no. 1983–93.
61. Wiston Arch. no. 1570–89.
62. Wiston Arch. no. 1586–7.
63. Kingston parish register.
64. Wiston Arch. no. 4409.
65. Wiston Arch. nos 1542–68.

Chapter 11: The Nineteenth-Century Village

1. For a comprehensive account, see Pamela Horn, *The Ravel Poor* (London: Hutchinson Social History of England, 1980).
2. Wiston Arch. no. 1965.
3. Wiston Arch. no. 1738.
4. On these rearrangements, see Wiston Arch. no. 1967.
5. See ESRO XA 24/1; Adams Mss, Wiston Arch. 1617.
6. Wiston Arch. nos 1832, 1619.
7. Wiston Arch. nos 1846, 1847.
8. Wiston Arch. nos 1593, 1591.
9. Kingston parish registers.
10. Hodson family papers include James Hodson's account book.
11. Wiston Arch. nos 1897–1900.

12. Wiston Arch. nos 1591–1600.
13. When Kingston Manor was sold in 1832, it fetched £17,020. See Wiston Arch. no. 1755.
14. Supposing family earnings were about £45 a year and that Thomas Rogers V provided employment for 25 of the 40 labourers in the village (Census 1831, ESRO, PAR. 408/11/1).
15. Chambers and Mingay, *Agricultural Revolution*, p. 83; also Pamela Horn, *The Ravel Poor*.
16. Wiston Arch. nos 1848–9. In the mortgage documents and in his memorial in the churchyard he is called Thomas Rogers of Southover.
17. Wiston Arch. no. 1593.
18. Wiston Arch. no. 1592.
19. Wiston Arch. no. 1635.
20. Wiston Arch. nos 1992, 1983–9.
21. ESRO, LTA, 1825–31.
22. Wiston Arch. nos 1887–96.
23. ESRO, LTA, 1831.
24. ESRO, Enclosure award for Iford and Kingston parishes, 1831.
25. Wiston Arch. no. 1763.
26. Chambers and Mingay, *Agricultural Revolution*, Chapter 4.
27. M. A. Lower, 'The descent of Wiston', *SAC*, V.
28. See the WSRO 'Catalogue of the Wiston Archive'.
29. Wiston Arch. no. 1759.
30. Wiston Arch. no. 1757.
31. See pencilled notes on the Maitland 'pedigree' in Wiston Arch. no. 1758.
32. Wiston Arch. no. 1619.
33. Wiston Arch. no. 1920.
34. Wiston Arch. no. 1977.
35. Wiston Arch. no. 4435.
36. Wiston Arch. no. 1802.
37. ESRO, LTA, 1780–7.
38. Wiston Arch. no. 1804.
39. Wiston Arch. nos 1805–7.
40. Wiston Arch. nos 1820–8.
41. Wiston Arch. no. 1992.
42. Wiston Arch. nos 1983–9.
43. Wiston Arch. no. 2000.
44. Wiston Arch. nos 4417–21.
45. Hodson family papers. James Hodson's account books indicate that he paid his rent through an agent called John Smith in the 1850s.
46. Wiston Arch. no. 4420 for example.
47. On stock numbers, see Kingston Farm valuation of 1852 by Shoesmith (Hodson family papers). On rent, see poor law rate collection books 1840 (Hodson family papers).
48. The 1852 valuation of Kingston Farm was £4682 (Hodson family papers). There had not been much movement of prices since 1834 and Henry Rogers may be presumed to have stocked the farm to somewhere near the same level.
49. The records of the Newhaven workhouse show that no Kingston resident was

admitted there in Henry Rogers's time – and not many at any other time (ESRO, G7/14/1–2).
50. Kingston graveyard and death register.
51. Catalogue of sale for stock on Birling Farm in 1837 (Hodson family papers).
52. He sold out at Falmer in 1852 (Hodson family papers). See below.
53. Account books in Hodson family papers.
54. Poor law rate books in Hodson family papers.
55. Information from T. J. Hodson, Esq.
56. Death register.
57. Kingston churchyard.
58. ESRO, 1861 census.
59. Death register.
60. Hodson family papers; notice of sale at Falmer Court Farm, and Schoesmith's valuation of Kingston Farm.
61. ESRO, 1861 census, Kingston.
62. Hodson family papers. Book entitled *Bank a Rent Book*.
63. Hodson family papers. Notice of Sale, 1872, annotated with prices realized. Also Schoesmith's valuation, 1852.
64. See Hodson family papers. Valuation of Stacey's property at Kingston, 1895.
65. ESRO, PAR. 408/11/1, 1831 census.
66. From birth and death registers and Hodson family papers, poor law rate books, ESRO, 1861 census.
67. Comparison of births and death registers with data from Mr Gayler, aged inhabitant in 1973.
68. G. M. Trevelyan, *British History in the Nineteenth Century and After: 1782–1919* (London: Penguin Books), p. 155.
69. See E. J. Hobsbawn and G. Rudá, *Captain Swing* (London: Unwin, 1969).
70. See *The Poor Law Report of 1834*, edited by S. G. and E. O. A. Checkland (London: Penguin Books, 1973).
71. T. W. Horsfield, *History and Antiquity of the County of Sussex* (2 vols, Lewes, 1835) i. 27.
72. ESRO, PAR. 408/31/1, Overseer's notes, 1814.
73. Data from ESRO G7/2a/1–4, Ledger of Newhaven Poor Law Union.
74. ESRO, G7/14/1–8.
75. Kingston poor-law rate book.
76. Register of births and deaths, 1837–1900, Brighton registry.
77. Ibid.

Index